JULY 1990

STAN KENTON

THE MAN AND HIS MUSIC

STAN KENTON

THE MAN
AND
HIS MUSIC

Lillian Arganian

Artistry Press
East Lansing, Michigan

Stan Kenton photos on front and back covers courtesy of a Kenton friend.

Typeset by Inco Graphics, Mason, Michigan, United States of America. Printed by BookCrafters, Chelsea, Michigan, U.S.A. First Edition. Additional copies may be ordered by writing: Artistry Press, P.O. Box 1571, East Lansing, Michigan, 48823, U.S.A.

Library of Congress Catalog Card Number: 88-72084.
ISBN Number: 0-9621116-0-0.

Artistry Press
East Lansing, Michigan
United States of America

1989

To my friend Karl Keyes
who encouraged me to write this book
and to my beloved cat Louie
who nurtured me through the writing of every page of it.

Acknowledgements

My grateful appreciation is extended to every participant in this study, for his or her gracious sharing of time, thought, trust, and memory, as well as generous hospitality. All interviews were done live and on location in the spring of 1982 except for those with Dick Shearer and Mike Suter, which took place in Detroit, Michigan, in the fall and winter of 1979-1980, and that with June Christy, which was done via tape recording because of Ms. Christy's unavailability due to illness during the author's stay in California.

Most special thanks go to Leon Breeden, for sharing with me precious materials only he had access to, for his personal, guided tour of the Stan Kenton Archives and beautiful Stan Kenton Hall at North Texas State University, and for his personal encouragement and support.

To Dick Shearer, for my first interview, at a time when his loss was still bewildering and painful, and for his many helpful suggestions. To Bob Gioga, for showing me his Kenton collection and for giving me his own copy of the first Stan Kenton arrangement in the first Stan Kenton book: "Adios." And to his wife Dorothy, for the authentic California dinner.

To Shorty Rogers, for a very special autograph inscribed on the actual manuscript paper used for the Innovations Orchestra. To Dalton Smith, for showing me the Los Angeles city lights. To a connection of contacts that helped me track everyone down. (They know who they are.)

To John J. Swain, director of bands at Olivet College in Michigan, for access to 15 scores of music by Kenton and his arrangers, where Kenton seemed to pop right back to life, in those great, sweeping phrase marks.

To Ken Anderson, of Anderson's Camera Center in El Monte, California, without whose gentle persuasion to buy a certain little camera none of the pictures taken by the author in this book would have been made.

To JoAnn Cribley, Tim Brown, and the Composition Department at Inco Graphics in Mason, Michigan for their invaluable guidance, suggestions, accommodation, flexibility, and great work.

To Scott Stewart, for permission to observe every phase of the intricate workings of the Madison Scouts Drum Corps.

To Jack Elliott, for a recording of The Orchestra and for background material on The New American Orchestra.

To Hank Levy, for allowing me access to his studios during live recording sessions and for permission to observe him conducting his jazz bands.

To Ross Barbour, for the genuine California orange blossoms.

To Randy Taylor, for his special interest and assistance.

To Ken Hanna, for the gift of two of his rare recordings.

And to Stan Kenton, for giving me so much through his music and personality, and for enabling me to see the great state of California, a wonder that might well forever have been lost to me if I had not written this book.

Contents

Palm trees, Balboa Beach, California. (Photo by the Author.)

Introduction

Balboa Beach. June 14, 1982, 9:35 p.m.
Site of the Rendezvous Ballroom.

A more perfect setting could not be imagined for what happened here 41 years ago. Dramatic and colorful, it's a stage set for the launching of something of great moment.

A pier runs to the left of the site into the incredible green sea, now darkened. From its edge lovers could turn to face the expanse of miniature gold city lights in the distance to the right, the exotic silhouette of romantic palms to the left. Walking back, they would hear the roaring Pacific, crashing to shore in giant bursts of white foam, hissing away in huge swirls.

And, roaring back, the bold, brash new music of Stanley Newcomb Kenton and his Orchestra, a scant 300 yards away in the Rendezvous Ballroom on Ocean Front Boulevard.

They began here, the five musical decades of Kenton's life, as he progressed from playing in other people's bands in the mid-1930s to putting together his first orchestra at the end of 1940. A booking on Memorial Day, 1941, and through the summer of that year gave his young band the solid footing it needed before heading East. It was to be an international career before it ended with his death on August 25, 1979, and though he stipulated in his will that there be no "ghost band" there is Kenton music being heard everywhere in the world today, through the quicksilver scattering of his ideas that have danced into so many corridors of music they can never again be contained.

Stan Kenton the Man was a figure of complexity and simplicity; of contradiction and straight-ahead logic; of enormous psychic awareness and sensitivity; of characteristics at war with each other but at home within the same person, a seeker of the farthest frontiers of music and imagination. If he had to be summed up in one word, the word would be: *Innovator*.

Stan the Man's music was daring and brilliant. Exquisitely tender and pensive. Quick-paced. Exotic. Lush. Sensual. New. Different. Polytonal. *A*tonal. Massive. Emotional. Unleashed. If it had to be summed up in one word, the word would be: *Exciting*.

Stan Kenton *was* his music.

No phase of it was left untouched by the man, from playing piano, composing and arranging to leading the band, expanding its horizons, stretching and nurturing his musicians, promoting his concerts and records, *making* his own records and organizing his own direct-mail organization, speaking for jazz, entering the world of education and fostering the art form in an extensive clinic program in colleges and universities that lasted twenty years.

Married and divorced three times, Stan fathered three children and at one time owned a beautiful home in Beverly Hills. But his calling was his music and his true home was the road. And so it has not been the intention of this book to present the life of Stan Kenton in biographical or chronological form, but rather to touch upon key ideas of his musical thoughts and to ask questions—some of which will remain unanswered—as to his aims, directions, and ultimate achievements as a twentieth-century American musician. And to see what his life and music were all about by discussing their facets with some of those most closely involved—his musicians—and their interactions with him.

Whether sidemen, arrangers, composers, vocalists, educators, a combination of two or more of these, or related through kinship of idea or admiration, all were part of the Kenton orbit and understood its sphere of influence. From the early meeting in 1934 with Bob Gioga, who played on the first Stan Kenton Orchestra, through Dick Shearer and Mike Suter, who played on the last, they cover the entire span of his career. A strict chronology was not followed because many of the characters came in and out of Kenton's life in more than one period, but the book should be seen to have its own logic of presentation as the story unfolds.

1

It may be helpful to keep in mind certain key times in Kenton's career as a guide in tracing the progression of the several phases of his innovations and developments. While most big band leaders were content to settle into a specific style and trademark, Kenton explored. For Kenton the adventure could not be too extreme. Many will remember the revolutionary *City of Glass* from the late forties-early fifties period. Written by Bob Graettinger, this unusual concert work would not have been touched by any other band leader of the time, nor probably any symphonic conductor. The author has seen some of the Graettinger charts in the Kenton Archives at North Texas State University, courtesy of Leon Breeden, and the courage it took to take on one of those—*graphs,* for graphs are what they are—is unimaginable. That Kenton championed this music alone guarantees him a place in modern American musical history. But that was but a single episode in a highly episodic life.

Kenton's birth, long considered to be February 19, 1912, in Wichita, Kansas, was established as December 15, 1911 by Dr. William F. Lee in his book, *Stan Kenton: Artistry in Rhythm* (Creative Press, 1980). Both dates continue to be observed in celebrations and tributes. Kenton spent his early youth in Colorado and moved with his family to California, where after a time they settled in Bell.

Kenton has said he became addicted to music at the age of fourteen, following a visit to his home of his cousins, Billy and Arthur, who impressed him with their playing of jazz. Even before that, he'd had piano lessons and used to fall asleep at night with radio headphones over his ears. Young Stanley formed a combo in high school, called the Belltones, who played dances and parties.

For several years he played in territory bands and in speakeasies, working his way up from fifty cents a night to forty dollars a week. Meeting Everett Hoaglund in 1934 seems to have been a turning point; perhaps because he learned from the man's professionalism, or perhaps because some of the musicians he met at this time later went with him.

By the autumn of 1940 Kenton had made the decision to go off on his own. He formed a rehearsal band, wrote his theme song, composed original charts and arrangements of standard tunes, cut several dubs, lined up his own bookings, premiered at a Huntington Beach ballroom, just north of Balboa. Kenton and his men substituted one night at the Rendezvous in Balboa for the Johnny Richards band, and through a mysterious set of circumstances inherited the summer job there when the owner cancelled Richards' band and hired his.

At some point in the early forties the band picked up the name "Artistry in Rhythm." It was an active band, changing personnel with the coming and going of its sidemen into the armed services. In the autumn of 1947 the "Progressive Jazz" Orchestra was formed, centering on the music of Pete Rugolo, with its many striking influences of classical composers such as Bartok, Stravinsky, Ravel, Debussy, and Milhaud.

Balboa Pier. (Photo by the Author.)

2

Pacific Ocean, Balboa Beach, California. (Photo by the Author.)

Stan's highly creative "Innovations" Orchestra was put together at the end of 1949 and premiered in 1950, going on tour in 1950 and '51. It was the most unusual idea of its time, and probably comes closest to what Stan was striving for all his life, continuing in the experimental vein that predated it in the Progressive Jazz concept and that went on after it. Long before he had one he'd dreamed of a band that played concerts instead of dances. Sprinkled throughout this book is a quote in his words made at the time of the premiere of this new phase of his music. Though the time frame of its formal existence was relatively short, the idea was a lasting one.

Jazz greats were the stars on the famous "swing" bands of the early- to mid-fifties, when performers such as Lee Konitz, Lennie Niehaus, Frank Rosolino, Gerry Mulligan, Charlie Mariano, Maynard Ferguson and many others seared into the consciousness of impressionable young musicians who knew they "*had* to" join the Kenton band one day. For the Kenton band was always its own catalyst for attracting future musicians to it, just as it made the reputations of those who were associated with it. Known as "New Concepts of Artistry in Rhythm," the band took Europe by storm in the first of Kenton's many trips abroad in 1953. In 1959 Kenton first became involved with jazz clinics at the universities, an involvement that developed into a passionate commitment that endured all the rest of his life. Many feel it was his most important achievement.

Two widely differing musical ideas and a brainstorm found their conception in the sixties: the "Mellophonium" Band, or "New Era in Modern American Music" Orchestra, of 1960-63, which recorded such fabulous discs as *West Side Story* and *Adventures in Time,* both written by Johnny Richards, was one. The "Neophonic" Orchestra, which premiered at the Los Angeles Music Center in 1965 presenting some of the most original music ever written for an American band, was the other.

The brainstorm was the creation of Creative World, a Kenton organization that started as a promotional vehicle and later developed to pressing and distributing its own records. Its importance in keeping interest in both Kenton and jazz alive cannot be overestimated, for the sixties saw the rise of rock to dominating proportions on the popular music scene.

Rock crashed head-on into Kenton in the seventies and lost, in that Kenton simply superimposed "the Kenton sound" onto it, through such records as *7.5 on the Richter Scale.* Kenton also became entranced with the time revolution of the seventies, instigated by Don Ellis and carried on by Hank Levy, bringing on a whole new but still very much Kentonesque sound.

Stan Kenton's amalgam of twentieth-century European classical influences with jazz in his own original compositions, such as "Shelly Manne" and "June Christy," produced works of startling quality and interest. Many of his works have never been recorded, perhaps never heard. He could be maddeningly modest at times.

3

Madcap humor was as much a part of his life as were the clashing of chords and brass choirs. A classic favorite was his disappearing act. Stan would mysteriously vanish while leading the band, as stealthily as a fox. Moments later he would reappear—through the parted fronds of a stage palm!

The Kenton band of nearly forty years hurtled through the night in one gigantic card game. Only the players changed, while Kenton stayed on. A remarkable rendering of the Kenton philosophy turned up on the back of some score sheets, dated Dec. 1966, during Leon Breeden's researches at NTSU, which he very kindly shared with the author. In Stan's own writing were these words:

A bus is many things to a band over and above transporting it from engagement to engagement and place to place.

It is serenity—it belongs to the musicians and they belong to it. It carries not only the musician, but their (sic) *necessary personal items such as clothing and other objects contributing to his being in addition to the most important reason for his very existance* (sic) *and his justification for living, his musical instrument which is his identity.*

A bus is more important than a hotel room. A hotel room is temporary. The bus is permanent. A visit to a restaurant is a fleeting intermission.

A musician's seat on the bus becomes his personal area both above and below & is so private that no one infringe(s) by placing anything foreign to him in his retreat.

A bus is refuge and escape from the outside world.

A bus is a symbol of a musician's dreams and aspirations. It can become a sanctuary of elation and satisfaction or a den of despair and disappointment all determined by how and in what manner he and his horn have performed. A bus can be anything from a horror chamber from which there seems no escape to a vehicle taking him to the highest level of exalted achievement.

A bus is sometimes a dressing room a warm up room a library a place of meditation, on it dreams of the future take shape and foundations are lain to help them become realities.

A bus is a recreation center a rumpus room a private meeting place in which no one is admitted unless their interests are common.

Talk and conversation is in almost every case is (sic) *dominated by discussions revolving around music. Occasionally talk drifts away to other things but only for a moment then back to music.*
'I feel this way'
'I dig that'
'I find that'
'My taste tells me'
'He thinks'
'They thought'
What do you do
What are your feelings
etc. etc.
—*One nighters*—
Constant movement.
Travel—eat—play music—travel eat sleep travel et (sic) *play music and the cycle continues.*
No one remembers where they played last night or where they play tomorrow. It is only today that counts. The day of the week and the date of the month is forgotten, sometimes even the month itself.
—*Hit & run*—/ *Goody box/ Water jug/ Rules/ Root/ Beer Coolers/ Tire checks/ Day sheets/ Laundry/ A.C. & Heat/ Iron lung/ Coffin/ Chops/ Axe & horn/ Misfits/ Numbers/ Anticipation of the job &/ Crowd raport.* (sic)

Kenton's legacy reaches far beyond the glossary of supertalents who spent time with him and went on to great success in their own careers, people like Art Pepper and Mel Lewis and Conte Candoli and Stan Getz and Laurindo Almeida and the whole encyclopedia of them. To borrow a quote from Hank Levy in his own chapter, that's "just touching the *top.*"

The Kenton Wall of Brass is *thriving* in the hundreds of international drum corps who pour onto the fields every summer playing richly orchestrated arrangements with full colorations of brass and percussion. "Kenton music lends itself to our art form," Scott Stewart explains. Stewart is director of the Madison Scouts, who favor a decidedly Kenton style in their jazzistic approach, balanced horn line and warmth of interpretation. Madison drives people crazy whenever it performs "Malaguena," won an international championship with "MacArthur Park," and has played other Kenton favorites. The Blue Devils of Concord, California, a consistent international finalist, has ripped into "Pegasus"; the Garfield Cadets of New Jersey have done a medley from *Adventures in Time*; Les Eclipses of Canada has done music from *Cuban Fire;* the Crossmen from Delaware County, Pennsylvania, and others have done "Artistry in Rhythm"; the Freelancers, of Sacramento, California, and others have performed "Malaga." But whatever the work being played, a Kentonesque concert of brass comes right at the wildly cheering throngs of appreciative fans at every show, in dauntless presentations of fire and talent highlighted by intrepid soloists.

Coincidentally, these young people *also* ride on the bus, do one-nighters, and live on the road, at least during the summers.

Kenton's legacy of new American music and his propensity to experimentation is somewhat more difficult to trace, though interesting ideas have been attempted by The Orchestra in Los Angeles, whose name was later changed to The

4

New American Orchestra, following the departure of co-founder Allyn Ferguson. Some of the problems and concepts of such a venture are discussed in the chapters on Ferguson and Jack Elliott, present director of the orchestra. Some similarities with Kenton's Neophonic exist, however, such as writers Russ Garcia, Bill Russo, John Williams, Morty Stevens, Dave Grusin, Dick Grove, Oliver Nelson, Lalo Schifrin, Bill Holman, Gerry Mulligan and Ferguson. Also Claus Ogerman, who wrote an arrangement for the Neophonic, Manny Albam, who wrote for Stan at the time of his Innovations Orchestra, and Don Sebesky, who played trombone with Kenton. Musicians common to both orchestras are George Roberts, Bud Shank, Bill Perkins, Vince DeRosa, Art Maebe, Richard Perissi, Lloyd Ulyate, John Audino, Henry Sigismonti, Chuck Domanico, Gene Cipriano, John Lowe, Virginia Majewski, Gerald Vinci, and Shelly Manne (as a guest soloist).

Many people feel that a decided Kenton influence exists in the far more sophisticated kinds of music being written for films and tv. Academy-award winning composer John Williams, for just one example (*E.T., Close Encounters of the Third Kind, Star Wars, The Empire Strikes Back, Return of the Jedi, Superman, Indiana Jones and the Temple of Doom,* and the music for the L.A. Olympics), was one of Stan's Neophonic writers.

Even more exciting is the direction being taken by people such as Bud Shank and Bill Russo, now Director of the Contemporary American Music Program at Columbia College in Chicago, Illinois, in erasing the dividing lines between jazz and classical music in brand-new creative ways. Both were with Kenton during his Innovations period and learned from the experience. Where this direction will ultimately lead is a fascinating question for our times.

Stan Kenton willed all his music, that is, the scores and charts, to North Texas State University, in Denton, Texas. Why he chose to do so will be seen in the chapters on Leon Breeden, Gene Hall and Bobby Knight, as the background and structure of their fine jazz program are explored in some depth. Gene Hall, one of the principal originators of the jazz clinics in 1959, founded the NTSU program in 1947, the first of its kind in the country. Leon Breeden continued its development from 1959 to 1981, bringing great honors to it and earning prestige and recognition for his efforts. North Texas' 1 O'Clock Jazz Lab Band was chosen by Kenton to appear with the Los Angeles Neophonic in 1966, was the first university band ever to appear at the White House, in 1967, and was the official big band at the Montreux International Jazz Festival in Switzerland in 1970, among other honors. Breeden has his own extraordinary story to tell concerning his relationship with Kenton and the future of the music at NTSU, a heartening one for all Kenton fans.

Bob Gioga was a close friend of Kenton's, tracing their friendship back to the Hoaglund band in 1934. He played baritone sax and was band manager for 12 years, from 1941-1953. George Faye joined for a year and a half in 1942 and played tenor trombone. Buddy Childers came on as trumpet player in January of 1943 and was with Kenton over a span of 11½ years. Pete Rugolo, composer and arranger and closely identified with Kenton's "Progressive Jazz" period, joined the band in 1945. June Christy was vocalist in April, 1945 for two years and also made several tours and recordings. Shelly Manne was Kenton's drummer starting in February, 1946, off and on until 1952; Milt Bernhart played trombone in the band off and on from 1946 to 1952; both came back for the Neophonic. Bill Russo was trombonist and composer-arranger off and on from January, 1950, through October, 1953, returning to write for and conduct the Neophonic in 1966.

Shorty Rogers was trumpet player and composer-arranger on the band in 1950, stayed for a year and a half and continued to write for Kenton afterwards, including a ballet for the Neophonic. Jim Amlotte joined as trombonist in 1956 and was band manager from 1959-69; Dalton Smith was lead trumpet player off and on from 1959-1970; both were involved with the Kenton clinics and the Neophonic. Bud Shank came on in late 1949 for two and one half years, played in the Neophonic, taught in the clinics and was involved with the Collegiate Neophonic in 1967.

Mike Suter was bass trombonist in 1963 and again from 1973-75 and in 1978. He was both a student and a teacher in the clinics and is a close friend of Dick Shearer's. Shearer was band manager and trombonist for the last 13 years of the band, though he left on August 21, 1977. (The band broke up on August 20, 1978.) A joint chapter on Shearer and Suter in addition to individual ones has been included, since they triggered each other's memories in many details.

Hank Levy, Director of Jazz Studies at Towson State University in Towson, Maryland, composed for Kenton chiefly in the seventies, though he was on the band for six months in 1953. George Roberts was bass trombonist on the Kenton band from 1951-53 and again later on; he had his group of forty trombones play for the dedication of the Kenton Memorial in Balboa in September, 1981. Ken Hanna, composer-arranger-trumpet player, began his long association with Kenton in 1942, writing some of the band's finest charts in the seventies. Ross Barbour sang with the Four Freshmen, a group that made several appearances, tours and recordings with Kenton. The Freshmen, still concertizing, though without Barbour, proudly claim to have owed their style to the Kenton sound. What is surprising is the number of groups who imitate the *Freshmen*—and who therefore are perpetuating the Kenton sound as well.

Big bands are enjoying a resurgence in popularity, which assures a future to the new ones being formed, some of which have a Kentonish verve and brightness about them. Kenton records are being played on radio both by deejays on the new shows and by long-time advocates of his music. Perhaps none can equal the devotion of Randy Taylor, big band host on Miami University public radio station WMUB in Oxford, Ohio, who plays a special 4-hour all-Kenton show every Friday night from 7 to 11. Taylor, former Kenton archivist, began the practice as a memorial tribute in August, 1982, and has continued it in response to public demand.

Memorial concerts testify to the enduring values of Kenton's music and the loyalty felt to him by his fans. At Clarenceville High School in Livonia, Michigan (affectionately dubbed "Montreux North" by host Dick Purtan) one of the first such concerts was held on February 19, 1982, with Dick Shearer fronting the band.

By 7:30 p.m. the lobby was jammed for a performance scheduled to begin at 8. By 7:35, after the auditorium doors were opened, almost all seats were taken. Guests sat back and surveyed the scene: Blue seats, aqua carpeting. Orchid lighting on the stage, set up to show a piano at left, where Kenton would have sat, congas nearby and percussion at back left. Rows of aqua-and-tan chairs poised like sentinels. Saxophones parked, slightly aslant, trombones "face down" behind them. A pleasing, sensual avant-garde look about it all. The audience, mostly dressed in sharp, youthful, sporty attire, looks alert and intelligent.

Opening remarks, and then Shearer whips the band into a crescendo that threatens to tear the walls down, leading into Willie Maiden's "A Little Minor Booze." In a rainbow of colors and moods, he takes them through "Here's That Rainy Day," "Minor Riff," "Two Moods for Baritone," "Opus in Chartreuse," "Body and Soul," "Roy's Blues," "Street of Dreams," "Intermission Riff," "Send in the Clowns," "Stompin' at the Savoy," "Yesterdays," "Opus in Pastels" and "Peanut Vendor." The second half of the program goes quickly, and suddenly it's time for The Theme. Pianist Chuck Robinette does it proud: weaving Kenton music in and out as he spins the haunting threads of *Artistry*. Everyone anticipates what's coming and tries to prepare for it, but with the electrifying entrance of the saxes a universal chill slips through the audience like a single emotion: "*Baa*-baa . . . ba-ba-ba-ba *baa*-baaa . . ." Before it is over there are few if any dry eyes either on stage or anywhere in the room. And the realization dawns that "Artistry in Rhythm," like its creator, has become immortal.

In his own ways and by avenues that will perhaps not be felt for some time in all their scope, Stan Kenton was the greatest force in twentieth-century American music.

His sweeping sense of music favored extremes in dynamics and tonal expanse, tormenting crescendos to ear-splitting highs, tension and release. It became its own genre, consuming the categories of "concert jazz" and "classical jazz" and adding enough character of its own to be labeled unto itself.

No one can measure the effects of the priceless gift he bestowed upon people and how it contributed both to their own flourishing and to new forms of American music: the gift of *listening*. It was a selfless, most generous form of encouragement. In the total freedom allowed his composers and arrangers to create, his band became a vehicle for their creativity; but by a curious reciprocity everything that passed through it somehow became "Stan Kenton music." Kenton was influenced by the musicians who came to him, but none left his band untouched by the Kenton experience.

Stan the Man had the integrity of his own conviction and would gladly have dispensed with the need for money and sacrificed all his time to artistic endeavor. He was not satisfied to cater to the public taste of his time, but insisted on going in his own direction, whoever listened or did not.

Stan Kenton's music was the headiest combination of love, emotion, intellect, form, freedom, boldness and fire ever known.

It still burns, its sparks igniting life wherever they touch down.

Balboa Beach, site of the Rendezvous Ballroom. (Photo by the Author.)

This orchestra is dedicated to the development

of a truly American style of musical expression.

Dick Shearer. (Photo: Courtesy of a Kenton friend.)

1 Dick Shearer

I'm sitting here with my friend. Mike and I are watching a Zulu movie on tv. Mike was on the band with me. I'd hired him. We're sitting here watching the thing. All of a sudden on the bottom of the screen, where they give the weather, it said: "BAND LEADER STAN KENTON PASSED AWAY."

We looked at that, blinked, and it came back again. We got on the phone and immediately called the hospital in Los Angeles and they confirmed it with me. I called Audree (Kenton's personal manager at Creative World in Los Angeles) and she said they'd kept it quiet, they didn't want the press to get on it. And I'll be damned—I talked to her for about forty minutes—the minute I hung up the phone CBS from New York called me. Put me on the air right away. I have an unlisted number—how had they found out where I was? Next day the Free Press called and they did a big thing. And Christ I wasn't worth a damn here at all.

It hit me hard. Every time I'd hear something on the radio I'd get tears in my eyes. WWJ put me on the air, and we had a long, really nice conversation, for about an hour and a half, with people calling in. WWJ is an all-news station, but the guy played a bunch of music.

L.A.: You hadn't known that he was that close to dying?

SHEARER: No. They kept it a secret from me. He'd been in the hospital about six days with the stroke. Nobody knew. They wanted it that way because we've had problems before with the press, when he was sick.

L.A.: What would they do?

SHEARER: They would exaggerate things. When we went through this last time, when he got sick and was away from the band, naturally we wanted to keep it from the press because of the promotion we were involved in. We've done this before. We were on the road. Everybody knew the band was very well organized, and—I'm not blowing smoke at myself, but they knew if I was there everything would be fine. So we wanted to let the guys know little by little instead of panicking everybody. The office was swarmed with telegrams and phone calls from around the world . . .

L.A.: He was on tour at the time?

SHEARER: Yes. We were in Reading, Pennsylvania. In fact, we pulled up at the hotel, and it seemed it was like about two hours later the hotel manager—it was a night off—called me and said, "You have to come downstairs right away." I said, "What's the problem?" He said, "I have to see you right away." So right away I thought, well, one of the guys is screwed up. They got drunk and made a mess in the restaurant. You know, all those typical things that can happen. Normally Stan and I were always together, on our night off. We were only, like, two or three doors apart. After we arrived I went up to my room, then left to take care of some business in town. When I got back I got the call.

"Come down here right away." So I go downstairs and he says, "We just had to take Stan away in an ambulance. We found him outside. He fell on the cement."

L.A.: Was anybody with him at the time?

SHEARER: Nobody was with him. He'd got out of the room somehow. He'd gotten into a panic. They discovered in the subsequent operation that he had two brain clots. Nobody was sure at the time whether the blood clots came first and then he fell in the confusion—it's one of those mysterious things we'll never know. We were on the ninth floor. He had got outside of his room, and he went down the exit—the inside fire escape, or the stairwell—and ended up on the fifth floor, where the parking garage was. And he couldn't get back in, so he was walking around in a daze. This led us to believe that the brain clots had hit, and in the confusion he evidently was trying to find me or somebody and went out the wrong door, and tried to get back up and tripped and fell.

9

That's when they took him to the hospital. Then they called me. I got there right away. He wasn't—he didn't know why he was there. He was in a complete state of confusion.

L.A.: I just can't see the man that way, I don't know why.

SHEARER: About three or four years before that he had another serious problem where he had an aneurysm, and we almost lost him. They say sometimes when you have something like that— you know he had a plastic tube in his groin area from where it happened— that sometimes these will cause blood clots.

L.A.: Elsewhere.

SHEARER: Elsewhere, later on. So we never knew. He was in the hospital four months after that. The fall had caused a skull fracture. And they had to do brain surgery. We were very lucky that of all places Reading, Pennsylvania had one of the great neurosurgeons in residence. This happened in '77. He got well again, and got his strength back, and the band went on the road last year (1978) for seven or eight months. But he decided he'd have to take the band off, because it was just too hard on him. Brain surgery is a major thing. At certain times his memory wasn't good at all.

L.A.: I can't believe he'd go back on the road after a thing like that.

SHEARER: He's always been that way. He did after the aneurysm. He did it one time afer an exploratory operation that backfired—went back on the road. A very strong man. So after this thing, a year or so ago, he was doing really well. You talk to any doctor, they will tell you he had a memory problem. Sometimes he couldn't remember who you were. Like a five-year period. He'd remember everything beyond five or six years ago, but he didn't remember some of the guys who were on the band in the last period of time. And then he would remember.

L.A.: I want to ask you a strange question. Because I have a feeling he didn't lose any of the musical stuff that he had.

SHEARER: Oh no.

L.A.: I'm convinced that there's—just as there are parts of the brain that control the eyesight and other specific functions, I'm sure there's a music center up there. For music only. And I base it on a number of things. Once I saw a tv program. A guy had an accident, or a stroke or something, and couldn't talk anymore. But his sense of music was unimpaired, and he could sing. For myself, I can go to sleep at night and sometimes hear music in my head all night long.

SHEARER: Um-hm.

L.A.: I'm thinking that even though he had brain surgery, and forgot parts of his life . . .

SHEARER: It came back.

L.A.: . . . the music thing must have been absolutely intact.

SHEARER: The music thing was there. They told me at the time—Stanley told me later, even, himself. In the hospital, he didn't know who he was. He'd go down to therapy, and the doctor would say, "Do you know who you are?" He says, "No. Not really." "You're Stan Kenton. You're Stan Kenton, a very very famous band leader." This was a very short period he went through, of course. You know, you're talking about a matter of weeks or something before he finally realized what was going on. When he got back to L.A. then he started to fool around with the piano. He would forget things, but he still had the musical ability.

L.A.: Did he conduct the orchestra at this time?

SHEARER: Oh no. I'd have to check my records—I thought I'd never forget the date—but it seemed like it was around May. May, June, July, August (of 1977). He finally started playing again around, oh, I think maybe around the end of August. He started to fool around with the piano. Now he wasn't with the band.

L.A.: He went to a piano and the music was all there.

SHEARER: Um-hm. Then he knew exactly who he was, what was going on, and this and that. He knew the band was out without him. August 21st was when I cut off the theme. That's the last time the band was together until he took it out again January of '78.

L.A.: What do you mean, you "cut off the theme?"

SHEARER: My last night conducting the band. We were doing "Artistry in Rhythm," and I gave the cut-off. We were off for five months after that before he took the band out again.

L.A.: And then he took it out himself.

SHEARER: By that time I'd left, and most of the band had left, to do other things.

L.A.: But they got together again?

SHEARER: Ya, different guys. They were on the road last year (1978) for eight months. And that was it. They went off in August and the band never went back again.

L.A.: It's just incredible the number of bands he had and the continuity of his life in music. Why do you think there was this affinity to music and almost nothing else?

SHEARER: He believed in his music. He had a very big dedication to it. He had a tremendous amount of integrity. When he started the band it was during the height of the big band era. Miller, Dorsey. And he wanted to do his own thing. He had a completely different band.

L.A.: Stan's desire for a concert orchestra goes back to his early twenties. During the time that you were with him, was there still the conflict between hiring out for a big dance and concert jazz?

SHEARER: We did a lot of dances. Seems like whenever there was a heart fund or big charity event they always liked to have the big name band.

L.A.: Some people even argue that he killed the dance band business.

SHEARER: Charlie Barnet said that, he killed the dance band.

L.A.: Probably others did too. But then he said, "You're darn right I did. Who in hell wants a dance orchestra?" It was never a broad enough definition for him, was it?

SHEARER: He wanted to get the band out of the dance halls and into the concert halls. We were always considered a concert jazz band. He didn't want to be a dance orchestra. That's something he had to do in those days. He said if he killed the big band business how come he survived? How come Woody Herman survived? Count Basie?

L.A.: Even they're playing concert dates more now than they are dance dates, aren't they?

SHEARER: Um-hm. Duke Ellington. You think about all those bands now, that are still here.

L.A.: So he really saved big band jazz rather than destroyed it.

SHEARER: They all went into the jazz clubs, and the concert halls. We still had to play dances. *They* still have to play dances. But the majority of the work now is in concert halls. Ninety percent of our work was strictly concerts and clinics. Where people would *listen*. Or a night club, where they'd listen.

L.A.: That was the whole point, wasn't it? So you could be more experimental, in your concerts?

SHEARER: Sure. You don't have to worry about people dancing. You can sit back there, and you can *listen* to the music. We used to play dances, he used to get so . . . He'd say, "Dick, oh, we gotta play this horseshit again!" (Laughs). We'd play a dance somewhere, and we'd sit there. Brass section would have to play everything soft. Put the mutes on, trumpets down an octave, trombones soft, saxophones sub-toned . . .

L.A.: Trumpets down an octave?

SHEARER: Oh *yes*. Everybody'd be playing soft. In about two sets, you could see it's just fryin' his ass. He'd look up at me and he'd get that smile on his face. He'd look out there. He'd look at the brass section. He'd look out there . . . Then he'd go *(gestures)*. "That's it! *Play!*"

L.A.: The famous Kenton Blast. Terrific.

SHEARER: We had a good dance book, but no, we'd have to do that type of thing and then they'd still be too loud and then we'd—he was never a fan of doing dances.

L.A.: Why would he do them? Just to . . .

SHEARER: Well, you get booked by the agency. You have a dance job somewhere some Saturday night that pays five, six thousand dollars. Nobody wants to turn that down.

L.A.: So it was mainly for the money, and to keep going.

SHEARER: Um-hm.

L.A.: But he preferred concerts.

SHEARER: Um-hm. Some nights he would kind of lean back, put his arms on the piano, and just listen to the band.

L.A.: He would marvel at his own group, wouldn't he?

SHEARER: Oh yes.

L.A.: I used to see that myself. He'd be conducting, and then he would turn around and *grin* at the audience, this great big grin, as if to say, "Isn't that *great?*" (Laughs.)

SHEARER: And many a night he'd come and say, "Damn! I think I'm gonna go out and buy a ticket!"

L.A.: To his own orchestra?

SHEARER: Yes. (Laughs.)

L.A.: Could you tell when Kenton was about to go off in a new direction?

Would something happen, say during dinner, where you would notice that he was getting in the mood to try a new idea?

SHEARER: No. That would happen all the time.

L.A.: It was just part of his being all the time?

SHEARER: Um-hm. We would talk sometimes . . . well I remember one time we were in L.A. at Shelly's Manhole. And Stanley decided he didn't like the saxophones. Just never cared for the sound of the saxophones. So he wanted to try an experiment. So we wrote a bunch of new arrangements that were written for ten brass, rhythm section and *one* saxophone. It would double everything. So we got and rehearsed this stuff and it just was a bunch of garbage. (Laughter.) And he looked at the band, he looked at me, and he says, "This's a buncha shit, isn't it. Pass it in." So much for *that* experiment. Both he and Johnny never liked the saxophones. That's why they were always changing around.

L.A.: Johnny Richards?

SHEARER: Ya. Most bands had a conventional two altos, two tenors, and baritone saxophone. That was the standard thing. With Stanley they finally changed it around to alto, two tenors, two *baritone* saxophones. Which, you know, would give it more weight. And one of the baritones would also double on bass saxophone. So you had this very sonorous sound coming from the saxophones. A very *low, thick* sound.

L.A.: What was he after?

SHEARER: He just wanted that particular sound. That's also when the band went to five trombones, and out of that three tenors, two *bass* trombones. And one of the bass trombone players played tuba. A very rich, textured sound.

L.A.: Was he doing this kind of thing all the time?

SHEARER: Oh ya. He'd always change around. It's like the band, when it was very very hot, in the forties, when it was *the* band, right out of that period he went into the Innovations. Where he got the strings. Brought in all the screwy music. The Graettinger stuff, and all the far-out stuff. And people went *"Huh?"* Or *"What?"*

L.A.: Did you know Graettinger?

SHEARER: He died before I even met him. Or died before I was even playing— it seemed like he died around 1954.

L.A.: Did you play *City of Glass* with the orchestra?

SHEARER: No. That was done in the fifties. I have the record. I know it very well.

L.A.: It took tremendous courage for Kenton to do that.

SHEARER: I still won't listen to the whole album. I have to listen to one side, then I'll cool it for a bit . . . . .

L.A.: Well the thing I love about it is that I've heard some contemporary classical music . . .

SHEARER: It's not even *near* that good.

L.A.: That's my point. I wish Graettinger were still alive. Did anything ever happen to him, was he able to make any kind of name for himself? I never heard of him after that.

SHEARER: No.

L.A.: That's a strong argument right there for Kenton being the figure of our time, because he knew enough to give Graettinger the chance to do this.

SHEARER: Guys in the band thought he was crazy. "What is this screwy stuff we have to play?" Stan said occasionally he almost thought he was going to have to get a baseball bat in his hands to rehearse the music. He said, "You're gonna *play* it."

L.A.: Did Kenton believe in it himself?

SHEARER: *Yes.* Took it on the road, lost $125,000 with it, went out the next year, lost another hundred and twenty-five . . .

L.A.: Just playing it in concert?

SHEARER: They took it out twice.

L.A.: That to me is symbolic of his whole attitude, the *City of Glass*. Because that's the most far-out music I've ever heard.

SHEARER: Oh yes. The band was . . .

L.A.: They didn't like it.

SHEARER: Well, one thing, it was very difficult to play. Extremely difficult.

L.A.: It *sounds* like it's difficult to play.

SHEARER: And when you think that that album was basically done by a bunch of jazz musicians, if you want to use that term . . . *Classical* players couldn't even do it.

L.A.: I was surprised to hear Kenton introduce *City of Glass* on his *Artistry in Tango* album from the late forties or early fifties—it sounds as though he's introducing it to the public for the first time. And he says, "Here once again is a variation on a theme. This is Bob

Graettinger's expression on 'You Go To My Head.' " And he says something like "Don't listen for *melody;* listen for *sound.*" That was interesting.

SHEARER: They never did the whole *City of Glass* on the road. They would do movements from it.

L.A.: It's probably too much to expect of the audience.

SHEARER: Oh yes. And always after they played that, he would follow it with "Opus in Pastels," in which the saxophones play their pretty thing, you know. So everybody can just: *phew.*

L.A.: In many ways, Stan Kenton seems to loom as the largest musical figure of our time. How do you feel about that statement?

SHEARER: I've always felt that. But a lot of people won't accept it.

L.A.: Perhaps they haven't really thought about it.

SHEARER: He has probably contributed more leaders to the jazz world than anyone.

L.A.: Is this because they were good to start with and they got their grounding in him and then were able to go off on their own?

SHEARER: That's not the whole story. It used to be years ago you went through all the bands. And finally if you got to the Kenton band, you had made it!

L.A.: What makes that a viable statement? What did he have in his band to offer a musician that somebody else didn't have?

SHEARER: The music was so much more of a challenge.
L.A.: Sophisticated.

SHEARER: It was very sophisticated. It was very difficult. The trumpet players were playing very high. The trombones were roaring. Nobody was doing that type of thing. It's the only band in the country that's ever used ten brass. Most of the bands use eight brass. Four trumpets, four trombones. Stanley was five trumpets, five trombones. Time when he had the four Mellophoniums there were fourteen brass. Nobody's used to a band that large. Nobody on the road. For the Neophonic he had five saxophone players who doubled everything in the world—I mean it looked like a *music store*—bass saxophones, bass clarinets, alto clarinets, piccolos, bassoons. We used four French horn players. Then we had a regular rhythm

section: piano, bass, drums, and triangle. We had a huge percussion section. Those guys back there played everything from timpani to the wind machine to—anything you could imagine.
L.A.: Wind machine!
SHEARER: Yes. That's a kind of thing you *fffffff!* (*Blows.*) Sounds just like the wind. We did an album, called *Stan Kenton and the Los Angeles Neophonic Orchestra.* It won the Grammy that year.
L.A.: It wasn't just the composition, though. One thing I loved about him was his experimentation with time.
SHEARER: The time, the color.
L.A.: Wasn't that great?
SHEARER: Yes.
L.A.: I loved that.

SHEARER: That came out of Don Ellis, who was the big instigator with the time movement, and we got on it.
L.A.: So many kinds of things seemed to be going on in Kenton's head all the time! New arrangements. New changes of pattern in the instrumentation in the band. New kinds of music.

SHEARER: We were always looking for writers. New music. Sometimes of course we got stagnated. We'd play the same stuff night after night.
L.A.: And he'd hate that, right?

SHEARER: Well sometimes he would forget. He would end up in a trap, with all the same stuff. Finally I'd have to say, "Stanley, I DON'T WANT TO PLAY THAT ANYMORE." There was a joke that went on. We did this thing called "Hey Jude" which was a big thing with the kids. It's on the *Redlands* album. We played that and played that to death. One night we were going someplace and I stood up and I said, "Stanley." We were out in Texas. "Listen, we're gonna play this 'Hey Jude' one more time tonight." I says "If we don't retire this chart, you see that spot over there," I says. "We're gonna dig a hole." (Laughter.) "Now there's two things that can go in that hole." I said "One is 'Hey Jude.'" I said "The other is you. Now we're gonna have to wait after the concert. You let us know what we're gonna do with that hole."
L.A.: God. Would he listen to that?

SHEARER: Ya, sure he would. He was gettin' tired of it too. Good Lord, I remember some times, some hollering sessions we'd have.
L.A.: What would you holler about?

SHEARER: Sometimes the personnel. And the music. You spend so much time on the road you lose perspective. It's like the old movie, "If It's Tuesday, This Must Be Belgium." You're never really aware of getting in a rut. Even Stan.

L.A.: You must have got into many all-night rapping sessions with him, where you wouldn't want to quit because it was time to go to bed.
SHEARER: Oh yes. Or we'd go the other way, where we knew it was time to go to bed, depending upon how busy the schedule was, what we had to do. There were times when he was very well organized. We used to do "hit-and-runs," where we'd work the job, pack up, change our clothes, get in the bus, stop somewhere and get something to eat, and maybe go three hundred miles that night. Naturally everybody would be drinking, having a party on the bus, trying to unwind and all that. We used to work so hard, and of course the music is so physically demanding. When we worked, we worked. When it was time to play, boy we played. And we had fun. Finally everybody would go to sleep and later you'd wake up, you'd pull in someplace 7:30, 8 o'clock in the morning, and *oh!,* your mouth felt like all the frogs in the world went through it. And *oh,* you'd feel miserable, and this and that, and you'd look up. And there's Stanley standing in the front of the bus. In the same suit he'd had on. Not a wrinkle in it! It looked like he'd gone out to the cleaners and got it pressed. You never could believe this! He'd be up there, hair combed, standing in the well. Bus would pull up to the hotel; we'd get out; the driver would be unloading, and Stanley would be handing you your suitcase.

L.A.: Had he been awake during the night?
SHEARER: No, he fell asleep too. But he'd wake up, look like he'd just had a shower and the whole bit. And here we're young guys, and we can barely walk.
L.A.: You know what the Kenton orchestra is before you join it. But then—how do you know how to produce that sound? What are you thinking when you first join the group and you go out there and he's conducting?

SHEARER: What I felt?
L.A.: What you felt, what anybody felt.
SHEARER: I could speak about what I felt okay because—I grew up, I started

playing the trombone and all that, and the first record I ever heard by the Kenton band was *Kenton in Hi-Fi*. It had just come out then. A friend of mine played it for me. I liked it. Took my allowance down to the record store and bought me a Kenton album. The only one they had at the time was *New Concepts of Artistry in Rhythm,* which is the "Prologue" album. Where he talks about "This Is An Orchestra." So I put that on, and right away I said, "This fool is talking about my album. What is this?" I started listening, and heard the band. Heard Frank Rosolino. I said, "Boy, that guy's pretty good." Then I heard the first trombone player Bobby Burgess come in. I said, "*What?*" I must have listened to that twenty-five times.

L.A.: How old were you?

SHEARER: Then? Oh I must have been fourteen. Yeah, it was '54. I heard that thing and just wigged out. And I said, "That's the way I'm gonna sound." I started buying Kenton albums and Kenton albums. It led to every other thing. That's all I wanted to do. I knew all the Kenton trombone players. By the time I got into the band I had all of them in my head. I could play anything Kai Winding ever did, anything Milt Bernhart ever did.

L.A.: Were you planning to be a trombone player even before you had heard of Kenton?

SHEARER: Oh yes, I've always wanted to be a professional player.

L.A.: Kenton was more of a catalyst, then.

SHEARER: Um-hm. In turn, Bobby Burgess was one of my heroes, with Kenton, and then I heard the Ted Heath band, which was English. Then everything started to happen. I did all the stuff in L.A. I'm originally from there. Did all the sessions, worked with all the bands, and then there was an opening in Stan's band. I knew the road man. We'd worked together in some other outside bands, and record dates and things like that. He said, "You want to go out this summer with us?" and I said "Are you kidding? I've waited all my life." We got into rehearsal. First thing Stan called for was "September Song." *I* didn't even look at the *music.* I'm look-ing right at Stanley now. I went "Ba-bo-doo-da-da-da." He heard me play it. And he says, "God *damn.* What's *this?*" And that was *it.*

L.A.: Really?

SHEARER: I knew it from memory, from the records. Almost everything they've ever done. He called up "Peanut Vendor" and all that stuff, and I knew it and that was it.

L.A.: You're a book yourself, what with the Kenton history and your own association with the band all in your head. You saw all the trombone players come and go.

SHEARER: Oh ya, I hired 'em.

L.A.: When was Winding with the group?

SHEARER: That's 1946, '47. Then Bernhart came in, Bob Fitzpatrick, Kent Larsen, Bobby Burgess, Bart Varsalona. Christ, I got 'em all. I met 'em all.

L.A.: You were with him the longest.

SHEARER: I had that chair thirteen years, you know? And played lead trombone. That's the one I played (looking at trombone). And I'd say

Stan Kenton, with Dick Shearer (trombone) at North Texas State, '70s. (Photo: Courtesy of a Kenton friend.)

when I left the Kenton band I'd put it up on the wall, and I did.

L.A.: Can I touch?

SHEARER: That's the dummy. Guys'd say, naw, I'd say, "No, when I leave the band I'm gonna put that horn on the wall," and I have.

L.A.: You'll never play it again?

SHEARER: Once in a while I'll get it down just to . . . .

L.A.: Did you feel that he took something of you when he died?

SHEARER: I felt something happen, yes. I wasn't worth a shit. Pardon the expression. When I left the band, it was something I had to get away from. I'd spent so long there. The band was off for five, six months, and I just had to do something different. I was getting tired.

L.A.: What in particular?

SHEARER: It was just the pressure. I had to take care of the band, I had to talk to promoters, I fronted the band, I did all the talking. I was the one who hired the musicians, did the paper work, booked the rooms, did all that stuff. I had to worry about everything. I started juicing real hard. Those four months I put on forty pounds, which I still haven't taken off yet. Forgetting to eat, going out later and having three or four hamburgers; that's all you had time for. And I said I don't think I should continue my life like this.

L.A.: That must have been a painful step for you, though.

SHEARER: It's just something that happened. Stanley was still recuperating, so we got over it gradually. I didn't want to go back on the road. I turned down Basie twice. I'd always wanted to play with Basie. Always wanted to play with him, just to play that happy music.

L.A.: He's very different from Kenton.

SHEARER: Oh yeah. And I just said, "No. I'll have to turn him down." I'd talk to Stanley occasionally on the phone. The whole time I was off the band I would think about him. I missed him.

SHEARER: Did he talk to you ever in philosophical terms about what music meant to him or what he was trying to communicate to people through music?

SHEARER: Stanley—to him music was always something that you would think about. We'd talk about it. Music should have emotions. How does it stir you? What does it do for you? You can't just sit down and listen like you can to some of these tunes, "I Wonder Who's

Been Making Waves On My Water Bed" and all this garbage. He always had to think about what the band was doing. There was a restaurant we used to go to in New York. A big steak house we loved. Very popular, packed all the time. This was ten years ago. We go in there, and they're playing *Cuban Fire!* Somebody said "What the hell are you playing this stuff for?" It wasn't at Muzak volume, you could *hear* it. The owner said, "Listen, if they don't like what I'm playing in here . . . Besides, they start eating faster, they drink a little bit more. Next thing you know they're starting to think about what's going on. Then they leave. This stuff *stimulates.*" That was his theory.

L.A.: I never heard anything, now that you mention it, anything by Kenton that didn't affect me exactly that way.

SHEARER: He led the ballads, sometimes, you know, the pretty emotion—but you'd still have to think about it. You're not talking about just three chords. Music to Stanley was like a one-act play.

L.A.: How is it like a play?

SHEARER: You tell a story with the music. Or you paint a picture. There's a climax, a release.

L.A.: It happens in everything he did.

SHEARER: Everything. The ballads, the simple ballads. It'd start off very soft, and then the trombones would come in. Then the piano, then the saxophones, and then finally the brass would come in.

L.A.: Would Kenton sit down and figure out how to produce that?

SHEARER: No. He would never dictate to anybody what to write.

L.A.: How would he get a sound like that, then?

SHEARER: It's the way the band played. It's the way we'd interpret the music. And as far as the way we would play—he'd never have to tell us what to play, how to play.

L.A.: How is that *possible?*

SHEARER: We just knew. It's the style of the band, it's something that, if you've listened to it, you know what makes the band.

L.A.: You're saying that it was just something within every musician.

SHEARER: Right. Stan was the first band leader who never dictated to the band how he wanted things played. He left it up to the lead players. Like before,

with Dorsey, he used to say, lead trumpet, you blow this short, you play it this way, and so forth. Stan never had to do that. He would say things just now and then, you know, think of this thing, it's this way. Think of this piece of music as doing this. Think of it very broad, which means the notes will be long instead of short. That kind of thing. That's all he'd ever say. And he'd rehearse the band until we'd get it down.

L.A.: Somewhere I read that in order to get a sharper sense of rhythm he'd ask the players to count the "ands." "One-and-two-and-three-and . . . . "

SHEARER: We'd do that mainly on the ballads. 'Cause we would play things so slow . . . .

L.A.: They're pretty slow, aren't they.

SHEARER: And he would say, now subdivide those things. That way you would make the time come out much more precise. And it's not lazy then. And the band would play, basically, without vibrato. It was a very pure, straight sound. We had occasions, like I would use it on the top of the section on a lead part, just toward the very end of a note, to give it a little warmth. I've seen parts the guys have done where it'll say something like "a la Dick Shearer." On a trombone part. Some ballad, and what they're talking about is a style of playing that I have on a ballad. You know, do this on a certain note. It's not all written; it's just something you have to know, you've listened to records.

L.A.: What is the Kenton sound?

SHEARER: It's a very . . . thick form of orchestration.

L.A.: Thick meaning that more instruments are used?

SHEARER: More instruments, more of the colors of the chords . . .

L.A.: Color. Tone color. Let's talk about tone color.

SHEARER: That's what makes the sound, is the color. It's very thick.

L.A.: Thick as opposed to loud?

SHEARER: Yes.

L.A.: It's a fatter sound.

SHEARER: It's a fatter sound. It's using *more* of the chords.

L.A.: Using more of the chords.

SHEARER: Right. From the very bottom all the way to the top.

L.A.: Bill Russo used to say that when he first heard the Kenton band he sat in the audience and just drank in those nine- and ten-note chords.

SHEARER: Um-hm.

L.A.: Is a typical chord an octave?

SHEARER: Oh no. It can go over an octave.

L.A.: Is it typical for jazz to have the ninc- or tcn-note chord?

SHEARER: Usually you have seven- and nine-note chords. Like you'd say C-E-G-*B-D*, which is now *above* the C, F-A, and you're back to C again.

L.A.: Is this typical of Kenton or . . .

SHEARER: Oh, yes.

L.A.: Or is this typical of all jazz?

SHEARER: It's typical of all jazz. But Stanley used to really voice out the things like that.

L.A.: And make them louder.

SHEARER: Um-hm. Most bands are in a tradition of what we'd call four-bar block-style writing.

L.A.: What's block-style writing?

SHEARER: In which you'd have, let's say, I'll use C-E-G-B-flat. Four notes. Then you'll voice it all the way down the same way. You'll have the trumpets . . .

L.A.: Voicing is what, giving parts to the various instruments?

SHEARER: Right. You'll have the trombones play the same thing the trumpets play, an octave lower. The saxophones will be in there. That's the basic style of writing, where it's all blocked.

L.A.: If you're an arranger, you write chords, and then build on that?

SHEARER: Um-hm.

L.A.: But a musician in the Stan Kenton orchestra would see more than chords.

SHEARER: Oh, that's only when you improvise, now. When you play, the music is written out.

L.A.: An arranger would only write a chord for someone who's going to . . .

SHEARER: Improvise.

L.A.: In Kenton's music, then, most of the time it must be written out, because that's where the arrangers would come in.

SHEARER: Oh yes. When you hear the ensemble, the whole band playing, that's all orchestrated. When you hear the individual soloist, you know unless he's playing a strict melody line, he's improvising.

L.A.: When you compose something, are you back into the chord thing, do you come up with a chord and then work it out?

SHEARER: Yes. You decide how you want to orchestrate that. You write a theme. As you're writing the theme, of course, you know what chord changes you want to use.

L.A.: That's fascinating. Because the chord is the make-up of the orchestra.

SHEARER: Um-hm.

L.A.: Each line of brass or whatever carries a different note of the chord?

SHEARER: Um-hm.

L.A.: You work it out, and that's called voicing?

SHEARER: Right.

L.A.: Okay. And Kenton's use of that would differ from, let's say, Count Basie's.

SHEARER: Oh, yes, it's a much thicker sound. More instruments.

L.A.: More voicing of the chord.

SHEARER: And . . . right. Like the Basie band a lot of times would use just a straight seventh chord, while we'd get involved in the ninth chords. The eleventh chords. Then you could *alter* those notes *in* those chords.

L.A.: Building dissonance right into the chord.

SHEARER: Right. Instead of using a very simple chord a composer might want to use a more complex chord, a very colored chord, which will have more notes to the chord in it. As the band got more experimental and added more colors, we started using what used to be considered "very rare" chords all the time.

L.A.: And as new musicians came on the character changed also, didn't it?

SHEARER: Right. Stan used to have a very short sound on the trombone until Kai Winding came along.

L.A.: Most of Kenton's music is arranged, and he himself has been heard to say he couldn't stand the idea of swing. Most of the jazz criticism leveled against him is precisely that—that he didn't swing. If jazz can be defined as being a combination of improvisation and swing feeling . . .

SHEARER: But he *did*.

L.A.: He did what?

SHEARER: He *did*.

L.A.: He did have swing feeling?

SHEARER: Oh *yes*.

L.A.: Not all the time. Wait—how do you define swing?

SHEARER: Now we're getting into . . .

L.A.: Elements of jazz.

SHEARER: . . . We're getting into personal things.

L.A.: So swing can be anything you want to make it?

SHEARER: To me it can be. I mean if it's got that pulsating rhythm. Like the Basie type of swing is totally different from ours.

L.A.: What are the differences between his and yours?

SHEARER: Ours is more ponderous.

L.A.: It's not as relaxed, either.

SHEARER: No. when you deal with a lot of horns . . .

L.A.: It's a whole different thing.

SHEARER: . . . and the thickness of the chords . . .

L.A.: Jazz really needs a much broader scope, doesn't it. If you think of something like Stan's *Concerto to End All Concertos*. That's absolutely gorgeous, especially the twelve-bar theme written for trumpets in fifths, near the end.

SHEARER: Part of that was originally written around 1942, that Stan used for a theme for a show that he did. And then later on he reorchestrated it, and did the whole work.

L.A.: You mean that particular theme?

SHEARER: No, it was some other part of the *Concerto*. I think it was the trombone playing, that pretty thing: *Doo-doo-dee-doo-deee, . . . doo-dee-doo-doo-doo-dee-doo* . . . . .

L.A.: It's beautiful.

SHEARER: Then he did a whole composition around that, the whole *Concerto*.

L.A.: Was he doing any composing at all, later?

SHEARER: From what I understand he'd written a couple of things. He wrote a thing called "The World We Knew." We were always on his case to write.

L.A.: Stan was a master at psychology, wasn't he?

SHEARER: He would always have a way to introduce the audience to something that would make them aware, even if they wouldn't understand it. He would say, "We'd like to have you become very much interested in this new piece of experimental music." And right away the people'd go, "Oh, this is *new*." Even though they wouldn't like it, they'd go, "OH."

L.A.: They would dutifully listen, right?

SHEARER: Yes. And Stan had a very big belief that the mind controlled a lot of things. And the emotions. Like if he was getting sick he knew there was something that had to be wrong. He would say, "I got something bothering me, Dick. I've got a cold." He'd come back a couple of days later, and he wouldn't have his cold anymore. He rarely ever even took an aspirin. He was very much in control of himself, up to a certain point. When you think of all those years that he really abused his

15

body, still he never had a problem. The man was in his sixties—he'd never even been in a hospital until he was sixty years old! He hardly ever sneezed.

L.A.: Do they know what caused the stroke?

SHEARER: What happened, as I learned later, was that he got up to go to the bathroom one night, and fell. He hit his head. That brought on the stroke. It was strange—that exploratory operation they did on him in 1971—they left something in him that they shouldn't have. He had to go back and get that re-operated on. Then he was fine. Then pouf, the aneurysm hit. And the brain surgery in '77, and then this last thing.

L.A.: What's amazing is that, through all those years, with musicians coming and going, having wives and children and leaving the band and being replaced by others, with things sometimes falling by the wayside, Kenton endured.

SHEARER: It was his life. That's what he wanted to do. Everybody thought the band was pretty much on its way out around the late sixties. Then we came up and started the Redlands thing. Did that album, *Jazz Orchestra in Residence.* It's one of the classics. Stan believed that's where the future was, with young people in the universities.

L.A.: Last time I saw him, in 1975, he did seem to have a lot of young musicians in the band. Why would the personnel change?

SHEARER: They'd get tired. Tired of traveling.

L.A.: So they'd drop out and you'd get others.

SHEARER: Ya, I'd call somebody on the phone and say, "Hey. Got an opening. Come on."

L.A.: And what would they say?

SHEARER: "NO SHIT?!" (Laughter.) You know. Pardon me, but you know.

Or: "You're putting me on!" I've had things happen some nights, one of the guys would be sick, so I'd call somebody. I really didn't know 'em. I said come on we'd like you to play for the night. I called one guy I never will forget it . . . and I said uh . . . "I'm calling for Stan Kenton. Uh, we need a tenor player for tonight." "Who is this!" (Laughter.) I said this is my name. He says, "Come on, Ralph, is this you?" I says "No this is Dick Shearer." He says, "Don't give me that crap!" And he'd *hang up* on me!

L.A. Good grief! Then you'd call him back and you'd straighten it out, right?

SHEARER: No! *No!*

L.A.: (Laughs.) He never believed you and you never called him back?

SHEARER: *No!* I had a guy—it happened a couple of times, and one night a guy did show up at a gig and said, "Oh, I didn't know! I thought it was my partner! He's always doin' weird stuff like that to me."

L.A.: So many of them came to see him as a father figure.

SHEARER: He's my son's godfather.

L.A.: . . . And he seemed to like that.

SHEARER: Very much so.

L.A.: They obviously respected him.

SHEARER: Um-hm.

L.A.: It must be that in the beginning you were in awe of him.

SHEARER: Yes, I really was. We went out, the first time, for three or four months in the summertime, and it was something I enjoyed very much, playing all the music that I had listened to. It was like I'd been there all my life.

L.A.: Did you find it difficult to take your eyes off him when he was conducting?

SHEARER: I would watch him quite a bit, because I really knew what he was doing.

L.A.: What do you mean by that?

SHEARER: Sometimes the way he would conduct certain things—some of the guys weren't really familiar with the way he would do things.

L.A.: How would *you* know what he was doing?

SHEARER: I figured it out very quickly. I knew pretty much what he wanted.

L.A.: There's a story that the classical conductor Fritz Reiner, when he wanted a great big fortissimo from the orchestra, simply said, "Gentlemen, when I give you the cue I want you to give me everything you have," and he went—you know, like that—*(makes a tiny gesture)* and there was this *blast.* What was it like with Kenton?

SHEARER: Sometimes he would give very big gestures. And sometimes he would give things, like a cut-off, he'd get that twinkle in his eye and go—*(gestures)*—which is hard to describe on a tape.

L.A.: Would he keep eye contact with you?

SHEARER: Oh yes, all the time. He always had eye contact.

L.A.: It must have been more than eye, though. I must have been his whole being.

SHEARER: He had the eye, but he had the physical thing.

L.A.: So it's the charisma of the leader himself. It's not written down anywhere.

SHEARER: No.

L.A.: There's no way you can repeat it. He's going to remain . . .

SHEARER: . . . Oh, he's a paradox. It's one of those things you never can figure out. He'd get up there with the band, and boy you would just . . . *Cccceeewww.* You could *feel* the energy. Nothing was ever more exciting than when he put those arms out. And he stands six-foot four . . . .

GIOGA:

It was the spring of 1934.

We had a rehearsal that afternoon and Everett Hoaglund said,

"We've got a new piano player. Stan Kenton."

And here he is, just a skinny kid.

We looked over there and

some of us said "Hi, Stan."

I don't think any of us had played with him, or heard of him before.

We had a very good band. As a rule,

they didn't get the second-rate musicians,

or have to.

So we figured he must be good.

He sat down

and played

and he had a real—

when he touched the keys, you knew he was playing the

piano. He really set the musical tempo.

The rhythm section really felt it.

And when we were through rehearsing,

everybody felt that they had a good change there.

17

2 Bob Gioga
and George Faye

L.A.: Change from what?

GIOGA: The fella that we had before was an excellent pianist, but he was the type that was very flowery. He wasn't trying for rhythm, he was just an exhibitionist mostly on the piano. In a band, the rhythm section should not be flowery. Let somebody else do the improvising.

FAYE: When I came out here to California in '34, Hoaglund was *the* one. The top band.

Bob Gioga and George Faye, outside Gioga's California home. (Photo by the Author.)

18

GIOGA: The band that I was in before was Henry Halstead's. Bands usually change personnel every once in a while. Phil Harris, who later had his own orchestra, was playing drums. We played all the big spots, Fatty Arbuckle's Plantation in the Hollywood Roosevelt, the St. Francis in 'Frisco. I was with him for three years. After three years he let the whole band go, except the trumpet player and the lead sax. I joined Hoaglund's band, and I'd been playing with him down at the beach there, at Balboa, for about three years, like in '31, '32, and '33 before Stan came. So Stan thought, since he knew I'd been playing with him for so long, that I must know what I'm doing. We had a few other new guys, too, that had been playing a year or two professionally. I'd been playing eight or ten years.

L.A.: So Stan looked up to you?

GIOGA: He thought I knew what the score was.

L.A.: How did your close friendship get started?

GIOGA: I was renting a house down in Balboa, at the point. Fifty dollars a month, in the summer, for a furnished house. That was pretty good. I had a roommate named Bill Covey, who played lead alto in the band and who was exceptionally good. Bill led three lives—in one *day*. I had a phonograph and Bill had lots of records. So after work Stan used to come down and listen to the records. Bill was a big supply of information. He knew everybody who was playing, who they were and why they were doing this. And that's what Stan wanted to learn, why they did this and why they did that. Like Duke Ellington and other bands. Though Stan didn't go for Dixieland. We'd work from 8 to 12, and after work Stan would come down to listen. And then he'd drive home to Bell. So one night he said, "Gee, I wish I didn't have to go home." I said, "Gosh, we've got an extra bed here. We've got twin beds in one room, and a double in the other. Gosh, stay with us." Gosh he loved that. So for the rest of the season he stayed with us. It was pretty nice.

FAYE: Stan was a gentleman. He was one of the few orchestra leaders I could really call a gentleman: Stan, and Ray Noble, and Dave Rose. I can count 'em on one hand, the guys that I really respected as leaders.

L.A.: In what way? The way he treated his musicians?

FAYE: Yeah. He was gentle. He treated you like—

GIOGA: Absolutely.

FAYE: You know, he had respect for you. And didn't put you down. If he said anything it was constructive. He did everything he could for the guys. 'Cause he wanted his band to be like a family, I think. I joined his band at the Tunetown Ballroom in St. Louis on their first trip East in 1942. I'd been with Jerry Wald's band for six months, playing third trombone. I got a call to go down and

"ADIOS"—first chart in the first book of the first Stan Kenton Orchestra (bari sax part), 1941. (Courtesy of Bob Gioga.)

work with Stan. And here I get on lead. What a difference! I remember up at New Haven, we were working up there, after a job one night we were walking down the street, Stan and I and a coupla guys, and he says, "Boy, you sure have improved over how you played when you first came with the band." I says, "Aw, really?" I said "I always played like that." You know, I didn't realize myself that I was improving that much. But Stan noticed it. I believe him, because when I played the bottom horn all the time, I never had a thing to do. No solos, no nothing. Stan was enough of a gentleman to compliment me. Which encouraged me. Which was great. You need that.

L.A.: This is really exciting. You were there when he first put together his band, and as an experienced musician yourself you must have noticed certain things about Stan that were different right at the start.

GIOGA: That's right. When Stan organized his band, I did all the copying. Things were pretty tough around 1939. I was working down in San Diego and then I really came back here. It was cheaper living. Stan met his wife (Violet) down in Balboa in '34 when I met my wife, and they became friends. When we were with Hoaglund they used to come down and dance. So anyway, later on, about '39, Stan went up in the mountains, to Idyllwild, and wrote arrangements, and asked if I would copy them.

L.A.: Where's Idyllwild?

GIOGA: About twenty miles from Palm Springs. Stan would come down once a week with about three or four arrangements, and I'd transpose 'em and copy 'em for the 12-piece orchestra, whatever it was. Then after he got out about forty numbers, then he got a band together and made some test records.

L.A.: What impressed you about his arrangements at that early time? 'Cause you would have seen him progress from that stage to the Progressive Jazz Orchestra. You were with him until '53.

GIOGA: For one thing, they didn't sound like Basie. They didn't sound like Benny Goodman. They didn't sound like any particular band. In fact, at the first rehearsal, I remember we had two basses. And that was kind of strange.

L.A.: He wanted two bass players?

GIOGA: For that small band. But that didn't last. I didn't think it did anything, and I guess he didn't either, but I guess he was trying . . . .

FAYE: Trying. He was experimenting, he was always experimenting. That's Stan for you.

GIOGA: Stan had new sounds. In those days, the clarinet doubling with the lead alto was kind of the Benny Goodman sound, or the Artie Shaw sound. I think Glenn Miller also had that. And everybody thought that was real nice.

L.A.: (Laughs.)

FAYE: But Stan's first band had the short staccato sound: Rrrah!-pa-pa-pa-pa-pa. Almost everything was like that. It kind of kicked, you know? He got away from it eventually, when he started going more progressive. I joined the band when he was still doing that, playing that style. And I guess just starting to get away from it a little bit. It was enjoyable.

L.A.: One hears a lot about Stan's use of certain trombone patterns and unique saxophone voicings. Was there some of this in the beginning?

GIOGA: The band wasn't a large band to start with—we just had five brass and five saxes—so he had a number of tunes where he featured just the saxophones and the rhythm, like "Opus in Pastels" and a couple of others. Jack Ordean, our lead alto player, had a vibrant tone. He really played from the heart.

FAYE: He had a lot of drive. He got right into it.

GIOGA: You have one person like that, that's playing the lead, and then you have a fellow in front that's giving it to you . . .

FAYE: Stan, yeah.

GIOGA: In other words, when you're playing, he just doesn't stand there like Lawrence Welk and move the baton . . .

FAYE: He gets excited. Like the reed man, like Jack was.

GIOGA: He got really into it. "Let's—Let's express ourselves." So—

L.A.: So that made Jack Ordean play even better than he would have played.

GIOGA: It made him really pour it out even more than he was used to playing. And of course the saxophones went right along with him. You know, you hear this guy blowing, you go right along with him. After we were on the road about a year, Stan used to feature a good loud baritone saxophone, to fill the bottom.

L.A.: That's your instrument.

GIOGA: Right. And I'll tell you a little story that will show you what I mean. I

Hollis Bridwell, Jack Ordean, Red Dorris and Bob Gioga (not shown: Ted Romersa, left of Bridwell) on the bandstand at the Rendezvous Ballroom, opening engagement, 1941—Stan's first sax section. (Bridwell was replaced by Bill Lahey when the band left Balboa.) (Photo courtesy of Bob Gioga.)

Stan Kenton and his Orchestra at the Palladium, Hollywood, California, December 1941, first engagement following Balboa and two weeks of one-nighters to Portland, Oregon. (Photo: Courtesy of Bob Gioga.)

had a friend back then who also played baritone saxophone. He was one of the best baritone men out here. I'd played in his band in high school in 1923 and '24. He went into the studios, 'cause he was so good, so far ahead, where I just went into dance bands. He doubled on all kinds of instruments. Where the good brass men back then were making eighty-five dollars on a big program every week, he was making like a hundred and forty, with all his doubles baritone saxophone, bass clarinet, flute—he had about four doubles. Arrangers want you to have these doubles, because sometimes when they can't get ideas they'll use different instruments...

FAYE: It makes a lot of color in the arrangements.

GIOGA: Different colors, ya. They'd write in about four bars on bass clarinet or flute. So after I'd been playing with Stan and we'd come into town, this guy would come over to my house and say, "What kind of a mouthpiece are you using now?" (Laughs.) "Let me try your mouthpiece." He'd want me to show him how I was doing it, because he said

"They're asking me to try to get the tone that you get."

FAYE: Get a little more body.

GIOGA: I was blowing louder than the usual baritone man, and that's what they wanted. They wanted to hear the chord.

FAYE: The loudness. When I joined the orchestra, we had three trombones. It seemed to me like Stan used the trombones to get a lot of bottom sound. Things like "Eager Beaver," you could hear so much bottom. I'd get dizzy when I got through playing that number. I was losing all the oxygen, blowing that thing. (Laughs.) Believe me. I would get dizzy. But it was great. It built up your chops. And it made you play better. Oh, everybody played better.

L.A.: You played tenor trombone?

FAYE: Tenor trombone, yeah. The other two trombones were Bart Varsalona and Harry Forbes, and then later he added another one, so we had three tenors and a bass trombone. Four.

GIOGA: When he got his band together, Stan used local musicians, mostly

men who were out of work. I don't think anybody'd been with an Eastern name band. He could have got musicians that had been with big bands.

L.A.: Is that what he wanted to do? Choose his own musicians?

GIOGA: Ya. He wanted people that would play what he wanted to play. He didn't want somebody that had his own style. Everybody was willing. They liked the sound. They wanted to play this style. Having all these new guys, when we played, Stan very seldom played piano, he was always up there just leading the band. And really waving his arms, he was really feeling it. And you could see—you were playing, too. We had so much enthusiasm. As a rule you might have two people in a band who had some enthusiasm, in the average orchestra, large orchestra. In fact, most of them are depressed, because they're not getting as much as the guy sitting next to them. We got on national radio while we were at Balboa. I guess it was a Sunday, when there wasn't too much else of interest on radio to listen to. So

21

we got a lot of reaction from the East, inasmuch as the band *was* different, if nothing else. When we left for the East on our first tour, everybody was really on their toes.

FAYE: Everybody was really kickin' right along. We *enjoyed* doing what we were doing, that was the thing.

L.A.: What made it exciting? Was it Stan's own belief in what he was doing?
GIOGA: No—I think it was just the music that we were playing *was* exciting. It might not have been real progressive at that point, or something exceptionally new, but it had a lot of rhythm, a lot of feeling. There was no piano playing— we just had three rhythm, so it couldn't have just been the rhythm. Everybody was—was—

FAYE: Everybody was *driving*. Everybody was interested in what was happening, and getting a big *kick* out of it. Because it was good music. It was good.

It was good arranging. As far as we were concerned. And we were all like just driving like *Stan*. Trying to get something new going here.

GIOGA: Ya. And I think people *sensed* that. It was just like today, the young people sense that feeling, and like these rock bands today, you know, people don't know about music, I mean these kids, they just feel a bunch of beats going, and they think it's wonderful. I think it was probably similar to that. They *felt* it. And everybody was very excited. We could see the people loved it. So we even gave more. Stan was deriving from the cut-and-dried music that was being presented in the thirties. Artie Shaw, Benny Goodman with his clarinet and four saxophones—it was all wonderful jazz, and they actually didn't all sound the same, but it was sort of a stereotype, they were all the same type. This was the first thing that was *different*. The more we got back East—people there were just overenthusiastic about it.

Those that had heard us on the radio. We were on radio quite a bit then.

L.A.: Weren't there a couple of concerts before May 30, 1941?
GIOGA: We played at Huntington Beach, there on the pier. But it was before they got the job.

L.A.: Why did they consider Balboa the opening of the Stan Kenton Orchestra? Instead of . . .
GIOGA: Well, it was really the first *steady* job that we got. Gosh it must have been about eight months or so before, that we made records. Up at Music City. And the band was quite different then. I don't even remember that Jack Ordean was in the band at that time. That's when we had two basses.

L.A.: What were Stan's work habits like? Did you observe him while he was composing?
GIOGA: When he first came to live with us, down at Balboa, I had a 22-foot

Kenton band and dancers at the Rendezvous Ballroom. Easter Week engagement, about 1947. (Photo: Courtesy of Bob Gioga.)

22

Stan Kenton at the helm, sailing on Balboa Bay with his band, '40s. June Christy is in front row; Bob Gioga is in dark cap, second row. (Photo courtesy of Bob Gioga.)

racing sailboat. I'd take it out every day, usually about 8 in the morning. There'd be all these people that had danced there the night before, and they had found I had a sailboat—these people I didn't know would be waiting on the dock. I had my own wharf, which I rented for five dollars a month. Today you couldn't get it for fifty. I'd take out the boat and sail all day, really getting my kicks. Stan would come by in the afternoon—he'd be at the ballroom, arranging, trying to figure things out. Never went swimming. Oh, occasionally, the three of us—Bill Covey and Stan and I—would go down on the beach, maybe about once a month. We'd go down on the beach, and lie there and throw the baloney. Covey was such a great musician. Played clarinet just like Benny Goodman. He was doing radio shows at seventeen. He got me in on the Bing Crosby show.

FAYE: We did the Bob Hope show one season. Entertained troops, traveled all across the country.
GIOGA: We'd do the show on a Tuesday, then fly to our next job, then fly back.
FAYE: Join 'em for the show. We had Frances Langford, Jerry Cologna . . .

GIOGA: And we had the Three Stooges with us for about a month.
FAYE: But Stan couldn't wait to get *off* that show. He felt it was holding him *back*. They tried to make a comedian out of him, writing lines for him on the show. And he didn't enjoy that.
GIOGA: No, he didn't.
FAYE: I could see it. He really didn't like it. Boy, he couldn't wait until he got out of that. Stan was one of those guys that was driving. And he kind of knew in a way what he wanted. He was *progressive*. He just wanted to get away from that, and start something new.

GIOGA: He wanted the music to grow. And he was in a stalemate there, because they wanted a certain type of music. We even had five members of the band sing the introduction.
L.A.: "Thanks for the Memory"?
FAYE: It was "Poor Mirium." It was a toothpaste commercial. I sang with the group, and Red Dorris and Dolly Mitchell.
L.A.: You mean the orchestra sang the commercial?
FAYE: Yes.
L.A.: (Laughs.)
FAYE: Yeah. It was *good*. You're laughing now, but we went to rehearsal, we

went to the studios one week. We played it back, and I was *amazed* how *good* it sounded. I know Buddy Childers was in it. He didn't even know he could sing, but when he—they were paying seventy-five dollars.
L.A.: (Laughs.)
FAYE: We knew we'd make more money! It was good for us, really.

GIOGA: Stan would be going day and night. It was unbelievable. We'd quit a job at 1 a.m., and he'd drive 400 miles to the next job. He'd have radio interviews, and go to the department stores to promote his records.
FAYE: We did some movie shorts, too.

GIOGA: Ya, a whole bunch of them. When I left the band in 1953, I didn't think he'd last another three or four months. Maynard Ferguson and I were sort of rooming together. Maynard said "Well I'm gonna leave after the Palladium" and I said "Gee, I've been thinking about it, too." I said "I don't think Stan can hold up." He was burning himself up.
L.A.: How can a person live like that? What was driving him?
GIOGA: He wanted to make the music—progress in some way . . .

23

FAYE: There are people like that. We recorded "Artistry in Rhythm" the first time he recorded it. Right here in Hollywood.

L.A.: What did you guys think of the theme?

FAYE: Oh! Fantastic!

L.A.: Did you know that it was going to become immortal? (Laughs.)

FAYE: I loved it. I just thought it was great. It started out like—so fast. (Tapping finger.) *Taptaptaptaptaptaptaptaptap Da-daaa, dadoodeedee, dee-dee . . . .* The rhythm is double time, you know. I've always liked the theme, I mean—it was great.

L.A.: You mentioned Dolly Mitchell and Red Dorris. Who were some of the other singers with the band in those days?

GIOGA: Kay Gregory was our first girl singer. Helen Kerr—she wasn't with the band very long. Gene LaSalle. We had a singer, Helen Huntley, who only lasted with the band a month. They wouldn't let her on the air, in New York. I never got the complete reason why. Eve Knight was another. She was with the band about four or five months. Anita O'Day. Gene Howard. Kay Brown, who was Maynard Ferguson's girlfriend. June Christy. Gosh, he had a bunch of 'em. We had a jazz violinist at one time, too.

L.A.: You *did?*

GIOGA: Otvos. Harold Otvos. We picked him up in the East somewhere. Somebody suggested it—"Here's the greatest jazz violinist"—and he *was.* He was *fabulous.* Funny thing, nobody ever mentions it.

L.A.: What period of time was this, that he was with you?

GIOGA: I can't remember. He was with the band about six months. He was the nicest person a person could meet. Like when we were traveling on the bus, if anybody wanted a sandwich, he'd say, "Let me get it for you." He always wanted to run errands. And he was so sensational. We had no arrangements for him. Stan would just say, "Okay, Hal." Stan never auditioned any musicians, either. If somebody had recommended him, he figured the fellow knows what he's talking about. Even if he didn't accept him, he must have some quality or this person wouldn't recommend him. So he usually turned out quite well.

FAYE: Stan Getz was with us in 1944. Baby-faced boy. What a memory that guy had. He told me, after two weeks, he never took the library out. Had a photographic memory.

GIOGA: No, it was the third day.

FAYE: Third *day?* Oh God. That's worse.

GIOGA: There was another guy— Eddie Meyers, took Jack Ordean's place on lead alto. He was from one of the radio stations. It used to bug Stan—this guy was always looking at him, never at his music. We never rehearsed our numbers. We could get a new man and he'd play it right off. Eddie could read about four bars ahead.

FAYE: You can read ahead, you see, you can see your music ahead, if you practice that. Instead of reading each note, you can read ahead to see what's coming.

GIOGA: Eddie's sitting in the middle, there, looking down, up, around, at Stan, never at his music. Stan said "What *goes* with that guy?" (Laughs.) "I was watching him, and he just came on the band, how can he tell what *music* he's supposed to read?" Well Stan Getz was like that. He joined us after we left the Palladium and were going up the Coast, playing one-nighters. They'd want to hear certain tunes, those that

Jazz violinist Harold Otvos, featured with the Stan Kenton Orchestra, summer 1946. (Photo courtesy of Bob Gioga.)

24

we'd recorded and played on the air—usually about 35 or 40 tunes. Sometimes we'd change them around, skip from say letter E to something else. I sat on the end, and Stan Getz sat next to me. I'd say "Jump from B to F" or something. It was marked, but just to be sure, you know, that he doesn't slip. The next night I said the same thing, "Jump from B to F." He says "*I* know *that.*" You know, like, gosh, you told me yesterday, what're you, what're you doin'? You know, I've been told. So he kind of brought me down. Now, the third night, we were moving on to different ballrooms, and the band boy sets them all up, we've got these nice gold-and-white stands—five of them for the saxophones right in front, and the piano and guitar over there—and Stan Getz takes his stand and puts it over back of the orchestra. So we're all set up, ready to go. And Stan walks up, you know, 8:30. He looks over at Getz and he walks over and says "Hey, where's your stand?"

Getz says "I don't need it." "What do you mean, you don't need it?" "I know the whole book." Stan says, "That doesn't make any difference. You go get that stand. We want a *picture* here." Getz was the biggest baby.

L.A.: Mr. Faye, how long were you with the band?

FAYE: A year, year and a half. I made some albums with Stan. I was married at the time, and I decided when I got to Hollywood the last time I'd had enough traveling. So I stayed right there and I went right on staff at radio station KHJ. Then later I had a contract at United Artist studios, and everything started falling my way. I started free-lancing at all of 'em. It was just unbelievable.

L.A.: And what are you doing now?

FAYE: I'm with this group, forty trombones. We rehearse every Saturday morning, from 9 to 1, at Orange Coast College. It's with George Roberts, who's just about the greatest bass trombone

player of all—he was with Stan about four years. Forty trombones and a rhythm section. And you should hear it! We're gonna give a concert on May 2nd.

L.A.: What's the name of the group?

FAYE: Bones West. I'll tell ya. You should hear this thing. We play jumpin' things, swinging things. "Have You Met Miss Jones" and "New York, New York."

L.A.: My gosh. Just imagine what Kenton would have thought of it.

FAYE: Ohh! He would have wanted to *write* something for it.

L.A.: (Laughs.) He would, wouldn't he.

GIOGA: Anything that's progressive...

FAYE: Anything that's progressive, yeah. Oh, boy! In fact, we do play some of his things. You know what? You know what I like about Stan? The legacy that he left. When he passed away, he didn't want anybody going around saying This is so-and-so with the Stan Kenton Orchestra. I thought that was great. There's only one Stan Kenton.

Stan Kenton and his band. Red Dorris, Chet Ball, Eddie Myers, Duane Tatro, Bob Gioga; Gene Englund, Joe Vernon, Harry Forbes, Ray Wetzel, Bart Varsalona. (Photo: U.S. Army Air Corps. Courtesy of Bob Gioga.)

L.A.: If you had to pick three or four qualities about him that you remember more than anything, what would they be?

FAYE: Ohh. I think he was a dedicated man. He was an honorable man. And he was fair. And he was interested in the guys that worked with him.

L.A.: Took a personal interest in their lives?

FAYE: Took a personal interest in everybody, ya.

GIOGA: And he really did.

FAYE: He did, really.

GIOGA: Even if he hadn't met your parents, if he hadn't seen you for a couple of months or longer, the first thing he'd ask was "How's your father doing? How's your father, and your mother?" You know? And it really wasn't that it was a—a line with him. He actually was interested in how they were. Incidentally, Stan's mother was one of my wife's best friends. They were very close.

FAYE: I went over to see him at Dis-neyland at one of his last appearances there. I hadn't seen Stan in years. I came over, and he was sitting there with some people, and he got right up and he came right over and gave me the biggest hug. A big bear hug. I was so—I was just thrilled. That he would even bother.

GIOGA: I don't want to cut you, but I did the same thing and he *kissed* me.

FAYE: (Laughs.)

L.A.: (Laughs.)

FAYE: Well he didn't kiss me, but I was

Stan Kenton, backstage at the RKO Theater in Cleveland, Ohio with an admirer, 1945. (Photo: Courtesy of Bob Gioga.)

Above: Stan Kenton in trio with Bob Kesterson, bass; Johnny Boch, drums; 1945. (Photo courtesy of Bob Gioga.)

Left: Stan Kenton, on *Metronome* cover, '40s. (Courtesy of Bob Gioga.)

glad to get the hug from him! It was a real bear hug. He was a giant, you know? And it was just like in the forties, people came to listen. He set it up that way, so the first set would be a concert. He'd announce it, and the people would sit down, right on the dance floor. Or stand around. The next set he'd say, "This'll be a dance session here." And he'd play dance music, a lot of dance numbers that he had arranged. It was great! Then next session would be a concert, and the last one would be a dance. Played four sets, and that was it for the night.

L.A.: You say it was like that in the forties?

FAYE: Yeah! They'd be standing 50-deep out there.

GIOGA: Ya.

FAYE: Listening to the band! Like it was a concert. Even at a dance! You know? They'd stand twenty-five, fifty deep. I've seen it happen.

GIOGA: I started a scrapbook, for the first year of the band. My wife Dorothy was Stan's personal secretary for eight

BAND LEADERS

JUN.
15¢
K

KRUPA
STOP-ACTION SHOTS

SINATRA...SINATRA...**SINATRA!**

KITTY KALLEN
Full-Color Pin-up Pic

COMPREHENSIVE RECORD REVIEWS

STAN KENTON

Cover Art, Stan Kenton on *Band Leaders* magazine, '40s. (Courtesy of Bob Gioga.)

years, and whenever there was any throwaway stuff, I would accept it. We can look through that.

L.A.: (Looking through the scrapbook.) Look at these headlines! *Balboa Contribution to Jazz Unsung. The Band Sensation of the Nation.* I love this: A quote of Stan's in the headline: *"We May Not Be The Best, But We're Surely Different."*

FAYE: (Laughs.) *"We're Surely Different."*

GIOGA: Here's a nice quote from an article by George Frazier, a jazz critic, in April, 1942: *"Stan Kenton's Band Will Be Devastating, and Nothing Can Be Done About It."*

L.A.: *That* sums it up, doesn't it?

FAYE: (Looking at photo.) I didn't know you doubled on trumpet!

GIOGA: I played at the Pavilion in Balboa with the Trojan Tooters, in 1925. I played trumpet with one band, nothing but trumpet. I think I had an oboe there, too.

L.A.: What's that picture of Stan on the cover of that music? "How Could You Do That To Me?" I don't remember that song at all. Is that a song that he wrote?

GIOGA: No. They just put his picture on it for some reason.

L.A.: Why?

GIOGA: We never played the number or anything. I've got about a dozen of these. Different pictures—er songs—that wanted to use Stan's picture.

L.A.: To sell the thing?

GIOGA: Yeah. They had to put *somebody's* picture on it, so . . .

L.A.: But why Stan Kenton?

GIOGA: I don't know. (Laughs.) We never even played that. It says "Featured by Stan Kenton and the Orchestra" but . . .

L.A.: You were the band manager with Stan for twelve years. What did that involve?

GIOGA: I sort of ran the bus, which means I just told the guys "We're all here, let's go." And I had to get the rooms and the transportation. We'd get these three months ahead of time—ninety one-nighters. I'd write ahead for rooms, six doubles, six twins and six singles. And of course some of the guys always wanted singles, but they'd have their wife in with them. (Laughs.) It was really a problem. Sometimes some of the guys would get some girls that hung around the band that weren't too legitimate, and some of the wives that weren't going on the trip would see this when they saw us off and would tell their husbands, "If THEY go—you *stay.*" So I'd have to go in the bus and tell them, "Gee, we're sorry, we just can't let you go. We've had some objections." But Stan was good about letting the wives travel with us. When we left for the East we had about three wives and a couple of kids and a cat and I don't know what else. And if anybody wanted to take a girlfriend—and Bart Varsalona usually did—

FAYE: Yeah. (Laughs.)

GIOGA: . . . it was all right with Stan. Before our first trip East, we'd known him for many months by then, he said "We're goin' back East. We're gonna have a lot of competition. I don't care what you guys do off the bandstand. But when you get on the bandstand, I want you guys to be *blowing.* That's all I ask."

L.A.: During this time you would have seen the development of the brass section, from three trumpets and two trombones to a full ten brass. And the filling out of the famous Kenton sound, the development of the chord.

Opposite page:

Stan Kenton, cover photo, *Metronome* magazine, 1947. (Courtesy of Bob Gioga.)

28

JANUARY, 1947 25¢

M*etronome*

THE REVIEW OF THE
MUSIC WORLD

COMPLETE RECORD SURVEY
ALL STAR WINNERS
LOUIS ARMSTRONG
DIZZY GILLESPIE
HOAGY CARMICHAEL

STAN KENTON
BAND OF THE YEAR

GIOGA: Yes. Well you start out with simple harmony, the lead, say, and two harmony parts—in simple music, like in cowboy music and things like that. But in more modern music, you have a third harmony part, which can be a seventh or a sixth. In some modern music, you have five or six notes sometimes.

FAYE: They write 'em real—get a real tight sound, a real close harmony sometimes sounds real dissonant, because they like the sound so close together. But overall the effect is great.

L.A.: Well then as you went from three trumpets to four and then five, and from three trombones to four and then five, you added notes to the chord, you added an interval in the writing?

GIOGA: Ya. It made it sound fuller. The lead trumpet would play the melody, and the two underneath would play the first harmony and the second harmony. When they got to five trumpets, they could add the seventh and they could find different notes to add to the chord, along with the fifth and the third. Actually all good arrangers do that. In Kenton's band, Gene Roland had a lot to do with it. He was on and off the band several times, and sometimes when Stan said "We need an arranger" I would say "Gee, how about Gene again?" "Gene?!"

FAYE: Bob was Gene's biggest booster. (Laughs.)

L.A.: Why did you like Gene Roland?

GIOGA: 'Cause he was a character.

L.A.: (Laughs.)

FAYE: He really was!

GIOGA: He didn't care about money, or anything. He cared about—well he liked women.

FAYE: And music.

GIOGA: I used to room with him occasionally. It was really a little bit *frightening*. He's the type that, after work, he doesn't think of going to the hotel or anything. He's out for some excitement. *Anything.* I remember once—I forget where it was—it was some big town. But a lady came up, a nice-looking lady—and said to Stan, "I'd like the band to come over." I think she said she had a cafe, somethin', like that. I forget how she put it. And Stan, during the evening, said "We're all invited out after work." So we got off about 11. He says "We'll all go over there together." It was downtown someplace. So we went up to this place. And—all walked in. It was a real nice place. Some nice-looking

women, y'know, there, and uh—like we were kind of waiting there, our hands out like this, like, "Where's the food?" y'know. I forget how it got going, but it was a little bit embarrassing. Nobody knew what to do—some of the fellows were quite naive about the whole situation—except Gene Roland! (Laughs.) He knew what was happening all the time! And finally, the lady said to Stan, something on the side, and like Stan was surprised—he didn't know—it was gonna turn out *that* way. It was really a house of ill repute. (Laughs.) I don't know whether—I guess—I guess uh—I guess we were gonna have special *rates* or *something.* You know?

L.A.: (Laughs.)

FAYE: (Laughs.)

GIOGA: But Stan was a little embarrassed about it, so—we were all kind of looking at the girls and—and not knowing where we were going to sit for dinner or what. But anyway. Stan came over. And we all huddled around him. He said "Well—there's a little misunderstanding here, and—" Gene says, "Well, listen, Stan, I'm gonna stay."

L.A.: (Laughs.)

FAYE: (Laughs.)

GIOGA: (Laughs.) And he *did.* I think Stan said, "Gene, you don't have any money." He says, "Stan, I'll see you in the morning." And he did stay. As I remember, we all disappointedly walked out, and back to the hotel. And Stan said "Gee, I didn't know, I'm sorry, I didn't know it was gonna be like that." We used to have some wild times. We'd go to a restaurant, and when it came time to pay the bill Stan would only have a fifty-dollar bill and would ask for my help. And I would peel off a hundred- or a five-hundred-dollar bill, and the guy would gasp. Serves him right—he was a real El Cheapo, charging us thirty-five cents just for bread for our dinner. Or we'd be shopping in some little grocery store somewhere, usually late at night, and these guys are like all over the place, down the aisles, and the manager would be very nervous and watching us. So I'd say in a good loud voice, "Okay, now don't steal anything." Then he'd *really* get nervous. And we'd go to the check-out counter and I'd pay for it with a $500 bill.

L.A.: (Laughs.)

GIOGA: Stan was so good. If all the rooms at our motel were taken up through some sort of mistake he'd be the last to see to his own needs and would think nothing of taking his satchel and

going down the block to another motel—after his musicians were seen to.

L.A.: It sounds as though you had some wonderful times. Whatever made you leave, in 1953? At that time you were the last original member.

GIOGA: My dad was getting old and I figured—figured I should check out, give somebody a chance—actually, there were so many good musicians around, I really felt a little bit embarrassed.

L.A.: My gosh. I bet he was sorry to see you leave. Maybe I should ask, what *kept* you on the band for all that time, while others were coming and going so much?

GIOGA: Stan and I were close friends. I love music. I would have worked for nothing. In fact, when we were back East I—occasionally I'd buy an MG Roadster. I'd had one out here, when we were working the Palladium, and I'd sell it when we left—when we flew—we were on the Bob Hope show and we flew to Kansas, and I saw one in a showroom. They had two of 'em, and they couldn't sell 'em in this college town. It was cold in Manhattan, Kansas. So I said, "Well, gee, I just sold mine, but I'd be interested. We're leaving tomorrow morning." This was like on a Saturday. And he says "I'll sell you this for cost." And he showed me the thing. It had a heater on it, that's all. It was $1665. I said "Well how about the tax and license?" "That's five dollars extra." So I bought it. And I drove it a lot. I was supposed to ride with the bus, but we'd go for a couple of weeks and like I told the bus driver—the bus driver says "You'd better get that thing out of the way, you know, 'cause when I start going, I don't want you in front of me." And I said, "Listen. If you ever pass me, there's a five-dollar bill in it for you."

L.A.: (Laughs.)

FAYE: (Laughs.)

GIOGA: And he never passed me, for many, many, many times. But I always had a standing line waiting, you know, the wives would get so tired riding on the bus, they wanted to get out and see the world a little bit. Sometimes I would even take, instead of staying on the main highway, I'd take some secondary road, where you'd go through New England and all the beautiful country. Coming down, we were going to Atlantic City, that was my downfall. Had the top down.

FAYE: (Laughs.)

30

GIOGA: One of the wives was riding with me. Like I said to her, "You know, I'm getting paid for this. And here we are. Enjoying the sunshine, look, it's so beautiful, look at the scenery. Tonight, have a good dinner, and then get on the bandstand with the greatest band in the country. Play for four or five hours. And then, have a room in a nice hotel. And I get *paid* for this. I can't *believe* it."

FAYE: When the music business is right, there's *nothing* like it. There's nothing like it.
GIOGA: Just about that time, a dark cloud came over . . .
L.A.: (Laughs.)
FAYE: (Laughs.)

GIOGA: . . . and all hell broke loose. And—I had the side curtains stacked in the back and I couldn't figure out how to—I stopped, pulled over right away and I said "See if you can put up the side curtains." I started putting up the top, and just then, the bus went by, and everybody was leaning out the window! *Horns,* people waving . . . .

Bob Gioga and George Faye, outside Gioga's California home. (Photo by the Author.)

Buddy Childers. (Photo courtesy of Buddy Childers.)

3 Buddy Childers

CHILDERS: *Stan had to save some money on the second orchestra and that cost him in personnel, especially in the strings.*

L.A.: *You mean the first Artistry in Rhythm orchestra versus the Innovations?*

CHILDERS: *No, I'm talking about the first Silly Symphony.*

L.A.: *The first what?*

CHILDERS: *Silly Symphony.*

L.A.: *(Laughs.) Silly Symphony? You mean Innovations I and Innovations II.*

CHILDERS: *Is that what he called them?*

L.A.: (Laughs.) Yes.

CHILDERS: I called them the Silly Symphony. And I had a very good reason for calling them that. Because that year we had a coal strike. John L. Lewis pulled everybody out on strike, and Stan started this 45-piece orchestra . . .

L.A.: (Laughs.)

CHILDERS: . . . and—we're rehearsing it—while we're in the middle of a rehearsal a national emergency was called, closing down all places of entertainment, all athletic things, and everything, and we went out and did a tour in the middle of winter. Back East. Now if that ain't a Silly Symphony I never heard of one. It cost him hundreds of thousands of dollars.

L.A.: I heard he lost $250,000 on both of them.

CHILDERS: Well he had to try to save something on the second one. I doubt he lost that much on the second one. In 1950 already things were tough for a big band, and we're talking about 16 or 17 men. For us to go out with *45* is kinda *silly*. But it was only silly financially.

Musically, it was a magnificent thing to do. I don't think anything any better has ever been done. It was one of my two favorite bands. My other favorite was the Bill Holman band of '52-'53, the Gerry Mulligan/Bill Holman band. Gerry opened the way, but Bill was the one that really did it. Gerry wrote about a half dozen things for the band. Stan hated 'em. The band loved 'em. Stan would play 'em, but he's standin' there, shakin' his head, he couldn't figure out why we loved it. Soon as he'd get off the stand I'd immediately call the tunes, and if he was late coming back, like sometimes he'd have to collect the money and stuff like that, we'd play the charts he hadn't let us play. It started in 1950 with Shorty Rogers.

L.A.: Though Shorty wrote some of those classic things like "Maynard Ferguson" also.

CHILDERS: "Maynard Ferguson" was a *masterpiece*. The "Art Pepper" thing—incredible. Two wonderful things. The "Maynard Ferguson" piece was so perfectly presented. It laid such a challenge on Maynard to play—but he

did, like, *doo-wee-dee-dee-doo, wee-dee-dee-doo, wee-dee-dee-doo, WEE-dee-dee-doo*—the hardest thing. It was gorgeous. It was tailor-made for Maynard, and it just stretched him to his limits. All the way. In every way it was gorgeous. It was perfect.

L.A.: Did anyone else ever play it?

CHILDERS: No one has ever attempted to play it.

L.A.: Wouldn't you think that he'd play that in his own orchestra?

CHILDERS: Why?

L.A.: 'Cause it's a nice piece of music. It was written just for him.

CHILDERS: It was also written for a whole string section and a whole bunch of things that his orchestra doesn't *have*.

L.A.: That's a shame. That's my one regret about some of this music.

CHILDERS: It was written for forty-five people, and his band is what, he's got six brass, three saxophones, and three or four ryhthm. He's got a 12- or 13-piece band. He could not possibly play that with his band and have it sound right.

33

Stan Kenton — Metronome's Band of 1946

Stan Kenton and his Band of the Year, 1946, *Metronome* magazine. (Courtesy of Bob Gioga.)

L.A.: That means it'll never be heard again. Probably.

CHILDERS: Nope. No that was the only time it was supposed to be heard.

L.A.: I guess as a trumpet player you'd have a finer appreciation of it than most of us. What special qualities would you say a person needed to play in the Stan Kenton orchestra?

CHILDERS: Uh . . . . Insanity.

L.A.: (Laughs.)

CHILDERS: You've got to be kind of crazy to want to do it. Long on dumbs. If you're long on dumbs, it helps. Because you don't know that it's too hard, so you go ahead and do it.

L.A.: You mean you're—how does the saying go—too stupid to be scared.

CHILDERS: Something like that, ya. What happens is you feel good one night so you play a high G and you do something or you take something up an octave. The next thing you know, some writer comes in, he's written something a little similar to this but it doesn't feel right and it doesn't play right on the horn, but he's written it for you. I wanted to play trumpet in that band. I was a kid. I was a talented kid when I joined the band.

L.A.: You were the prodigy. Sixteen years old when they picked you up in St. Louis.

CHILDERS: Yes. I lived in Belleville, Illinois with my grandmother. The first time I saw him was actually in September of 1942. That first night I told my girlfriend, "I'll never be good enough to be in this band." I went up to him at break and asked for his autograph. He says "What's your name?" I says "Marion," which is my real name. He said "Okay." Wrote an autograph out to me. Then something happened to me within the next two months. Several things. I got called to join a couple of bands. Then when they saw how young I was they changed their minds. They didn't ever hear me play. But there was just something changed in my whole thinking. I realized what was happening. I was getting calls to work with bands in St. Louis and everywhere, all over. Suddenly I realized I was a good player. And so the next time I saw Stan, two or three months later, I had a confidence that I had never had before. He was appearing that night across the river in St. Louis, Missouri. I went up to him—the war was going on then, and I decided that if I was gonna get a chance

to play I had to do it then—I had a lot of childish ideas—I went up to him and I said "Stan . . ." He said "Hi, Marion, how are you?" Just like that. *Wo.* This man remembered *me.* Stan had that faculty. I said I wanted to audition. And he said "Well certainly."

L.A.: Isn't that pretty nervy for a sixteen-year-old kid to do? Or was that par for the course?

CHILDERS: It's stupid. You know. When you don't know any better, what are you gonna do?

L.A.: Did you have quite a reputation in high school for being a good player?

CHILDERS: Ya, by then.

L.A.: So even though you knew how good the Kenton band was, you had confidence in your ability to handle it.

CHILDERS: I knew I was good enough to do it. I mean I felt that I was. He said "Can you come over here about Tuesday afternoon?" Or Wednesday or whatever it was. "Sure." He said "Well don't you have school?" I said "Don't worry about it."

L.A.: (Laughs.)

CHILDERS: I went in, and he put me in the lead trumpet chair. And I said "No, I'd rather play—I didn't come over here to play the lead trumpet chair, I just want to . . ." He says, "No, go ahead."

L.A.: You mean to audition?

CHILDERS: Ya.

L.A.: Wow.

CHILDERS: Well you figure out later on, that's how you tell what a fella can do. Give him something to do. And I had a particularly good day reading. My adrenalin was roaring that day, naturally, and everything just kept poppin' at me so quickly that I didn't get a chance to get that nervous. I played probably well over my head that particular day. Afterwards I said, "But Stan. That's not what I came to do. I just want to play solos with you." And he said "You want to play solos? You play jazz?" "Ya." And he said "Well the rehearsal's over. Can you come back some night this week, Friday night?" "Ya." So I did. I came back.

L.A.: What was it like for a young kid in those days to join a band like that?

CHILDERS: As a matter of fact they gave me a terrible time. The people in the band. When I joined it. Because I was a kid. I had to pay my dues. They were real nice to me until I became one of them. Then they wouldn't let me be one of them. And I would never advise any kid to go on the road. It's just nothing. It really is wrong. Stay with

your own people. But—the meanness and everything else, I lived through all of that. I wouldn't ever want to do it again. I didn't want to do it that time. Once I was there I was there.

L.A.: What did they do that was mean?

CHILDERS: Oh just everything. It's the way they treat you. Nobody would talk to you. Nobody—the butt of all jokes. I was very naive. I wasn't a hip kid. I was a country hick. I really was. And I'd been taught if you were—you know, everybody told the truth all the time. I was with guys who dealt from the bottom of the *deck. Literally.* They took my salary, week after week.

L.A.: That *is* mean.

CHILDERS: Stan Getz, too—they took his. And *Pete Rugolo's.* They took *his.*

L.A.: Why, was he a naive kid?

CHILDERS: He wasn't a naive kid, but Pete was a very lovely—as he is today—a lovely, beautiful, gentle, wonderful man. He just liked to stay on everything when he was playing poker. If he had two cards, that was enough to stay on. It didn't have to be a pair, or anything else. Pete just, every week, donated his salary. I finally figured out who did what, and when any of those guys dealt from the bottom of the deck, I just turned my hand over. I would never play against them. It was very simple.

L.A.: You didn't take over lead chair right away, did you?

CHILDERS: No. At first I took one of the guy's places, John Carroll. He was going off to be tested for the draft. And he came back 4-F and about the time he came back Chico Alvarez had to leave. He was one of the last original members left. And Chico had to leave; Chico they accepted. So I stayed on in that chair. But I started playing some of the lead. One night, a few months later, we were playing a dance at the Shrine Auditorium out here, it was the last tune, when three of the guys laid out to play a high note that wasn't written, and I was the only one playing my part. Stan cut the band off, he says, "You, you, and you, you're fired. You—" pointing at me—"you're my new first trumpet player." He changed his mind about one of them later, but I was supposedly his lead player. He had doubts about it later on, I think. Got somebody else and tried to make him the lead player, but I still wound up being the lead. That's the way it worked out. He kept trying to get somebody else to replace me while I was there for the next two years and finally

35

said "Oh well," 'cause I was doing . . .

L.A.: Why was he trying to replace you?

CHILDERS: *I* don't know. He'd get somebody else to play lead and would listen from out front and say "Gee that doesn't sound any better" or whatever. So I was the lead player.

L.A.: Does the lead trumpet player play jazz solos also?

CHILDERS: Well, I did. At that point—now they do, ya. In those days it didn't happen. I mean you had the guy play first, the guy play solos, and never the twain shall meet. But that changed. You know. There should never have been anything like that. But the music business was very very young at that point.

L.A.: In the beginning they were two separate things.

CHILDERS: If you played jazz solos you were a jazzer, and if you played first trumpet you were a first trumpet player. That's the way it was. The first trumpet player was usually the guy who had the most training and had never learned to play jazz. The jazz player was the guy that just sort of came along and picked up the horn and had to learn to read notes while he was in the band. They accepted a lot of mediocre section work in return for his solo work. I was part of a group that was coming along that was doing both.

L.A.: Were there other trumpeters that played solo also?

CHILDERS: Sure. Pete Candoli did.

L.A.: Boy you must have really worn out your lip.

CHILDERS: No no no no. You find ways to rest. Or you get strong. You're young, you don't know any better.

L.A.: How'd you handle those high notes, up in the stratosphere? Blacking out, and that kind of thing.

CHILDERS: You just learn to live with it.

L.A.: So then the writers would see what you could do and they'd write for that.

CHILDERS: They just kept writing harder and harder things, and because they wrote harder and harder things, you had to learn to play 'em.

L.A.: Any composer in particular?

CHILDERS: Pete (Rugolo) was very good at that. And then things like Bob Graettinger's original *City of Glass* were impossible to play, but we did. We learned to do it. So it wasn't impossible, it just seemed that way.

L.A.: I didn't know there was more than one version of *City of Glass.*

CHILDERS: It was only performed three times. We played three successive concerts, successive nights, at the Opera House in Chicago. That's the only time we ever performed that. That was the 1946-47 band, with Shelly Manne and Eddie Safranski and Ray Wetzel . . .

L.A.: That wasn't part of Innovations, then.

CHILDERS: No, this was prior to that, this was the Artistry in Rhythm band, the band that won the *Look Magazine* Band of the Year Award in 1946. That was the original *City of Glass*. The one that was recorded was six years later. And had been rewritten so many times none of it was recognizable from the original. Graettinger I know would know within his own mind the themes were there, but he wove things in and around each other to disguise everything, everything was disguised. When we played his things, something I couldn't understand but we'd play, I would say at first, "Well that stinks." Then later I said "No. I don't know whether it does or not. I'm gonna have to reserve judgment on that 'til *I* learn more. And when I learn enough maybe I'll come to a—maybe if I listen to this two years, two months from now, or two years or twenty years, I'll be able to make a decision on whether that's musical or not. Whether it's good, and it's just my lack of knowledge."

L.A.: That's amazing.

CHILDERS: With Graettinger I would say that he was very very—he could have been a very important composer. He was so introverted, I don't know if anyone ever really knew him.

L.A.: What was his music like to play?

CHILDERS: I felt that he had a tendency to overwrite everything. He overloaded everything. Yet he heard everything that way. He could hear all these things. But he would wind up adding so many little things that you'd have all the half-tones, you'd have every possible beat of every possible . . . I would say every possible division of a beat, covered with somebody playing from beginning to end always, on everything he wrote. And it would just be to a point that only he would know which part of that melody that wove in and out of—it's like plastering the whole thing across the wall and hearing it all at once and letting the melody—there is a *melody* in there. But he would be the only one that—although some of it, it was quite atonal music, to some degree. And we'd have some of these parts that were *dee-DEE-da-DA (sings atonal phrase)*—We'd be going like *you* are. And he'd say, "Can't you hear that lovely *melody?*" He would say. "Can't you hear that beautiful melody." I said, "He really means it. And he's not nuts. He's a very intelligent man. So—I have to reserve judgment on this until later."

L.A.: From Bill Holman to Bob Graettinger. You certainly covered the spectrum of sounds on the Kenton band. How long were you on it altogether?

CHILDERS: Eleven and a half years, or let's say covering a span of that time, from when I joined in 1943 through 1954. And at certain periods I also played with Woody Herman, Les Brown, and Tommy Dorsey. I actually went through all of the different styles, major style changes of the band. It didn't change much from 1953 on. The band was a year and a half old when I joined it. They still had a little bit of the original Balboa band when I joined it, but already it was changing. They had a lot of different sidemen in it. A lot of guys from the East. It went through all kinds of changes. At one period after Glenn Miller died—I think it was Gene Howard's idea—they had the clarinet band, in which they voiced the five clarinets exactly one octave higher than the five trumpets and they played things together. It was the most horrendous sound you ever heard.

L.A.: (Laughs.)

CHILDERS: It was *horrible.*

L.A.: How long did he have that set-up?

CHILDERS: About a year, we messed around with that thing. And then we—when we came out of that—that was from maybe late '44 or early '45 through '45, and then in '46 we became the Artistry thing, the Artistry in Rhythm thing. We decided we would go all out to be a jazz band.

L.A.: Didn't he consider his first orchestra Artistry in Rhythm?

CHILDERS: No. That wasn't the name of it. That didn't happen until later.

L.A.: What did he call the first band?

CHILDERS: It was just Stan Kenton. That's all. Stan Kenton and His Orchestra. The Artistry of Stan Kenton and His Orchestra. It wasn't Artistry in Rhythm then. There was no *name* to the *theme,* even. Until he did the Artistry in Rhythm logo, or whatever you want to call it, title, at that point. Then he called his theme song "Artistry in Rhythm." Possibly he had called it that before—but I don't think so. Well in 1943 we recorded it and he called it "Artistry in Rhythm" then—it had not had a name to my knowledge before then. But the band was not the Artistry in Rhythm of Stan Kenton until later.

L.A.: What would a typical band rehearsal be like?

CHILDERS: *(Starts laughing hysterically.)*

L.A.: Why is this man laughing?

CHILDERS: He used to pass out charts, and he'd say, "Well, let's see what we can do with *this* one." Every now and then Gene Roland would come out of—what's the proper word—let's say, *seclusion*—and he would have maybe forty or fifty things that he had written while he was in seclusion. He would show up, and there we were, and Stan would say, "Okay, guys, we're gonna start rehearsing—" We'd rehearse three

or four—we would be doing one-nighters for weeks and then we would get into a place where we're gonna be sitting down for a week, and resting a little bit, and instead of that we'd rehearse every night after the job, and two or three afternoons . . . .

L.A.: After the *job?*

CHILDERS: Oh, sometimes. Sometimes we'd wait a half hour or fifteen minutes for everybody to clear out, and then we'd rehearse for two hours.

L.A.: You're kidding.

CHILDERS: Or come in the next afternoon. You've got a week, you think you can really settle back and rest and relax and get some sun and all that stuff, and it didn't work out that way. 'Cause you

would wind up working all week trying to get through all these Gene Roland things just in the hope of finding another "Jump for Joe." You never found one.

L.A.: Would he go straight through, or would he . . .

CHILDERS: Oh we'd go—we'd—(laughing)—Gene was beautiful. Once I copied one of his charts. He would use one sheet of score paper and a half—that's like 12 bars. Then he had about three pages of written instructions for all the bars. Like, "Second tenor, for bar 24, copy the third trumpet part for the first half of the bar," and then the second alto part of another bar for something else, and he just had all these written instructions, and it was an absolute mess. It would have been so much easier to write it out, but his game was to put it all on these two pieces of paper and make all those instructions. Those are the instructions most writers give to themselves, they write it on the score paper. Everybody used to moan when Gene showed up. 'Cause he would continually show up with a whole bunch of charts . . .

L.A.: You wouldn't go through *all* of them, would you?

CHILDERS: Oh yes! Stan was very patient that way.

L.A.: It's interesting that you lasted for such a long time on the Kenton band, whereas other trumpet players sometimes would leave after a short period—six months, a year, a concert . . .

CHILDERS: Some of 'em could play, some of 'em couldn't. I used to get into fights with Stan over the hiring of trumpet players. We went out one time with seven trumpets, Conte and myself and five others. Stan asked me to pick three out of the other five. We disagreed about one of them to the point that I threatened to leave if he stayed—that's the only time it ever came to that. I fought so hard for that band to be musical.

L.A.: During all that time I guess you got to know Stan pretty well.

CHILDERS: The longer I was there the less I knew him.

L.A.: How is that possible?

CHILDERS: It's very simple. The better you get to know somebody, the more you realize you don't really know him.

L.A.: You mean there's more than meets the eye?

CHILDERS: That's right. I was always glad he never went into politics.

L.A.: (Laughs.) Why?

CHILDERS: Because he would have been *king*.

Stan Kenton at the mike, '40s. (Photo: Courtesy of Bob Gioga.)

L.A.: He had that kind of mesmerizing effect on people?

CHILDERS: Are you kidding? He sold people—he used to stand out there and make announcements that went on for God knows how long, use words that he didn't necessarily use correctly—uh—and he would use like the—he would hear a big word and it would mesmerize *him*—

L.A.: (Laughs.)

CHILDERS: . . . and he would start using it over and over and he would just like lay these things out, and he would make these announcements and I'd go *"What'd he say?"* Then he would *shove* a bunch of music down the people's throats that they didn't understand or know what it was, but he sold the whole thing and became what he set out to be. The number one jazz name in the world.

L.A.: Think that's what he became?

CHILDERS: Well—there's an awful lot of people who do. My opinion isn't too important. But I know that everywhere I go in the world I'm known because of him.

L.A.: Is that right.

CHILDERS: And it's been twenty-eight years since I left that band.

L.A.: You mean they hear Childers and they say "Oh, you were with Stan Kenton"?

CHILDERS: That's right.

L.A.: And they automatically respect you for that?

CHILDERS: That is right. In fact, in Europe is where I find the most people know me. I was over there last November (1981) with the Toshiko Akiyoshi-Lew Tabackin band. And I ran into, almost everywhere we went, I ran into—somebody came up to me and said "I remember you, I saw you in 1953 with Kenton." "I saw you in Hamburg" or "I saw you in Frankfurt" or "I was at one of the concerts at . . . "you know, one of the places we played. I was told by two guys in Paris, at the last big auction at this place in England, my two albums brought the highest price. Not because they're the best albums. You can't get them, and because of my association with the Kenton band. That's all. Wherever I go, I'm still associated with that band, despite the fact that I've made records that I consider much better than anything I ever did with that band. Records with Toshiko, with Quincy Jones, Billy Byers, Pat Williams, with Oliver Nelson, live in L. A., with the Bob Florence band, live at Concerts By The Sea. They know me for these things, but the Kenton stuff is what they love me for. It's weird to me that that's what

I'm remembered for.

L.A.: That 1953 Kenton tour in Europe was the band's first, wasn't it. What was it like?

CHILDERS: It was wonderful. I never worked so hard. That was a rough tour! We did 55 concerts in 45 cities in 33 days. (Pauses.) Think of that. Fifty-five in 45 in 33.

L.A.: It *does* sound *impossible.* (Laughs.) Would you say that being with the Kenton band helped you in the rest of your career, then?

CHILDERS: It's been more of a hindrance than a help.

L.A.: It has?

CHILDERS: I find that there's more expected of me than I'm capable of.

L.A.: Isn't that a good thing?

CHILDERS: Not really. No.

L.A.: It makes you work harder, and you don't want to.

CHILDERS: No, because you go and you do your very very best . . .

L.A.: And they say now that's a starting-off point.

CHILDERS: And they say, gee, that's not what I expected. I expected—if you could ever nail them and say What did you *really* expect? they couldn't tell you.

L.A.: What do you do besides jazz concerts?

CHILDERS: Studio work. And I'm doing a lot of clinics. I represent a music company.

L.A.: Is this in any way similar to the Kenton clinics?

CHILDERS: It's a development from it. It has nothing to do with anything that Stan did, but had Stan not done these things, it may not have existed today. I mean, if he did nothing else, if he had succeeded in doing nothing else, that one thing that he's done to help jazz education is enough to make him immortal. And he did, Lord knows, a hell of a lot more than that. I mean just that one thing is more than any other one person did for jazz.

L.A.: During the years you were with him, were you witness to changes in the man himself?

CHILDERS: Some. Ya. Sure, we all change as we grow older. Stan became intrigued with psychology, to the point that when he disbanded his orchestra—the first time, in 1947—he said "I'm going to become a psychiatrist." And he found out it took 13 years.

L.A.: (Laughs.)

CHILDERS: Minimum. That wasn't going to stop him. But it's a lot easier to just start a band again and play psych—you know, play doctor with the guys in the band. Stan went through a lot of

therapy, with one guy in particular. I can't remember his name, but I remember *him* very well—who, as far as I was concerned, was *very* suspect. They say the most screwed-up people of all make the best therapists. He certainly fit *that.* Stan changed from that. He played a lot of games—we all do when you're on the road. Who's to judge what anybody does? Really. None of us are perfect. I think mostly what he did—he did a lot of good things for a lot of people. He made millions of people happy, for a lot of years. He gave thousands of young musicians a chance. He certainly gave thousands of young musicians a lot of inspiration through these camps and things that he set up. I think he was more responsible than anyone, through his earlier efforts, in helping get the school thing started, that's going on yet, and the educational system, the jazz program that's in the educational system, that they never would have considered. It was his charm. I mean he was a man.

L.A.: Are you happy you knew him?

CHILDERS: Oh, hell yes. Hey, he was—he was my surrogate father for a lot of years. Which wasn't fair on my part to put him there. And it wasn't fair on his part to have volunteered for it in the first place.

L.A.: Maybe you needed someone, being so young like that.

CHILDERS: Yeah. And if it weren't for writers like Pete Rugolo I wouldn't be near as good as I got to be. Pete was one of those who believed I could do anything he wrote. So he did it, and so I learned. You put it down, well I'll have to learn to do it. There were some very demanding things in Stan's band. They made me the trumpet player that I've become.

L.A.: What about Kenton as a composer and arranger?

CHILDERS: He was a brilliant arranger and composer. He wrote a couple of things in that album that the first Silly Symphony made that were just absolutely *brilliant.* There was one thing that was the trombones and the strings. It was so *gorgeous,* I mean—it *inspired* me. And the other one that he wrote, he had everybody who wrote for him, all the best writers in the world that were available, he had them try to write something for Shelly Manne. And nobody could. He went home and wrote it, and it was a masterpiece! That "Shelly Manne" thing is a *masterpiece.* He said, "Oh, this is just a piece of crap, I just dashed it off." ". . . . . *Yeah. All right, Stan."*

Today the cultural music in America is European dominated —

governed, almost entirely, by European tastes and standards.

4 Pete Rugolo

*Let's say the trumpets
would be playing
C, D-flat, D, E-flat, and E,
all half-steps apart.
Clusters, for certain effects
in maybe a piece that
I thought should have that.
Not to scare anybody.*

Pete Rugolo, at his California home. (Photo by the Author.)

L.A.: People talk about the Kenton sound as having tension. Does that kind of writing contribute to that?

RUGOLO: That contributes. Tension is also having the brass all playing double forte. And the rhythms—exciting rhythms against each other—that creates tension. The band had excitement, and Stan loved that. He didn't hold back at all when it came to that.

L.A.: "Progressive Jazz" and "Pete Rugolo" are probably interchangeable words in most people's minds, since you introduced the concept to the Kenton band and to the world. What are the components of Progressive Jazz?

RUGOLO: Dissonant harmonies, influenced by the people that I liked at the time, such as Stravinsky, Bartok, Milhaud, Hindemith. Completely different harmonies, more classical, modern, very contemporary. And rhythms. I started introducing 5/4 rhythms, and also 7/8, 6/8, and 3/4, into not only original music but in arrangements like "Over the Rainbow," dance band music. There were very dissonant chords in tempos you could dance to.

L.A.: What's a dissonant chord composed of, say from C to C?

RUGOLO: From C to C I might have all eight notes played at once. Or three chords . . .

L.A.: All eight notes played *at once?*

RUGOLO: Sure. Sure.

L.A.: Wow.

RUGOLO: A dissonant chord. Or a C chord against a D chord against an E chord maybe, three complete chords. Each—I'd have the saxophones maybe play a C chord, a C major seventh chord or whatever it was, and against that I'd maybe have the trombones play a D chord and then the trumpets an E chord. Many times I'd have, in the saxophones, C-D-E-F-G, just the first five notes, all played at once, and voiced that way for a C chord. Or half-steps apart. Really dissonant. Clusters of notes. So you'd have a very dissonant sound.

L.A.: Did you perceive the Stan Kenton band as being a likely vehicle for trying out new music?

RUGOLO: Stan saw that I was capable of writing some things that he'd never heard before. Even in the beginning, while I was writing things in the style of the band, imitating him, I also wrote some new things that he heard that he liked. That's one reason he liked me. He encouraged me to write anything I wanted to write. He was very good about that. He never ever hardly

changed a note. And he would be very patient. He would try very modern things, and he'd never say, "No, gee, that's too wild," or "The ending is crazy," he'd say, "Let's try it" or "Let's work it out." And that's why he was so nice. Not only to me. To all the composers and arrangers in the band. He encouraged them; he was very wonderful that way.

L.A.: It's been said that when Stan first looked at the compositions you presented to him he felt he had met his alter ego. That the two of you wrote so similarly he sometimes mistook something *he'd* written for something *you'd* written. How could that be?

RUGOLO: When I first joined the band, some of the early things that I wrote I tried to write like Stan. The very early things. They were all based on a lot of the records I'd heard of his. I copied his style quite a bit. The only thing I had to go by were his records—I never heard the band personally at that time. I was in San Francisco. I heard all his new records and I loved the band. And I started copying them right off the records and then we would play them in the Army band.

L.A.: Oh, were you director of an Army band?

RUGOLO: Yes, I had a band in San Francisco. Fort Scott, it was called. At the Presidio, San Francisco.

L.A.: So even the Army bands were playing Stan Kenton music.

RUGOLO: They were things like "Reed Rapture" and "Adios" and all his first records. I had all of them. I just copied them as best I could. When we played these things our band sounded like Kenton's band. It wasn't anywhere as good 'cause the caliber of musicians wasn't too good, but we had a lot of fun playing it. And they all loved to play that sound.

L.A.: What did you like about the sound? Why were you enamored of the band?

RUGOLO: It was completely different. Up to that time the bands that were around were the Benny Goodmans and the Glenn Millers, Tommy Dorseys. I liked the voicings and just the general spirit of the arrangements.

L.A.: Back then he had a smaller band than he ultimately wound up with. Two trombones . . .

RUGOLO: . . . three trumpets, five saxes, and four rhythm, with himself. I liked the way he voiced the saxophones, and the ensemble voicing where he used

the saxophones as the bottom of the orchestra. He had very deep voicings. And then developed all that, played it together. He had a syncopated style at that time. I liked all the offbeat things.

L.A.: All the "Artistry" things.

RUGOLO: The only "Artistry" things at that time were "Artistry in Rhythm" and "Artistry Jumps." We wrote the other "Artistry" things after I joined the band. "Artistry in Bolero," "Artistry in Boogie" . . .

L.A.: You brought something very much of your own to the band. The complete tenor of the band changed. You joined it about '46? Or earlier?

RUGOLO: Yes. I think '45.

L.A.: Your first meeting with Stan must have been quite exciting. You had an arrangement to give him?

RUGOLO: I first met Stan when I was in the Army. That was probably in 1943, since I joined in '42. I had a chance to get into the Army band in San Francisco, and since that was close to my home up there, I decided maybe I should go. Stan was playing at the Golden Gate Theater in San Francisco. I saw the concert, saw the band play. Watched every show. Finally I went backstage and was introduced to him. I was wearing an Army uniform and I had three or four arrangements under my arm and I just finally got enough nerve to wait for him to go backstage. I gave him the arrangements to try. He took them and I didn't hear anything for I don't know how many months. Then one day I got a call. I was still in the Army then. It was from him, and he said "We've tried your arrangements, and they're wonderful. When are you getting out? You have a job as soon as you do." Next time I saw him was a couple of years later; I was sent to be discharged to San Pedro, and they happened to be playing at the Palladium there. I went backstage to see him, see if he remembered, and he said "Oh, sure!" and "Do you have anything new?" I'd been writing some new things for Stan and I'd brought them. And they rehearsed them. And he loved them. The first ones I'd given him were just exactly like Kenton would write—the off-beat style, exactly his voicings, and everything. Now the new things were more my things, although they sounded like Kenton too. He liked them and said "As soon as you get out of the Army, the job's yours." So I was discharged in '45 and they went on to New York at the Meadowbrook and I flew and joined the band the day I got out of the Army.

L.A.: The day you got out of the Army!

RUGOLO: Right. I couldn't wait, I was just so excited. After a few months with the band I started to write the way I really wanted to write. I started to do some modern things the band had never played before. With different time changes. They had never played anything before with a 5/4 bar in it, or 6/4 or 7/4. I started using tone colors with the band. Mutes, and not all the brass playing together. Two trumpets playing one thing and two trumpets playing something else. Also a lot of classical sounds. I started to fool around, experiment. And he loved it. We had a lot of tempo things. They were more concert pieces than dance, you couldn't dance to them.

L.A.: Were you part of an influence then on his wanting to do concert jazz rather than dance band jazz?

RUGOLO: I guess I was the one that started it because of the pieces that I wrote. Later on when we added the strings and did the Innovations tour, that was strictly concerts. But for a while the things that I wrote they called Progressive Jazz. And we started to do concerts at all the colleges, opera houses, Carnegie Hall and all the major halls. We called it "An Evening of Progressive Jazz." We played some of his regular things, but most of them were concert pieces that I had written, most of them, maybe 95% of the things were the things that I wrote at that time.

L.A.: And you recorded one of my favorite albums, *A Concert in Progressive Jazz,* in 1947. It's absolutely fabulous. Those are your compositions.

RUGOLO: Yes.

L.A.: I'm sure you used all the orchestra parts like the colors of a palette when you were composing; you didn't necessarily favor one instrumental color over another?

RUGOLO: No, but I tried to think of the band, the style of the band, and we featured a trombone a lot. That seemed to be the sound of the orchestra. So I'd have trombone solos, especially when we had good players like Milt Bernhart and Kai Winding. Then when we had Vido Musso in the band I wrote things for him and we featured him. When Art Pepper was with the band we wrote things for him. We wrote things for everybody. And the band had a style, so we tried to keep it that way. We used a lot of saxophone choruses. We didn't use woodwinds at all in the regular dance orchestra, even in the Progressive Jazz things. Stan didn't like woodwinds.

Although at one time, just when I joined the band, they were using clarinets, five clarinets voiced above the trumpets. That's when Gene Howard was writing a lot of the things. They were trying to get a different sound for pop tunes that they were recording. It never really lasted. They tried it for about a year and then went back to the saxophones. With the Innovations, that was something else—we started using flutes and oboes and all the other legitimate instruments, French horns and tubas. But the dance band he kind of just liked to have a certain way. Any sound that you wanted. In other words I wrote, experimented with all sorts of tone colors and harmonies and stuff—that didn't bother him. But he kind of just liked the saxophones and the trumpets and the trombones. That sound.

L.A.: Did he have a favorite composition that you'd written?

RUGOLO: A lot of things he played more than others. A little piece called "Interlude" he played a lot, and then people started to like it. It was very simple. He played that for years, even after I left the band.

L.A.: "Interlude" is a classic!

RUGOLO: Things like "Safranski" and "Artistry in Percussion" he would play quite a bit, 'cause Eddie and Shelly were in the band. Many of the other pieces we just played because we had a lot of air time in those days. People couldn't dance to "Impressionism" and things like that, but he was always good about playing them on the air.

L.A.: I'm sure he *preferred* that. Most people agree he'd much rather have gone into the concert jazz strictly and forgot about dance band music altogether.

RUGOLO: When we did play hotels the band was so loud that, especially for the first hour, when they were eating dinner, we had to mute everything and play everything soft. That's why I wrote "Interlude," something that had no trumpets at all in it, that he could play during the dinner hour. And I made a lot of little dance arrangements that they could play, that were kind of simple and still sounded like Kenton, so it didn't sound like any other band. But he preferred the exciting pieces. He loved the brass. He loved to hear that brass wall in front of him. I think that's one reason he liked "Love For Sale" a lot, because when the brass started to play at the end, that just screaming, high brass, he just loved that, and the percussion going.

L.A.: At what point did the Latin rhythm come in?

RUGOLO: When we hired Laurindo Almeida, I started to write some Latin-type things for him, and then also for Jack Costanza. Then bands like Tito Puente started to get popular, and the mambos started coming in. We influenced a lot of those bands, 'cause we were playing Latin things *before*—not mambos, but we were using bongos and Latin rhythms. I started experimenting with them and Stan liked them; it gave a little excitement, and he liked the colors. Naturally when all the Latin bands were popular we continued using them.

L.A.: But you're a forerunner rather than a copier.

RUGOLO: Yes.

L.A.: I was wondering if maybe having lived in California, with its strong Hispanic population, and listening to pure Latin music, which is so exciting . . .

RUGOLO: I'm sure, 'cause we used to go listen to quite a few bands in town, and Stan liked them very much.

L.A.: You were quite close to him. How would you rap with each other about music? How would you interrelate when it came to composing?

RUGOLO: We worked together a lot even when we were driving in a car. Usually we worked either at his house or down at Capitol Records, where they'd give us a little room when we knew we had to do a record date and needed some piece. He might have got an idea for a melody, and then I would maybe finish the melody, or maybe I had a melody and we would work together. He'd like it, and then we'd add to it. And then we'd say "Let's call this . . ."—whatever it is—'Collaboration,' " the one we wrote together. And he would sit down and we'd write a sort of a map. We'd say, "Let's start off with the brass intro, two bars, four bars, then piano first chorus." He would write a map and we'd talk about it. "Then let's have a trombone chorus the next chorus, then let's have a saxophone chorus, an ensemble, and let's build in the end." I'd look at this map, and he'd go away and I'd write the thing. Of course I would change it the way I felt it should be. But it gave me an outline of what he thought, and I'd follow it pretty closely. I added more if I wanted it—if it's "Interlude," I'd want a different ending, or if I didn't want the saxophone here I would put it someplace else. As I composed the piece, naturally, it grew. We did that a lot. We would just get together and talk about a piece, or we'd like a melody, and we'd either finish it together or he would start and then he'd get busy and I'd finish it, and that's why we put both our names on it—and then we talked about what kind of a piece it should be. Or if he needed a fast opener, like the arrangement I did of "Lover." We had to play a theater, I remember, and he needed something really to start off fast. He'd say, "Okay, let's take 'Lover' and write me the wildest arrangement you can on it and . . . "

L.A.: "Write me the wildest arrangement you can on it"? (Laughs.)

RUGOLO: Ya. Because he wanted it—it was originally a waltz, you know. He wanted a real fast arrangement of it. So it worked out fine.

L.A.: I *guess* you got a wild arrangement of it.

RUGOLO: Yeah. We used that a lot. Or he'd say "Write a piece for Vido." Or "We need a piece for so-and-so." And being Italian, I'd say, "How about 'Come Back To Sorrento'?" He said "Fine." So then we'd get together and talk a little bit about it and then I'd just go ahead and write it. But we discussed quite a bit of music. My originals I more or less did on my own. I'd want to surprise him. Or I'd just got an idea let's

say for a piece like "Impressionism," or whatever it was. And I would write it and bring it. He had no idea and the band had no idea. They'd never heard that type of music before. But they were all wonderful, they appreciated it. A lot of them, truthfully, didn't like my arrangements, because there were people in the band that liked modern music and others that liked just swinging arrangements, Basie-type things. And they would balk down that we played so much of my things, because they didn't really swing. They weren't *supposed* to; they were supposed to be just concert pieces. Luckily there were some others in the band who wrote that way—Shorty wrote some things and later on Gerry Mulligan contributed and then when Stan got Bill Holman, naturally the guys liked him, because—

L.A.: He swung.

RUGOLO: Well ya, and most of them would rather have that type of band. Most of them I don't think really cared for the Progressive Jazz band. They appreciated the music, and they did like to play interesting pieces, but I don't think their hearts were in it. They just loved to play something that really moved.

L.A.: Stan always had a battle with that.

RUGOLO: *He* liked it and I liked it.

L.A.: *He* liked it. That's the important thing. You can get swing in any band. And you can only get Stan Kenton-Pete Rugolo-Bill Russo, that particular quality, in the Stan Kenton sound.

RUGOLO: It was a wonderful thing for the band. It sold records, and it was good for him. When we did the Progressive Jazz concerts we were sold out in every city. Carnegie Hall, Chicago Opera, every place, you couldn't get in. I think it was the most popular band ever.

L.A.: All this creativity in the forties and fifties, yet you still had to make concessions to the popular trade.

RUGOLO: We sold quite a lot of records from 1945 to 1950. Then later on everything changed in the record business. They kept telling him to try things—try an album with Tex Ritter, do an album of vocals. Everybody singing "September Song." It was all right for one tune, but the guys didn't really like to sing; they felt funny about it. But listen, the whole business was if you sold records, then your band would make money. You would draw crowds. Everything in those days depended on selling records. That's why Stan would go to a disc jockey and plug his records. And he'd go to a music store—God, I guess he never

Stan Kenton in one of his many radio interviews, probably late '40s. (Photo: Courtesy of Bob Gioga.)

slept. While we were sleeping he would do these things.

L.A.: Where do you suppose he got his stamina?

RUGOLO: He was a big man. Nobody could keep up with him. He was just going all the time. I don't know how he did it. In those days promotion was very important. I guess some of the big band albums are doing better now, but for a period there you couldn't give them away.

L.A.: Don't you feel, especially in light of your really original kind of composition and the other things he did, that Stan should not be confined to the image of a big band leader, that what he did was so much wider in scope?

RUGOLO: Yes, I think so. He was open to anything, he really was. He was so good to Graettinger. His music was so advanced. But he heard something in it. You know, he was so good. He supported him for years, he paid him every month, to live, he was—he was good to everybody, to Johnny Richards, he gave money—and he didn't demand anything. He wasn't the kind who would say "Jesus, I paid you a thousand dollars and you haven't written a note!" He never would say that. Whenever you brought something in was fine. But he had all these people under salary, whether they worked or not. For a whole year. If they didn't write a thing, they got paid every week. He was wonderful to people like that. To composers. He knew that they needed the money, and whenever they could come up with something—they weren't the type of composer who could write an arrangement every day. Like Graettinger took a long time, he took great pains in everything he wrote. He would take six months on one piece. But when it was finished, it was something unusual.

L.A.: Did Stan actually like that kind of music? Or was he just trying to experiment?

RUGOLO: Ya, he liked it. He heard something in it. That's why he had so many different people writing for him. He appreciated everything. All the different styles. Certain things he liked about certain arrangers. He liked Johnny Richards very much.

L.A.: What about Kenton as a composer? As a composer yourself, what do you think of, say, *Concerto to End All Concertos?*

RUGOLO: That was a great piece. It was written in the forties, even before I joined the band. I loved those pieces— *Concerto,* "Painted Rhythm," "Artistry Jumps," "Eager Beaver." They were great. That's what made the band.

L.A.: I'd like to understand the jump between his composing those works and then such advanced things as "Shelly Manne" and "June Christy," which are really far-out, terrific pieces.

RUGOLO: He wrote those later, when we started the concert orchestra and he tried writing for strings. "Theme for Sunday" was really nice. When I joined the band he didn't write a note for four or five years. Then when the band broke up, in '49, and we came out here and we decided to do the Innovations tour, that's when he started, he sat down and started to write some modern pieces.

L.A.: By then he'd been influenced by you, right?

RUGOLO: By me, by all the other people who were writing—Richards and Graettinger and Russo. But Stan had his own style. He liked certain composers, too, classical composers. But everything he wrote sounded like Stan Kenton. He had, really, his style of writing.

L.A.: Stan had some actual formal study in the classics, too, didn't he, with Charles Dalmores and Paul Held.

RUGOLO: He started to study again after the band broke up for a while and he had some time on his hands. He started to write. Later on he wrote a lot of the dance arrangements. Standard tunes, like "Street of Dreams." They would record every once in a while, and he would write all the arrangements. They were all very good. He had a real style for writing for saxophones.

L.A.: I thought his favorite instrument was trombones.

RUGOLO: Trombones, everything, but he wrote a certain way for saxophones. You always knew it was his arrangement.

L.A.: Much is made of the point that the two of you could be interchangeable and that you made the same sound. Would Stan have had the capacity to write something like "Mirage"?

RUGOLO: No.

L.A.: He would not.

RUGOLO: No, I don't think so. Or some of the other pieces. He could write modern music, but not like that. I would say, I could copy him more easily than he could copy me. But he wouldn't want to; he never really wanted to copy anybody. He liked certain sounds and I guess he probably was influenced by *somebody,* but he really wrote the way only he could write.

L.A.: You admired him as a composer, then.

RUGOLO: Oh sure.

L.A.: And as an arranger.

RUGOLO: Sure. He never really had a chance to compose an awful lot. You know, serious things. But I think he could have if he really devoted himself.

L.A.: Do you think he would have, if he'd had more time?

RUGOLO: If he'd had the time to do it. If everything was going all right, and if he really said, "Look, I'm going to just now take a couple of years off and try to write some serious music." He didn't have a chance to write a lot, you know. He was busy twenty hours a day. He was the greatest man on the road. Always traveled with the band, never flew. Either the bus, or for years he had a car and I would drive with him. And—he just didn't have any *time* to write. *I* didn't have much time to write, truthfully, because the five or six years I was with the band he wanted me along every night, he'd like me to come to the concerts every night. And I didn't have time to write because I was traveling all the time. But there were times when I had to write things, like when we'd come to L.A. and we knew we had a recording session and needed four or five arrangements. So I'd get in a hotel room, find a piano, lock myself up and write 'em.

L.A.: After your five years with the band, you continued to write for him?

RUGOLO: I settled in New York, and when the Innovations started up I came out and was with him again. For a couple of years I contributed, whenever he needed something. After that he would ask me to do something, and anything he wanted I would do. The last ten years or so I didn't write anything for him.

L.A.: But your influence has been a lasting one. You mentioned your attraction to the modernists. Where did you get your formal training?

RUGOLO: I studied at Mills College. I studied with Darius Milhaud for two years. I got my master's degree there.

L.A.: What did Milhaud teach you that you applied to your own music?

RUGOLO: Studying with him I became accustomed to more new music. As a teacher he taught the basics. We had to study counterpoint and Bach and everything, it wasn't just modern music. I learned a lot from him in many ways. Even being *around* him for a couple of years and hearing his music was wonderful. He created, he was an originator. He created what they call polytonality, which means more than one key at once. He'd have two, three, four, five things going on in different keys. Or two chords against each other. And I used an awful lot of that in my writing.

L.A.: Was there a lot of that in *The Creation of the World* that he wrote?

RUGOLO: There's quite a bit of that. I guess with that he tried to write a jazz piece. It sounds a lot like Gershwin; there are snatches almost of "The Man I Love." But he wrote it before "The Man

L.A.: You think because Stan admired the Impressionists . . .

RUGOLO: I don't think he was conscious of it at the time he wrote it.

L.A.: You don't?

RUGOLO: I don't think so. I'm *sure* he didn't copy it. It's only the first few notes that are similar, and those intervals have been used a million times.

L.A.: The popular song, "Softly, As In A Morning Sunrise," is that adapted from *Daphnis and Chloe?*

RUGOLO: Oh we liked it very much, sure.

L.A.: There's a place in Stan's "Shelly Manne" that sounds like it's from the third movement of the Bartok *Concerto for Orchestra.*

RUGOLO: It could be. He liked Bartok. He liked Stravinsky. I would make him listen whenever we had time. When he was off, you know. He liked all the modernists very much.

L.A.: What particular pieces did you

Pete Rugolo, at the piano in his California home. (Photo by the Author.)

I Love," before Gershwin. *Creation* was written in the nineteen-twenties, and that was way before Gershwin. But he always liked jazz. I used to take him with me—there was a ballroom where all the name bands came once a week. Every Sunday there'd be a name band, and I'd have to play piano there, with the house band. We would play from about 7 to 9 and then bands like Jimmy Lunceford, Tommy Dorsey, Duke Ellington would play. Milhaud would sit there and just love it.

L.A.: What about "Artistry in Rhythm"? There's a lot of discussion about that being from Ravel's *Daphnis and Chloe.*

RUGOLO: It's very similar to it.

RUGOLO: I never thought of it.

L.A.: Some people claim that "Artistry in Rhythm" is right out of that. Others think it's from *Daphnis and Chloe.*

RUGOLO: Well, again, it's a phrase of music that's just intervals. There are so many pieces that sound the same.

L.A.: What do you think of "Artistry" as a trademark for the band?

RUGOLO: Oh it was perfect. It was perfect. It couldn't have been more so. When you heard that theme everybody knew who it was. People loved it.

L.A.: Am I correct in detecting Stravinsky's *Rite of Spring* as being a pretty strong influence, both in you and in Stan Kenton?

play for him?

RUGOLO: Well I think he liked all the early Stravinsky a lot. He liked *The Firebird* and *Rite of Spring* and *Petrouchka* and the *Symphony in C.* He also liked Ravel and Debussy and the Impressionists. He liked Bartok very much. I know he liked the *Concerto.*

L.A.: Were you ever around when he would extemporize on the piano? Just for relaxation?

RUGOLO: Oh sure. He liked to doodle around.

L.A.: Every so often on the records his piano introductions sound a little more beautiful than usual. They seem to show a classical influence.

46

RUGOLO: It became a style. All the bands at that time had a style that right away gave away who the band was—Glenn Miller, Benny Goodman, Les Brown, Claude Thornhill. The style for Stan was starting almost every piece with the piano, start the thing off with the rhythm section. And the bass would follow. Then we featured certain people, like the trombone sound, and the saxophone sound. And then naturally the brass sound.

L.A.: When you say brass do you mean only the trumpets or do you mean trumpets and trombones?

RUGOLO: No the brass sound was—well the trumpets—they had their own sound, but the ensemble sound, the *big* sound.

L.A.: The whole thing.

RUGOLO: Ya. It was very exciting to hear that whole band blow really triple forte.

L.A.: You're telling me. (Laughs.)

RUGOLO: Ya. Boy.

L.A.: Were there differences between the Progressive Jazz Orchestra and Innovations other than the addition of strings? Or was it the same genre, I mean, experimental, different, polytonal . . .

RUGOLO: It was similar music. But the Progressive was more of a dance sound. I wrote a lot of strictly concert pieces that you couldn't dance to but then I also wrote a lot of arrangements that you could dance to that had the progressive sound in it. Very modern arrangements, intricate arrangements. A lot of vocals for June Christy to sing. Sometimes I wondered how she ever could sing with that background. She was amazing. She had a terrific ear.

L.A.: And the Innovations bore a similarity to the Neophonic of the sixties, except for the strings?

RUGOLO: It's all similar. Sure.

L.A.: You added a whole new dimension.

RUGOLO: Right. Other people had used strings before—Tommy Dorsey, Artie Shaw—but not that way in a dance orchestra. We tried to voice very much like a modern composer. "Conflict" had quarter-tones in it. "Mirage" started off with just a drone, and just kept building. It started off with hardly anything, just sustaining notes, and then kept building, and different things would happen, tone colors. Then it really built towards the end, with the brass coming in. It was really something.

L.A.: Would you consider your association with Kenton the height of your career? Creatively?

RUGOLO: Yes, uh-huh. Though I did write a lot of good music in the last twenty years in television. You don't always hear it, because it's behind dialogue, and under fires and racing and all that. The hard part is that you don't have enough time. And there's a lot of stress. But there are times when you can write anything you want, if the picture demands it. You can really write anything and get by with it, much more than you can in making records. I've been doing television and movies for the last fifteen to twenty years.

L.A.: What tv shows have you written for?

RUGOLO: I've been very fortunate. I've had a lot of big hit television shows, like *Run For Your Life* and *The Fugitive*. I was able to write jazz for those. I've done almost every major tv show. I've written so much music. When I work I work so hard, I work six months without stopping. Forty minutes of music a week is like writing a symphony.

L.A.: Where do you derive your creative inspiration from?

RUGOLO: I like to listen to a lot of music. I'll do one composer at a time. I'll have all the scores, and I'll browse through Stravinsky one week, then the next week Bartok, then the next week maybe Schuman—all the modern—I like Samuel Barber. I like the American composers very much. I'll hear something there and maybe I'll write it down to remember what it is, or it might start off some idea for me.

L.A.: What place do you think Stan Kenton has in 20th Century American music?

RUGOLO: He will live because he had that sound. He always tried to have a good orchestra. He kept that band going whether he was losing money or not. He always tried to maintain and play good music.

L.A.: Good as opposed to popular.

RUGOLO: You have to give him credit for always trying, and wanting good music. He never said "We're going to stop all this crazy music and make some money and just play what the public wants." He always tried to play new music and give composers a chance to write whatever they wanted.

L.A.: What will you miss the most about him?

RUGOLO: I'll miss *everything* about him. He was so good to me. I can't say enough about him. I know what he went through. He was really a wonderful man. I liked him personally. I liked everything about him, truthfully. He was so good to everybody, so kind. Not only to the children, but to the wives on the bus and everyone else. He would help anybody that needed it. No one really knows how many good things he did.

5 June Christy

Stan and I would sit at the piano and we would find a comfortable key for me to sing a certain tune in. And then he would raise it. At least a tone, where it would be almost uncomfortable for me to sing with just piano. But I learned, after some time, that he knew what he was doing.

L.A.: What was he doing?

CHRISTY: The Kenton band, as everyone knows, was *not* a subtle *band*. There were special challenges in singing with the Stan Kenton Orchestra. There was, obviously, a situation with the volume. I think that's one of the reasons that Stan was selecting keys for me to sing in. And by changing the keys, by raising them that way, he enabled me, when I did hear that tremendous volume behind me, to have the strength to sing up to it, and even sometimes over it. Because I was singing more or less at the top of my range, rather than at what I would have considered a more comfortable key. But I was so excited at being with the band that there didn't seem to be anything that I certainly couldn't cope with. I was floating on clouds of—(laughs)—of just great *joy*! And I really didn't consider the challenges that much, I just looked forward to going to work every night. Or every day, whatever it was.

L.A.: What was your first meeting with Stan like?

CHRISTY: It's difficult to even say— how do you describe *exaltation*? I was so excited at *meeting* Stan even. This was in the office of General Artists Corporation—that's an organization that handled Stan. I knew that Anita O'Day had left the band and he was without a girl singer. So I went to the offices of GAC and sat there and sat there, thinking that he might come in looking for a singer. And of course he did. I say of

June Christy. (Photo: Courtesy of Bob Gioga.)

June Christy and Stan Kenton, 1947. (Photo: Courtesy of a Kenton friend.)

course, that's out of line, because later I learned that's the *last* place he'd be likely to be found. But he was looking for a singer. And I had my little test record under my arm. And I asked him if he would be kind enough to listen to it. Which he did, he went into the inner office and listened to the record.

L.A.: What thoughts were going through your mind while he listened?

CHRISTY: I was so excited at the very thought that he might *like* the record. And so *dejected* on the other hand at the fact that he might *not* like it—that I became frankly quite ill! (Laughs.)

L.A.: He must have been impressed. We all know the final outcome!

CHRISTY: As it turned out, he asked me to come to the theater where he was working and he and I made some kind of arrangement. It wasn't necessarily the most *satisfactory* in the whole world. He said to me, "We'll give it a try. Maybe for a few weeks. We'll see how it works

out." But that was better than nothing, you know. So you can see, he was quite cautious with me at first. He didn't want to give me *too* much encouragement in case he had to *fire* me, I suppose. But as it turned out, as you well know, I lasted for quite some time with the band. (Laughs.)

L.A.: Yes, to the everlasting gratitude of millions of us.

CHRISTY: In fact, that was a sort of a funny thing between us. Years later, when we were on our way to one of the many disk jockey shows he and I did together, I recalled that conversation. I said "Stanley, do you realize that six weeks have long since come and gone and you still have not told me that I am definitely with the band?" He laughed and said "Well, you are."

L.A.: It's good to know we haven't been *imagining* it all these years. Did he encourage your development as a singer?

CHRISTY: He encouraged me as a singer as he did everyone on the band. He developed a lot of character and a lot of talent in that band, because he wasn't afraid of giving people their—their own rope, so to speak, and he encouraged people to be themselves. And he provided the spotlight as often as he possibly could, for anyone he felt was deserving of it. Which is a pretty nice thing to be able to say of any band leader.

L.A.: Do you recall your first years with the band with any special fondness?

CHRISTY: That was probably my favorite time with the band. I had never been with a big band before, and found myself with one of the most popular bands in this country, perhaps even in the world. And the first record I recorded with the band was a million-seller, which was something that I had not expected, as I don't suppose Stan did either. (Laughs.) But everything was just going so beautifully! And every-

49

thing was just almost too good to be true. In fact I remember having written in my diary—doesn't every eighteen-year-old kid have a diary?—that all of this was just too good to be true, and that eventually of course I would—I would be *canned,* you know. I just couldn't believe that I was fortunate enough not only to be with a great band but with the band I would have *chosen* to be with had I had a *choice.* But really, almost all of my time with the band was a favorite with me.

L.A.: What did you most enjoy about it?
CHRISTY: The feeling of friendship that was almost always with the band. Very seldom did we have people who didn't fit in, I mean emotionally. In fact it was Stan's thought that no one is irreplaceable, so if we did find someone that — or rather he did find someone that didn't seem to move with the band and, you know, didn't like the climate of the band, he was usually replaced soon enough, and usually by someone who was musically even more superior.

L.A.: You were with the band on its trips abroad. How would you describe Europe's response to the Stan Kenton Orchestra, and to you?

CHRISTY: It was *fabulous!*

L.A.: That must have been a very exciting experience.

CHRISTY: It was overwhelming, really. We were a young enough band, and certainly I was a young enough person, to be overwhelmed by their response. And it never failed to excite me and I don't think it failed to excite the band, either, because no one is that blase,' you know, when you're met with that kind of a reception. You pretty much respond to it. We went through Europe so quickly that if there were any highlights I certainly don't remember them. We were doing an *impossible* task. Two shows a night in two different *cities* a night. Which meant that most of what we saw of Europe was the inside of a *bus.* Because we would do a concert, get on the bus, eat some cold sandwiches, and arrive at the next town, and play that city, and then, if we were lucky, check into a hotel and move out the following day. But most of the time we weren't even that lucky, we got back on the band bus and went to the next city, and so on and so forth.

L.A.: Probably no American popular singer in our history ever had to cope with such challenging, difficult music as you did during Stan's Progressive Jazz and Innovations periods. Can you give some insight into all that—rehearsals, performances, and the like?
CHRISTY: I guess I didn't really consider that there was anything challenging or difficult in the music. I just was swept along. I had always been a fan of the band's. And so when Rugolo and Graettinger and people of that sort began to write for the band it was just easy for me to go along.

L.A.: What about those strange tonalities and weird key changes in some of the works that Pete Rugolo and Stan Kenton did for you—Stan's "June Christy," and Pete's "This Is My Theme," for example. How did you cope with that? Why did they want to use your voice in that way—what did they have in mind?
CHRISTY: There *were* some very very difficult pieces and some of them I don't think I did very well. In fact some of them I think are total bombs. When Stan presented me with "This Is My Theme," I said, "Well I don't see how

June Christy, posing in front of poster for the Innovations Orchestra, 1950. (Photo: Courtesy of a Kenton friend.)

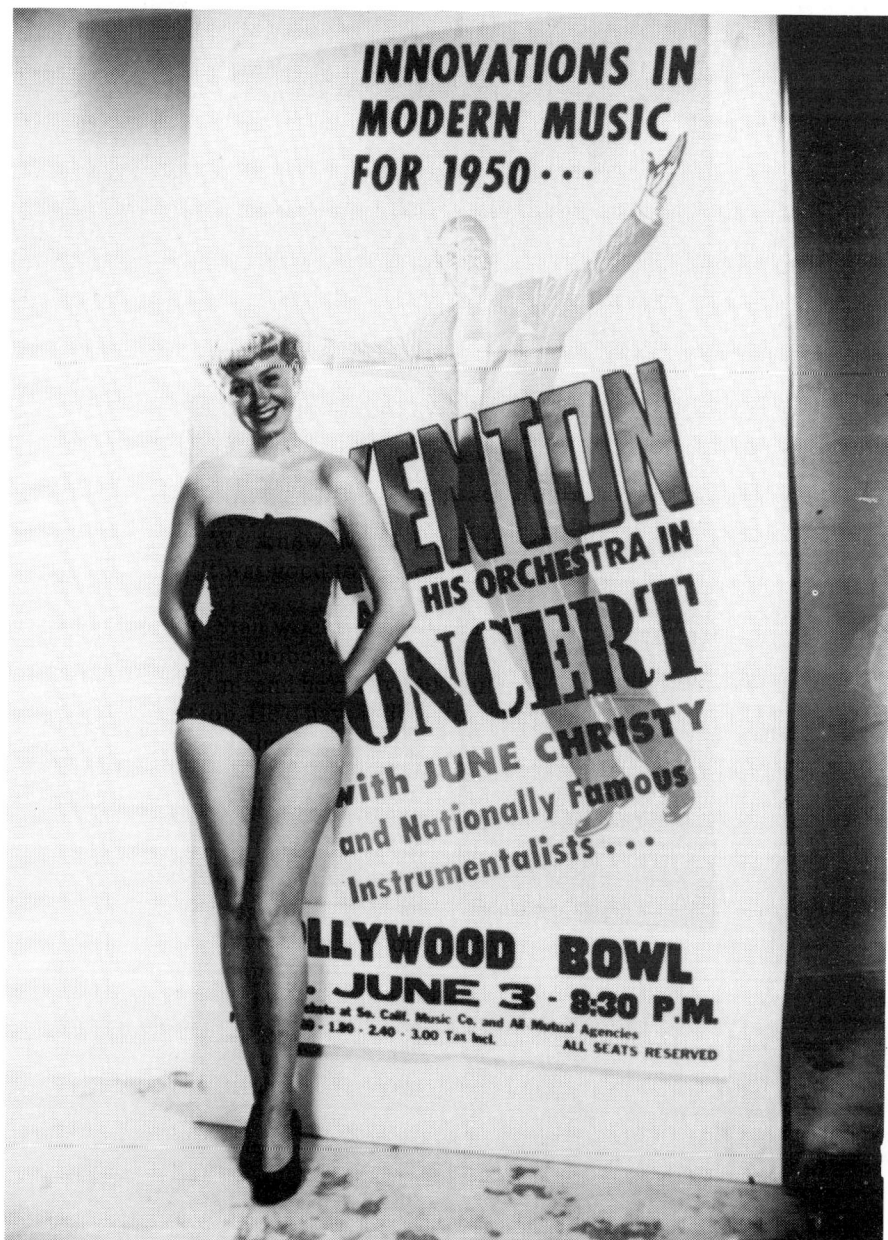

50

that is ever going to work, because I was never much of an actress," and it seemed to me that that's what it called for. But his explanation was simple. He said "I think of your speaking voice as the same as your singing voice." And of course he smoothed that all over. But what I did do, when we went to record "This Is My Theme," I said, "This is going to be so embarrassing, and I ask that you put a kind of a thing between myself and the orchestra," because I didn't want the band seeing how very embarrassed I was. And also I made him promise me that I would never have to perform that work in public. And he gave me his word, and I never did have to.

L.A.: Was there any particular reason why Stan made an album called *Duet,* in which he plays piano accompaniment to your singing?

CHRISTY: I don't think Stan actually wanted to record that album. I think it was Capitol's way of getting him to— well to begin with *Duet* and then eventually to make a record of his own to be called *Solo.* And I'm not sure that he really enjoyed doing that album—nor am I sure that I did, either. But it was fun doing it for me, because I've always liked Stan's accompaniments. Stan's always been a good accompanist. Many people don't realize that, because he hasn't done a great deal of it.

L.A.: One of the trademarks of Stan and of his band was their sense of fun. What were your fun times? Can you recall any particular incident or event?

CHRISTY: Yes, there were lots of fun times on the band. Perhaps all of them were fun times. Memory is kind to you that way. You sometimes forget how terribly tired you might have been, or upset about what happened the night before, or something. The Road Shows with the Four Freshmen were a lot of fun. There were so many incidents. One of my favorites sounds like something out of a B movie. But take my word for it, it really did happen.

L.A.: I'll believe anything. (Laughs.)

CHRISTY: It was our bus driver's birthday. That is, at midnight that night it was going to be his birthday. So we had found out about it and we in the band, those of us on his particular bus—at that time we had two buses—had gotten him a lighter and had it inscribed and we were kind of looking forward to midnight. And the driver was driving as usual and the guys in the band got their horns out secretly. At the stroke of midnight they began playing "Happy Birthday To You." And—I think they got kind of carried away with it, because Lee stopped the bus and we all got off— all of them still playing, by the way— and stopped at a little cafe. There was a policeman on the beat, I remember, and he just looked at us and shook his head. I don't think he'd ever seen anything like that before. Probably hasn't *since.* The man who was running the all-night cafe I *know* had never seen anything like that before. We all waited on ourselves and rang up the sales and when it was all over we got back on the bus and went on.

L.A.: Just a typical day in the life of the Stan Kenton band.

CHRISTY: Yes. (Laughs.)

L.A.: Other than forays into the strange, what most impressed you about Stan Kenton?

CHRISTY: I think the most impressive thing about Stan was his strength as a leader. He had qualities that are unique. They spoke of strength. I've often said if Stan had set out to be President of the United States, nothing could possibly have defeated him. He would definitely have won. Because he had that kind of charm. And strength. And I imagine that almost anyone who's ever worked with Stan would say pretty much the same thing. Stan was not always the warmest person on earth, although for the most part he was. But that wasn't his major forte, I don't think. I think his strength as a leader was.

L.A.: Did your association with him affect your musical style and career to any great degree?

CHRISTY: Yes. I was only eighteen when I joined the band. And that was my growing up—I grew up with the band.

L.A.: What about the direction of your life?

CHRISTY: I met the man that I love on the band—that's Bob Cooper, of course— and we married. And are still married. So the direction of my life was altered by my association with the band too.

L.A.: What will you most remember about Stan Kenton?

CHRISTY: His diversity as a personality. He changed a great deal from time to time, sometimes for the better, sometimes not. And his strength. It was always there.

Milt Bernhart in his office, Hollywood, California. (Photo by the Author.)

6 Milt Bernhart

One. One rehearsal. We come in, and everything there is brand-new. And everything there is very difficult. I looked at this stack of music. Marty Paich wrote a concerto. Twenty-page concerto. Lalo Schifrin wrote something like that. They had something of Johnny Richards. It was very hard. Stan wrote two to three things—really killers. I didn't want to come back for the concert. I figured, you know, who needs this?

Somebody told me the next night it was sold out. When the curtain went up, first thing I saw in the first ten rows was every well-known composer and musician you'd ever heard of. Dizzy Gillespie. Count Basie. George Shearing. Andre Previn. You could see their faces.

We started this concert. And I began to realize that we'd be lucky if we lived to the end of it. Stan got lost totally in the middle of something and we began to shout the bar numbers to each other. Somebody's yelling across the stage, "We're at bar sixteen." About forty times during the concert I was convinced, I can't play any more.

We finished it, bleeding. I mean bleeding. On the way out a lot of people were saying, "Good God. That was unbelievable." Apparently it was a memorable night.

Stan wanted full houses for new pieces of music nobody had ever heard, a whole concert of them. That's asking a great deal. He really didn't like nostalgia. So that was his dilemma. He would have liked to have lived to have seen the whole thing become the biggest success that ever happened. It was really not in the cards. That Neophonic Orchestra was—horrendous. I played one concert and then I quit. After the first concert I refused to go back.

L.A.: Why?

BERNHART: I never went through anything that difficult in my life. It was just too hard to bring off. Next time Jim Amlotte called I said "Jim, no, I'm sorry." And he said "Oh Stan's gonna be really unhappy about that." I said "I suppose. But he'll find somebody else." Stan always did expect the utmost from you. It was expensive. He couldn't keep it there. Even to get the concerts on the stage of the Music Center in Los Angeles was an uphill battle. I'm not sure any of us ever got paid. It was a gargantuan accomplishment to get through that first performance. Came the end of the concert, somebody that I knew, a musician in town, said he was there, and he said that the feeling in the audience was something like being at a football game. You were pulling for everybody to make it to the twenty-yard-line. And he said that they cheered every time something happened that they knew we were up against. I had left Kenton's band years before. It takes a certain kind of endurance that you build to do that kind of thing. Most of us were in the same boat. We'd been playing a lot different kind of music. I was playing in the studios, where mostly you underplay. Rarely overplay.

L.A.: How long were you at the studios?

BERNHART: For twenty-some years. I've had the travel agency for ten. You know, it's funny. There were back in the fifties and there always have been people that can play in dance bands that were capable. Not a lot of them, but some. A few. But they couldn't even get near the studios. There was a definite stigma attached to jazz musicians. That they couldn't read, that they didn't show up on time, that they were dangerous and that they—

L.A.: Dangerous? (Laughs.)

BERNHART: . . . That they couldn't play music. I mean, a score by Dmitri Tiomkin was usually symphonic music, and it had to be played on the spot. It requires very, very sharp abilities. You really need to have symphonic training to play scores for motion pictures. They just wouldn't even consider a man who came from a jazz band. And the turning point was, it really was the turning point, was about 1953. I was playing at the Lighthouse, in Hermosa Beach. And Shelly Manne, Shorty Rogers, Bob Cooper, Jimmy Giuffre, we were the group. Shorty was making a lot of records. Jazz records all over the place. So it turns out that there was a movie completed that starred Marlon Brando. The one about the motorcycles, *The Wild One.* They had already signed up an old-line music man to do the picture who didn't know anything about jazz. He was going to write a standard score— big chases and a lot of strings and stuff. But Brando sat in somebody's room one day and said "That's not what I want." He put on a record he'd gotten of Shorty Rogers. He said "*That's* what I want." He had such power that there was nothing for them to do but to come down to the Lighthouse and see what was going on down there. So one day I'm aware that the place is full of people that you don't see normally at the Lighthouse . . .

L.A.: (Laughs.)

BERNHART: They were all dressed up. They're *there.* They weren't going to take any chances. So they watched us— for *weeks.* Came down on Sundays and stayed all day. Watching us. You know, what do they do, why do they—*really.* I think Shorty, or somebody, knew what they were there for. So we showed off. Played a lot of different kinds of things. Then they hired Shorty Rogers to help this man with the score. Shorty got paid, but they didn't give him credit on the screen. We were added to the studio orchestra at Columbia Pictures. First time I saw the inside of a picture studio was that picture. Myself and Shelly and Bob Cooper and Bud Shank and a couple of trumpet players that had never gotten in before. It was a sensation. After that, we were all busy.

L.A.: Did your playing with Kenton through the Innovations period help to prepare you for that? So much of the music had a classical quality.

BERNHART: That's correct. Yes. Yes, the program of the Innovations was a symphonic program.

L.A.: One of my utter favorites of that period is Bill Russo's "Solitaire," which you played and recorded. Jim Amlotte is wild about that too.

BERNHART: That's deceivingly simple music, that kind of writing. It's exposed. Harmony is something that the arranger or composer determines, and if he has imagination, he finds things. That's the difference between pedestrian and creative. Bill Russo always was very original.

L.A.: Among the people who wrote for trombone in Kenton's orchestra, was he one of your favorites?

BERNHART: Sure, we were very close friends from youth. We both come from Chicago. I've known him since we were in high school. Also Lee Konitz was part of our gang. We had a group of kids. We happened to discover each other. We didn't go to the same school, but there was some kind of a band and pretty soon you know who plays, they find each other. Bill Russo was younger than we were, about two years younger. *Brilliant.* Had an IQ of two hundred and something. Both his parents were attorneys, and they imparted to him all that intelligence. I think he had already graduated from high school and was in college when I first met him. He was fifteen.

L.A.: Fifteen, in *college?*

BERNHART: He was in college, yes. He was one of those. A genius. As a matter of fact, his major in college wasn't music. It was something like psychology, something on an intellectual plane. He was always adept as a musician.

L.A.: Was he composing when you knew him?

BERNHART: Oh, sure. "Solitaire" was written about that time, when he was fifteen or sixteen.

L.A.: I can't believe it.

BERNHART: The record was made in 1951, and he'd had it in his portfolio for a number of years. I had played it in the band in Chicago. We didn't have the strings. It was written for jazz band. He had a number of things like that and he brought them to Stan. Stan certainly recognized his talent.

L.A.: You were on the band before Russo?

BERNHART: Yes, I joined the Kenton band in '46.

L.A.: Right at the bridge between Artistry in Rhythm and Progressive Jazz. That must have been a really fertile time.

BERNHART: I guess it was. Sure. Yes. Yes, when I joined, the book had a lot of dance music in it. Of course, it was better than pedestrian dance music. In 1946 Stan recorded *Concerto to End All Concertos.* He'd been playing it for a long time, and he finally recorded it. It required that people had to stand there and listen to it.

L.A.: Was that just about the turning point between dance music and listening music?

BERNHART: Ya, I think so. So that

required that there be a concert period. And that was something new, to do concert pieces that people couldn't dance to. But they *still* tried to dance to them!

L.A.: What, to *Concerto to End All Concertos?*

BERNHART: (Laughing.) Yes! Well, it had a lot of tempo changes, but people were out there dancing. You get a dance hall, there are a lot of people that don't come to dance. And Stan knew that. That's why he realized that it would be hypocritical to say this is a dance band, that that wasn't what he wanted to do. He wanted to play concerts. But the dance halls were the places that were most available, and it was a difficult situation for him.

L.A.: You mean his desire for concert jazz actually goes back to the '40s period.

BERNHART: Oh sure.

L.A.: And that evolved through the years.

BERNHART: Certainly. Once in a blue moon, they'd be able to set up a concert. One of the first was at the Hollywood Bowl here, in '48. I think it was one of the first times the band played to an audience that sat and listened. And it was such a success that that changed his whole thinking. From then on he never really could go into a ballroom and feel happy.

L.A.: Was that the Progressive Jazz Orchestra?

BERNHART: That's correct. The Hollywood Bowl sold out. Twelve thousand or more people came. It was the first time Stan had ever had a band play to that large a crowd. That was *listening.* Came to listen. And it really did.

L.A.: Did Stan talk to you about that?

BERNHART: He talked a lot about it. But actually, I never got social with Stan. It was just a policy I picked up from older musicians that I respected who had been telling me over the years, the best policy is not to get too thick with the leader. I went my way, and he went his, and our conversations were limited. We had a very good understanding about it. I think he respected me for that.

L.A.: Before joining the band, had you heard Stan's music?

BERNHART: Sure. I heard them a couple of times live, in Chicago. He came into a theater in Chicago with his first band, his first trip back East. It was 1942 or '43. I had heard his name. I read *Down Beat* religiously, so I knew that this band from California was making a trip East. So we went to the theater, and we were all impressed by the way they played, which was very clean. And Stan. He was an impressive man to see. Standing there. Most band leaders left something to be desired. They might be great players, but most of the time they had no personality. But Stan had a personality, a very engaging personality. He really looked great in front of the band. And you know something, they were playing *Concerto to End All Concertos.*

L.A.: How did it happen that you got on the band?

BERNHART: Practically a storybook. I was drafted into the Army in 1944. There were Army bands all over the place, but I couldn't get into one. When I was shipped to the West Coast I left my horn at home; I'd given up. I was at Fort Ord, which is where they prepared you to go overseas. Everybody that was with me ended up at Okinawa, and most of them didn't come back. Okinawa was terrible. They were just pouring guys into that place, and they were being killed. And I had no doubts about my ability, I was not much of a soldier, so . . . On this day, that we were to leave, get on the boat, we were going up to San Francisco, standing there with packs on our backs, suddenly somebody called my name. It turns out there were two bands at Fort Ord, and somebody on one of them had been medically discharged. A trombone player. The day before. They went through the list of people on the post who could fill the bill. When you were enlisted in the service, you put down what you had done and they assigned a number that covered what you had done. There was a number after my name, and it said "trombone player." They went down the list and came to "B." What if there'd been someone whose name began with "A"? But mine was the first on the list. It's miraculous. They took me to the band barracks, and I'm in the band. Everybody else went to Okinawa. The band had in it two of the original members of the Kenton band, a saxophone player, Red Dorris, and Harry Forbes, a trombone player. Red Dorris was very close to Stan, and they asked for his arrangements. So we played Stan Kenton originals in the Army band. When the war ended Dorris and Forbes rejoined the Kenton band, and about three weeks after that, there was an opening. Forbes recommended me. Bob Gioga called me in Chicago and said they'd be at the Eastwood Gardens in Detroit. I arrived in Detroit, got to the hotel where they were staying around 7

o'clock. It was late. Everyone had left for the Eastwood Gardens, which was quite far from the hotel. I wouldn't have known where to go. But Stan waited for me. Himself. He was waiting in the lobby for me to show up. That impressed me. The whole thing was unbelievable. I've thought many times, on somebody's finger pulling my name, everything in my life changed.

L.A.: Did you play much in high school?

BERNHART: Oh, sure, but I had no intention of being in jazz. Nowadays they teach kids to play jazz on the stage. But that was out of the question then. That was considered, you know— terrible. Don't mention those things. My intention was to get in a symphony orchestra.

L.A.: What attracted you to the trombone?

BERNHART: As a matter of fact, I wasn't really attracted to it. I started in elementary school on an instrument that was available, because we couldn't afford anything. That was a tuba. I was pretty small, but I played that tuba for a couple of years, and I really liked it. I figured it was a challenge, and it is. Later on my folks said to me "We can buy you an instrument, but it can't be a tuba; that costs too much." So the next thing in order seemed to be the trombone.

L.A.: You're kidding! (Laughs.)

BERNHART: I really wasn't that thrilled about it, either. The trombone has a lot of things about it that make it very difficult to play. It was always a trial, very, very, very hard. You have to practice a lot and give up any kind of outside life if you really want to play it.

L.A.: How long were you with Kenton, not counting the Neophonic concert?

BERNHART: Off and on from 1946 to 1952. In 1947, if you'll recall, Stan had a nervous breakdown and disbanded the band. We were in Alabama. Everybody went in a different direction. I went back to Chicago and later ended up with Boyd Raeburn's band in New York. That went on until about September of that year, and then Stan reorganized his band and I rejoined him. In 1948 we played all over and then I left in the middle of the year because I was tired of the road. I came out here, to California, to try to get into the studios, but it was impossible. So then I joined Benny Goodman for about a year, in 1949. And left them when Stan started his Innovations, in late 1949-50. I came back and stayed with him until 1952.

L.A.: Then you were probably associ-

ated with Kenton through the most creative periods of his life.

BERNHART: Well, that's hard to say. I thought his best band was about 1955. That had Lee Konitz on the band, and Zoot Sims, and Gerry Mulligan was writing for him. Lee wasn't too happy then, but it was good for him, there were good things for him to play, and it was a better swing band. It was a jazz band more than Stan had had before. The arrangements swung more.

L.A.: One can't always tell from a record, but at a live performance a soloist has a lot more time for improvising. How much of the time would be devoted to jazz improvisation, where the soloist could really do his thing?

BERNHART: Not too much time, unless it was a featured number, where a man was out front and played the whole number. I'll give you a hint of how he felt about it. It was maybe the best example I've ever had of how Stan felt about individuals playing as opposed to the band playing full, with the big sound. We had an arrangement of Cole Porter's "Easy to Love" in the book that we would play toward the end of the evening, when it got quiet and people were just dancing. It had a trombone solo for most of the tune, and saxes playing melodically. Last eight bars it went into a big finish, with crashing pyramid chords just at the very end. On this one night, maybe the last five minutes of the night, Stan said "Okay, play 'Easy to Love,'" and he walked off the bandstand and went to the back of the ballroom—I could see him, talking to the owner of the ballroom. But when we were about three beats away from the ending, he suddenly wheeled and—like a *gazelle,* in *three leaps,* with those big legs—made it to the bandstand. So he could be there to conduct the last part of that arrangement. He was in his glory. Cung! bang! gung! That was what he enjoyed. It was his life.

L.A.: What about the creativeness of the Innovations period? Did that appeal to you?

BERNHART: Certainly. Absolutely. We played so many different kinds of music that it required more than just being a jazz musician. It required lots of symphonic, legit symphonic playing.

L.A.: When you joined in 1946, that was when Kai Winding was there. For the short time he was on that band, he just made a tremendous impression with people.

BERNHART: Yes, he was the star. He

had a way of playing that was his own. Stan was really terribly enthusiastic about him and Kai was really the major player on the band.

L.A.: The whole band?

BERNHART: Major soloist. Sure. I sat next to him for about a year. And it was a good idea because I picked up what he did. In my own way. Stan wanted that style. A loose kind—he didn't want somebody that played like Tommy Dorsey. He'd had lots of trombone players that played like Tommy Dorsey; he didn't want that.

L.A.: In musical terms, what's the difference between Kai Winding and Stan Kenton versus Tommy Dorsey?

BERNHART: Melodic. Tommy Dorsey's the greatest player of the melody. Tommy Dorsey played a melody almost mechanically, except that it wasn't. It's not easy; it's very difficult to play as perfectly as he played a melody, because it requires something that I've never heard with any other trombone player. Usually they slip around and smear and things, but Tommy played every note in tune, and made it beautiful, made a very beautiful sound. Unique. His control was unbelievable. He overcame the trombone. But there's no point in trying to imitate him, and Stan knew it. And besides, it didn't do anything for him. He wanted to hear more—personality. *Add* something.

L.A.: How was Kai Winding different?

BERNHART: Kai played growls and slips and turns and . . .

L.A.: What's a slip?

BERNHART: Well just fall, like falling off of a note—whatever he felt like playing.

L.A.: Style.

BERNHART: And Stan thought that was great, because that was the person speaking.

L.A.: I've always thought the Kenton trombones had a *beautiful* melodic line. Evidently he wanted to create his *own* sound. Get away from Dorsey through this Kai Winding style, into something he could call his own. After Winding left, then, you became the lead trombone?

BERNHART: Yes. In 1947, when Stan regrouped. I was told before the band started that Winding would not be on the band. I wasn't so sure I wanted to go back and just be his associate. But he stayed in New York and that changed my attitude. I took his place.

L.A.: What was Stan like to work for?

BERNHART: He was not hard to work for. You had to play, but there was no show of temperament. I've been on some bands where that's the case, and the morale goes way down. With Stan, he was always the nice guy that you saw. He was a nice man. A good man. Sometimes his business decisions caused him to suffer—maybe he needed to suffer. He seemed to have some need to punish himself from time to time. But to work for him was fine. He was great in front of the band. It was a pleasure playing for him.

L.A.: What business decisions?

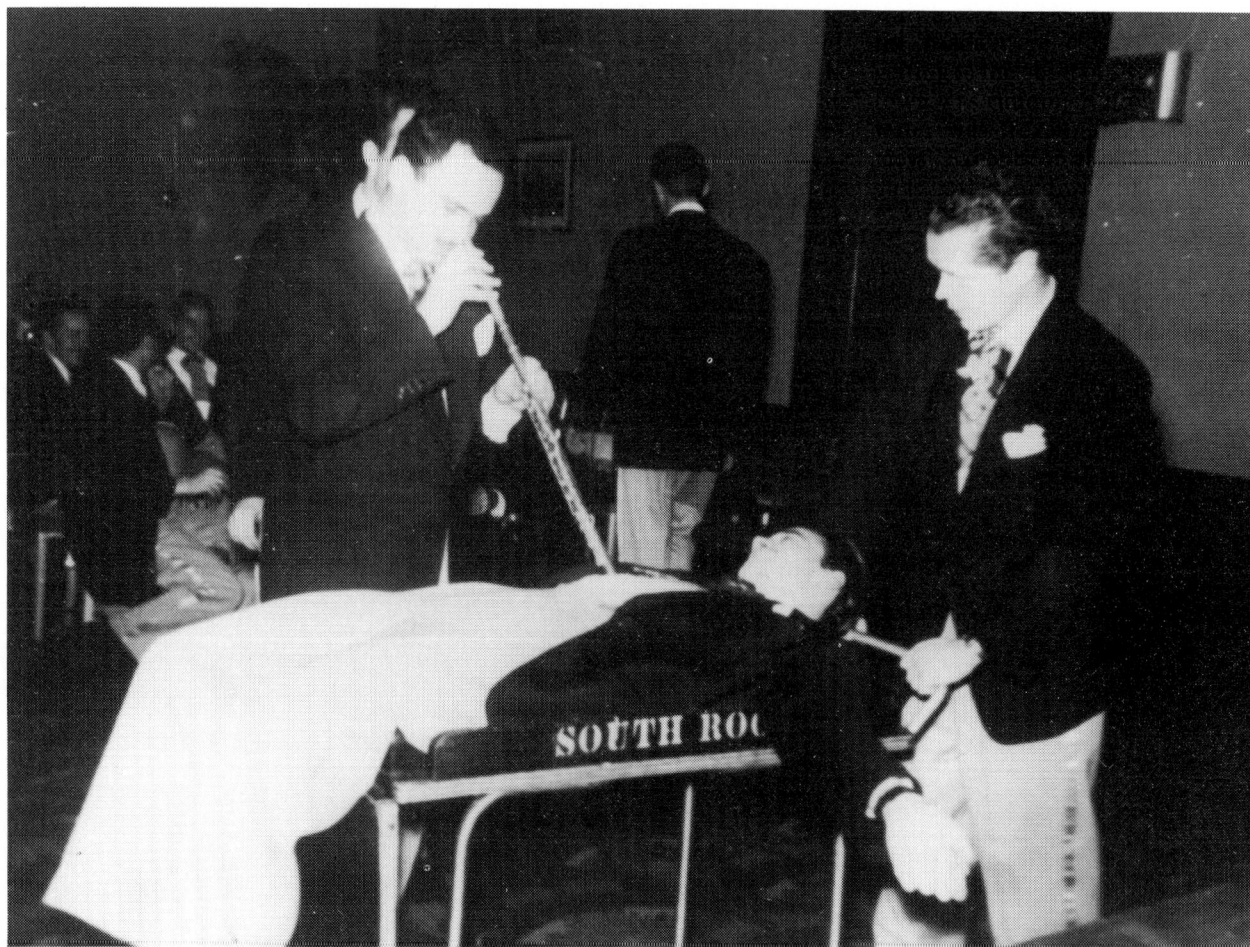

Kenton band members Milt Bernhart and Eddie Safranski, clowning around at the Hotel Pennsylvania, New York City, in 1951. (Photo: Courtesy of Bob Gioga.)

BERNHART: Stan had an opportunity, in 1948, to do his own radio show. We were playing Carnegie Hall, and as I walked around backstage I heard him discussing it with his then-manager, Carlos Gastel. Ford Motor Company would sponsor an hour show, once a week. All he would have to do would be to play a couple of popular songs; the rest of the hour he could play whatever he wanted. But Stan said no. I'm standing out there; it wasn't a dream. Carlos says, "Stan, you realize what this *is*. It gives you a chance to stay in one place, and build something and have a resident orchestra, and play as much of what you want to play, except—give in a *little* bit." Stan said, "No, I'm sorry. I won't subvert my art to that sort of commercialism." Just like that. Carlos and Stan split after that. Carlos had had to work pretty hard to get them to agree to it. What's ironic is that about ten years later, Stan did do a tv show here in Los Angeles, where they played rinky-dink arrangements, and after five weeks it flopped. That was a low point for Stan. On top of that, in order to secure a place to do this show, he took a lease on the Rendezvous Ballroom in Balboa, refurbished it, for twenty thousand dollars, and then, after the show flopped, he simply gave the ballroom back to its owners, having fixed it up for them. Stan also had this strange perversity in his personality, this strange fixation about old standards not being what they were and times changing—yet he was a believer supposedly in change in music. It's an old story. People in his position, every day they're on the road with the band, they're too concerned with finding a place to eat and sleep and play the job, and get a new trumpet player or whatever, to even look at a newspaper and know what's been going on.

L.A.: With all that traveling, did Stan favor some part of the country more than any other?

BERNHART: No. He didn't know one part from another. It was just the road. It didn't matter.

L.A.: I find it hard to understand how he could leave a gorgeous setting like California to go through snowstorms in Chicago and all that.

BERNHART: That's what you had to do when you had a band. You've got to go someplace else. Once in a while we'd be in a snowstorm, couldn't play the job. Somehow or other they'd book him into places where you'd have to know it was going to be snowing. We'd run into big problems. We were stranded several times. Once we were stranded a week in Milwaukee. Five-foot-high snow. All the roads were closed. It was really getting to the point of a real danger—the town was running out of food, and the water was frozen, and it was really a mess. Except for about a half a dozen guys in the band who played cards.

L.A.: (Laughs.)

BERNHART: Who never looked up.

L.A.: (Laughs.) Never looked up?

BERNHART: For them it was great.

L.A.: What did you most admire about Kenton?

BERNHART: Oh, that he was dynamic. And he *was*, you know. And he was interested in people. He really was interested in people. The man had a photographic memory for names. That's why they liked him. He was—he didn't look off over to the side or something when he was talking to you, he looked right at you. And he would listen to you, he'd want to know what you thought.

L.A.: Do you ever still play the trombone?

BERNHART: I've got news for you. I'm gonna play it on Easter. Once a year.

L.A.: Play what?

BERNHART: A brass quartet I wrote.

L.A.: You wrote a brass quartet?

BERNHART: Sure. We're all capable. You know something? A trombone player that sat next to me for several years—Harry Betts—never wrote a note for Stan, but all the time he was there, Harry was one of the best writers I've ever known. As soon as he left the band and came into town here, he began writing, and that's what he does. He's one of the best.

L.A.: How come you guys never wrote while you were on the Kenton band?

BERNHART: No one ever asked.

Shelly Manne, outside his California home. (Photo by the Author.)

7 Shelly Manne

Stan was fascinated with the sounds I got off the drums. I always had an inquisitive way about playing the instrument. Of trying to get different sounds from the drums, more musical sounds, the way the timbres would blend with the orchestra to create new colors. Sometimes I'd experiment and it would work. Stan would know it. He'd tell me. And sometimes I'd do it and he'd say "Leave that; that's great! I love that sound."

L.A.: What are the colors in that group of things you have there?

MANNE: You have a choice in cymbals, sounds of cymbals—the way you tune your drums—your use of hands—use of other percussion instruments. Brushes, sticks. There's a lot of timbres on the drums that create a lot of creative sounds; a lot of imagination has to be used. And I did use a lot of imagination in Stan's band, in creating a lot of these sounds.

L.A.: Is there a total freedom in the drummer's mind? Sitting there with all this beautiful equipment, like a smorgasbord of instruments, do you have this freedom—

MANNE: You have to be careful. You can become over-indulgent and a little self-indulgent. The music should always be the primary thing. You should always use your instrument to make music, not use the music to show off your instrument.

L.A.: Boy that's got to be a fine line to know how to do.

MANNE: Well—(laughs)—yes it is. It's what separates the men from the boys.

L.A.: It's such a fascinating palette of colors. You're saying that you can't be like a baby and choose a little of this and a little of that. You've got to have a higher goal in mind as far as the music is concerned.

MANNE: The music has to take you where you want to go. You have to listen to the music and add something to the music.

L.A.: To what the others are playing.

MANNE: Yes. That dictates to you the kinds of things you want to do.

L.A.: Did all that freedom to experiment in Stan's band broaden your own ideas about what you wanted to do?

MANNE: Of course. His charts were very challenging. They made me reach a little further than I thought I was capable of.

L.A.: As far as ideas and what to do with them.

MANNE: Right. And that broadened my musical knowledge, too.

L.A.: What about the relationship of the drums to the other instruments, the blending and contrast, did it add to that?

MANNE: Right.

L.A.: Do you carry this over now in your playing?

MANNE: Yes. Yes.

L.A.: What do you do now, do you have your own trio?

MANNE: Ya, I've been working with a trio mostly.

L.A.: Who are the other members?

MANNE: The set trio has been Mike Wofford on piano and Chuck Domanico on bass. Last night at Ventura it was Roger Kellaway and Monty Budwig.

L.A.: Do you play mostly around this area, in California?

MANNE: We toured Japan last year. I'm going back to Japan in October. I work as an individual sometimes, and I go to festivals. Whatever comes up. If there's something I want to do, I go.

L.A.: The rest of the time . . .

MANNE: I'm here. I work a lot of the studios. Well I did—I'm not as busy now as I used to be at the studios. The experience I had with Stan's band really helped me prepare for studio work.

L.A.: Why? What do you have to do to prepare for studio work?

MANNE: Read. You have to be able to read. And because Stan's music was, in a way, classically oriented, it helped me for the studio work that I did, because I could step into a lot of different situations and hear what needed to be done. I became very adaptable at different kinds of music. His band helped me in that area.

L.A.: Do you play clubs often?

MANNE: Well this week I'm going to adjudicate at the Collegiate Jazz Festival at Notre Dame University, then play a club in Westwood for four days, then Studio City for two days. Then I have a couple of albums to make.

L.A.: When you adjudicate, what do you expect to hear?

MANNE: Swing.

L.A.: It comes back to swing.

59

MANNE: That's right. If you don't have time, you don't have anything. Everything is based on time.

L.A.: Time and swing aren't the same thing, though, are they.

MANNE: No. That's right. But . . .

L.A.: But you want to hear swing.

MANNE: I want to hear it swing, and I want to hear the band play in good time.

L.A.: You're more interested in hearing that than you are in . . .

MANNE: That's the most important *thing.* If it's not there then the whole band falls apart. Even Stan Kenton's band.

L.A.: What is it, a kind of pulsation?

MANNE: Ahhh . . .

L.A.: It's more definite than that.

MANNE: It's what makes the band play together. Then everybody has a good time. They don't necessarily have to swing, everybody, but it helps if they do. But swing is an abstract thing. I mean you can take five guys and they can all be equally talented—one guy'll swing his fanny off and the other guys'll just play good time. And not get that feeling that makes you want to get up and tap your toes and clap your hands.

L.A.: What's your impression of the young talent you hear coming up?

MANNE: That there are very few individuals, stylists in music today. Even with the thousands that the schools are putting out. You come up with a couple of handfuls of great players out of all these thousands of musicians.

L.A.: Some of the younger drummers that came on in the seventies would talk about how difficult it was with a band as large as Stan's as far as the volume in sound coming out of it, how difficult it was to be the dominant figure and keep it together. Now the role of the drummer in the band—any band—is terribly important. But I would think it would be even more so in a band like Kenton's.

MANNE: Well it was hard to swing that band.

L.A.: Did you want to swing it?

MANNE: *Yeah,* I did.

L.A.: But Stan didn't like his band to swing too much.

MANNE: Ah, no. His band moved more by sound than by time feeling. But I wanted it to swing. I tried.

L.A.: Did he ever say, "Shelly, stop that"? (Laughs.)

MANNE: Oh, no. Never. But he knew when it would swing, and he enjoyed it too. He had a great band after I left, the band that had Zoot Sims on it, and Mel Lewis and Lee Konitz. I mean that was a great band, the one that Bill Holman

was writing for. That was a totally different kind of band. That was a swing, more of a swing band than the others. The others—the other bands, like the bands I was on—they bordered on classical feeling, almost. But using jazz musicians.

L.A.: Did you enjoy it?

MANNE: I enjoyed it. But I don't think I enjoyed it any more than getting in a band like Woody Herman's and swinging.

L.A.: I would think you'd have more of a palette of sounds to work with.

MANNE: I did. That's the part I enjoyed.

L.A.: But you'd rather swing.

MANNE: Ya. Right. That's what jazz is about.

L.A.: Kenton's view of jazz is quite different from that of a lot of other people. Some argue that the kind of music he played couldn't even be called jazz.

MANNE: Ya, I may have to go along with that, to a point.

L.A.: That it's not jazz?

MANNE: It's jazz-oriented, yes, because of the players he's using. He's using jazz players to interpret the music. So it's going to have a jazz feeling. But the essence of jazz is a small group. Like you heard last night, at the club at Ventura. That's what it's about. We go on the stage and we don't *know* what we're going to play. And it happens spontaneously, empathy happens between three or four, five musicians. And they get really swinging and total improvisation . . .

L.A.: *Total* improvisation.

MANNE: . . . in a free—well, built on a definite melody line or something, you know. But—that's what it's about. You take that and you put it in a big band and build around it. And you get a jazz band. The nucleus of a jazz band, Stan's or anyone else's, are the guys who want to play jazz. They would interpret Stan's music in a certain way. Those particular people that Stan hired that were great soloists were merely the nucleus of what was happening in the band. And he recognized that. But he also had people in the band—as were the soloists—who could contribute ensemble-wise to the band with their individual sound. Like the way Kai Winding played is the way the trombone section played in the band. I can't stress that enough. He was the lead trombone player. They were interpreting him, and he was interpreting Stan's music. And the way I played in the rhythm section. There

were four guys in there, but the way I interpreted the music, he made use of that, that creative thing that we gave. That's what I mean. In the ensemble playing. But these people were also very capable of getting up and playing great jazz solos, too. The soloist was as important at getting the band's sound in solo playing as in the ensemble.

L.A.: That's interesting. With arrangements written out . . .

MANNE: The arrangements are only a jumping off place for the soloist.

L.A.: Improvisation and freedom come in when the soloist gets his turn.

MANNE: Exactly, right. And then you're back to the small-group jazz feeling again.

L.A.: Did you ever clash with the composers and arrangers whose style, shall we say, veered from that?

MANNE: Oh, sure, at times we must have said "Hey, man, this doesn't swing. What are we gonna do with it?" We knew that he was writing pieces featuring certain people that were important to the band—and important to him.

L.A.: In "Shelly Manne," the piece that Stan wrote for you at the time of the Innovations, what is the construction—it's an arrangement written down, and then there are portions of it where you're supposed to improvise?

MANNE: Yes.

L.A.: So whoever played it would have the same . . .

MANNE: Freedom.

L.A.: How did the writing of it come about? Stan wrote it after you joined the band. Did he just spring it on you, or did you have some input into it?

MANNE: We talked about how "Shelly Manne" should be before he wrote it. It was the same as with "Artistry in Percussion," where he'd said "What would you like to do?" and I said "I'd like to do something where the drums take the melody. Not just a drum solo, but where the drums are an integral part of the melody." One of the main things about Stan's music was that he wrote for the people he had. He didn't just write music; he wrote with them in mind. The Stan Kenton sound, like the trombones in "September Song" and those things, was Kai Winding's sound. Stan recognized the creative thing that Kai gave to the band and utilized it; from then on that sound was Stan Kenton's sound. So for "Artistry in Percussion" he put me together with Pete (Rugolo) and we came up with that idea and Pete wrote it and orchestrated it. And when I talked to Stan about the "Shelly Manne" thing, I remember that I said something like "I want to do something different. I'd like to do something almost in a ballad." Which had never been done, using drums, before. With triangle sounds and cymbal sounds and all the pretty percussion sounds we could get.

L.A.: Is "Opus in Timpani" a different work from "Shelly Manne," or the same work under a different title?

MANNE: I don't know "Opus in Timpani."

L.A.: Stan wrote that for the Neophonic. You played in the Neophonic—

into how the band should sound and play certain things. Of course if he didn't like it, if it was away from his train of thought, he would change things. But he let us have input into the band. A lot of the charts weren't that creative to start with, but they developed that way. We would be able to change things, as we played them, night after night. Somebody would do something else and we'd leave it in, because it sounded great. It's just like "St. James Infirmary," the comedy number, evolved. You know, it was originally a number for Stan to sing. Arrangement. Everything. And one night he sang "I went down to the St. James Infirmary" and a guy, somebody

L.A.: Let's get into this input thing somewhat. Was it the same with you as with Winding, as far as your contribution to the Kenton sound?

MANNE: Stan always gave us the freedom, when he had really creative players, to contribute. When he liked what he heard he utilized it and wrote for that sound. It was something that happened naturally. Like when I joined the band and started—you know how they would play the theme song and he'd start out with just the cymbals roaring? And then he'd bring the band in? You know, he'd point to the drummer and get more. That was my idea. That's the way I played it. I started doing that and

Shelly Manne, playing with his trio at a club in Ventura, California. (Photo by the Author.)

evidently you did not play timpani, just drums?

MANNE: I played timpani in the Innovations, but no, not in the Neophonic.

L.A.: So I guess it's a different work altogether. Did you like "Shelly Manne"?

MANNE: I loved it. I thought it was unusual. The great thing about Stan was his flexibility, and his willingness to let the musicians, the sidemen, have input

yelled in the band, "Why didn'tcha get a hotel room like the rest of us?"

L.A.: (Laughs.)

MANNE: And the next thing you know the whole band went bananas. And Stan loved it. And it became a big deal. It became a whole big comedy routine. We used to get *wild* on the stage. I would dive off the back of the stage and . . . it was fun. We enjoyed it. It kept the band loose.

he liked it. It was a big sound and then a fanfare, it was all conducted.

L.A.: How did it develop into the big production number that it eventually became? I've heard it go thirty minutes or longer, at a live performance.

MANNE: We started at the Click Club in Philadelphia, messing around with the theme. We'd get into a rhythmic thing that he liked. And we played it different every time, sometimes. It just evolved. These things just evolve

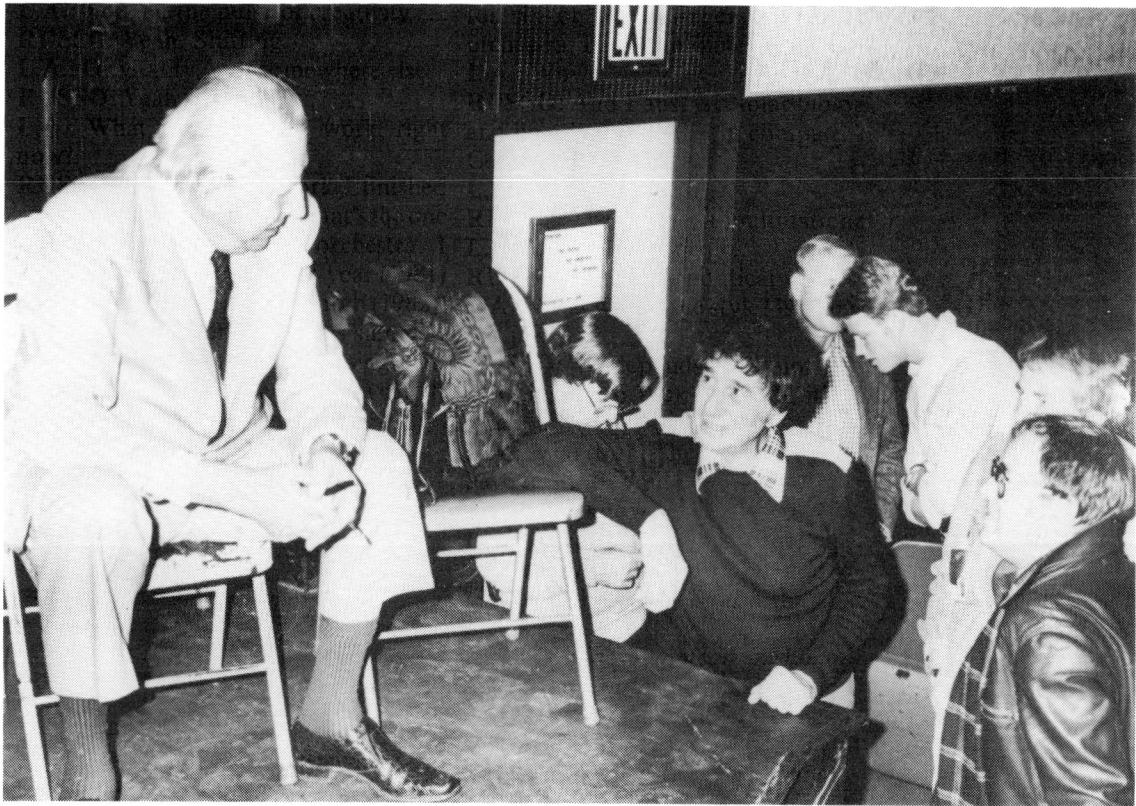

Stan Kenton, in his last public appearance, at California State University at Northridge, December 1978. In picture are Shelly Manne (in dark sweater) and Buddy Childers (in leather jacket). Cal State presented a special "Tribute to Stan Kenton" with its jazz band. (Photo: Courtesy of Shelly Manne.)

naturally. It wasn't written. It was all practically a head arrangement. The extended version. Except for the original version of "Artistry in Rhythm," which was Stan's arrangement. The real fast tempo?

L.A.: Which starts off without any kind of cymbal or anything. What was it that you had that so impressed Stan, do you think?

MANNE: I was a stylist. A strong stylist. I had an individual way of playing. He recognized that and made use of it. After I left the band Stan used to buy cymbals to try to duplicate the cymbal sound that I made.

L.A.: How did you meet him?

MANNE: Stan was in New York in 1946, looking for a new drummer. He'd had Ralph Collier and Joe Vernon and a number of others. I was working on 52nd Street, building a reputation as a jazz drummer. The guys brought Stan down to hear me one night. Afterwards he came to me and said "I'd like you to join my band. We're playing at the Adams Theater in Newark." I said "I'll have to talk to my wife about it." 'Cause I was doing fairly well in New York—

not making a lot of money, but doing what was important to me; I was playing. But I knew about Stan's band. When I heard the early recordings, with that chopped-off *ba-da-du-dit-dit-dit-dit* kind of playing, I wasn't crazy about it. But I knew the band was getting hot. And it was changing. He was hiring a lot of good musicians. My wife was working—she was a Rockette at the time. We had to decide. She said yes, let's go. Of course I knew it was a good opportunity for me. 'Cause I'd been with a number of big bands before that; I'd made some kind of reputation playing in big bands before the war—Bobby Byrne and Bob Astor and Joe Marsala and Raymond Scott and Will Bradley and Les Brown.

L.A.: You must have been a prodigy at the age of *two* to have had all that experience.

MANNE: No, I didn't start playing until I was eighteen.

L.A.: *Eighteen?*

MANNE: Yeah. I hadn't been playing very long.

L.A.: How did you get attracted to it?

MANNE: My family was musical. My dad was a drummer. But he never taught

me anything. He didn't want me to do that. I always wanted to be a jazz drummer. I just knew that's what I wanted to be. I started off playing saxophone. I wanted to be a jazz drummer and come hell or high water that's what I was gonna do. (Laughs.)

L.A.: But you were eighteen already when you made your choice on that.

MANNE: Well no I made my choice before then, a little before that, but that's when I really started playing in earnest.

L.A.: That's an interesting point, your recognizing the promise of the Kenton band.

MANNE: It wasn't what was going on back East, which we were all involved in. Stan definitely had a style. An individual style. I joined in February of '46 at the Adams Theater and I never regretted it. It was a great experience being with him. I was with the band six years.

L.A.: Straight through?

MANNE: No. When Stan broke up the band in '47 I went with Jazz at the Philharmonic. I played with Woody for a year. Then another time I left because I

62

wanted to play in a small band and hired my own group for a while, with Bill Harris. That wasn't working out. So finally Stan asked me to come back and join the band for the Innovations and I did. I left the band after that, in 1952.

L.A.: Why?

MANNE: I was just tired of traveling. I felt it was time to move on to another place. I had things I wanted to do, some experimenting on my own I wanted to do, playing with a small group. It was just time, you know?

L.A.: What kind of experimenting?

MANNE: A looser way of playing, a more melodic way of playing the drums. I had a melodic way of playing the drums on Stan's band, but you're very limited when you're in a big band, making something meaningful happen ensemble-wise out of four notes that are written on the page. I wanted more of an outlet to create as a soloist and as an individual within a small group. I wanted to get back to the basic jazz concept. That's all.

L.A.: What do you feel Stan did for you personally, for your career and . . .

MANNE: My God, you know, my career blossomed with Stan Kenton.

L.A.: Is this just through exposure with his band?

MANNE: It was a combination of things. Getting the chance to explore what I could do. Having an outlet, a showcase for our talent; Stan gave us that. The band really started becoming popular, and got a direction, a set direction, in writing. That was one of the great things about Stan. He had an individual style, an individual way of writing for the band, of using writers who could interpret the way he felt so that the band would have its own style and sound. As the band grew in popularity so did the individuals within it— guys like Kai and Eddie Safranski and Buddy Childers and myself. The kids in those days knew every guy who played in the band. They knew the guy who played fourth trumpet, fifth trombone. I started winning polls, I started becoming very well known. My reputation really flowered.

L.A.: Did you have a good personal relationship with him?

MANNE: I think we loved each other. I know he loved me, and I did him. I always felt a close tie with Stan. Always. I hardly saw him in the later years, but when we did see each other, it was a very strong feeling. As long as I knew he was there, I felt good about it. He loved doing what he was doing, and that was what was important.

Shorty Rogers, outside his California home. (Photo by the Author.)

64

8 Shorty Rogers

It's funny. Yesterday I had to go to Universal Studios—I'd done some work on a pilot show, and they wanted me to come in and check it out—all the musicians are friends of mine, and they had a pretty large band there. I stepped through the door (laughs) and as soon as they saw me one of the trumpet players played the intro to "Maynard Ferguson"! "Ye-tuil-ya, tuil-ya, tu-tu-tu-tu-tu!" It's been thirty-four years since I wrote that.

L.A.: You wrote that for the Innovations Orchestra?

ROGERS: Yes. We were on the road, and I remember, Stan got me on the side and said "I'd like to have you write a piece for Maynard, and we'll call it 'Maynard Ferguson.'" We were in Lincoln, Nebraska. I needed a piano to try things out on. I finally wound up at the YMCA there and I said, "Do you have a piano?" (Laughs.) They said "You can go in this room. If people come in, don't let 'em bother you." One of those things. But I wrote the whole thing, to my memory, I wrote it in that one day.

L.A.: In the YMCA.

ROGERS: Yes. Then later, on the Innovations tour, we got to New York City and Stan said to me, "I'd like you to write a piece for Art Pepper. We'll call it 'Art Pepper.'" And he said "I want you to take as much time as you need. We'll go on the road, and you stay in New York a few days, or as long as you need, to write it." I wasn't used to being treated this nicely. (Laughs.) So I stayed in New York. I think I was there about six days.

L.A.: Six days. It's a beautiful work.

ROGERS: To this day it really means a lot to me. Not only as an important memory but for the tremendous reward I got back from hearing it, and hearing Art; how marvelous he sounded then

and how great that record still sounds today.

L.A.: Was Innovations your first meeting with Kenton?

ROGERS: That's when I was invited to join the band, but I'd met Stan actually earlier. The first band I played on when I graduated from high school was Will Bradley's band. I was seventeen. Let's see, it must have been 1942. That's where I met Shelly Manne, too, who later figured in my getting with the Kenton band. We were playing at a ballroom in Boston, alternating with Kenton. It was a new band from California, and there was a lot of talk about him. I met him then just briefly, you know, like hello, shake hands. But that's the first time I heard the band, too, and it really impressed me. Some years later, in the late forties, Buddy Childers and Shelly and myself were with Woody Herman's band. Woody was in the process of disbanding, and a few months later Stan was organizing the Innovations, the large orchestra with strings and all that. I remember Shelly and Buddy and Pete Rugolo talking to Stan and saying, "Let's get Shorty on the band to play and do some composing and arranging."

L.A.: How did you know Pete Rugolo?

ROGERS: When I was with Woody's band, we were playing in Birdland in New York City when Stan's band came

to town and Pete came down and heard us. I had really just started arranging. I mean I had written in my life maybe four or five arrangements. But Woody's band played something I'd done and Pete liked it and came up later and introduced himself and was really nice. Said it was a nice arrangement and Woody should announce that I wrote it. Woody didn't do that at that time.

L.A.: Does he now?

ROGERS: I think he does. But this was at a time when I don't think he announced anyone. That was one of the basic differences in Woody and a characteristic that Stan had that I appreciate so much. But Pete said "Ask Woody to mention it," and I said "I'm lucky to have a job here. I'm gonna cool it." (Laughs.) Pete was a very well established composer at that time and I really took it as a great compliment that he would take the time to talk to me and encourage me. Through all these years he's been just a dear friend, just a great guy.

L.A.: What piece was it of yours that he heard?

ROGERS: Maybe it was "Keen and Peachy," a thing I wrote for Woody's band. Or "Keeper of the Flame," something I wrote way back at the beginning of my career.

L.A.: What do you suppose it was that he heard in the music that made him think you'd be good for Kenton?

ROGERS: Woody had a great band. If he heard anything it was probably due 90% to the players. (Laughs.)

L.A.: Ohhhhh . . . now Pete Rugolo wouldn't be fooled by that.

ROGERS: No he just—I think it was a natural instinct I have of writing some things that were kind of swinging, that the guys could get their teeth into and really . . .

L.A.: This is a curious situation, because you entered the band at a time when Stan got away from swinging and went into Innovations.

ROGERS: Yes.

L.A.: How would you have made that adjustment, that change of style?

ROGERS: Well, you know, it's interesting. In between the time I'm talking about, that Pete Rugolo came up and talked to me and before I joined Stan, in those years I studied composition very diligently with Dr. Wesley LaViolette out here, and possibly . . .

L.A.: At the University of California?

ROGERS: No, it was at his own house. Jimmy Giuffre, who wrote "Four Brothers" for Woody's band, had studied with him, and Nelson Riddle and a lot of jazz guys. But I feel between the time I first met Pete Rugolo and the time I was invited to work for Stan's Innovations Orchestra I had grown as a writer, as a composer, retaining this instinct for swinging, more of a cookin' thing, but also growing more into some of the sounds that Stan was used to. It was kind of a marriage of those two elements, more ambitious orchestration and composition but still a swinging thing. I think when Shelly and Pete and Buddy spoke to Stan about hiring me it was with the idea of getting more swinging things in the book so it would have more variety. I never asked, I just feel that that would have been part of what they discussed with him.

L.A.: Were you planning to study with LaViolette before—I mean you didn't know that Stan would call you.

ROGERS: Oh no, no, it was just . . .

L.A.: A coincidence.

ROGERS: . . . for my own growth. A few friends of mine were studying with him and I respected their work a lot and previous to that I was a self-taught composer and arranger. See I just taught myself . . .

L.A.: Another California genius. (Laughs.)

ROGERS: (Laughs.)

L.A.: Except that you're from Massachusetts.

ROGERS: It's weird—I grew up in New York City, where I went to the High School in Music and Art and had four years of intensive music training, including theory and some of the teaching that would prepare you to be a composer. But I just wanted to play jazz on trumpet. And I thought all this writing and music theory was just a waste of time and I wouldn't do any homework. It's a strange thing that as a kid I really turned my back on this part of music. I wound up making my living at it and my whole life is wrapped up in it now. By the time I was in the Army, I had some kind of hunger to get some music paper and write something on it. I wrote a few things for this Army band I was in. But it was all self-taught up to that time.

L.A.: What did LaViolette do for you as far as teaching you new things?

ROGERS: He specialized in teaching counterpoint, and jazz music, up to that time and to a great extent still today, is chordal music, chords and voicings, and the thick chords of polyphonic music. Counterpoint is just linear music, single lines that intermesh with each other, that harmonize with each other and complement each other. The main thrust of his teaching was counterpoint, but he also taught orchestration. I mean his teaching was strictly in the symphonic, legitimate field. So whatever gift the Lord gave me or the other guys in jazz, we would just do what felt natural to us and kind of mix it in with LaViolette's teaching.

L.A.: That's fantastic.

ROGERS: But mainly, we would do a lot of writing. Take paper and pencil and write all over it. That's one of the things you have to do.

L.A.: In your arranging for Kenton, did he specify what he wanted you to do, for example, in the voicings?

ROGERS: No. He wouldn't invite you to arrange for him unless he had confidence in what you could do, and he would want you to do just what you felt was natural to you. I mean for him to even tell you—I never talked to him about it, but I just feel as a person that his compassion would be such that he didn't want to inhibit you. Like with chords and voicing, he wouldn't touch that area. He would talk to me—I called it like a layout plan—and it's just general things, and he never would demand it of you; he'd say, like with "Art Pepper," "If it feels good," you know, in those terms, "maybe start out real slow. If it feels good. And then, you

know, build it up, and maybe there could be a cooking section, a swing section, let Art improvise." Just some general things. It could have happened that he would talk in those terms. But as far as, on this chord, give it this voicing, no, he wouldn't touch that at all. Stan appreciated his composers and arrangers and was vocal about it. Getting back to the thing with Woody, when Pete Rugolo said "Shorty, why don't you get Woody to say that you wrote it, so people will know?" Woody plays clarinet and saxophone and that's the world he grew up in and lived in, and his peers wouldn't make a big deal about arrangers or composers. It's nothing derogatory, it's just the way it was at that time.

L.A.: Then why is Stan Kenton different?

ROGERS: Stan is an arranger and composer. And he just has a reverence and a love and a different type of insight into that element of creating music. He knows what it is to get out a piece of paper and sweat over it and get notes on it. So he just appreciates it more than a non-arranger, a non-composer would. He'll tell people about it and he'll be happy—"I got this guy to write for my band, he's great, and I want the world to know about it." And I'm very thankful he treated me that way. He would talk about me not only in front of the band but in the interviews he might have. I can't really express in words what a precious thing it was for me to hear a guy of his stature speak that way about me and the encouragement it was to me. I was a young guy trying to get off the ground. I'll never forget it. He made me feel like a *mensch*, a man.

L.A.: I've heard musicians in the band say things like no matter how good they were, he made them better. Maybe it was the same among arrangers, then.

ROGERS: It definitely was. It was a natural instinct with him, a love for other guys that did the same thing that he did.

L.A.: As a composer yourself, what did you think of Kenton as a composer?

ROGERS: I think he was a great composer. I think there's possibly another element to him as a composer that is of more importance than a lot of people attach to it. I think he was kind of a turning point in jazz and American music. You can look at jazz music before and after Kenton. Before, certain things were going on. When he came he changed the direction. He brought a bigger sound. He pioneered the element

66

of mixing jazz and so-called serious classical music together. I think as a composer he was just a marvelous individual, original; but I think this other element is equally as important, this turning point.

L.A.: Taken altogether, Stan Kenton's contribution could be considered a whole new genre of American music.

ROGERS: I would agree with that.

L.A.: A combination of jazz with the classic, with the experimental, that's just a whole new American style that nobody has ever labeled.

ROGERS: Right. In a way, in the late 1920s Paul Whiteman was a turning point. He brought in George Gershwin and popularized his music. But that music was really more classical-oriented than jazz-oriented. There was no improvising in *Rhapsody in Blue* and some of those great things.

L.A.: That's more classical with jazz . . .

ROGERS: Jazz flavors, ya. But with Kenton's music, the proof is that as time goes on, as years go by, it either fades away or becomes more valid and more important. And I believe Stan's whole life and everything he did are becoming more true and more valid. You know the old saying, old wine gets better. It's certainly true in him. And the dedication he had to music and to his band—if there's anyone with more dedication, someone will have to point him out to me. I mean he was a guy that literally bet everything on an idea. I wish I could say I have that kind of courage. It was a natural instinct with him, go for broke. (Laughs.) Can't hold back. But it was great to have worked with a guy like this. Someone could do a study—it would be kind of wild, but there's a bunch of things that Stan was the first to do. For instance, in the Innovations Orchestra he had Franklin Marks write for the band. Now to my knowledge that's the first time 12-tone music was written for a jazz band.

L.A.: And Bob Graettinger.

ROGERS: Sure.

L.A.: Kenton's heart was really in this Progressive thing, wasn't it.

ROGERS: Yeah.

L.A.: He seemed constantly to be involved with opening new perspectives on things, with his musicians and arrangers and audiences.

ROGERS: Yeah. We'd go places where people would want to hear the standards, and Stan would play 'em for them, but he'd say "We have these new things, why can't they latch on to those?" It's a principle of life and Stan

sure was a subscriber to it—a hunger to always be growing in his art.

L.A.: Some critics have said that Stan Kenton music isn't jazz. If the essence of jazz is free-flowing improvisation, can a written arrangement, no matter how creative, qualify as jazz?

ROGERS: The concept is changing. Guys write jazz, write it down on paper, but only the jazz players that are capable of improvising can really play it with the right interpretation. And execute it correctly, and get the right sound. In a given piece without improvising, it's still jazz to me. It's a question I'm sure you've run into, and not everyone's going to agree on it. You can go on into infinity. That's one of the interesting things about jazz, there are these points that just can't be agreed upon. The final analysis is the way you react inside to it. I think it's a spiritual thing.

L.A.: As an arranger you were probably hired to bring in the element of swing, but you've done some far-out writing too, haven't you?

ROGERS: Before writing "Maynard Ferguson" I had written a thing called "Jolly Rogers."

L.A.: Which had a different name at first.

ROGERS: "Expression from Rogers" Stan first called it, and he changed the title a few times. We had all these strings there, and I had never written for violins. (Laughs.) So when I wrote "Jolly Rogers" I just left the strings out. (Laughs.) But the band loved it. It was a good change of pace. There were a lot of very serious things, and this was just kind of a down-to-earth jazz thing, with some improvising. It served a good purpose in the repertoire. But I've written some 12-tone things. It's just the joy of trying to grow, go in unexplored areas. Areas that other people have explored, maybe, but that I haven't. Yes, I want to get in there and look around.

L.A.: Tell me about *The Invisible Orchard,* that you did for the Neophonic. Tell me what this means: "In the heart of this apple there dwells a seed and inside the seed dwells an invisible orchard." What were you getting at?

ROGERS: Well, from one seed that you could take from an apple, adding the element of time to it, you can plant the seed and get an apple tree. Then from each apple you take the seeds, and if you add enough time to it you can cover the whole planet Earth with apple trees. I feel it still makes sense. It was just something I was into at the time.

L.A.: How did you express that in music?

ROGERS: It was a suite of several pieces, eight or ten pieces. I felt it was a ballet. It's interesting because Stan—I didn't remember 'til right now—and it's part of him—when we did this with the Neophonic Orchestra it got just a great reception. People stood up and the newspapers and so on and so forth really praised it. And Stan loved it. And he said, next season, the next season for the Neophonic Orchestra, he wanted to present the whole ballet, with dancers, ballet dancers, and do the whole thing. It was a dream in my mind; not thinking in the scope that Stan would think in, I thought of it as a ballet for the inner eye—(laughs)—that you could sit down and listen to and in your inner eye you could picture it all. But he said we're gonna do the whole thing on stage. And he put me together with a choreographer, Earl Barton, and we had a few meetings. That's as far as it went. But there was Stan again. Go for it. Go for broke.

L.A.: Is it 12-tone or aleatoric?

ROGERS: No, it's . . .

L.A.: Conventional?

ROGERS: Conventional—uh, at that time, avant-garde . . .

L.A.: Avant-garde conventional? (Laughs.)

ROGERS: (Laughs.)

L.A.: There's a new genre right *there.* (Laughs.) It's been suggested that one avenue for continuation of the Neophonic idea might be in the New American Orchestra out here. What's your feeling about that?

ROGERS: I would say that Stan was quite a bit more ambitious.

L.A.: Than what they're doing now?

ROGERS: Yes.

L.A.: In other words, they don't carry the experimental vein far enough?

ROGERS: No. Whereas Stan's avenue was experimental jazz, some of the musical roads they go down are film music. Where Stan's main objective, really, was a jazz objective, theirs is more a variety of things.

L.A.: Have you written for them yourself?

ROGERS: I haven't yet. But I'm going to talk to Jack (Elliott). I've been writing some things for this church I go to. I'm starting to get together a cantata-type thing, an oratorio for a hundred-voice choir and a big orchestra that would do well with them. We're doing one for Easter. I also did one for Christmas.

Score sheet from the Innovations Orchestra. Writing is that of Shorty Rogers. (Courtesy of Shorty Rogers.)

L.A.: How long are these works?

ROGERS: About fifteen minutes.

L.A.: And you wrote them for your church?

ROGERS: Yes, it's right here in Van Nuys, called Church on the Way. We have a lot of musicians. Pete Candoli plays lead trumpet.

L.A.: You have a trumpet in your church?

ROGERS: We have a whole trumpet *section*. We have a hundred voices, and over thirty musicians.

L.A.: Is this another example of California influencing the whole rest of the country?

ROGERS: Right now you could count it on your hands, but it's growing. Don Lamphere, who's a tenor sax player that was on Woody Herman's band with me and who was a very close friend of Charlie Parker, is up in a town in Washington, and he sends me cassettes of things they do at his church. We were a bunch of wild guys a few years ago. Don's playing soprano sax and tenor and has a few marvelous trumpet players. He's doing some wild things. It's all jazz. I think some great things are going to come out of the church. And it's great, it's to bring glory to the Lord. And when you go all the way back, that's what the original function of music was.

L.A.: What I can't get over is a modern composer writing music like that.

ROGERS: Yes. (Laughs.) It's great. I've been in music my whole life, but this is just another experience.

L.A.: When you joined the Kenton band in 1950, were you on for a straight length of time or did you leave and come back?

ROGERS: I stayed with him about a year and a half. But after I left the band as a player, I continued to be associated with Stan. I did some arranging and some things after I left.

L.A.: You still played trumpet while you were composing on the band?

ROGERS: Yes, I was a playing member of the band all through that.

L.A.: Which trumpet did you play?

ROGERS: We had five, and we switched around. I was never a lead player, never the first trumpet chair.

L.A.: I'll bet you're grateful for that. (Laughs.)

ROGERS: Even when I sing in the church, I sing harmony parts.

L.A.: All those stories I hear about blacking out.

ROGERS: Yeah. No, I never had that kind of stamina. Even when my embouchure was at its strongest—I could play a lot of high notes, but any chair other than the first could be a chair where you could get some jazz solos, do some improvising, and that's what I really wanted to do. Going way back to when I was a kid in high school and didn't want to study. I just wanted to play jazz.

L.A.: What's it like being a trumpet player in the Stan Kenton orchestra?

ROGERS: Pretty wild. (Laughs.)

L.A.: It's got to be exciting. That's the top of it.

ROGERS: It's hard work. As long as I played, my physical ability as a trumpet player was never in the shape it had to be to keep up with that trumpet section. (Laughs.) The fifth trumpet part was high notes that guys can't play. (Laughs.)

L.A.: The *fifth* trumpet part.

ROGERS: Yes. (Laughs.) Yeah there'd be unison parts where you know they'd be way up in the stratosphere.

L.A.: (Laughs.) Stratosphere.

ROGERS: Yeah. (Laughs.)

L.A.: Where did you go after leaving the Kenton band?

ROGERS: I got a job at the Lighthouse down in Hermosa Beach. By this time I was married and we had three children and it was really the first time I could stay in town and have steady work here.

L.A.: You formed your Giants, then, right? A real group of all-stars.

ROGERS: Most of them were right from Stan's band. And here's another little glimpse of Stan Kenton the person. I had done my first album, with Art Pepper and Shelly and a few guys, maybe three or four guys from Kenton's band. It was one of the early jazz albums done on the West Coast and it attracted a lot of attention. It was done by an independent production that sold it to Capitol. Then I got a call from RCA. They wanted to sign me up, and they wanted an album made that would fit the title *Cool and Crazy*. I said great, a chance to do that with a big band. It was Shelly, it was Maynard Ferguson, it was Buddy Childers, and Pete Candoli, and Art Pepper and Bud Shank and—it was the whole Kenton band. So I went to see Stan. I said "Stan, I have an opportunity to do this big band album, but I'd like to use—"and I named the guys, 80% of them from his band. I said "Stan, I don't feel comfortable with it; I feel like I'm raiding your band. I don't feel right about it." And he said "Forget it. Take 'em! Bless you. Go." He encouraged me and gave me his approval. That's the person he was.

L.A.: How long did you have the group?

ROGERS: Well the big band was actually put together just for recording, and like occasionally I'd do a concert, but it was late 1953 that the Giants that I worked with all the time—it was actually just five guys—was a partnership between Shelly and me. Shelly had left Stan's band and was working at the Lighthouse with me. The Lighthouse became a kind of first stop after you'd left Kenton's band when you'd come in town to work and stay. Bud Shank, Frank Rosolino, Bob Cooper, Stan Levey later—they're all guys that came off Kenton's band and tried to establish a working situation here in town. So Shelly and Jimmy Giuffre and I and a few of the other guys were at the Lighthouse, and we left and went on our own. That became the little Giants orchestra.

L.A.: How large was the big band then?

ROGERS: I think about sixteen, seventeen. It was five saxes, four trumpets, four trombones, and rhythm section. Maybe fourteen or fifteen.

L.A.: Did it sound a little bit like the Kenton orchestra?

ROGERS: It sounded like a mixture of what I was at that time: Kenton and Woody. Those two elements together.

L.A.: Are any recordings available?

ROGERS: They're being reissued in Europe. In France and especially England, they're very popular. They're on the best-selling charts. I had a jazz album of the Giants three years ago that became number one on the jazz charts in Europe. (Laughs.)

L.A.: Great! Is your work mostly in the studios now?

ROGERS: Yes. At a certain point I was phased out of being a trumpet player and into being a composer and arranger, and it gradually got so busy, I had so much writing to do, that there was literally no time to play or practice anymore.

L.A.: What shows have you written for?

ROGERS: Some feature pictures, and in television some years back I worked on *The Mod Squad, I Spy,* and *Starsky and Hutch.* More recently, *Vegas* and *Love Boat* and some of Aaron Spelling's productions. Every week, television's full of 80 new shows. There isn't time to keep track of it. But I'm practicing my horn, wondering if I should get back into that.

L.A.: Do you think you might form another group of your own?

ROGERS: It may be something I'll get into, because of the reaction in Europe.

I've been getting calls. It'd be fun to do that kind of traveling.

L.A.: Anyone who was with Kenton on the one hand brought him something and on the other has taken something away. Sometimes it's hard to tell who got the most out of what. Obviously he benefited from the fabulous talents of people like you who were with him. But then maybe being in the presence of somebody like that who gave you the opportunity, the freedom to write what you want, set your career in a certain direction. Do you have any thoughts on that?

ROGERS: I know that I got the most out of it. I can look at my career so to speak as a before and after situation. I was doing well before, but Stan is the one who really drew attention to my work. I still talk every week to a few of the guys who were with him. They're like brothers to me. That's where I met them. We're members of the same family. Stan is still here. You can't erase it; it's part of our lives, and we're the better off for it. We're the fortunate ones that had a chance to be with this guy.

L.A.: Was it something to do with creativity, or is it more personal?

ROGERS: It's both.

L.A.: How would you assess his impact on the American scene?

ROGERS: It's a living thing. If we just keep our eyes and ears open we'll see his impact, his influence. I anticipate seeing more of it, seeing it grow in stature. The legend, the validity of his work and his life—it's an ongoing, live thing.

L.A.: In other words the Stan Kenton sound did not die with him.

ROGERS: No. No. No, you hear it in different ways. You can hear it on some big pop records, rock things, that have a big brass sound. Like Earth, Wind and Fire, you hear some brass things where the figures are different but there are some sonorities and voicings that are related to the Kenton sound. Now how did that come about? You know, the arrangers who are doing that are younger guys. Maybe when they were kids they heard some Kenton thing. Another interesting question you can ask is: Who's gonna take his place? You come up with a blank. See. There's no one like him.

9 Bill Russo

RUSSO: *Stan, I think with good reason, favored, out of all the people who wrote for him, Pete Rugolo. And I think Pete Rugolo was Stan's Billy Strayhorn, was his alter ego. And was the person who most clearly reflected what Stan himself sought.*

L.A.: *Don't you think you come close to that too?*

RUSSO: *I think I was second.*

Bill Russo, in his office, Chicago, Illinois. (Photo by the Author.)

L.A.: When I think of some of your compositions, such as "A Theme of Four Values," "Egdon Heath," and "Dusk," I just have the feeling that that's exactly what Stan wanted to be doing.

RUSSO: Yes. I would say I was closer than anybody at that time to what he wanted. Including Johnny Richards, who was more flamboyant in that respect, and more attractive to Stan, but—but also, Johnny was a little classical in a way that wasn't quite what Stan had in mind.

L.A.: Did Stan have a personal favorite among your works? Or did he like everything you did?

RUSSO: Oh no. Some things he didn't like at all. They were never played. He loved "23° North." And then another piece he liked, because the band tolerated it, was "Sweets." He played that a lot.

L.A.: I'd be interested to know something of your working relationship with Stan. It must have been extraordinary.

RUSSO: Yes. Here I was, a very shy, awkward, idealistic young man who knew none of the things about proper presentation or good titles or how to build a piece up, and so on and so forth, who knew very little about that, who was involved in an extraordinarily refined cool jazz, that is, the Tristano thing, who, although more tutored than Stan himself, was not very tutored either at that time. John Williams, the film composer, refers to us all, including Pete Rugolo, as primitives. Here I am, holding Stan up to the highest ideal standards, and probably being a great pain in the neck to him much of the time. On the one hand. And then on the other hand, here Stan is dealing with the only member of the orchestra during that period with intellectual pretensions along the lines of his. So it was a little complicated for him as well as for me. A bright, young... arrogant is not exactly the word but ... bumptious boy. And a brilliant leader and politician and co-ordinator. It would be unfair to say that it was personal conflict, the situation that led to my leaving the band, but there's something in that. It would be untrue to say that I left because he and I were competitive. But there was some truth in the matter.

L.A.: I always understood that he absolutely *loved* your music. And preferred it to that of many others, such as Bill Holman.

RUSSO: I think he probably did, yes, 'cause I was closer to him. Bill was

writing wonderful pieces, but they were in the idiom that Stan hated. Basie, and . . .

L.A.: Do you think there might have been some conflict because you were so close in what you were both trying to do?

RUSSO: Um-hm.

L.A.: That might have led to what you referred to as a complex situation?

RUSSO: Sure.

L.A.: He admired you, obviously, and your work.

RUSSO: Also I was one of the few people on the band, and he knew it, who was going to become a leader.

L.A.: Really. He could notice that in you.

RUSSO: Ya. He said it on one of those albums, I think it was *This Is An Orchestra*. He said "He wants to lead. And he will." That's true. I have had many orchestras. I had my own theater. I produced works. Conducted all over the world.

L.A.: He must have been sorry to see you go.

RUSSO: He was.

L.A.: Did he come right out and say it? Did he try to keep you?

RUSSO: He did, actually. We were all so exhausted from the touring. Especially the European tour. That took a lot out of us.

L.A.: Milt Bernhart told me that you wrote "Solitaire" when you were about fifteen years old. Can that possibly be true?

RUSSO: I was pretty young. I don't remember exactly how old I was. I know Stan played it with the band in '46, '47—so I would have been eighteen at that time.

L.A.: *Performed* it when you were eighteen. Which means you had to have written it earlier.

RUSSO: *(Reaches for a score.)*

L.A.: That's it! That's "Solitaire"! What's it doing in your office?

RUSSO: I was thinking of rewriting it.

L.A.: Rewriting it!

RUSSO: Ya.

L.A.: For what?

RUSSO: For different instrumentation.

L.A.: What instrumentation?

RUSSO: I don't know. I've just been thinking about it. I'm doing something for the Greenwich Village Jazz Festival and I thought it might be nice to do that piece.

L.A.: What would you do to it? Would you leave it the same and just have different instruments playing it?

RUSSO: Different instruments, that's all, ya.

L.A.: You would not change any of the harmonic structure.

RUSSO: No.

L.A.: That's fabulous.

RUSSO: Actually I played "23 Degrees North and 82 Degrees West" at a couple of the college graduations here, as an opener. It went over very well.

L.A.: I'm really glad to hear that. Was "Solitaire" the first work of yours that Stan heard?

RUSSO: Yes. I wrote it for the Innovations Orchestra.

L.A.: You mean you re-orchestrated it for full orchestra?

RUSSO: Yes.

L.A.: What was his reaction to it?

RUSSO: I think he liked it. He decided to record it, so it must have been . . .

L.A.: How would he show it when he liked a piece? Was he flamboyant about it? Or just quietly told you he liked it?

RUSSO: I would say he was pretty appreciative, actually.

L.A.: Would you be the one to present this piece to the orchestra, or would you just give the arrangements to him and he would rehearse it?

RUSSO: He would rehearse it. I remember one time, I can't remember the piece, when he said to me, "Bill, it must have been a beautiful morning when you wrote that."

L.A.: When was the first time that you can remember composing? Evidently you've always been involved with it in some way.

RUSSO: I must have started in 1943. At the age of fourteen, fifteen.

L.A.: What got you started on composing music?

RUSSO: My father was a musician. Became a lawyer. His father was a violinist, who escaped from Europe as a little boy.

L.A.: Classical musician?

RUSSO: Ya. Well classical and roadhouse and whatever he could do. And then all my uncles played instruments. All eight of them. And one of my uncles was a conductor at the Palace Theater, here in Chicago. Danny Russo. So I was around music a lot, even though nobody wanted me to go into it. I formed this experimental orchestra I think in 1946 called An Experiment in Jazz. And Pete Rugolo came to hear it one time. In 1948 or '49. And he recommended me to Stan, and that was it. So he discovered me. A very nice man. I know him to this day.

L.A.: I understand that a lot of that went on with Stan Kenton—somebody would just have to say a good word for you . . .

RUSSO: Um-hm, um-hm. That was it.

L.A.: Had you heard Stan's music yourself? It was pretty new at that time.

RUSSO: Well when I was a very young boy, a high school boy, I often went to vaudeville houses to hear the band. I loved it. Although I was in a different school, I was a Tristano-ite. I came out of a highly refined, elegant, fast, cool school of jazz, so I was torn between those two pleasures.

L.A.: Between Stan Kenton . . .

RUSSO: Between Stan Kenton and Lennie Tristano. And in a way I may have served to reconcile some of it. Mostly through Lee Konitz, who I brought into the band with me.

L.A.: Somewhere I read about how Lennie Tristano would compose music while walking around his apartment, that he read books like *War and Peace* . . .

RUSSO: He was blind. So he read by braille.

L.A.: He read books like *War and Peace* by *braille?*

RUSSO: Right. Or they were read aloud to him.

L.A.: That's amazing.

RUSSO: Yes.

L.A.: There was a connection, then, between the three of you, Konitz and Tristano and you. I believe you went to school with Konitz?

RUSSO: Lee and I went to the same high school. And we studied with Lennie.

L.A.: You mean you both came to Lennie individually or—

RUSSO: No, I came to Lennie through Lee. I think he and I were probably his first two students.

L.A.: No kidding.

RUSSO: Yes. He taught jazz improvisation. And he was the first person to do so.

L.A.: He was the first person . . .

RUSSO: In the world.

L.A.: How did he relate that to the blues movement coming out of the South? Or is it related to that?

RUSSO: I don't think it is. He would have you write out a jazz solo. Actually construct a jazz solo. You would play it for him. And then he would discuss it. In terms of its forms. It was a wonderful way to develop your compositional skills as well.

L.A.: You mean you would improvise . . .

RUSSO: You would improvise into a written solo. You would improvise until you got it into a given shape and then you would write it down. Very interesting way. The purpose of that was to get you to analyze and understand what you were doing enough so that you would repeat your improvisation.

L.A.: But isn't improvisation an instinctual thing?

RUSSO: Yes.

L.A.: You would try to get your instinct analyzed . . .

RUSSO: Right.

L.A.: . . . so you knew exactly what you were doing?

RUSSO: Right. Well so that you could do it better.

L.A.: I read somewhere that you introduced the Lennie Tristano concept into the Stan Kenton orchestra.

RUSSO: I did.

L.A.: Tell me about it.

RUSSO: Well it's complicated, because first of all the band members themselves were not particularly sympathetic toward anything except toe-tapping music. The band obviously was a very hot band so they—they were a bebopping band. They wanted to play Count Basie was the truth of the matter. They didn't like Ellington, they didn't like Stan Kenton, they didn't like any of this really hot stuff. On the one hand. On the other hand Stan wanted to do pieces that had production values, that were really hot and theatrical. And that had some of these classical resonances. But Stan started to, as of maybe '52, when the band got more New York and more—became more of a so-called jazz orchestra, Stan became intrigued by the idea of making a jazz band. More of a jazz band, with Conte and Frank Rosolino and Bobby Burgess and so forth. So it was a very schizophrenic time for the band. Actually the band played Pete Rugolo's music, I thought, far better than they played Gerry Mulligan's music or Bill Holman's music. 'Cause in a way they didn't have the feeling of the—they didn't have the feeling that they sought. It's a strange circumstance.

L.A.: Well why would he want to get into more swing-type jazz when he had all this other exciting thing going for him?

RUSSO: I don't know. And they were very demanding. So anyway, despite those two forces, I every once in a while would write a piece that was very Tristano-like. But it wasn't until Lee came in that I was able to really do some things that more accurately reflected the Tristano influence.

L.A.: Does Tristano-ish mean cool intellectual?

RUSSO: More eighth note, more soloistic. More like a jazz soloist. Written, but more like a solo artist.

L.A.: When Lee Konitz was in the orchestra, it had more of that kind of sound to it.

RUSSO: Um-hm.

L.A.: When you first heard the band, it was the Rugolo influence.

RUSSO: Right. I was very excited by the band. It was an exciting band. In the forties it was a very exciting band.

L.A.: Then after Pete recommended you to Stan, you came on the band. Right about the time the Innovations Orchestra was formed.

RUSSO: It actually was January of 1950. I came on with Maynard and all those people. Stan I think or Pete just called me up and said "Would you like to join?" I said "Sure." Oh then I wasn't composing. It was a funny thing.

L.A.: You joined as a trombonist?

RUSSO: Ya. I didn't want to compose any music. I'd made an agreement, a pact, with Lennie Tristano that I was going to concentrate on my horn and just play for a while. So it was ironic. Here I was with this magnificent instrument available to me to write for.

L.A.: But there was a period right after the first Innovations tour that you left the band. Why?

RUSSO: I think it was because it was my intention to be with the Innovations. I wasn't interested in being on the road with what at that time he called the dance orchestra. I wanted to wait until the next Innovations.

L.A.: How did you know that he'd even *have* another Innovations Orchestra?

RUSSO: He said he would.

L.A.: But he'd lost a hundred thousand dollars on it! (Laughs.)

RUSSO: Ya I know.

L.A.: He *said* he would even though he knew he'd lost money?

RUSSO: Oh yeah. Ya, he was very pure about some of those things.

L.A.: Then you remained with the Kenton orchestra after the second Innovations and through the European tour and left in October of '53?

RUSSO: Ya.

L.A.: And returned and wrote for the Neophonic, in 1966.

RUSSO: Right. I also conducted the Neophonic.

L.A.: In your own work?

RUSSO: In my own work and for other works. I conducted a whole program.

L.A.: Is that the reason you left in 1953? Because you could see that he wasn't going to repeat that kind of music for a long time? Or, as far as you knew, ever again?

RUSSO: (Pauses.) The reason I left is that Shelly Manne was recording an album with two of my pieces—"You and the Night and the Music" and "Gazelle," with Art Pepper and Bud Shank and a very good band in L. A. And they played it so beautifully that I realized that I wanted to be in a situation where—I may have been wrong, by the way—I wanted to be in a situation where I could control the rehearsal of my music.

L.A.: You couldn't do that with Stan Kenton.

RUSSO: Not on the road. It wasn't Stan, it was just that we were on the road; we were working too hard. And it was a very unsympathetic milieu for me to be in. Most of the people would infinitely prefer to play Gerry Mulligan or Bill Holman's pieces. Which I understand. But I felt very put upon, and so it wasn't personally rewarding for me to write for that band. I suppose if I had been more career-oriented, as most everybody is, and has to be, today, I would have stayed in the band a while, because I had a terrific situation: I was writing music, writing a lot of music, and being paid very well, and so on. But I also wanted to study. I wanted to study with a real composer. And I did, with two composers, subsequently. So there were a lot of impulses involved.

L.A.: Whom did you study with?
RUSSO: John Becker, chiefly, who was an old-time, avant-garde composer out of the Ives-Ruggles-Carpenter school.
L.A.: Didn't Stan, though, champion your cause in his orchestra? Wasn't it typical for him to go with the new even when his players recoiled against it?
RUSSO: I suppose I wanted to write longer works.
L.A.: Another really outstanding work of yours from the Innovations era is "Halls of Brass." You wrote a lot of great music on the Kenton band.
RUSSO: Thank you.
L.A.: But you don't write like that anymore.
RUSSO: No. Isn't that interesting.
L.A.: Why don't you?
RUSSO: Why do people change?
L.A.: You don't want to anymore? I know that you're very eclectic. There's a fascinating section in your latest record, Street Music, where there's a kind of counterpoint going on among members of a string trio. What are you doing there, with that? You're using classical

form to play jazz music?
RUSSO: Um-hm.
L.A.: I never heard anything like that.
RUSSO: My blues idiom. It's a full string orchestra, and that part is a solo violin, solo cello and solo bass. It's more blues, to make a distinction. As a matter of fact, it's non-jazz blues. Jazz-blues has a different chord progression. Same idea, 12 bars.
L.A.: How did this change in your writing style all come about, anyway?
RUSSO: Well the biggest thing that happened in my life after Stan's band was, first of all, I studied classical music. And then I wanted to write some classical music. I wrote the Second Symphony for the New York Philharmonic and Bernstein . . .

L.A.: That's the one called The Titans?
RUSSO: Yes. Maynard Ferguson plays the fourth movement.
L.A.: What's it like? Why isn't there a record of it?
RUSSO: There was almost a record of it. I had it taped. It's going to be published, the score, finally, after 25 years.
L.A.: When it gets published then you'll make a record of it?
RUSSO: Not necessarily. Usually you record it and then you make a score. It was also played by the Chicago Symphony.
L.A.: That's a classical symphony, I assume.
RUSSO: Yeah. I suppose. Bernstein thought it was jazz, but it isn't. And then, in the late 1960s, I got very, very interested in vocal music. And most of the jazz musicians, and Stan Kenton's fans, don't know what I'm talking about. I understand. But something happened. I suppose I'm an opera composer now. I've written fifteen full-length vocal stage works. Then another thing happened, too. I really became absolutely seduced by Ellington, and what he was doing. I finally came to understand it. I spent some time with him. I was writing a piece for him and the San Francisco Orchestra when he died.

L.A.: A little while ago when you were talking about Count Basie you mentioned Ellington in the same breath with Kenton rather than with Basie. Which is not something many people do.
RUSSO: Well Ellington and Stan's orchestras had serious intents. Serious is the wrong word, but . . . . Basie's band is a wonderful, wonderful band. But it's essentially a delight, pleasure, and ve-

hicle for improvisers. But Ellington's band was a piece in which the composition was very important. Very very important. Improvisers were good, but they were utilized to a lesser extent. In a good sense. But Ellington's music I suppose interested me so much because of the variety and subtlety and wit and humor, none of which are characteristics of Stan's music.
L.A.: Some of the music on record with the Stan Kenton orchestra strikes me as being very moody. And classical.
RUSSO: Right.
L.A.: But you've written classical music too.
RUSSO: Yes. Yes. I'm a real maverick.
L.A.: Do you get criticized for that?
RUSSO: Ya, I get criticized for being a maverick. The jazz people feel that I've betrayed them sometimes. And the classical people feel that I'm a poseur and a fake. So . . . .
L.A.: (Laughs.)
RUSSO: It's interesting. I wouldn't trade it for anything else. Sometimes it's very painful.
L.A.: You can't get accepted by any one group as one thing.

RUSSO: No. I would have trouble getting money from the National Endowment for the Arts in either category. People think if you aren't doing just one thing you're somehow false.
L.A.: You've even done some rock.
RUSSO: Yes.
L.A.: I have two conflicting statements from you. In 1961, in an article with Teo Carol, he championed the rock cause, and you did not. Then in 1969 you wrote a rock opera. Did you suddenly decide just to give it a try?

RUSSO: Well during the late sixties the life went out of jazz. Think about it. The jazz musicians were demoralized and jazz had come to a dead end in many ways. The only jazz that was flourishing, I thought, at that time, was the black nationalist jazz, toward which I was not so sympathetic, partly because I wasn't a part of it, although it was far superior to some of the dadadada dididididi stuff that you heard in general jazz. So there was really no place to go in the jazz world. And at the same time I'd gotten interested in theater. And I heard some rock and roll stuff that I really loved—Jefferson Airplane, Beatles, Rolling Stones. Mostly white groups. I think a lot of what went on in rock and roll, also, was the white answer to the blacks. Okay, all right, jazz is yours. You won't let us in it. Critics won't agree that we can make any contribution, so—we'll go with this music that the blacks have left behind, rhythm and blues and that stuff. Anyway, I found the same sort of enthusiasm and care among the young rock musicians that I had found among young jazz musicians when *I* was a kid. I mean they really cared about it. Whereas my contemporaries in the jazz world were just demoralized and unable to figure out what to do. And they were looking at their watch more often than they were looking at their music. So—I said goodbye.

L.A.: You felt the pulse of creativity . . .
RUSSO: Yeah. Shifting.
L.A.: Or vitality, was somewhere else.
RUSSO: Yeah.
L.A.: What is your latest work, right now?
RUSSO: Well the last work I finished was called *Urban Trilogy.* That's the one I did with Jack Elliott's orchestra. I finished it at the end of last year (1981) and we performed it this March (1982). It'll be on NPR sometime this summer. Then in addition I'm writing a singspiel, a musical comedy, whatever you call it, for six or seven singers and a small orchestra. Based on the *Faust* legend.
L.A.: Wow.
RUSSO: And Faust is a solar biologist, and he sells his soul to a company like Con Ed or AT and T.
L.A.: *Wow.* (Laughs.)
RUSSO: The devil is a multinational.
L.A.: Oh that's fantastic.
RUSSO: It's a very political work.
L.A.: What will be the style? Is it rock or is it jazz?
RUSSO: It depends. It's not a real relationship to rock and roll, it's jazz-istic . . .
L.A.: A mixture. The critics are going to have fun with you.
RUSSO: I know.
L.A.: What about your other operas, *The Jamaican in London* and *John Couten,* which is based on the *Othello* theme?
RUSSO: *The Jamaican in London* is jazz. *John Couten* is half and half. Iago and his wife are jazz singers. Othello and *his* wife are classical singers. It's written for a jazz orchestra with strings, full orchestra.
L.A.: So it's jazz *and* classical?
RUSSO: Um-hm.
L.A.: Wow. (Laughs.) That was performed a few times, wasn't it.
RUSSO: Yes. On the BBC and then here in Chicago.
L.A.: I've been trying to understand whether The New American Orchestra in Los Angeles is the natural progression from Kenton's Innovations and Neophonic ideas.
RUSSO: Yes.
L.A.: You're one of the composers who has written for both—actually *you've* written for all three—along with people like Russ Garcia and Claus Ogerman.
RUSSO: I've heard his music. It's beautiful.
L.A.: What is *Urban Trilogy* like?

RUSSO: It's in three movements, for full symphony orchestra. There's a little improvisation in the second movement, by tenor saxophone. A couple of times I use jazz drums. But there's no jazz rhythm section in it. I wanted very much to get away from that feeling of that jazz-band-with-strings, which has haunted many—experimental, or whatever word we use for Neophonic, Innovations, orchestras of that sort. And it's in this quirky new idiom that I've evolved, which is that I freely move within—how can I say this. I've never said this before. I have no hesitation about doing eight bars of absolutely classical and then eight bars in a jazz

Bill Russo, in his office, Chicago, Illinois. (Photo by the Author.)

variation on that. In the past the rapprochement between jazz and classical has been of a piece. The composer has tried to make a stylistic amalgam of the two. Now, I'm not concerned about amalgam anymore. I don't mind successively alternating those in the same piece. I never had the guts to do that before. Somewhere along the line I figured that out. Whether it's correct or not, or fruitful, I couldn't say.

L.A.: What made you decide, do you think, to forget about amalgam and go into this more original idea?

RUSSO: Well this way instead of constantly putting the two musics at odds with each other, and conflicting, and doing an almost dada-surrealistic simultaneous conflict, I'm able to take the most lyrical aspects of each. I suppose that's what drew me toward it.

L.A.: You want to be more lyrical now.

RUSSO: Ya. My big aim is to, as they say, get the cork out. Really say what I really want to say, which is very difficult, because we are all subject to terrific pressures. The people we work for. Other composers, especially among classical people. Intellectuals. My aim now is to write music that is really beautiful and understandable and still has underpinnings that will make it continue for a while. Which is the way a lot of music used to be written. I mean that's the concept behind Mozart, surely. And behind Ellington, I might add. So I'm absolutely disinterested in the avant-garde. It's very interesting to me, personally, but I don't care to do anything avant-garde.

L.A.: You're enough of a maverick that you'll switch to *something,* sooner or later, won't you?

RUSSO: I might. I might go into prepared piano or some electronic tapes. I don't think so. I've been able to write eighty-four opus numbers because I don't do much else besides that. I mean I make a living, somehow, but I don't . . . I'll get pontifical for a second. I'm very concerned about the moral and religious aspects of music. Two years ago I wrote *A Shepherd's Christmas,* about the birth of Christ. I'm concerned about works that help to maintain the good

life. They have some political concomitant or some sense that the world will get better. I've always had that feeling. And now I'm starting to have a sense of how to do it.

L.A.: Do you feel that Stan Kenton had a long term influence on you? Or were you pretty much going in your own direction and just passed through his orchestra at the time?

RUSSO: Musically?

L.A.: In any sense of the word.

RUSSO: Through him I got a real sense of relationship to audience. Which is a very, very useful thing to have. Which I hadn't had before. Through him I got a sense of the power and vitality of doing something that you really believe in. As I already did and still do. Musically, I think what I learned from him although I may not have realized it until much later was how to connect with an orchestra, with an audience better. And to use titles that dramatize or explain a piece rather than titles that I tended to use, which were not so good. Like "Ennui." Which means "boredom." That's a terrible title.

L.A.: I *like* it.

RUSSO: That's a terrible title. It was used much over his objections. He was absolutely right about it.

L.A.: What would he have called it?

RUSSO: I don't know. But I learned some things about the presentations of one's material in a clear, cogent way. Personally, I learned a lot about *noblesse oblige,* about how being the leader means you have responsibilities.

L.A.: What's the responsibility to the audience? I understand to the men in your group but what responsibility do you as a leader have to your audience?

RUSSO: To give them a show, to be on time, to present the very best you can, and not to be too long or too short in the sets that you play. To pace the pieces, to put them together, to have a sense of what they're ready for and available for. And then, to the members of the orchestra, to take care of them, to smooth them out when they're ruffled—in a good sense—to *attend* to them, to nurture them. To let them grow. And at the

same time structure them. So I learned a lot from him.

L.A.: How do you see Stan's place in twentieth-century American music? That's a broad category, but Kenton obviously goes beyond big band jazz in the many things he tried to do, in trying to form a new American music.

RUSSO: Well separate impact from reality for a while. 'Cause some people think that only if a music bears fruition can it be considered important. For which reason you might say that Bach wasn't an important composer. Because his music didn't have any influence after he died for another hundred years. So disregarding that element I would say that he and Ellington were the principal jazz orchestra forces in the twentieth century. Have been, will be. Then—as far as . . .

L.A.: Is that the reality or the impact?

RUSSO: That's the reality. Then the impact—I think the impact was great but is not seen now, because the racism has been so rampant.

L.A.: Racism?

RUSSO: Ya. His music has suffered so much from racism, from anti-white sentiment. Among blacks *and* whites. Especially during the last thirty years.

L.A.: Is that a fair thing to say about it, though?

RUSSO: No. No. It's a different direction.

L.A.: Rather than everybody playing the same kind of jazz, he tried to create a new kind of music.

RUSSO: I couldn't agree with you more. But that's not clear to people. Also there were a lot of excesses that came out of Stan's band. A lot of those blaring brass groups that you hear are corruptions of what Stan was doing and tend to confuse the ear with what he really had in mind.

L.A.: By trying to imitate him they miss the mark altogether?

RUSSO: Yes, but they imitate him not for any purpose except to make money. It was the same with Debussy for a long time. Debussy and Ravel. Same thing has happened to Stan. When the air clears, and the racism subsides, and we move, I hope, into a better world, then his true contribution will be revealed.

10 Jim Amlotte

L.A.: From your vantage point, I'd like you to tell me just what it was that would have enabled Stan Kenton to suffer through his setbacks and then turn right around and launch into something absolutely brand-new and risk-taking again. What kind of character of a man would do that?

AMLOTTE: That's Stan's make-up totally. Never be defeated, never look back. One thing I've learned from him: yesterday is yesterday; it's over. And that was totally his belief.

L.A.: During your time with the band, from 1956 through 1969, you would have witnessed not only the Balboa financial bust of 1958 but also the disastrous tour in England the year Kennedy died. Didn't Stan go home and brood, or feel depressed, or anything?
AMLOTTE: I'm sure he brooded, but he didn't dwell on things like that. It was the same with the Grammy Awards that he won. They were fine for the moment. But he never had them hanging on the wall. If someone wanted them, he could have them. I have four or five at home now.
L.A.: What were the Grammys for?

AMLOTTE: *West Side Story* was one. *Adventures in Time* was another, in '61, '62. Nice awards that were given to him and the band. But after it was over, he couldn't care less about looking at 'em and reflecting on it. Tomorrow. It's got to be tomorrow. That's why, if he was down for any particular time, it was not for long, not for years. Maybe six months or so to recoup and rejuvenate his thoughts. Then he'd come up with something new and different, and go straight ahead.
L.A.: Would he talk to you about these things? As road manager you must have been pretty close to him.

AMLOTTE: He talked occasionally about his direction. Once he considered moving from L.A. to New York, when there was a chance to get the *Tonight Show*.
L.A.: Have his band do the *Tonight Show*?

AMLOTTE: Not the band. Stan would be the leader of the show's band.
L..A.: And make a lot of money.
AMLOTTE: Right. Yup. That wasn't his concern.
L.A.: But he did toy with the idea for a while.

Jim Amlotte, outside Carmelo's Jazz Club, Sherman Oaks, California. (Photo by the Author.)

77

AMLOTTE: Yes, we talked about it. He wanted to know what I thought of it. He brought it up several times.

L.A.: California is *so* beautiful. It's like saying no to Paradise to leave here. Why would anyone do it?

AMLOTTE: I think you have to be a part of that type of work to understand. To stay here and do nothing as far as playing is concerned leads to boredom. And if your livelihood is such that it takes you on the road, you have to do that. He appreciated the beauty that was here, but that didn't make money for him, money to do new things with or to pay the bills. Albums won't sell unless you're out there promoting them. It's different for jazz people than it is for rock stars or pop artists. People assume you've disbanded if they don't see you live for three years. As for the rigors of the road, you overcome those. The few hours of sleep you miss one night you make up the next. Stan took me to so many great restaurants it was unreal.

L.A.: Maybe it's irrelevant, but two of Stan's band managers were trombone players and one played sax. That might be surprising to one who would think of the high trumpet as being a Kenton trademark.

AMLOTTE: If you study the music, the whole sound of the Kenton band is made up of the sound of the trombone section. In a sense, the tension comes from the trumpets up above. And then the color, the real nice color that Kenton is known for, is the trombone color. Because of the five trombones.

L.A.: How did that develop, structurally? They started with just two at Balboa. By 1942 they had a third.

AMLOTTE: One big influence in the early days was Gene Roland. Gene was there as a writer, and started writing arrangements and suggesting to Stan that we needed four trombones. And he suggested, I *think* Stan told me this, the fifth trombone. Gene was writing some low notes that extended into the bass trombone range, but were being played by a tenor. So it led logically to adding a bass trombone. They might have talked about it, realized there were more possibilities as far as sound and voicings and colors. And Stan was all for that. Knowing him, he'd say, "Yeah. That's a nice, good rich sound." He was really a guy who liked bottom heavy, the bottom sound.

L.A.: You knew Gene Roland?

AMLOTTE: Sure. Gene was a musician who had a great deal of talent. His bag is blues. And he's dynamite at it. Great writer. He did the *Adventures in Blues* album for Stan's band.

L.A.: Is there a "Kenton sound" that's strong enough to be an influence of and by itself on American music?

AMLOTTE: Oh definitely.

L.A.: There is.

AMLOTTE: Definitely. During the time the Neophonic was formed, the man who was in front of it was Stan Kenton. Composers who were called together to write for it—Hugo Montenegro, Johnny Williams, and the others—are down at Stan's house on Alta Drive, sitting in the rumpus room in the back. They're being told the idea of this Neophonic Orchestra—what they're going to do, what the purpose is: to present American jazz *however they want*. Maybe with a touch of the classical —*however*. Compositions should be in the category of seven minutes, or twenty minutes, or whatever length you want. We don't have money—can you donate your time? You can use score pad. Copying will be paid for. So these guys donated their time, and their energies, creative abilities. Just the fact that these composers are *there* and Stan is at the *head* of it means they're not going to write Lawrence Welk- or Ray Anthony-type music. It's Stan who's in charge. Composers are thinking of what Stan's thoughts are, what his type of music is. They're gearing their music towards Stan's ideas.

L.A.: Kenton's influence on the world would be ten times as great as it is if the recordings of all those works were made available, instead of just the ones on the albums.

AMLOTTE: The charts are around.

L.A.: I'd give anything to hear them. You played in the Neophonic Orchestra, right?

AMLOTTE: Yes. Besides playing I was very much involved in the administration of it, the very foundings of it.

L.A.: Which had to have been a real headache. (Laughs.)

AMLOTTE: But it was fun. It was a big cost undertaking. You go to the musicians' union and ask to have a special scale, so you can survive. With the vast amount of music being written and the time it takes to rehearse all this material, the musicians that are in that large orchestra have to be paid. The musicians' union would not give me any help. "No, this is it, this is our standard pay rate." Okay. It's done. Next you want help from reviewers. You have to pro-

mote it, put it in the papers, get on the phone and get subscriptions—just as The Orchestra did later. Now when the concerts are presented, there's a couple of guys who do reviewing. And they're very influential people.

L.A.: In Los Angeles?

AMLOTTE: Nationally. World-wide. One of them, Leonard Feather, is a big influence. He could have been a big, big help where it was needed, in the reviews that he did after the concert. He could have helped the Neophonic survive. Really survive. Instead: zappo. Down the drain. Now this is umpteen years later, and he's praising the New American Orchestra. Not totally, but he's not putting it down as he did with the Neophonic.

L.A.: How does the New American Orchestra compare with the Neophonic?

AMLOTTE: It's the same format.

L.A.: What about the other writers? Did anyone praise it?

AMLOTTE: Art Seidenbaum did a good review on Stan, at the very start of it. Harvey Siders was another—praised the orchestra up and down. Did excellent, good reviews. But those names weren't as heavy as Leonard Feather's. To attract outsiders, to fill three thousand seats for so many concerts, other than the fans, you won't do it with negative reviews. People won't spend the money to go see it.

L.A.: Right about then, or just before, was when Stan had resumed classical studies with Dr. Paul Held, wasn't it? Around 1963-65?

AMLOTTE: Right. We used to hang out then, and he had just taken a lesson from him. Held was a Wagner specialist and authority. That's when we recorded the Wagner album.

L.A.: Why do you suppose Stan didn't spend more time composing?

AMLOTTE: I think he found it hard and tedious at times. When you're on the road, it's very hard to write. You're out for four months, going night after night. You finish three hours of a concert and come back to the hotel room, and you really don't want to write. It takes pretty stiff training in one's mind to condition oneself to come home at midnight or later and not hang out with the guys, have a drink and relax. And there wouldn't be enough time between tours, what with two weeks off for Christmas, let's say, to let the creative juices flow. You need to rest.

L.A.: It had to be a conscious choice on his part to do that.

AMLOTTE: Sure it was.

L.A.: He must have known he had it in him to write. There are people like that, talented in a number of ways, but who seem to be drawn in a certain direction. Does this mean that he preferred to be—what would you call him, a jazz educator—rather than a composer?

AMLOTTE: Um-hm. Right.

L.A.: Do you think that's his biggest legacy, then, that he got into all these schools and colleges?

AMLOTTE: Definitely. Definitely. And whether he's gonna be recognized for it or not, I don't know. I hope so. It's through his library, his love for educating young people, that he's giving back what the colleges gave to him.

L.A.: You mean attending his band concerts?

AMLOTTE: Getting a lot of musicians from North Texas State. Getting a lot of musicians from other schools, that were training these people to be jazz musicians. To help those kids get to be better musicians, he spent *time* at these col-

leges. He gave his library to North Texas. I remember being down at the house on Alta Drive in Beverly Hills. And here's a whole wall, about half-way up, all the way across, *stacked with arrangements,* in the garage. And Stan said, "Jim, we gotta pack these up and send 'em to North Texas. So we're gonna go through 'em and see what we're gonna keep." Many of them at that time were Gene Roland's, 'cause he was just feeding and feeding the library! We had played them; some were good, some were not things that Stan wanted. So it was all packed up and shipped down there. But this is where he was such a big influence.

L.A.: How many people do you think he reached that way, as students?

AMLOTTE: Ohhh, many many *thousands.* Really. You can go to, I would say, any stage band in the United States and find a Stan Kenton arrangement in that library, in that book.

L.A.: It's probably an impossible question to answer, how many universities he reached, if you were doing at times several one-day clinics at several different schools in a *week*.

AMLOTTE: The one- and two-day clinics were mostly in the seventies, though we did a couple towards the last two years of my time with the band. But he believed in that so much.

L.A.: Taken all together, it must be hundreds of colleges.

AMLOTTE: Oh, I'm sure. Yes. I'm sure there are.

L.A.: And if he had hundreds of colleges and hundreds of students at hundreds of colleges, over a 20-year period, you're talking about several hundred thousand students.

AMLOTTE: Right.

L.A.: That's a big influence.

AMLOTTE: That are being influenced by the sound of the Stan Kenton band. And looking up towards the guy who's the leader of it. And that's gonna rub

Stan Kenton with young students at a clinic at Redlands, California, '60s. (Photo: Courtesy of a Kenton friend.)

off. Right? Really, it's gonna rub off. By performance and— One of the things I'm kind of proud of, that I really look back on and think about, is the part I played in helping Stan get the clinics going again. Stan at first was part of the National Stage Band Camps that were started by Ken Morris, the ballroom owner out of Terre Haute, Indiana. With Stan's association it became known as "The National Stage Band Camp, Featuring the Stan Kenton Clinics."

L.A.: These were the clinics held in 1959 and '60 at Indiana University and then in '61 at Michigan State?

AMLOTTE: Right. Dr. Gene Hall from North Texas State University was part of that, and the North Texas band was the in-house band for the first two years. The Stan Kenton Clinic was a big feature of the camp because it was a selling point. Kids *came* there because of his name attraction.

L.A.: And you later added the University of Connecticut, at Storrs?

AMLOTTE: Yes, and Denver, University of Denver. I think what we might have done was one the first year, two the second, three the third, and then four. Southern Methodist and the University of Nevada were in there. The Kenton band became a part of it, and I was a part of that as far as seeing to it that we were there, we were on campus, and every guy within the band had a job to do.

L.A.: You were the manager of the clinics?

AMLOTTE: With the band. Not the campus. Not that part. That was still Ken Morris's. That went on for about four years. And each time, the third year, the fourth year, Stan would say, "Jim, we're not getting a fair account of this." Stan *donated* everything. Gave his time, and while the band was there on campus, not making any money, he had to pay every guy his weekly salary. And Stan's not playing any concerts to make up for this; a week here at Michigan State, a week or two at Indiana, for that period of time no money came in. So it got to where he asked me, "You think we should continue next year? Do it again?" I said, "Well, he promised to give us a read-out," a count of what was supposed to be the financial report. It never came. Finally one day, we were in the South someplace, and Stan called me to his room. He had this letter that he had composed, and he had been downstairs and had somebody in the hotel office type it up. He said, "Read this." It was

his dissociation with the National Stage Band Camps. No more was he going to be connected with it. No longer could they use the name "the Kenton Clinics." That was it.

L.A.: Then he went off and did the clinics on his own.

AMLOTTE: That's where I took a part. For two years I bugged him. "Stan, we've got to do the Kenton Clinics. I'll help. I'll get it started." He'd say, "Nah." Though he knew I had some education. Well it was during the Neophonic concerts—probably the second or third one that we were having at the Music Center—and I was sick. He stopped by my apartment in Sherman Oaks, knocked on the door, came in—I'm lying in bed—I had the flu or something. He greeted me and we talked about this and that. Then he said, "Jim. I've been thinking. I want you to start the Kenton Clinics for us." I said "Fan-tastic! I'll get well, and I'll go!" That's when I started . . .

L.A.: (Laughs.) "I'll get well and I'll go." Right then.

AMLOTTE: Ya. I wanted to get 'em started. I knew how important it was. I wanted to help him continue doing the thing he believed in. I went to Redlands, and I surveyed the school and talked to the people out there. And more or less put it together. We had the first one of the Stan Kenton Clinics there. Then the next year we went to San Jose.

L.A.: Then 1966 at Redlands was the first actual Kenton Clinic. On his own.

AMLOTTE: Right. That was his own, from then on.

L.A.: Was it known then as the Jazz Orchestra in Residence?

AMLOTTE: There was an interim of about three years between the National Stage Band Camp clinics and Redlands, and those went on for two or three years. Then there was another interim of a couple of years—and I had left the band—until they resumed and that title, Jazz Orchestra in Residence, came about. Maybe '69, '70.

L.A.: So the one is called Kenton Clinics and the other is Jazz Orchestra in Residence. There's still a difference there.

AMLOTTE: Well—the whole thing might be under the title of Kenton Clinics. With the Stan Kenton Orchestra in Residence.

L.A.: It was evidently the same kind of thing only a somewhat different format.

AMLOTTE: Ya. I was involved with the administration of it, and helped set up the program for the whole week. Sunday afternoon was for registration. Sunday evening, ahead of the start of

the clinic, we gave a concert. The kids would just blow their minds hearing the Kenton band play. They're so ready for school the next day.

L.A.: (Laughs.) Psychology!

AMLOTTE: It really was. It's what I had planned. And I also had it set up so that every musician in Kenton's band would have a teaching role at the camp, doing a sectional, leading a band, or whatever, so these kids could rub elbows with them. I set up a rehearsal for the Kenton band every day from 3 to 5, and anybody who had new arrangements, bring them in, we'll play them.

L.A.: You mean the students?

AMLOTTE: Oh, sure.

L.A.: Stan Kenton's band would play new student arrangements?

AMLOTTE: Oh, sure! We wanted them! I wanted that as an incentive for them to write. To show those kids that we're not machines, we do make mistakes. And when we stumble over something they see hey, we're human. But I stipulated that every kid at camp *had* to attend a rehearsal. One hour, every day. From 3 to 4, or from 4 to 5. They had to come in, and take that as a class.

L.A.: I can't imagine anybody not wanting to.

AMLOTTE: Well—they might sometime have had enough feeling in their heads from all this material they're trying to learn in a week to want to go home and *write*. Or practice something that one of the teachers had told them. And forget about the rehearsal. But I thought that was very important. Another thing I tried to do was to set up, in the Kenton Clinic format, an *orchestra* camp. Have string players there at the same time, have arrangements for them, and make use of the material that was in the Innovations Orchestra.

L.A.: That would have been fabulous.

AMLOTTE: That hasn't been done. But there are some problems involved with it. When you deal with strings in a university, you're dealing with two different directors, two different programs: strings and concert band. So to put the two together, that's fine; musicians would jump at it. But who would lead? There are two egos, right there.

L.A.: I would think, for something like that, the band director.

AMLOTTE: Yes, but no way would the other one allow his strings to cross the border and have the other guy get all that credit.

L.A.: It's neat the way the clinic program works in cycles. I started my interviews with Dick Shearer. You hired Dick. Dick hired Mike Suter. Mike remembers studying with *you*. It's come full circle.

AMLOTTE: Um-hm. I remember another student I had. A young trombone player who had driven to Bloomington, Indiana, all the way from San Diego. His name was Graham Ellis. He was really enthusiastic, wanted to be part of the band, wanted to learn things. In addition to the regular program he wanted to take lessons with me, and to *pay* me for them. I said, "Forget it. You paid your tuition to *get* here. If we can work our schedules right, I'll be happy to work with you." On the last day he tried to give me money, but that's something that I couldn't even think of doing. Back when I was in college, in the fifties, there wasn't that big a jazz movement in colleges around the country. A senior would decide to have a dance band or a jazz band on campus and somebody with talent would write arrangements and they'd present their own concert. As far as being integrated into the music department, *no way*. But stage bands, from what I can find out, didn't start in colleges, they started in high schools. It makes sense to me. After World War II a lot of great musicians came out of the service and went back to school. Then from college they got teaching jobs in high schools. They're great band directors, but they also have this experience from having been in dance bands in the service. So they start, in high school, a fun band, a kicks band. A *stage band*, they called it. Jazz wasn't accepted in the high schools. The PTA wouldn't accept that word *jazz*. That's bad. Then, in a turnaround, the colleges picked up on the high school thing. Because some of these teachers left high school and went on to college for higher degrees, bringing the stage band concept along with them.

L.A.: Where did you go to college?
AMLOTTE: University of Minnesota, in Duluth. I'm from Cloquet, which is right near Duluth.
L.A.: Is that when you first heard Kenton's music?
AMLOTTE: No, I was in high school when I first heard it. I'm sure it was records. I played in a band. It just turned me on, totally. It was the start of his all-star bands—'48, '49, '50, '51—when

all the guys were winning the *Down Beat* polls, and his music was growing and growing. It was very experimental. It was *dynamite*.

L.A.: You heard the Pete Rugolo things.
AMLOTTE: Yes. "Monotony" and "Mirage" . . .
L.A.: "Cuban Carnival" . . .
AMLOTTE: All those things got to me. Then when I went to college I had to give a dissertation on some composer. The period I liked was the Impressionistic era—Ravel and Debussy—which is closely related to what Stan does, so I was very much stimulated by it. I'd get in front of the class and make comparisons, talk about Debussy chords and analyze what was being done in Stan's band. And these people in Minnesota, *they* knew nothing about Stan Kenton's Orchestra. I don't think *I* knew much about it either. But I loved it. And I buffaloed the teacher enough to get an A from the course, so . . . (Laughs.)
L.A.: Do you trace your interest in jazz education perhaps back to this period, when you were giving papers in college?
AMLOTTE: I think so. There's a need for it. Where there's a need you try to help.
L.A.: Did you join the band in Minnesota?
AMLOTTE: I came to California in 1954. I was doing graduate work in music at USC.
L.A.: Then after you joined the band in 1956, when did you become band manager?
AMLOTTE: About 1959. I was manager for ten years. At the time I was hired, Stan was still doing the calling, as he did for a few years longer. Three years later now, I'm taking on the responsibility of putting the band together. It's funny, thinking of it. I might have started something that Dick (Shearer) took over, with the hiring for Stan. I don't think anyone but Stan did it before that time. Stan would make out the payroll, when it came from Los Angeles, he'd stay up Sunday night and do it. After I became road manager I asked for more duties. I wanted to get more involved, to find out what went on. So then I made payroll. The only thing I didn't do, and most of us didn't, was fire. Stan did that. I was interested in him. I wanted to get more insight into him.

L.A.: As you did so, what impressed you about him?
AMLOTTE: I think his leadership. The good goals that he had.
L.A.: What were his goals?
AMLOTTE: To expose his music, to have more people become aware of it. I really think that was the biggest thing he wanted. That was his life. It had to be that.
L.A.: One of the most ingenious things Kenton ever did was to found his Creative World. Without that a great many people wouldn't have had access to his music. Except for places like Tower Records in L.A., it's not readily available in record stores. You were there during that time—don't you really feel Creative World helped him survive?
AMLOTTE: Yes. We left Capitol when they were no longer really interested in the jazz artist.
L.A.: By reissuing his old records, Stan got a whole new audience, I think.
AMLOTTE: It's true. Creative World also served as a newsletter promotion, giving information as to what the band was doing, when it was going on its next tour, what was happening with the guys and things like that. There was a mailing list of maybe 10,000 people.
L.A.: It may have started at that, but I believe it built up to 100,000. A great idea. And I think it saved him.

AMLOTTE: It was an excellent idea. And you're absolutely right, because when you deal with creative form—art, jazz—you have a limited following. It's not watered down. And it's sad, but most of the people in the world don't want to be strained that much. You're a minority when you're a follower of jazz.
L.A.: Stan had definite thoughts about that, about people who were involved in music, either at a young age, as fans, or as musicians, being more creative than other people.
AMLOTTE: I think it's true, because you're in a creative form of expression.
L.A.: Music per se or jazz as music? Or either?
AMLOTTE: Music at the high level. And jazz I put on the high level. It's very creative. It's *impromptu expression*. It's not like, say, a pop tune, in which you're not being asked to go beyond right there. You tax your brain to listen to Kenton.

Dalton Smith, outside Carmelo's Jazz Club, Sherman Oaks, California. (Photo by the Author.)

11 Dalton Smith

I'd been playing with Ralph Marterie's band about a month. We were in Cincinnati when Stan called me. You know how he talks. (Lowering his voice.) "Dalton, this is Stan." I thought, "Who's this?" I thought somebody was pulling my leg. I thought, "Oh, sure it is." And I hung up.

(Laughs.) My whole thing all my life was to play on Stan's band, and I hung up! And he calls me back, he says, "I'm serious, this is Stan Kenton." I says *"Wow."* He says "Can you join my band in two weeks? I know you have to give two weeks' notice." I says, "Stan, I'm not ready for your band." And I *hung up* again. So Stan calls Don Jacoby and says "Jake, Dalton says he's not ready for my band." Jacoby says "You hang up. He'll get back to you in five minutes. I'm gonna call that sonofabitch . . . ." (Laughs.) I was like twenty-one years old, twenty years old or something. Scared to death. So he calls me and he says "You call Stanley Kenton back and you tell him that you'll go on the band in New York in two weeks." So I did. Met him in New York. I took Bill Chase's place the next night. Chase later had his own group that was wiped out in an air crash, flying in their own plane. He had left Stan's band and he went with Woody Herman.

L.A.: Why would anyone leave Stan Kenton's band to go with Woody Herman?

SMITH: Because Bud Brisbois—do you really want to know?—Bud Brisbois played first trumpet and Bill wanted to play first trumpet and they were at each other's throats. It was a constant hassle, and Stan had said, "Look. Bud is the first trumpet player. He was when he came here. You guys have to work it out." So Chase couldn't handle it so he split. So that's when Stan called Jacoby.

Then when Bud left the band I moved up to first trumpet, and I stayed there for a number of years—18 albums and a lotta years.

L.A.: What was the connection between Jacoby and Stan Kenton?

SMITH: They were both innovators, and they were both teachers. Jacoby was a great trumpet player, played first trumpet with CBS in Chicago, a studio musician. He and Stan were good friends, 'cause he helped Stan a lot, and Stan helped him a lot through the years. I met Jacoby while I was going to school in Hattiesburg at the University of Southern Mississippi and he came down and did a concert with our band. He liked the way I played and invited me to come up and study with him at his house. He was very, very helpful and taught me a lot of things. It was about eight months later that Stan called him and said "Where can I get a real good trumpet player?" and Don said "I got just the guy" and gave Stan my number in Cincinnati.

L.A.: Where had you first heard Kenton's music?

SMITH: In high school in Mississippi. Heard a record—I think it was Bill Holman's *Contemporary Concepts* where they play "Yesterdays"—and I couldn't believe it. I was always attracted to the whole brass section. People used to say Stan liked to stand up there and get knocked down by that wall of sound, you know? That's what he

wanted. We never played so loud for anybody else. Or so strong. That's what he wanted to hear. You really got into it. You just felt like doing it. I used to black out on the stand. You know the theme in "Artistry in Rhythm" where it goes up to the high G? I don't know how many times I'd fall right off the stand when I played that. I left once for a couple of weeks when my kid was born, and Larry Ford took my place, and I said "You better play the theme tonight, so you get used to it," and he blacked out. We were in Detroit. And he fell off the bandstand, about eight feet. Just fell off.

L.A.: You really blacked out.

SMITH: Ya, you just go right out. It's called hyperventilating. Just from putting so much air into the brain.

L.A.: Is that like a sensation of fainting?

SMITH: You don't know it when it happens. You just go out.

L.A.: Would this happen quite often?

SMITH: Occasionally. Depending on if you'd had enough rest. If we were at a higher altitude. Everything affected it.

L.A.: That's what George Faye was saying about playing the trombone part; he'd get dizzy.

SMITH: Well, this is going just a little beyond dizziness.

L.A.: A trumpet has to be harder to play than a trombone, right?

SMITH: A trombone player wouldn't admit to that, but it is. Scuba divers have a word for it. It's called hydrogen narcosis. When you get too deep it forces hydrogen into the bloodstream and they call it rapture of the deep. You just swim off like a fish. And it's almost similar when you force that oxygen into the brain. And Stan's band was—well some players wouldn't play with him because of that. It was just too hard.

L.A.: It has to be the hardest book in the whole business, right?

SMITH: *I* think so.

L.A.: How was the Kenton trumpet section set up? The middle guy plays lead, right?

SMITH: Ya, that's the first trumpet. Then you've got two and three on either side of him, and four and five on the ends. What you tried to do, because the first was so high you needed the next high part right next to him, and the next high part right next to him on the other side, for support. You wouldn't want to sit next to the guy playing the lowest part, because it would be too difficult. It's hard enough as it was. And it would depend on how you set up. The fifth trumpet would set up on the side of the rhythm section. There's a reason for that. The fifth player played all the jazz solos, so he needed to be next to the drummer and the bass player and so forth, 'cause he played all the solo stuff by himself. And the reason he played fifth was because it was the easiest section part, so he could rest for the jazz solos. Nothing is as demanding in the world as the trumpet.

L.A.: Did that pattern hold for the other sections too?

SMITH: It's true with the trombone section.

L.A.: It was different for the saxophones?

SMITH: Yeah they just set up with the alto in the middle, 'cause he's playing the first part, and everybody has to hear him. See everybody has to follow the lead player, in whatever section.

L.A.: The alto player is the lead player.

SMITH: Ya. It was on Stan's band. With Woody it was the tenor player. With Stan's one alto-two tenor-two bari set-up, on either side of the alto you had a tenor, and then the baris, and one of the baris doubled on bass sax, which really gave it more depth. They all played solos. In the trombone section you might have two guys play solos, and the lead, like Dick Shearer, would also. But with the trumpet you've usually got a guy, he's doing all the high, hard work, and then you've got a guy who was doing all the solo work. And the other guys are just playing section parts.

L.A.: Did you come in on fifth trumpet?

SMITH: I came in as third trumpet, where Bill Chase was. Usually you work your way up, from third, fourth or fifth to lead, but I moved right to first in about eight months.

L.A.: You know the thing that really struck me as curious about the time that you were on the band was the number of changes in personnel in the trumpet section. My God there were a lot of them. Some of them would stay on for a year or two, but in your situation it would change every few months or so.

SMITH: We had guys stay on three and four years, like Bob Behrendt and a couple guys stayed two years . . .

L.A.: I'll refresh your memory, and then you tell me if this is average or not. Steve Huffstetter. Bob Rolfe. Larry McGuire. Ernie Bernhardt. Marvin Stamm. Norman Baltazar. Gary Slavo. Ronnie Ossa. Tommy Porrello.

SMITH: See now Tommy took my place the first time I left.

L.A.: Okay. Ron Keller. Buzzy Mills. Ray Triscari. Ollie Mitchell.

SMITH: Ollie Mitchell and Ray Triscari were never on the band. They were just hired to do the Los Angeles Neophonic concerts. Ollie played on the album, but I don't think Ray did, 'cause he couldn't make it or something.

L.A.: Gary Barone?

SMITH: Gary was on the band, yes. He played the jazz chair. He was very good.

L.A.: Bob Hicks? Tom Harrell? That's probably most of them. Keith La Motte. That must be fifteen players. That's a lot.

SMITH: Keith played mellophone. He wanted to play trumpet really bad. That's why he got on the mellophonium. Did you mention Ray Starling?

L.A.: No, these were just trumpet players. Did you hire for mellophonium?

SMITH: No. No, not really. Well yeah I did, actually, Lou Gasca I hired. See we had to get trumpet players who were willing to play mellophonium. That's why I came up with those guys.

L.A.: You mean they had to be able to double on both instruments?

SMITH: No. They all wanted to play trumpet. But we had to get somebody who would be willing to play mellophonium. We had one guy who wasn't a trumpet player, he was a French horn player who wanted to play the mellophonium. Dwight Carver. The rest of the guys were trumpet players we talked into doing it, really.

L.A.: They weren't happy about it?

SMITH: Well they wanted to play trumpet. But there were no openings in the trumpets.

L.A.: Is this because they're harder to keep in tune or they just didn't like the sound of it?

SMITH: It was a new thing. Stan and Johnny Richards had gone to the Conn company and had them design it and the whole bit. It was just a new thing and the trumpet players wanted to say "I'm a trumpet player with Stan Kenton." They didn't want to say "I'm a mellophonium player with Stan Kenton."

L.A.: (Laughs.)

SMITH: That's what the whole thing was all about, okay? Yeah, it was ego. It was really ego.

L.A.: Is that why they'd come on and stay a while and then leave?

SMITH: Yeah. Exactly. They would come on and play for a while, hoping that a trumpet player would leave and they could get that spot on trumpet, and we'd get somebody else to play mellophonium. We had to do a little wheeling and dealing just to get somebody to play those things, to tell you the truth.

L.A.: What did you personally think of them?

SMITH: I thought they had possibilities, but they were so out of tune, they were hard to play with and they were *so loud.* They used to make me work twice as hard, so I didn't like that. And intonation . . .

L.A.: To be heard above them, you mean?

SMITH: Well, yeah, to have a sound that, a top trumpet should kind of dominate them, and then that full trombone sound, which is really I think Stan's identifiable sound, the trombone section sound.

L.A.: Everybody says that.

SMITH: Yeah.

L.A.: Even more than trumpet, right?

SMITH: Yeah. I think so.

L.A.: And you're a trumpet player.

SMITH: Yeah. Except that he was always identified with a real high trumpet, also.

L.A.: I think that's the thing that people noticed first. Because it's the most obvious.

SMITH: It's the first mistake you'll hear. If the first trumpet player makes a mistake you'll hear it. All over the world. That's why that book was so hard. You had to play all that high stuff, and if you made one mistake, everybody knew it. If the first trombone player or the first saxophone player made a mistake, you might not know about it. They could kind of sneak by. But if we made a mistake—boy. So you're really on the spot more. That's why it paid a little more money.

L.A.: Was this really coveted by any trumpet player in the country? Was it considered the top band?

SMITH: It was for me. It was for me. Yeah, sure. Listen, there were so many guys that used to come around and wanted to play on that band, to play trumpet on that band. It was incredible. At one period it was like if you were a baseball player and you wanted to play with the World Champion New York Yankees. It was that same kind of feeling.

L.A.: The best.

SMITH: I tried not to be snobbish but I felt like when we'd check in a hotel somewhere and some other bands were there, people would be whispering "Hey. Kenton's band's here!" It was a prestige kind of thing.

L.A.: A lot of challenging work.

SMITH: That's *why* it was a prestige thing. They knew it was the hardest music around the place.

L.A.: Let's talk about what made the Kenton trumpet section distinctive.

SMITH: We prayed a lot.

L.A.: (Laughs.) I mean when you were blowing, and not fainting.

SMITH: I used to say, "Please don't let me pass out," you know. "Let me get through this."

L.A.: (Laughs.)

SMITH: It was awfully hard. But you know what? It was incredible. Stan used to look back at me when somebody would request something really hard and it would be our last number. We were out, we were wasted. And he'd look back at me, and I'd say, "Stan, we'll do it, one more time."

L.A.: How could you handle it?

SMITH: For him I could. That's the way we felt about him.

L.A.: When you've done the whole thing, which is what, almost a 3-hour concert, you've got to be completely winded.

SMITH: I was the last one to get up from my seat. I was always the last one to get up. Couldn't move.

L.A.: The evolving of that sound is a book in itself.

SMITH: There are a lot of groups today that use a lot of brass—Earth, Wind and Fire, Blood, Sweat and Tears, Chicago—only because of Stan, I think. Now it's not jazz, but it kind of came out of Stan's thing.

L.A.: And it came full circle when he did his *Chicago* album, playing music that they wrote.

SMITH: People go so far and then they want to stay in touch. Stan always wanted to stay in touch. For so many years he stayed in touch with the musicians and what they were doing. And he was an innovator. Dee Barton did some just incredible things, and Stan just kind of let Dee do it. Gave him a vehicle to do it with, which was his band. Dee could

Stan Kenton at the piano, in recording studio with Mellophonium Band, '60s. (Photo: Courtesy of a Kenton friend.)

85

write anything he wanted to. And boy he did! There's some hard stuff on that album, *Kenton Presents Dee Barton*. I didn't play on the album, but I played the whole thing later with Dee's band.

L.A.: You were on the Kenton band together?

SMITH: Dee came on the band when I was already the first trumpet player and he was a jazz trombone player. Dee and I grew up in Mississippi together. We were about the same age. He later became Stan's drummer. One night in Detroit our drummer had to leave—it was an emergency—and Stan called New York, he called Chicago, he called a lot of places. This was before he was getting people from North Texas State. You had to call a big city to get a really good drummer. Drummer and lead trumpet player were hard things to find for that band. 'Cause they were just too demanding.

L.A.: I've heard that, the most demanding thing was the drummer and then the first trumpet. Why was that?

SMITH: It was just so hard. For the drummer to keep a big band together like that, I mean really to keep it together, he had to be really strong and had to be really good. Really good.

L.A.: You mean he had to have a big enough ego to do it? Or do you mean...

SMITH: I think both, he had to be a good enough musician and a great enough drummer and he had to have a lot of ego to do it. It was a tough hard band and a tough hard book to play. It was very demanding. And the trumpet player had to have the range and the stamina to play it.

L.A.: What *was* that range?

SMITH: Whatever they wrote. Whatever they wrote you had to play it. It went—because of Maynard Ferguson and Bud Brisbois who'd been on the band earlier it went anywhere you wanted it to go, 'cause they could play anywhere.

L.A.: And once Stan had heard it, of course, he...

SMITH: The book was written for it. If he pulled up a chart that had those notes on it he had to play it.

L.A.: Do you remember the highest note you had to play?

SMITH: No, 'cause I blacked out right afterwards.

L.A.: (Laughs.)

SMITH: (Laughs.) Bill Holman was a great writer for Stan, 'cause he would build and build and build the way Stan likes. Four trumpets would be playing, just building and building, and then when they got to say four or five bars

Above and opposite page: Music Center Plaza, Los Angeles, California, site of the Neophonic Orchestra concerts. (Photos by the Author.)

from the peak, the first trumpet would come in. I would be resting up 'til then. And I would come in like "Ah-doo-*dee*-DAH!" That's what Stan loved; he loved that sound. I think that was his success, that note, and the writers would be hired who knew how to do that.

L.A.: To build to that big crescendo.

SMITH: Um-hm. That's what he wanted. He used to call it a wall of sound, and he loved that wall of sound. That's why he never had what you'd call a swing band, even though there were a few times we had a couple guys sneak in a swing chart just for fun, for the guys who wanted to swing a little bit. Stan was very classical, I thought. His piano playing shows that. He played in a very classical way. He never really got into

the jazz thing. I don't think he ever really liked it as much. But he enjoyed it sometimes, like Dee Barton would write a few things that really swung, and we played maybe one a night or something like that. And he enjoyed it, he liked it. Sure.

L.A.: Do you feel that Stan created a new form of music?

SMITH: Anybody's music comes from somewhere. Stan's music came from American jazz. But you could put him in a category all his own.

L.A.: Some people have tried to compare his genre with that of Paul Whiteman, but that misses the mark, I think. Whiteman dabbled in jazz, with a classical touch. Kenton's thing is very different. Can you imagine Paul Whiteman playing *City of Glass?*

SMITH: I can't imagine *anybody* playing it.

L.A.: (Laughs.) Or "Conflict" by Pete Rugolo.

SMITH: Or *Adventures in Time,* by Johnny Richards.

L.A.: Why *Adventures in Time*?

SMITH: It was the most challenging thing I ever played. It's the hardest thing I ever had to do.

L.A.: Did you like it?

SMITH: I liked some of it. I thought the mellophoniums took away from it because of their intonation hassle. But I'll tell you something. There's a perfect example on that album of what I was talking about, where the other trumpets play and build up and then the first trumpet comes in. That's a perfect example of how Stan liked people to write for his trumpets. 'Cause I could save myself—I was *breathing* all this time to get enough air. (Laughs.) These guys are playing, it's real slow. Shelly (Manne) could tell you. Shelly used to do an impersonation of Kenton kickin' off the band. Shelly would go *(whispering)* "One . . . two . . . three . . . *PKHOOOOM!"*

L.A.: (Laughs.)

SMITH: (Laughing.) 'Cause the band would just *explode* when he'd give a downbeat. If you listen to the big movie

(Photo by the Author.)

themes today, some of the guys that really got thcir start hcrc in the studios and have been scoring movies and stuff ever since wrote for Stan's Neophonic. Johnny Williams is probably considered the greatest writer-composer today in Hollywood. He wrote a thing for the Stan Kenton Neophonic, which we recorded. Stan's whole approach was to let the writers do their thing, and he made it work. He had to deal with them and he kind of guided them. That's just what I saw all the time I was there. And we only had two years, two short seasons. I think it could have been more successful if we'd had more time. I really do. It was such a new thing, and they didn't have money to sustain it for another year. If it had lasted longer it would have succeeded, 'cause it was great. The Neophonic thing was really unfortunately a low-budget thing to start with. We only had one day to rehearse for something that should have taken a week.

L.A.: I've never understood how you could do that.

SMITH: Even with the little rehearsal time we had, it was great. Word went out all over the world: anybody who wants to write for this, submit a composition, of *anything* you want to write.

Guys from Vienna, Canada, all over the United States . . .

L.A.: I've seen the list of composers. It's unbelievable.

SMITH: You know where that left us? I mean like *anything you want to write!* And they're thinking "Stan *Kenton.* Wow!" So right away the trumpets went sky-high. And right away everything— It was ridiculous. I used to go in there and sit down and say "Oh, no."

L.A.: (Laughs.)

SMITH: We actually needed two or three lead trumpet players, two or three second trumpet players. We needed time to rest, and we didn't have it. We had to play all day one day and the concert the next night. That was all the time we had, 'cause that was all the money they had. I would've rehearsed for free but the union wouldn't let us. So it was a killer. There were some times at the concert it wasn't quite as clean as it could have been. There was so much hard stuff there. It was a place for him to use, partly, all the musicians who'd worked with him in the past, and the new ones who would work for him in the future, and also to bring in anybody who wanted to write something that was valid—which he'd always done anyway.

What an opening! You know? Stan always got the best out of everybody, the writers, the players. Stan and Jim (Amlotte) and Dee and I sat down and picked the best tunes out of the first season for the album. That *Neophonic* record's great. It's one of my favorites.

L.A.: Do you remember Stan as being very happy and excited during that time?

SMITH: It was awfully tiring for him, I remember. A little frustrating 'cause he didn't have enough rehearsal time. It was a very hard job for him. I don't know that he enjoyed it that much, to tell you the truth. It had to be exciting for him, but I think frustrating too. But then a lot of things were.

L.A.: Because of all the problems involved?

SMITH: Yeah.

L.A.: You didn't have strings for the Neophonic, did you?

SMITH: Couple of times we had strings. Not too often, but I know we did on a couple of things.

L.A.: Do you feel the Neophonic music is along the same lines as the earlier Innovations?

SMITH: I think so. Except that when Stan formed the Innovations Orchestra, my understanding is that he said Okay, we're gonna have French horns and so many strings and this and this—that they were used to augment his band.

L.A.: It worked.

SMITH: It worked, but very few people were ready for it. The people who went to see symphonies weren't ready for it, and the jazz people kinda got turned off because it scared 'em. They thought, "Aw, man. That's not jazz."

L.A.: Mike Suter and Dick Shearer were saying that they felt perhaps the legacy of the Neophonic could be found in The Orchestra out here. How do you feel about that?

SMITH: That's a copy of it. That's Jack Elliott's thing.

L.A.: Do you feel this is what Stan wanted to do all his life? What he'd been looking for?

SMITH: I don't think he knew what he was looking for. I just think he knew he had to keep going. Whatever band he had at the time was the best band he ever had, every new writer was the best writer he ever had; that was his attitude. He couldn't ever go back. You'd have to yell and scream to get him to play some of the old things. 'Cause he just kept goin'

with the new stuff, the new stuff, all the time. Once we recorded a piece it was almost something else. It was like it was dead. We left tons of music at the Blue Note in Chicago when I first joined the band.

L.A.: *Left* it?

SMITH: We'd pull music out. He'd say "The book's gettin' too thick"; it was this thick, so he'd pull music out and we put it in boxes and left it. We came back about three weeks later to pick it up and somebody had stolen it. So nobody knows where that music went. Tons of music I'd love to have.

L.A.: My gosh. That's a shame.

SMITH: I had a piece of music, once, "Malaguena," where I would mark it every time we did another take at Capitol Records when we were recording it. We did it eighteen times in a row.

L.A.: Why? Couldn't they dub it back then?

SMITH: They could have. Stan never did that. He'd say "It won't sound the same." He wanted it to sound like a live performance. On one of the Lennie Niehaus tunes, "You Stepped Out of a Dream" or one of those songs, we did one take 34 times. One tune.

L.A.: Why so many takes? What would go wrong?

SMITH: Maybe a guy made a mistake. Or it wasn't quite like he wanted it or whatever. He'd stop and do it again.

L.A.: Speaking of ballads, just about my favorite record is *Standards in Silhouette.*

SMITH: That was the first record I did with Stan. The very first. I'd only been on the band a week when we did that.

L.A.: I think that's the most beautiful thing.

SMITH: It's more of a Stan Kenton sound.

L.A.: And my favorite song on there is "I Get Along Without You Very Well," arranged by Bill Mathieu. Whatever happened to him?

SMITH: I don't know. He sure wrote a beautiful thing there. Archie LeCoque played the trombone solo.

L.A.: You were one of those trumpets coming in after the slow part, where they come screaming in.

SMITH: Yeah.

L.A.: That must have been a big thrill for you. You weren't playing lead at the time.

SMITH: No, right. I was playing third.

Beautiful lobby of Chandler Pavilion, site of the Neophonic Orchestra concerts. (Photo by the Author.)

Bud was playing lead.

L.A.: You were watching Bud Brisbois play that?

SMITH: Actually I was shaking.

L.A.: (Laughs.)

SMITH: It was my first big-time album. We recorded that in New York, not L. A. It was one of the few record albums we did in a studio in New York, 'cause we were there working. And—I'd just come from Mississippi. New York *alone* scared me. Then Stan scared me worse. I mean, to do an album in a week. I was ready for the farm, you know? That was great. I remember that album. It's still one of my favorites. God, I remember that album. That's the one Bud Brisbois went up to a triple C-sharp on the trumpet. Triple C-sharp. That's off the end of the piano. It's off the *end* of the piano. No trumpet player in the world ever played that high, and he did it on that album. You listen to it. It goes like *(whistles off into atmosphere).* You'll hear it. It's like a little kiss on the end of it. Triple C-sharp. *Ppwhute!*—like that.

L.A.: That's on "Lonely Woman" I think.

SMITH: Scared the hell out of me.

L.A.: What did?

SMITH: Just him playing that note. I never heard anything like it. Never heard anything like it. Bud was on the band when they came down to my college and did a concert, and I remember all the music majors just sittin' there like *wow.* Couldn't believe it. That was '58, and I went on the band the next year. You know being on that band has just stayed with me from then on. Right up until now. I mean and it will.

L.A.: It's always a fascinating revelation to see what people feel they brought to the Kenton band and what they feel they took away from it.

SMITH: I heard Stan say something once. I know Kai Winding kind of started the trombone sound, but Stan told me "The guy that really gets the trombone sound, that I really feel is responsible for that really sweet sound, is Bob Fitzpatrick."

L.A.: What I like about the Kenton trombone is that foreboding quality, which is quite present in the *Standards* album, in Mathieu's arranging. What do you remember about him?

SMITH: He was actually a trumpet player on the band when he wrote that. Not a very good one. He was a good arranger, and he knew it, and Stan knew it. He wanted to play trumpet real bad. Stan really didn't want him on the band, but he wanted him to write for the band, so he let him play, too. Like one tour. And he played fourth trumpet and kind of stayed out of the way. He wasn't much help in the section. But that album is something else.

L.A.: What did Stan think of him as an arranger?

SMITH: Stan knew exactly what he was doing. That's why he let him play in the band. Stan couldn't have had him in the band if he hadn't been that kind of a writer, because it was actually taking away from the trumpet section a little bit. Stan didn't really want him to play on his own record, but I think he played on some of it.

L.A.: How long was he with you?

SMITH: A couple of months.

L.A.: Only a couple of months? And he wrote that beautiful music?

SMITH: Ya, well see that's why he wanted to be with Stan. He'd been studying Stan Kenton for years. He used to follow the band around, and say "Stan, you gotta let me play." Just kept on at it. Stan said "Okay." But see that happened all the time. You don't know how many kids have done it.

L.A.: Wanted to write for Stan Kenton?

SMITH: Oh, millions. I mean literally.

L.A.: Come on. Not millions.

SMITH: Ya. Think about it. Every college and everything. Guys come up and say "Stan. When can I write something for you?" Or "When can I audition for you?" We used to have people follow us. For miles. Hundreds, thousands of miles in a car, just hoping one of us would get sick and they could play. Every area that we went into there always were people that wanted to write and wanted to play, and Stan had to put up with that and he was always very nice about it.

L.A.: The Kenton trumpet section always seemed to have a lot of good arranging written for it.

SMITH: We had all kinds of combinations of voicings. Dee Barton and Johnny Richards wrote things that nobody ever saw before. Depending on the arranger, it was always a five-way part, but with sometimes two voices, or guys playing in unison, or a fifth apart or an octave lower than me, or this guy a half-step from this guy. That's where you got that tension. He would have tension in his sound, 'cause the notes were all close together, and then it would open up, and it would be a tension release. Stan always had a direction, and his direction was creative and new music. In a sense he was so complex, but in a sense he was

that basic. I think that's what contributed to people being able to come in and kind of fit in and follow along and still do their thing. Stan was compatible with that. That's why his music got very complex at times and sometimes his ballads were very simple and very pretty. I think that's part of the reason.

L.A.: And he had the largest chord, from the bottom to the top.

SMITH: Well that's 'cause he had the biggest band.

L.A.: No, I mean he liked the largest interval from bottom to top.

SMITH: Yeah, you know why? Did you ever figure that out?

L.A.: No.

SMITH: I figured this out once. Nobody ever told me. 'Cause his hands were so big. He could do that on the piano. He could play like this far at the piano with one hand.

L.A.: Did it all start with that?

SMITH: I don't know; this is what *I* think. I have no proof for this, but I think that's what he heard when he played piano. He kept doing this and it kept stretching. And every time they're going lower on this end, I'm going higher on the other end. That's the way he heard it. That's what he wanted, you're right about that, and why I don't know, but he heard that. He wanted more sound. I think the further he went, the more sound he wanted. I think he'd have liked to have added more people to the band later.

L.A.: With the most important positions on the band being drummer and first trumpet, did the three of you, Stan and you and Dee Barton, have some kind of psychic awareness of each other?

SMITH: Oh yeah. Sure. Not only musically but when anybody in the band was having a problem—a personal problem, anything—we all just knew it. Dee and Stan and I used to get together almost every night and discuss how things were going and what was happening. 'Cause Stan liked to keep things really smooth. And he did.

L.A.: What could you observe about the psychological workings of the man?

SMITH: First of all the way he used to come in and handle the guys I think is very important. Like my first night on the band, when I was so scared. He realized it. Nobody can really perform if he's scared to death. So he walked up to the first alto player, who was Lennie Niehaus at the time, and he says, "I'll bet you five dollars that the new trumpet player makes a mistake."

L.A.: He said that so you could hear it?

SMITH: Said it real loud. And Lennie pulled out a five and said "Okay." And then everybody laughed. Then I relaxed. That was part of his whole thing, the way he was able to get guys to perform who were soloists, or guys who'd been on the band a while but were maybe having problems at home or elsewhere. And he could do the same with audiences. This happened a lot when we played country clubs, and someone would tell him "It's too loud." He'd say, "Oh, okay." I remember one time we were at the Cherry Hill Country Club in Denver, where President Eisenhower used to go to play golf. So it was really a sophisticated place. They had the Stan Kenton band there only because they wanted to say "We had Stan Kenton here." So we played really soft for about an hour. I mean like really soft, everything down an octave or in mutes. Finally he says "Okay. Open up. Just a little bit. Just enough so people will start to say 'Oh, wow.' " Then he'd play soft again for ten or fifteen minutes. *Now* people are coming up and saying, "Stan—come on. Can we hear it?" So then we'd let them have something really loud. He would have the audience wrapped up. They would come and beg, "Stan, please play so-and-so." He knew us, and he knew the audience, and he got the best out of both. Another time we were playing really loud at a jazz club where there were Kenton freaks, people who were frantic over him. And they wanted more. But over and over again Stan called up a real soft, slow thing. And I said "Stan, they want—" you know. He says, "Even the audience has to rest, whether they realize it or not."

L.A.: Wow.

SMITH: Yeah.

L.A.: I've heard that he used to say "Always leave them wanting more."

SMITH: Yeah. Sure. It's good. They remember it then.

L.A.: Of the many attributes or aspects of the man, what about Stan would you think was most outstanding?

SMITH: I think Stan the leader. In a sense he was a teacher. I don't mean just music, 'cause he didn't really come around and tell me how to play the trumpet either. Some people couldn't handle that—maybe they had too many problems at the time, or couldn't be creative, or whatever. He never forced it on anybody, it was just there. I jumped at it, to me it just came—*whishht!*

L.A.: Were you on the band straight through from 1959 to 1970?

SMITH: No, I was off and on different times. Every time Stan would call me I'd come back and blow for a little while, 'cause I loved it so much. But when I did I'd have to give up jobs here. I'd make a lot less money with Stan than I was making in the studios.

L.A.: But you still found it worth it?

SMITH: Oh yeah.

L.A.: For what, the opportunity to be with him?

SMITH: Yeah, him, the music, and get to play that stuff. As hard as it was to play, it was fun. I loved it.

L.A.: That was a difficult time in Kenton's life, wasn't it, the late sixties?

SMITH: For the first couple of years it was. Then he got new things happening and new clubs started up. See it wasn't just the music. All the bands were hitting the pits, 'cause rock and roll took over. Even some of the ballrooms were catering to kids, with rock and roll and guys with a guitar who knew three chords. But Stan went right through it and kept innovating, which he always did, and pretty soon new clubs were opening up. Like during that period, I think '60 or '61, Basin Street East in New York opened and we broke all the records.

L.A.: In a way it was an exciting time, too, because of the start of the Kenton Clinics. Did you teach in those?

SMITH: As a matter of fact I taught at the first Stan Kenton Clinic Summer Camp in Indiana before I was even on the band. Don Jacoby was the trumpet teacher and I was his assistant. 'Cause Stan's band wasn't there that first year. We were there—the next year I was on the band and we were there. That first year they just used his name, and he showed up for a couple of days. It was the National Stage Band Camp Clinic and it was run by Gene Hall and Matt Betton. Betton teaches in Kansas someplace and he's been at all the Stan Kenton Clinics that I've ever been to since then. Stan came for a few days and talked to the students. I saw him, but I didn't really get to meet him. It was after that that I went on the Marterie band and it was after that that he called me. We did some clinics where we'd go for a few days and then we'd go on tour for a few days while the camp kept going and then we'd come back on that weekend and play a concert. We worked all during that period. We'd come in and out, working the area. Stan could have lost a lot of money if he didn't work.

L.A.: Those were pretty exhaustive schedules you kept.

SMITH: We used to go into like Kansas, and we'd get in in the afternoon, and say I would rehearse the trumpet players and lecture them, and Dick Shearer would take the trombones and he would lecture and rehearse them, and then we'd put the band together and Stan would rehearse their band and that night we'd have a big concert. We used to do that a lot of places. It was really a full day's work. Section rehearsals, individual study, group, you know, band rehearsals. And then they'd get to hear us—and all the time they're training for the weekend, the final day, where they present their stuff.

L.A.: I understand there were something like four categories of instruction: concepts of jazz music, individual and group instruction, rehearsal techniques, and jazz theory, beginning and advanced. Were you involved, then, with the group instruction on instruments?

SMITH: Ya. First of all we auditioned the kids. Like I auditioned all the trumpets. And then I put 'em in a category, like I'd take the best player and put him as first trumpet in the first band, and the next best player I'd put as first trumpet in the second band . . . .

L.A.: Oh I see.

SMITH: And so forth, all the way down. That way, all the bands were good. All the bands were real good. Just the first band was just a little bit better. And it's better, too, see, because a guy that's almost as good as this guy would rather play first trumpet in this band than second trumpet in the other. He'd rather play first there, 'cause he's a first trumpet player. So all the bands were fairly equal. Dick did that with the trombones and whoever was in charge of saxophones did it for them. Then each day I'd have a section rehearsal with each trumpet section from each band. Start early in the morning.

L.A.: Just the trumpets?

SMITH: Just the trumpets.

L.A.: Playing all five at the same time?

SMITH: Yeah. I'd work out their parts for phrasing, and intonation, and sound, and the whole bit. It was like a real lesson to them, you know? Then I'd have another group. Then we'd put it all together. I'd rehearse everybody's trumpet section, but also we each had one band, and we'd rehearse that band during the day. Then at the end of the week we gave a concert and we all tried to outdo each other. It was great. Oh, it was neat, and the kids played so well. But then Stan's band would come on and cause a commotion and wipe everybody out. (Laughs.)

L.A.: Would you play a certain arrangement?

SMITH: I always used Kenton arrangements, myself, with my band. Whoever had a band could pick their own.

L.A.: What would you choose?

SMITH: I used to like to do "My Old Flame," by Marty Paich, 'cause he was one of my favorites. It was the type of vehicle that I could use to get the most out of them. 'Cause that thing builds at the end—it'd really get them roaring. It would get the trumpet player really playing. And the drummer had to work his ass off.

L.A.: Something like "Rainy Day" would be good too.

SMITH: That's one I used to do too. Sometimes I'd use Dee Barton's things. What I always did was to make a guy play something just a little teeny bit harder than he could really do it. Just a little harder. Just to test him a little bit. Play something a little too high for the first trumpet player. A little too fast for the drummer. Or too technical. And just push 'em toward it, and boy they almost made it and boy they felt good.

L.A.: 'Cause they were taking on something more challenging! You didn't teach theory or these other things?

SMITH: No. All I taught was trumpet. If a kid had some special problems with playing the trumpet I would work with him. My lunch break, or his lunch break, or later at night after we finished. But you know what, that second clinic we did, we actually rewrote all the musical markings in jazz music. They were using old Italian opera-type markings, and I said "This doesn't make sense." We had a committee and we sat down and redid the whole thing. Dee Barton was very, very instrumental in pulling that one off. Came up with all kinds of ideas. I came up with new markings for the brass section. We did it so you could see real quick what the man wanted when he wrote it, and you'd know how to play jazz. We revamped it to make it fit jazz more.

L.A.: That's fascinating. I was wondering if, with personnel from Kenton's band running these clinics, they were more likely to influence these kids to the Stan Kenton sound, or ideas, or would they stick pretty much to straight principles?

SMITH: Most of these kids came to the campus *because* of Stan Kenton. So that's what they would ask, and that's

what they were really talking about. But, if you're gonna teach theory, theory is theory. Basic theory is basic theory, and even Stan had to learn that. And harmony is basic harmony. So they would teach that. But if a kid said, "Well how did you—on such-and-such a tune that you guys recorded—arrange the harmony in the sax section?" then the guy would show. And that would be Stan's thing. If they wanted to ask about something else, they'd show them that too. They could ask questions about anything.

L.A.: These were the week-long clinics. What were the one-day clinics like?

SMITH: A lot of our jobs were like, say, the University of Kansas, in Manhattan. That one stands out in my mind because it was really neat. The kids were great, and they had a lot of good musicians there. We pulled in at 11 in the morning after traveling on the bus all night, not really getting much sleep. Got out of the bus and went in and met all the kids and teachers and everything. Then they said "Okay, all the trumpet players go with Mr. Smith, here, and all the trombone players with Mr. Shearer"—I think Ray Reed was playing alto sax then. We all went to different rooms and we talked and they asked questions and I must have talked to them for about an hour. Then I had auditions for the band and picked the ones for each group and we rehearsed. All that in one day. *One day.* I think at this one place we might have had three or four bands. They would do two numbers each. I'd conduct my band, and Dick would conduct his, and so forth. Then Stan would come out with his band, and we'd have to run to get back in the band and play. And all the kids would sit down and listen. We did it like in a gym or something—it was just huge. A big auditorium, or something. *Packed* with people. The kids not only got to play, for their parents and friends, they got to sit down after that and listen to Stan's band. It was just—it was awesome. They used to have tears running down their faces. They used to chase the band . . .

L.A.: Really, used to have tears?

SMITH: They used to chase the bus. Ya, they'd run, with their horns, they'd be playing and come out, chasing the bus as we would leave. And Stan says "Sorry, we'd like to stay, but we gotta go, you know, we got 500 miles to the next clinic."

L.A.: And he did this kind of thing for twenty years, starting in 1959 right up until he died, in 1979. Incredible.

SMITH: But here's something else. I want you to think about it. Stan always said whatever band he had at the time was the best band he'd ever had. But all his musicians say the best band he ever had was when *they* were on it. Think about it. It's just that our egos say those things. Stan's thing was that he could never go back, he had to keep going forward.

L.A.: I can understand that.

SMITH: But to the guys that were on the band, like I always say, "Best band he ever had was when I was on the band." That's the way I felt.

L.A.: I liked the 1948 Progressive Jazz Orchestra myself. That was sensational.

SMITH: Ya but those guys, they didn't have it, you know?

L.A.: Didn't have as much—All right, now—let's try to be objective here! (Laughs.)

SMITH: They didn't have the *depth*. They didn't have the depth.

L.A.: What do you mean, the depth? You mean the capacity to play the . . .

SMITH: No, the depth. The range and the depth that—even the band was different then. It was closer to a swing band.

L.A.: They played the Rugolo things. You think your band was better than that?

SMITH: I don't think they could do the things we did. Those trumpet players could not have played the stuff that Bud Brisbois and I did. They didn't have the range, and they didn't have the strength. They couldn't have played it. 'Cause I still work with those guys. Still, one of my favorite jazz trumpet players is Conte Candoli. Still. The greatest.

L.A.: Well he goes back to '47-'48.

SMITH: I know. But he's the only one on that band that I would put in a section if I had to put one together.

L.A.: It's such a wide range, isn't it. From influencing young people in the clinics to evolving the kind of music he did to allowing creative individuals to flourish . . .

SMITH: Not only allowed them, he almost caused them to happen. You know? He really did. He really caused them to happen to be. They'd hear the band once and they'd get excited about it and come back five, ten years later. They'd want to write *because* they'd heard the band. It just turned something on inside of them. The way it did me, when I was just a dumb kid in Mississippi and first heard that music and thought, Man. This is a *record.* Second time I heard the band live was in Minneapolis, at an outdoor concert. Don Jacoby and I were standing there, listening. And Jacoby says, "You really want to be on that band, don'tcha." I says "I *am* going to." And you know what? Two months later I was.

L.A.: What did you like the most about it?

SMITH: For a trumpet player it was just the only place to be. If I spent the rest of my life trying to pay Stan back for what I've gotten from him I don't think I could ever accomplish it. If it hadn't been for him I'd probably—I know I would—be teaching in Mississippi. Instead, I'm one of the busiest trumpet players in town (Los Angeles). I was in Japan five or six years ago, with Quincy Jones and Roberta Flack. Stan is big in Japan right now. They're just learning about him. There was a kid, he'd been to our concert. Saw my name in the program, went home and got every Stan Kenton record that my name was on that he had. Wanted me to autograph 'em. And I'm autographin' them while the bus is movin', like real slow, out the window.

L.A.: You're kidding.

SMITH: True story. They're really into music over there. I'm telling you. All jazz, any kind of American jazz. They're hot on it. For so many years they were just starved for good American music. They just love it. We go over there we're like stars.

L.A.: So you think Stan's music will last?

SMITH: He's not only gonna last. I think, in a few years, because of what he did in the school programs and everything, he's gonna just start to grow again. When we go into the studios now we play a lot of things by young writers that are the same things I used to play with Stan. A little different drum beat, but the same figures, exact same things that I played before with Stan—fast figures in the trumpet, that kind of thing. A couple of these writers were from North Texas State and they had access to all Stan's music and they probably wanted to be on Stan's band. I think some day kids will do all phases of his music, all periods. Stan Kenton's music's gonna grow again.

Mike Suter. (Photo: Courtesy of Mike Suter.)

12 Mike Suter

We'd have the concert, and Stan would talk. He never would really address the whole group, except later at the one-day clinics we did. But the thing is, you'd be walking down the hall, you'd turn the corner, and there he was.

L.A.: And was that a mind-blowing experience?

SUTER: No, he wouldn't let you get that much in awe of him. He made sure you knew that he just was the piano player in a band that happened to be his.

L.A.: Really.

SUTER: I think he enjoyed the initial thing, where people would be in awe of him, but then he got tired of it real quick. He wouldn't let you do that, because then you couldn't talk to him, and he couldn't get to know you. But I dug it; I was more in awe of the guys in the band than of Stan. Stan would talk to you and everything else, but the guys in the band were doing the work. And for a junior in high school, some of the things they were doing were just beyond anything I could understand.

L.A.. What kinds of things were they doing?

SUTER: They were playing that *stuff*. And I couldn't understand how to do it. For less than $500 I got such an education it was amazing.

L.A.: That was for all the clinics? Room and board and everything?

SUTER: That was everything. Ninety-five dollars a week. My dad made it available to me to do what I wanted to do, and what I wanted to do was go to the Stan Kenton Clinics, as soon as I discovered he had 'em. I didn't even hear about 'em 'til 1962. I went to the Kenton Clinics in '62 and '63, all of them, starting with my junior year in high

school. In '62 I went to Storrs, Connecticut, then Michigan State, Indiana, and the University of Nevada-Lake Tahoe. In '63 it was Storrs, MSU, IU, the University of Denver, and the University of Nevada-Reno. There wasn't a question I couldn't get an answer to. The second year, Jiggs Whigham, Buddy Baker, Bob Curnow were the trombone section, Dave Wheeler and Jim Amlotte were the bass trombones. Buddy Morrow turned up one day, and we all talked with him for a while. Kai Winding showed up once during the first clinics, and we got a chance to talk with him. You could find out things, you could learn stuff. Plus you were playing.

L.A.: What would you ask them?

SUTER: "How the hell you do that?" And they'd show you. What I learned was not to be afraid of the horn. It's just a machine. And you make the machine work. I was a rotten bass trombone player. I didn't have any facility, any range, any technique. But with just the aura of sitting there next to, like, Jim Amlotte and having Jim say, "Oh, it's easy! You just do *this*," I made a hundred-and-eighty-degree change. Went from a rotten player to one that at least had some direction. In five weeks my playing got 200% better. In five weeks.

L.A.: Was it a question of improving your techniques, or did it involve other things?

SUTER: Basically it was just Amlotte getting the point across that it's no magical thing, you just do this and this and it comes out.

L.A.: What had been your problems with the instrument?

SUTER: I'd been doing it wrong for so long.

L.A.: What's the wrong way to do it?

SUTER: There's millions of wrong ways. And I was doing a lot of those wrong things. I never studied. That was my fault. I never had a teacher other than in band class in high school, things like that. All I knew was what I'd learned on records. I was doing a lot of things badly. My tone quality and my sound were so bad I couldn't make the tuning machine work. And Jim just said, "Well look, if you do this different, if you change this, if you change that . . ." Pretty soon I had a direction. I knew where I wanted to go. I knew what the recorded bass trombone sound was, but I didn't know what a bass trombone sounded like 'cause I'd never heard one played live. I mean, *I* didn't count. Hearing yourself, that's nothing.

L.A.: What had attracted you to the instrument?

SUTER: In the sixth grade at school we had four people who wanted to play trombone. We had three trombones and a bass trombone. I had the longest arms.

L.A.: From such simple beginnings . . .

SUTER: Our teacher promised me that in three weeks he'd have a real trombone for me. And in three weeks he did, but I wouldn't give up the one I had.

L.A.: What do you like about bass trombone?

SUTER: You're not one of the crowd.

L.A.: You mean you want to be different.

SUTER: Yeah. Any gorilla can play trombone.

L.A.: Um-hm. Does your friend Dick (Shearer) know you've made statements like that?

SUTER: Oh yes, I tell him, you know, if you can't play lead trombone, the rest of the chairs aren't worth playing; they're just garbage. The next solo instrument in the trombone section is the bass trombone. You're always doing something different from everybody else in the band. So it's an ego chair.

L.A.: This is really interesting. Rugolo and Kenton were always stretching out to the extremities of sound, the highest trumpet and the lowest-sounding trombone. And that's you.

SUTER: Yeah.

L.A.: What were they after? Was it a case of extreme just to be extreme? What kind of sound were they looking for? Or did they just want to stretch the music as much as possible?

SUTER: Well, it adds more colors to the palette, for one thing. If the lowest sound you make is three inches up the scale from what you can hear, those three inches of sound you're not going to hear. Let's use notes. If you really want to write something that goes down to a C, yet the lowest note in your band can only go to E-flat, you've got to give up that idea. You've got to modify it. So they were always into extending the range of the band, higher, lower. They could fulfill all their musical ideas that way.

L.A.: When did you first hear the music of Stan Kenton?

SUTER: It was in 1957. *Kenton in Hi-Fi.* A friend of mine had a brother, a senior in high school, who was a trombone player in the high school band, and was a Kenton fan. My friend and I were in seventh grade. We all three played trombone. One day we were at his house and he played that album, and all I could hear was that bass trombone in "Intermission Riff." And oh my God, the bass trombone player got to play a note all by *himself.*

L.A.: (Laughs.)

SUTER: And I liked that. I decided at age twelve that I was going to play in Stan Kenton's band. I bought *Kenton in Hi-Fi* on my own, and then started

picking up his records every time I'd see one. I also bought Ray Coniff records; he used bass trombones. Kenton and Coniff were the only two band leaders who used them.

L.A.: So you'd been playing a while before you heard this record.

SUTER: Yes, about a year and a half. But I had never heard anybody *play* it. I played bass trombone 'cause it *looked* different. I didn't know anybody really *used* those things. I thought they were for, you know, hangin' ties from, or something. I didn't know what it was *for.* I knew if I pushed the button I got a different note, but—half the time I didn't know what note I was playing, even. But then I heard what they were *used* for. So I started listening to Kenton.

L.A.: And you said you wanted to play in Stan Kenton's band, rather than just any band.

SUTER: I didn't say "wanted to." I said I was *going to.*

L.A.: You were *going* to. I take it there's quite a difference.

SUTER: Yes. Sure. The people who want to play in the band never get there. The people who decide they are going to play in his band, they're there.

L.A.: You were more interested in Kenton because he used the instrument, then, rather than being attracted to his sound?

SUTER: The sound didn't mean a thing to me then. I didn't have good enough ears to know it anyway. I wanted to play in his band only because he had a bass trombone.

L.A.: Did this change after you got in his band?

SUTER: I liked *him* more.

L.A.: Not the music?

SUTER: His music has never been special to me. I'd never listen to it to listen to it. I'd listen to it to hear certain things.

L.A.: What things?

SUTER: I like the energy, I like the fire, the verve.

L.A.: How long were you with Stan?

SUTER: Let's see. In 1963, when I graduated from high school, I was in the Kenton clinics when Dave Wheeler had something happen in his family, so he had to leave for a while. I was in the number one band at the time, so . . . "Well, as long as you're here, kid . . ." Jimmy Amlotte was doing the hiring at the time, and Stan okayed it. I played Dave Wheeler's chair for five weeks. I was totally incapable of doing it, but I

did it anyway. And a couple of other times. Then I came on the band in '73 and stayed through '75. That was my longest period, the period when I did the most to get my reputation. Then, in the summer of '78, the kid that was playing bass trombone—A. G. Robeson was his name—went into a hotel room with a bunch of hell's angels types and came out with a broken jaw, a split lip, and a broken nose. Kind of makes it hard to play. Real dummy. That happened in Grand Rapids. I got the call in Detroit and I finished out the tour. By that time Stan was—I mean, he had no right to be out there. But he was doing exactly what he wanted to do, so what the heck.

L.A.: No right to be out there because he was so sick?

SUTER: He was physically incapable of doing anything. The whole time I was out, that time, he never—he knew he knew me. But he had no idea what my name was.

L.A.: This was after the brain surgery?

SUTER: Yes. He'd play intro now and then. Then he'd just sort of sit and look at the band. We'd be playing along, and I'd look down, 'cause I was playing into his left ear all that time—and he'd be lookin' up at me, and you could just tell, he was thinking, "Who the hell is he?" He would get distraught because he couldn't remember people. I'd say, "Aw, forget it, Stan. Don't worry about it."

L.A.: This was '78 you're talking about.

SUTER: Summer of '78, yes. And I just—if he remembered, fine; if he didn't, fine.

L.A.: As a member of Stan's band, you were part of the clinic experience from the teaching angle as well as from the student angle years before. Were there similarities?

SUTER: Yes. The clinics were set up the same way. We were in the dorms, same dorms with the students. Stan did his best talking one to one. If you had a question you'd run up and you'd grab him and say, "Oh, Stan, I want to know this." And he'd talk to you. He would spend most of his time with educators. He felt the students would be best served by the musicians, in a structured atmosphere. And the Kenton Clinics were very structured. Stan had a good format from the beginning, which was to let 'em play professional arrangements, led by professional musicians, and let them be in contact at their will with professional musicians.

L.A.: During the week, any time of day?

SUTER: The whole week, they were all around you, you were just—you were brought into his world. His world wasn't superimposed onto yours.

L.A.: How would Stan approach youth? What was he trying to teach them? It must have been more than just how to blow an instrument. Was he preaching his gospel of jazz?

SUTER: Oh attitude.

L.A.: What attitude?

SUTER: A straight ahead professional attitude. Being honest in what you're saying and in what you're doing. Not saying things for political reasons. If you really like something, you say it. If you don't you say it's garbage. You don't flower it up.

L.A.: How would he project this attitude?

SUTER: By example, by the way he conducted himself. I think if we'd been called on for any reason to do something really dumb, and Stan decided it just wasn't right, he wouldn't do it. When I was on the band we had a chance to go out on tour with Tony Bennett and Sarah Vaughan. Stan turned it down. He would have had to take second or third billing, and that wasn't what he wanted to do. It would have meant a lot of money. But it wasn't what he wanted to do. So he stayed by his ideals and turned it down.

L.A.: Are you glad you knew Kenton?

SUTER: *Oh yeah, sure.* 'Course I am. I liked him as a person. I liked him as a person more than I liked him as a musician. I always felt there was much more style to what he did than absolute substance. And that the style had to do not with the music but the image.

L.A.: What's the Kenton style in the image?

SUTER: Uh, the big tall Ego, standing in front of a band, stretching from the baritone sax to the string bass player. And, uh, that very upright, tall, almost Satanic . . .

L.A.: *Satanic?*

SUTER: . . . look he would get. *Yeah.* Take a look at some of those album covers.

L.A.: (Laughs.) He's always smiling on the album covers. I think he's a genial-looking man.

SUTER: You apparently weren't close to him. He's got those big teeth, he looks like he's got a piano in his mouth . . .

L.A.: It's not a word that would have occurred to me.

SUTER: Well. You didn't play into his left ear for two years.

L.A.: No. Do you feel that he gave you anything in particular, that your association with him or playing in his group expanded your feeling for jazz or your personal style?

SUTER: I'm not a jazz musician.

L.A.: What kind of musician are you?

SUTER: A money player. I enjoyed immensely playing in Stan's band. But it did me a lot of harm, too. People think of me now as a jazz musician.

L.A.: You want to live that down?

SUTER: No. I want to incorporate it. I listen to everything. I play everything I can play. So in that respect it hurt me, because now I'm in that pigeonhole. But I got a lot out it, I got hundreds of things.

L.A.: What was the best of it, then, if that was the worst?

SUTER: The best of it, the best I got, is that I don't feel now that I have to be nice. Or friendly. I also learned from being on Stan's band on the road. I learned that being forthright and saying exactly what you think isn't always bad. 'Cause Stan never watered down what he thought. He knew exactly what he thought, and he'd say it. Stan almost fired me on the road once, between London and Edinburgh, 'cause he got tired of my saying what I thought. But I learned that from him—to say what I think and to follow through with what I believe in. And being with him was a good career decision for me.

L.A.: What have you been doing musically?

SUTER: I've got a fusion band that I'm working on. And Dick (Shearer) and I have been co-leading the Detroit Trombone Section, which is more a commercial band than a jazz band. I was on the road a lot before I joined the Kenton band.

L.A.: Who were you on the road with before?

SUTER: Motown band. Lots of things. Pee Wee Hunt. I *was* Pee Wee Hunt for a while, when he was sick. Pee Wee Hunt was 68 years old at the time and played trombone. I was 26 at the time and played bass trombone. They introduced me as Pee Wee Hunt and people would come up . . .

L.A.: They DID?

SUTER: People would come up and say, "Pee Wee, you're lookin' better'n you have in years!" "Oh! Thank you!" "You remember my wife Irma?" "Ya! How ya doin', Irma?"

L.A.: (Laughs.)

SUTER: The road was great. The road is a piece of cake. What's so hard about getting on a bus and sitting there? Or getting off the bus and doing what ten thousand other people in the country would give their right arm to do, and you're doing it. What's so hard about that?

L.A.: Some musicians absolutely hated it and would quit after a few months or a year.

SUTER: Oh. Complaining is part of your warm-up. I was naive enough to think of it as a great adventure. You've got a different life-style when you're traveling.

L.A.: I'll say. It's been known to break up a lot of marriages.

SUTER: It wasn't traveling that did that. The road isn't hard. That's just a carry-over from the Glenn Miller movies. All that stuff. Transportation is too well-refined to have traveling be that much of a hardship now. I enjoyed it. It was a once in a lifetime thing to be with a mover like Stan. But it was—it sounds like a paradox when I say it—it was great, but it was no big thing. It was what you made of it.

97

13 Dick Shearer and Mike Suter

SUTER: Southern Illinois, remember we did that?

SHEARER: And I had to go up and . . .

SUTER: Stan's ultimate band!

L.A.: Why was that?

SUTER: Thirty-seven hundred people.

L.A.: (Laughs.) What was this?

SUTER: They brought us to Southern Illinois University to play at the half-time.

L.A.: Oh, the Stan Kenton band? At half-time?

SUTER: It was their band day.

L.A.: You're kidding!

SUTER: So there were like 25 high school bands . . .

L.A.: Oh, wow.

SUTER: And the Stan Kenton band . . .

L.A.: (Laughs.)

SUTER: We played "MacArthur Park." Well fine. Pop-da-da-daa-dot-dot-dot-daa. You can't do that with thirty-seven hundred people. It went p o p-d o t-d o t-d a a-d u d u g u d u d u m-dot-dot. It was ponderous, it was terrible, the people loved it, and it was the perfect-sized band for Stan.

L.A.: (Laughs.) Thirty-seven hundred?

SUTER: He finally had enough people in his band!

SHEARER: And I'm the only one that went *Duh-duh-duh-da-duh-duh-duh-duh.* (Laughs.) I thought about that old joke.

L.A.: What's the old joke?

SHEARER: This piccolo player dies and goes to Heaven, and the Lord grants him one wish. Says he wants to play with great musicians. So *poof* there he's in the Grand Canyon and he looks up, and there's five thousand trumpets. Four thousand trombones. A thousand sousaphones. God only knows how many drummers, and clarinet players and all this. Goes up to the podium and plays that little solo march in "The Stars and Stripes Forever."

SUTER: You can imagine what it was like when they all came in after that.

L.A.: It would have knocked him over!

SHEARER: Would *you* like five thousand people playing two quarter notes in your ear?

SUTER: That's what was happening with Dick. It was him against literally the world.

SHEARER: I had a two-bar solo every time it happened. I'm the only one who played it. *Duh-duh-duh-da-dee-duh-duh-duh.* I'd walk up to the microphone and do that, just me and a couple of soft woodwinds, then I'd step back and all of a sudden WHAAACHHH! *Duh-duh-duh-da-dee-da-da-da. Da-da-daa-da-dee-da-da-da.* WHOH WHOH-WHOH WHOH-WHOH!

SUTER: It was really . . . it was weird.

L.A.: Stan must have loved it. That's his idea of a band, all right.

SUTER: We kidded him about it. We said he finally got enough people in his band to make him happy.

L.A.: A new high in tone color! Why do you suppose Stan favored trombones so much?

SHEARER: What he said to me was, when he was a young kid, and used to go down and hear the shows 'n' stuff, and he'd hear those trombones in the pit orchestra with that *sound* they used to get, he'd say "Someday I'm gonna have a band with a bunch of trombones." He loved the sound of it. He just loved that rich—that's why the band had a lot of low horns in it. Stanley always said, you need that bottom. You get a good bottom and the top comes out straight. That's why he had the trumpets up there.

L.A.: More people wrote for trombone, then, among Kenton's arrangers.

SUTER: We had more music in every chart than any other horn.

SHEARER: The trumpet book was two inches thick, the saxophone book was two inches thick, the trombone books were three-and-a-half inches thick.

SUTER: There were things you'd look forward to playing, like "Tonight." We played that maybe twice a month. There were three hundred tunes in the book. Once a month you played at least everything once. But some of 'em were killers, where you'd be playing nothing but whole notes. And it hurts to play whole notes.

SHEARER: Ken Hanna lives.

SUTER: Ya. Ken Hanna's stuff. Terrible for trombone players. All you're doing is playing long tones. And pretty soon the band's in Poughkeepsie and you're in Hawaii someplace, blowing your lung out.

L.A.: (Laughs.) My gosh.

SUTER: That's where "How's Hawaii?" comes from. That's what that means. Because you hyperventilate and you're sitting there in your chair and you're playing your pitch but you don't really know where you are sometimes.

L.A.: My gosh.

SUTER: Playing is physical.

L.A.: It takes a lot out of you.

SUTER: That's the thing Stan would do—he'd come up, there'd be a bass player sitting in his chair playing an upright bass, and Stan would walk along and hit him in the shoulder. "Stand up, so I can't knock you down." You'd hear that sort of stuff. And he'd talk about it at the one-day clinics. It's a physical thing. You've got to get involved with it. And he'd show 'em. He'd always use bass, because that was his little thing. He'd show how you have to embrace a bass, how you have to hold it, interact with it. And you have to do that with any horn. It's hard work. He used to talk about that—you can't swing with your brain, you gotta swing somehow with your body. You've gotta have some kind of physical motion in there.

L.A.: It's miraculous that the music never left him, even after his last illness.

SHEARER: First couple of times he sat down at the piano, everybody was nervous, wondering whether the operation had affected that. He sat down and started playing. "What's the name of that?" And it just came right out. At other times he'd get up there with the band, and couldn't remember the bridge to what he was playing.

SUTER: Ya, the chops were a trained reflex action with him. He never lost them. He never had a lot. But there were nights when he was the best emotional piano player in the world. I can't remember where it was in New York, but one night he played "Body and Soul" and the whole band missed the cue. Stan played his chorus and he looked up and gave his downbeat and there're nineteen guys in the band sitting there looking at 'im. Nobody made a move to pick up their horn. Nobody even knew that we were playing a concert. And that doesn't happen to me. I mean I'm not sayin' that for shock value. We all just blew it. We all just missed it. He would do that, once every three or four months. He'd get out alone and he'd play something really great.

L.A.: Some of the best piano music I've heard him do is on his *Chicago* album.

SHEARER: There's another album called *Stan Kenton Solo.* It's all just him and there's times in there where you can hear his whole life. It's very emotional stuff.

SUTER: It's the hardest one to listen to.

SHEARER: Ya. Hard to listen . . . .

L.A.: What did Stan like about you? He must have singled you out for some reason to be such a close friend.

SHEARER: I don't know. Just one of those things that happen. We'd get along very well. We had dinner together almost every night for years, and . . . you know, many a night we'd sit there and not say a word! At dinner. But he was perfectly content. All he had to do was look up, there was somebody there . . .

SUTER: I think that had a lot to do with it. I can speak about that relationship as an outsider. Dick did things for Stan that Stan didn't want to do. Dick took care of the hiring on the band. Stan did the firing. That was their agreement. But also, Dick made no other demands. I mean, one of the tests of a friendship is, you know, you can spend a couple of days together and not have to entertain one another.

SHEARER: Um-hm.

SUTER: I think long before they were friends, Stan trusted Dick. That allowed their friendship to blossom.

L.A.: Why were you so dedicated to Kenton?

SHEARER: I enjoyed it. It's what I wanted to do. I never thought about that when I joined the band, that I'd be doin' all that stuff someday. 'Cause he was a pain in the ass to me at times. He and I used to go around and around. I'd have to fight with him to go out, on our nights off. "Let's go to a *movie,* let's do *something,* come *on!*" Well I'd get 'im going. We'd go out and eat and we'd go see some band somewhere, or catch a film, or some concert, and he comes back and he says, "God *damn* that was great! We gotta do this more often!" Next time we had a night off, I hadda kick him in the butt again. "I gotta go see 'Hello Dolly.' " Pearl Bailey was doin' it. We were in Toronto. We had a night off from the clinic. And I had a hassle with him. We finally got him so he'd go down there, and I sent a note backstage to Pearl that Stan was there. And I'm lookin' over at 'im and he's just *smilin',* oh he's havin' a good time. Pearl got Stan up on stage, and everybody in the place stood up. And he gives me that look as he walks by me, and he gets up there, and afterwards we're in the dressing room. He just had a ball. But to get him to do stuff like that, he'd just as soon go to his room and get juiced.

L.A.: As band manager, you had quite a lot of responsibility toward the running of the band, didn't you?

SHEARER: I used to have to call and make reservations and all that, plus do the payroll.

L.A.: That's quite a load on you, isn't it? Plus playing the book.

SHEARER: Well it got to be a load. It got to be a little scary now and then. You lose $3,000, you wonder where it went. (Laughs.)

L.A.: (Laughs.)

SUTER: Did he think he was paying us a lot of money?

SHEARER: Well, you know . . .

SUTER: No I mean really, I'm not making a joke.

SHEARER: Oh, Christ yes, Mike!

SUTER: He thought he was?

SHEARER: That's one thing Stanley could never get straight in his mind. He was back twenty years ago. I fought with him for I don't know how long. I finally got the base pay up to $250.

SUTER: You know what happened last summer.

SHEARER: I know, it went right back down.

SUTER: It was the lowest paying band . . . in the world.

SHEARER: He thought it was a lot of money!

L.A.: The lowest paying band in the *world?*

SUTER: The lowest paying band in the world.

L.A.: How would he get away with that?

SUTER: People worked for 'im, didn't they?

L.A.: (Laughs.) That's what I'm wondering.

SUTER: There's no union on the road. Who're you gonna call?

L.A.: Would he pay more if you were stationary somewhere?

SUTER: No. You always got paid the same, no matter what. But I mean, if you went out with him, you knew beforehand what you were gonna get. So it was my fault that I got paid that little. I'm not saying it was bad. It just *was*.

L.A.: Maybe the prestige of it made it worth it.

SUTER: Whatever.

SHEARER: (Laughs.) That and a hot dog won't get you a cup of coffee. Here's a payroll sheet from 1968. That was the base pay then. A hundred and fifty bucks.

SUTER: 'Course now, motel rooms were—people will use this argument . . .

SHEARER: It was still the same ten years later.

SUTER: Um-hm.

SHEARER: The prices went up and everything.

L.A.: You mean out of that base salary you had to pay for your own motel room?

SHEARER: Oh ya.

SUTER: Ya.

SHEARER: Except we had a thing later on where anything over eight dollars the band picked up. So you knew it cost you fifty-six dollars a week for your room, and the band picked up everything else. That's why we started staying at Holiday Inns, Ramadas, nice places, where it would cost us—the band itself—up to sixteen dollars a night. The guys would pay eight of that and we'd pick up the rest of it.

L.A.: Was that fairly recently?

SHEARER: It got started around '70, '71. We used to give the guys their money back. They would pay their bill . . .

SUTER: Ya, we paid our own bills.

SHEARER: And I'd reimburse 'em.

SUTER: Every two weeks we'd get reimbursed.

SHEARER: With the exception of when we went to Europe, then we paid all the bills and got the money back from the guys later.

SUTER: At the same time I was on Stan's band—I joined for $250, plus overages—at that very same time Maynard was paying $400 and Maynard paid for the rooms. Woody paid $400 and paid for the rooms. We worked more and got paid less than any band. I joined the band, played the first

night at the St. Nicholas Hotel. Had a night off. Then worked 135 straight nights. I joined the band two days before Stan set his record.

L.A.: What record?

SUTER: A hundred and thirty-five nights without a break. We broke for Christmas.

SHEARER: You've got to have at least twenty to twenty-five grand a week, now. And you couldn't possibly earn that much. You're talking about five, six thousand dollars every night. To make that, you've got to have a hell of a good name.

SUTER: The worst part is, the recording company never made money. So guess who made up that money? The band did. The publishing company never made money. Guess who made up that money? The band did. So if the band made—the band was working for $2500 a night—what we made on the road went to support the entire Creative World. Not just the band. They made as much for the Kenton band as they would for Maynard Ferguson, yet their guys were getting a hundred and fifty dollars a week plus motel rooms more than we were.

SHEARER: And Stan was always broke! (Laughs.)

L.A.: Kenton's life story is peppered with the times that he could have gone more commercial and made the money.

SUTER: That's okay. That's what he wanted to do. And we chose to stay with him. The people who went on the band chose it—nobody held a gun to our heads. So we don't have any right to complain about it. And I'm not. I enjoyed what I did.

SHEARER: But the band was not one of the highest-grossing bands. That was part of the problem. They would book us for $2500 a night, $2,000 a night. We used to have a hell of a party every time the band broke $20,000. We didn't have too many of those.

L.A.: But he would do it because he wanted to play that kind of music, right?

SHEARER: Well, he'd try to keep working. It got a little bit better in the later years.

L.A.: That's what I think is heroic about him, to want to stick with his music even though it wasn't really commercially rewarding. How many people do you know who will do that?

SHEARER: (Looking in accounts book.) Okay, let's see. This week was $9970. We had a $6900 week. We had an $8,000 week. This was all 1968. Thirty-four hundred. At $3400, we were still on the road all week.

L.A.: How much did you have to pay the members of the band? About twenty people—that's $4,000 right there, isn't it?

SHEARER: The net payroll was $3,000. Not gross. Net. Which still had to be met on the Coast.

SUTER: But we never missed a payroll.

SHEARER: No.

SUTER: We were—

SHEARER: There were times when we were late. Gross, $8,000. *$10,000*. We must have had a hell of a time then. $9,000. $9,000. $7,000. This is still 1968. In 1978 it was better. We were probably around 19-20. When we'd go to Europe it would be another story.

L.A.: Why was that?

SHEARER: We'd make a lot more money over there. But then again we had a lot more expenses. Time we were in Rome, cost the guys eight bucks a night, and the hotel room was $40. So we picked up the other $32 ourselves. Stan did.

SUTER: When the band had the occasional five- or six-thousand-dollar job, the band didn't get paid any more.

SHEARER: No. See that's the way . . .

L.A.: Would it go to Creative World, then?

SUTER: Yeah, exactly!

SHEARER: It would go there, sure.

SUTER: It would go to Stan Kenton Incorporated. Or whatever you want to call it.

SHEARER: 'Course, some weeks we only worked three days. Well the band was paid for the whole week.

SUTER: Um-hm.

SHEARER: Bus expense. Every time the band'd fly somewhere . . .

L.A.: As long as you're leveling with me, tell me this: would a guy join the Stan Kenton band because it was the only offer he got?

SUTER: No.

L.A.: Or because he wanted to be in the Stan Kenton band?

SUTER: Ya. Um-hm.

SHEARER: You joined because you wanted to be in Stan's band.

L.A.: If you had three offers, and two of them were from Maynard Ferguson and Woody Herman . . .

SUTER: Yeah, if you were in your right mind you wouldn't join Stan's band. Businesswise it was the worst mistake I ever made. But like I said, I decided when I was twelve.

L.A.: You said it was because you wanted to play bass trombone. Is that the only reason you wanted to join?

SUTER: That's the only reason I wanted to join.

SHEARER: How many bass trombone . . .

L.A.: They don't have bass trombones in the other orchestras?

SUTER: They do, but they're nothin'.

SHEARER: Nothin'. They're *nothin'*.

SUTER: I mean, there's some substance to what was happening there.

L.A.: Would you say that Kenton created his own idiom, or wouldn't you go that far? Classical jazz, is there such a thing?

SUTER: Whatever it was, he made it himself. Ya. I would go that far.

L.A.: He's got his own definition of what he did, right?

SUTER: Oh ya. He had his own definition of what swing was.

L.A.: Isn't that why he doesn't fit neatly into anybody's category?

SUTER: That's true.

L.A.: Why they're always shaking their fists at him.

SUTER: Sure.

L.A.: Because he made his own kind of music.

SUTER: Ya. Um-hm.

L.A.: Would you call that classical jazz?

SUTER: No.

L.A.: Concert jazz.

SUTER: I'd call it Stan Kenton. I don't even call it jazz. I don't think Stan Kenton ever played jazz, or his band ever played jazz, after 1954.

L.A.: What would you call that kind of music?

SUTER: Stan Kenton. I'm not being evasive.

L.A.: Come on. You can't label a kind of music "Stan Kenton."

SUTER: I sure as hell can.

SHEARER: He used to call it "concert jazz."

L.A.: Nobody's ever put the whole picture together.

SHEARER: Nothing will happen about Stanley 'til about two years from now.

L.A.: And then what?

SHEARER: Then they'll get some kind of movement goin' and all of a sudden everybody's gonna realize what great things he's done.

L.A.: Stan's a cultivated taste. Not that many people in the United States even care about him, or know who he is. But the people who are involved in music do. Disc jockeys do. Musicians do.

SUTER: He used to say some little dumb things that just killed me. We played a concert in Jackson, Michigan, once, at Central High School. Somebody had let off a stink bomb. We smelled it, it was no big deal. It wasn't in the auditorium, it was in some other part of the school. And he was straight. We're playin' the thing, played the first half, came back for the second half, and he said, "I understand somebody let off a stink bomb in the school here. I understand some of you people thought it was the band. Well, I'm sorry somebody let off a stink bomb." He turned to walk back, took about four steps, turned around. Walked back to the mike, says, "*We* thought it was *you*." (Laughs.) I couldn't play the next two tunes.

SHEARER: He'd always say things like that. Sometimes he'd forget about how great some of the acoustics were. And he'd be straight as an arrow and he'd say something to me that would just floor me, and people in the front two seats are just *dyin'* laughin'. And he catches them out of the corner of his eye, he says (*whispers*) *"Can they hear me?"* And I says "Oh yes. Because you said it right into my microphone."

L.A.: (Laughs.)

SHEARER: He would do things to try to break us up. We were working some country club. The bandstand was up about this high, and there were bushes. We're playing some ballad, Stanley *disappears*. All of a sudden he peeks through the bushes, goes "VERY INTERESTING." That stopped the trombones. And when he'd tell us some corny joke just before the curtain would go up, he'd time it perfectly. Curtain would go up and he'd give the downbeat right at the punch line. Jamieson was on the band. That poor guy. I'd have to send him away, he'd start laughin' so hard. Took us twenty minutes to get through the first eight bars of "Rainy Day." He'd *always* do stuff like this.

SUTER: I got *him* once, though. It was in Michigan. We played up at Mott Community College. Their band leader had this multi-colored patchwork vest on. He came around. Bus pulled up to the clinic. He came out the door, waving at the bus, and he came running around to the side of the bus. And just as he reached for the bus door I said "Stan whatever you do, don't laugh at his vest."

L.A.: (Laughs.)

SUTER: Well that did it. Door opens— "Mr. Kenton, how are ya!" and Stan's just draped over the thing, tears running down his face. Poor guy never knew what hit him.

SHEARER: Oh I'd get him good. Any time someone would go weird he'd look over at me. "Dick! Are you behind this?" We'd alway do strange things when he'd have his back to us.

SUTER: He stopped the band one time in Springfield, Ohio. We were at the St. Nicholas Hotel. You had stolen Keim's mouthpiece. We were playing "Peanut Vendor." And Keim's sittin' there, with no mouthpiece. Stan got mad and stopped the band. "Who's got his mouthpiece?" Dick reached in his vest. Put the mouthpiece back. We started it again.

SHEARER: I was probably the only one to get away with it.

SUTER: I got Dick one night and almost got fired for it. Dick would drop a dime in your mouthpiece—then you'd blow, and nothing would happen. Dick told me that I would never get him. Well that was an immediate challenge.

SHEARER: Wrong choice of words.

SUTER: So this is like a year and a half later. We were in Jeff City, Missouri. We had some game that used golf tees in our rooms. I took a golf tee with me. We were playing "Intermission Riff." Two other tenor trombones go out front to play their solos. Dick stays in the middle. The two bass trombones move in to the inside of the section, so when the jazz players come back they can just sit down on the outside, 'cause it's the last thing before intermission, and it made the logistics of playing the chart a lot easier. So we moved on in. Dick turned around and was saying somethin' to the trumpets. I took the golf tee and put it in his mouthpiece. No big deal, he discovered that. 'Cause he always, always looked. So I took a dime, and it went: "CLANG!" And Dick's turned to the trumpets, he could see it went clang. He knew the dime was in there. I knew I had 'im. He picked up his horn and dropped the dime out. Stan was so mad at me. It was obvious who did it. None of us were playing. Sodersack and I were giggling, and I was on the floor.

SHEARER: And I was laughin'.

SUTER: Oh, he was mad. "I want to see you at the break." He bawled me out. I didn't pay any attention to any of it. (Laughs.)

L.A.: I suppose if it went on all the time, he really couldn't single you out.

SUTER: That band was like the *Waltons*.

L.A.: (Laughs.)

SUTER: We'd get to the hotel after the job: "Goodnight Stan." "Goodnight Mike." "Goodnight Stan." "Goodnight Dick." "Goodnight Dick." "Goodnight Mike." "Goodnight Tom." "Goodnight George." (Laughs.)

SHEARER: (Laughing.) It was *awful*. *You couldn't get off the bus for five minutes!* I forgot all about that.

101

It is true that American music must, of necessity, be the partial accumulation

of the best that has gone before us.

Ken Hanna and his wife at their home in El Cajon, California. (Photo by the Author).

14 Ken Hanna

HANNA: *When Stan formed his Neophonic Orchestra I called him and asked if I could write for it. I wrote "Tiare." I thought that would be my swan song, the last thing I would ever write. But a couple of years later something happened that led me back to Stan.*

L.A.: *What was that?*

HANNA: *I was shipwrecked in Mexico for a year. And during that time Stan and other people sent me money to keep me afloat, literally. The boat and me.*

L.A.: You're talking about *literally* shipwrecked or is this just a colorful way of speaking?
HANNA: Not at all. I was run aground in Mexico. Stan's A & R man, Lee Gillette, heard about it, and stopped in to visit me down there. He told Stan and they took up a little pool and sent me money. When I got back I went in to see Stan. He was putting a band together again and starting Creative World, making the break from Capitol. He said, "Why don't you go ahead and write something? Write 'Tiare.' You did for the Neophonic." I couldn't figure out what a tune like this would be doing on a dance album or in a dance band, but I wrote it. I knew what he was doing—he was just trying to get me off my butt. Then one day, I was clerking in a music store, just to keep the wolf away from the door, when I got a phone call from some guy in Cleveland. "Stan wants you writing for us." I was in Los Angeles, still living on a boat—not the one that got wrecked, but another one. Got a plane ticket, took off, joined Stan in Syracuse and stayed on the bus for two years.
L.A.: You had already written "Tiare" for the Neophonic. What did he mean, write it again?

HANNA: Score it down for the dance orchestra.
L.A.: Was this the late sixties?
HANNA: No, early seventies.
L.A.: Besides "Tiare," what did you write about that time?
HANNA: "Bon Homme Richard." That was for Dick Shearer. All within a year or two of each other I wrote "Lonely Windrose," "Fragments of a Portrait," "Beeline East," and "Theme for Autumn." "Tiare" was actually first written in 1948.
L.A.: All of your compositions seem to have change built right into them—I think that's why Stan must have liked your style so much. They start off in a certain way and then there are all these different kinds of progressions—changes of tonality, rhythmic changes. They add to the color of the Stan Kenton sound.
HANNA: This was what he liked so much in the later years, the idea of making almost every tune a concert piece.
L.A.: They *sound* like concert pieces.
HANNA: Sure. So that, if you didn't have something, or at least *try* to get something unique and unusual and different, in each arrangement, I don't think he was ever completely satisfied.

L.A.: Some composers cook with their material for years, and some others seem to get it all in a flash. In your own case, how long would, say, something like "Fragments of a Portrait" have been cooking in your head before they played it?
HANNA: In advance? Not at all.
L.A.: You got right down and . . .
HANNA: Just sat down at the piano and, in the course of doodling around, just working on melody lines, why, I came up with that, and then gradually it evolved into a full lead sheet. And then from there on I made the arrangement.
L.A.: How long does it take to make the arrangement?
HANNA: That depends. If it goes real well you can do something maybe in three days. Somebody else can do it in six hours.
L.A.: When did you first start writing?
HANNA: I started copying records when I was about sixteen.
L.A.: Did you always want to be a musician?
HANNA: No. I wanted to be a baseball player.
L.A.: Until you were sixteen?
HANNA: Even after. In fact, I became captain of the Kenton softball team.
L.A.: You did! (Laughs.) There must

have been a dividing point where you said well one of these has to be my career, and you chose music.

HANNA: Well—it seems as though I was always winding up in music one way or another. Somebody would call or I would stumble into something that led to music. It was in and out. A lot of it depended on finances.

L.A.: You got involved in it by listening to records and copying down what you heard, making arrangements, and you found that you enjoyed that?

HANNA: Um-hm.

L.A.: How did you evolve into the kind of composer you are now, with all that imagination and invention and creativity?

HANNA: You don't start out with that. You get there by listening to all types of music, and by practicing, analysis, and reproduction. A lot of it is just plain old copy-work.

L.A.: Are there people you particularly admired in composing that you perhaps wanted to emulate, or that influenced you in some way?

HANNA: Certain classical writers I've always liked. The Romantics. People like Debussy, Ravel, Ibert. Stravinsky.

And every dance band that ever came along, when I was studying music and getting started. So I was soaking it up, even though I didn't know it.

L.A.: Do you recall when you began to feel the urge or pull toward changing around the tonalities and the time structure in your compositions? I'm thinking of a work like "Beeline East," where, instead of playing the exact same thing all the way through for three minutes, it comes to a point where it slows down: "Ba-ba-BA-Bah!" and then you modulate it to a different tonality and pick up the tempo again.

HANNA: Kenton wanted every tune to be concert-length, so we'd be playing as a five- or six-, seven-minute number what other dance bands would be playing as a three-minute arrangement. Hank Levy's things run nine minutes.

L.A.: So this was because he wanted pieces that were more concertized?

HANNA: He wanted spark, he wanted the whole works. On every arrangement. If it wasn't strong, it couldn't get played.

L.A.: Do you have a favorite chord structure or arrangement that you use to experiment?

HANNA: No. There are patterns that

you get into. You don't mean to; you don't want to. But you get used to doing the same thing and pretty soon you say hey—Did I write that? And you go look up and see what you did two or three years ago, and your tune might be pretty close to the same thing. You might have written it twice, and didn't know it.

L.A.: What would be a typical pattern for you? You do a lot of different things.

HANNA: My patterns, my devices—like any arranger's—are always pretty much the same. I like to write for trombone solo, for example. Maybe because I played trombone originally, before switching to trumpet.

L.A.: Dick Shearer and Mike Suter were kidding about you. They were saying how difficult it is for a trombone player to play whole notes because they run out of oxygen, and pretty soon the band is here and they're in Hawaii. And one of them said "Ken Hanna lives!" They found your music beautiful, but somewhat challenging to play because of the wind problem.

HANNA: Good.

L.A.: (Laughs.) You don't care about that, do you. "Play it anyway, buddy."

HANNA: *Stan* never cared about it. He said, "Play it."

Ken Hanna at the piano in his home, El Cajon, California. (Photo by the Author.)

L.A.: They're not the only ones who said that.

HANNA: Trumpet players—they hated me.

L.A.: Why did they hate you?

HANNA: Too many notes, too high, too long.

L.A.: Too high?

HANNA: Um-hm. That was *their* complaint. But somebody else'd come along and give them the same thing, and they'd say, "Hey. *Great*." But remember, I wrote a lot of ballad things. And I would be thinking one tempo, which would be a reasonably playable tempo, and Stan would then slow it down to . . .

L.A.: A*ha*.

HANNA: . . . a *crawl*.

L.A.: (Laughs.)

HANNA: That means the notes get *longer*. Oh yeah.

L.A.: Well you're not to blame. (Laughs.) Kenton has said that you wrote most of the romantic ballads.

HANNA: Ya, well he liked to tag people with different titles, you know, so it was a good way for him to present me. On the ballad side.

L.A.: But ballads aren't the only thing you did.

HANNA: I guess I probably lean that way more than any other.

L.A.: "Bogota," I'm thinking of. On the London record.

HANNA: Most of what we recorded over in London that was mine had to be thrown out, because the recording quality was so poor. I've written lots of things that were never recorded, a lot of things that were never played. Stan was very unusual in that we always knew whether or not our arrangements were going to get played.

L.A.: How did you know that?

HANNA: At rehearsals Stan would let the arrangers and composers rehearse their own works. You could tell after the first hour. You just had a way of sensing it, that he liked it or he didn't like it. In the earlier days, in the forties, we would rehearse and rehearse and tunes would get played until they worked in. You had to take time to work tunes in. It takes time for an arrangement to jell. We worked our tails off to make sure that the arrangements were right, and a lot of them he really rammed home. In the later days it never happened that way. It was a weird change to see. 'Cause I was there for both times.

L.A.: In the later days he wouldn't give it time to jell?

HANNA: I remember one guy wrote six or eight arrangements, originals, for a record date. Stan rehearsed them for two days, picked them all up, and threw them into the trash basket. With a few choice words.

L.A.: You first met Stan, then, in the forties?

HANNA: I guess the first time I really became aware of Stan Kenton would be in 1941, when we listened to air checks coming from Balboa.

L.A.: What is an air check?

HANNA: That was the popular name used for half-hour and hour segments of the band playing from some ballroom, sometimes on transcription, sometimes direct, that were broadcast on the air, sometimes nationally. Every band had a special night.

L.A.: The exposure for the Stan Kenton band must have been terrific. I understand people would stay tuned to their radios for news of the war, and when the East Coast stations went off the air the Pacific Coast stations came in.

HANNA: He had a clear field. Stan came to my home town, Baltimore, in 1942, for a night club date. I had a band of my own then, and one of my musicians wanted to try out with Stan. He didn't make it, but he told me that Stan was looking for a writer. That's where my first love was. Always has been. So I went to the club and introduced myself to Stan. He suggested that I try doing a couple of sample arrangements and bring them to a rehearsal. This was a very unusual thing because I'd been turned down by everybody, practically.

L.A.: I can't believe it.

HANNA: Harry James . . .

L.A.: I can't believe it.

HANNA: Sammy Kaye . . .

L.A.: Why would they turn you down?

HANNA: In those days they didn't give you much of an opportunity to get your foot in the door.

L.A.: Why didn't they like your kind of music? I think it's fabulous.

HANNA: They'd never heard it.

L.A.: They hadn't heard it, but they wouldn't give you a chance anyway?

HANNA: No. No, they had their own writers, their own pet way of going, and you just, it was very difficult to enter into the writing end at all. In those days I would have written anything, for free, just to hear it played. So Stan was good enough to say, "Write something and let me hear it and bring it on in to our rehearsal."

L.A.: Was he merely looking for something new, or did he specifically need a writer at the time?

HANNA: He needed a writer. His other writers were back on the Coast, and he was doing his own writing. He wasn't really satisfied with the people who had been doing his writing for him. It didn't fit the sound that he wanted.

L.A.: The strain that you're talking about, that he was looking for, I can hear in your music. How is it that what you write sounds like what Stan wants to hear? Were you already writing in what we might call a Stan Kenton style, which he recognized and loved, or did you join the band first and then figure out what he wanted?

HANNA: I had an advantage of sorts. I did an awful lot of copying records in the early days of my writing. I would take these arrangements off the record to use in my own band.

L.A.: How do you do that?

HANNA: You sit down, with a lot of patience . . .

L.A.: You can *hear* all that?

HANNA: Yes.

L.A.: You can hear what everybody's doing on a record?

HANNA: You have to go slowly. You work with a piano and make the chords and the melody structure and so forth. So having done that often enough I could duplicate the sounds of Benny Goodman, Glenn Miller, Stan Kenton—you name it, I could come pretty close to the style that they had. And so in that way I was able to maybe jump in there and get his sound.

L.A.: Was the music you were writing for your own band substantially different from what you did for Stan?

HANNA: I was writing pretty much in the style of what you could say was standard dance bands in those days. Once in a while I took a crack at trying to do an original tune. It was a long time before I had the courage to really get in and write any of my own material.

L.A.: That started when you joined Stan's band?

HANNA: A little bit prior, but mostly with Stan and then on.

L.A.: What were those first two arrangements you did for him?

HANNA: I don't remember exactly. They were standards, one ballad and one rhythm tune. They had the Kenton sound because I used that same type of voicing, particularly in the saxes. He seemed to be very pleased with the results, and that led to our keeping in contact with each other. By mail, usually, or phone. As long as he was on the East Coast, he would send me tunes, and I would arrange them, whether for the vocalists or for the band, and send them back to him.

L.A.: In other words, you did not join Stan's band per se at that time?

HANNA: No. I was going to, but all of a sudden Uncle Sam was right behind me. So I enlisted in the Navy, and that postponed my joining the band for three and a half years. Stan and I had an agreement all during the war years that I would keep writing for him and send him the tunes. I was stationed in Baltimore, so that was fortunate. I had use of a piano, and one solid location where I could do all the work. So we kept in touch with each other. And I would go out and catch the band whenever they were close to Baltimore.

L.A.: When you joined, did you play in the band too, as well as write?

HANNA: Oh yes. In 1946 I joined on trumpet. I stayed for two years, then went back to Baltimore and taught for two years at the GI School of Music.

L.A.: What did you teach?

HANNA: A little bit of everything. Whatever somebody else didn't want to do, I did. I had orchestras to conduct, such as state bands, and taught arranging, composing, a little bit of theory . . .

L.A.: What do you teach, when you teach arranging?

HANNA: Everyone's talent and ability and understanding is at a different level. First thing you start out with is a grounding in theory. And build up from there to the use of chords and melodic lines and an understanding of transposition. During this time Stan had his Innovations Orchestra on the road, and when he passed through Baltimore he said "Why don't you come out to the Coast? I'm gonna put the dance band back together and you can start writing again." So I packed up, bag and baggage, and brought the family on out here. Since then it's been my home. In 1951 I went back to work for Stan for not quite a year, while he was putting the dance band together. But he had quite a few people writing for him then, Shorty Rogers and others, and he had as much music as he could use at that time. So in order to keep the family together I became a salesman, a purchasing agent, I did a little bit of everything. A few years later some friends of mine talked me into putting a band together out here. We spent a couple of years rehearsing it and cut a couple of recordings with it. I wrote "Bogota" for that band. We played a few dates locally, up in L. A.

L.A.: Then what happened to it?

HANNA: Money. Money happened to it. I got out of that and didn't do any more writing until the Neophonic. That's when I went back and called Stan and asked if I could write something for him.

L.A.: And that was "Tiare."

HANNA: That was "Tiare."

L.A.: What are some of the things you wrote for Stan in the earlier period?

HANNA: I remember vividly, the first original I did for Stan was about 1948, and that was "Somnambulism."

L.A.: The Progressive Jazz era. That's great.

HANNA: We were doing concert pieces then. He was getting into it in a big way. Where we all wore the ascots. I did quite a few arrangements backing up June Christy, and, in the early days, Anita O'Day and Red Dorris.

L.A.: Are you still writing?

HANNA: Yes, I'm free-lancing and doing a little bit of teaching. Every once in a while I'll do a semester up here at San Diego State.

L.A.: Whom are you free-lancing for?

HANNA: Anybody that happens to need some music at the time. Groups, singers, big dance bands.

L.A.: Why don't you do something on your own, form another orchestra or something? You're a wonderful composer. Your music should get more of a hearing.

HANNA: It might surprise you to know that I tried desperately about 1971 or '72 to get my own band together. Another one. I was hoping to go out and play a lot of the music that Kenton never played, actually.

L.A.: That you wrote that . . .

HANNA: That I wrote, that other people wrote. 'Cause we had tons of music coming into that band that was never heard. Literally.

L.A.: I've often wondered about that. With so many full-time arrangers and composers on the Kenton band at any given time, and so few pieces ever getting on record, one has to wonder whatever became of all the rest of the music that was written. Where is it, what happened to it. It'll never be heard, and that's terrible.

HANNA: Well I was very frustrated about the whole thing because doing the clinics I knew we had a choice of an awfully good bunch of good musicians. Excellent musicians.

L.A.: You mean students?

HANNA: Students. College, university people. They knew what they were doing. In fact a lot of them later on came to play with the Kenton band. Out of those clinics. And I wanted to put together a band composed of those people. I had a list seven miles long of people who wanted to get into it. I wanted to put a band out on the road. But Stan blocked me every step of the way.

L.A.: Why is that?

HANNA: Expense. I'm pretty sure, primarily expense.

L.A.: You mean you wanted to put it together for yourself or for him?

HANNA: For myself.

L.A.: But he was opposed to the idea because he thought you'd go under?

HANNA: Yes, I think that was the basic reason. He probably felt he couldn't help me financially, and where that kind of money would come from was anybody's guess, because by that time it was beginning to get a little bit expensive to take a band out on the road.

L.A.: What are some of your compositions that are not on recordings?

HANNA: "Sensitivo" has been recorded, I'm pretty sure, but I don't think it's been released. "Turido" I don't think has been released. "No Media Noche." "Montiya." "Morea."

L.A.: What kind of composition is "Morea"?

HANNA: Supposedly representative of the South Seas.

L.A.: Is it in classical style like your other works?

HANNA: It's got a little bit of classical form to it, but written for a dance band. "Westwind" is a ballad I wrote that ties in with "Morea." It's part of a suite I tried to do, dealing with the South Pacific. "Sensitivo" is a theme for trombone and piano, with the full band. "Querida." "Serapo." "Lazy Tiger." And I've done arrangements for "You Go To My Head," "This Is All I Ask," "You Must Believe," "Snowfall," "Wave," "The Song Is You," "Send in the Clowns"—not the recorded one, that's Dave Barduhn's—"Autumn in New York," and "Summer Knows."

L.A.: That's a pretty wild arrangement you did of "What Are You Doing the Rest of Your Life" that opens the *London* album. Just sensational. I guess that's on the *Brigham Young* album too, isn't it.

HANNA: Yes. *Macumba Suite* is also on *Brigham Young*.

L.A.: Hank Levy's compositions are on some of the same albums as yours. You and he were good friends, weren't you?

HANNA: You better bet your boots. He played in my band the first job he ever got, back in Baltimore.

L.A.: How did you meet him?

HANNA: We needed a saxophone player. He was the only one in town that had a baritone. So I hired him. We were always close from then on. Later, when I was stationed in Baltimore, I recruited him for the Navy.

L.A.: Is that doing him a favor? (Laughs.)

HANNA: (Laughs.) He came into the Navy, and I happened to be there.

L.A.: Did you influence each other?

HANNA: No. I don't think I had an influence on him. Although he played in my orchestra, I don't recall that he ever wrote anything for me at the time. It wasn't until he got into the Navy that he started writing. We were both interested in the same type of music. He was playing Kenton arrangements even in my band. I was out here on the Coast writing for Stan when he got out of the service, and I got him a job playing with Stan. He took Bob Gioga's place. Stayed for a few months, then left for family reasons. During that time he started writing for Kenton a little bit. Then later he got to writing for other orchestras back in Baltimore, and got into his business of school stage bands, writing for them.

L.A.: He's very important in the clinics, isn't he? Really believed in them.

HANNA: He's tremendous with the students. He's fabulous.

L.A.: You must have been a popular favorite when you went up to his college, Towson State, because of your friendship with him.

HANNA: Well no, he had so much going on there, and the Kenton band was so overwhelming to the students. Everybody got along with everybody; it wasn't a question of who had any more influence.

L.A.: It was really exciting to the students? It wasn't just a week away from home?

HANNA: They'd go out of their *minds* working. Never stopped from morning 'til night. They had to be recommended by their teachers to get there in the first place. We would mail out flyers to let them know about it at the different schools in each area.

L.A.: Most of them knew about the Stan Kenton Orchestra and what they would be getting into, and that was why they came?

HANNA: Oh absolutely.

L.A.: Would you ever get feedback as to how these clinics might have affected their lives?

HANNA: I've had some very good people who are turning out very good arrangements whom I hope we might have helped in some way. But you can only do so much in a week. The arranging thing is tricky; it's not like, say, a trumpet section where if a guy has problems you can straighten him out pretty fast. Incidentally, the clinics were very well supervised. The big ones, like at Drury, Towson State and Redlands, would have gone on for years longer if Stan had been able to continue.

L.A.: Did Stan have a favorite among your compositions?

HANNA: If he did it would have to be between "Tiare" and "Bogota."

L.A.: When you rejoined him in the seventies, how long did you stay?

HANNA: Almost until his death. Stan and I have always been very close. Twice when he was sick I went out and fronted the band. We were out there sometimes for about three months. It was a matter of just getting on and off the bus and doing the date where we were and trying to explain to all the promoters where Stan wasn't. 'Cause we didn't let anybody know. The band would have been down the drain. Promoters would have cancelled like flies. So we kept it going during those periods of his illness. Actually, for quite a while, maybe a year, the band wasn't really in existence. He was that ill. He kept going as long as he could, and then he just had to call it quits.

L.A.: What most impressed you about him? What do you feel was his biggest contribution to music?

HANNA: (Pauses.) You know you're asking for an awful lot there. I can't wrap up anything like that. One thing that was so fantastic about him throughout most of his years was his memory.

L.A.: For people?

HANNA: For people, for anything. Now that doesn't sound like it fits into a music situation. But I'll give you ten to one that if Stan hadn't had that fantastic memory, he might have been long forgotten. He made more friends by having such a fantastic memory. I met him, spoke to him for about fifteen minutes and came back three days later—he remembered my name. First name and last name. That's the thing that struck you. He would go back, year after year, to different places, where he'd played before, and he'd talk to a guy and say "Hi, Jack, how are you?" It would be *Jack*. Another thing was his ability to dramatize the music. Six-foot-four, arms like an eagle's wings—watching him conduct, he'd be all over the place.

That was very dramatic. And that helped put the music across.

L.A.: Brought out some more of the excitement that was already there.

HANNA: Ya. People'd look at that and they'd think, *Wow*.

L.A.: What about his impact on the American musical scene?

HANNA: I've heard other people say, and I agree with it, a lot of the voicings that they use now in television and movies, radio and bands, other bands, those voicings were not being used at all, the sound and the scope of the sound, until he started doing it. For so many years, the saxes in every dance band in the country played 1-2-3-4, and if you had a fifth, he doubled the lead. Wrote the score right down the chord. Always. Never any change. You could see a little of that branching out in the Miller sax section, where the saxes would open every once in a while. But Stan opened 'em up fast, and big. He opened up the brass. It couldn't get too big for him. And dimension. Every time he'd add a new man he was adding another dimension to it.

L.A.: That's adding an interval to the harmonic structure?

HANNA: Um-hm. Um-hm. Um-hm.

L.A.: Like a seventh or a ninth or a tenth? Something dissonant.

HANNA: It's not his alone—those devices have been used throughout the years by some of the classical writers. I don't know how far back we can go, but you'll hear it in recent classical writers. He got more out of a dance band than had been tried. He heard certain sounds. When I first joined the band, we all used vibrato. When I was last with the band, *nobody* used vibrato. He wanted that cold, icy feel of . . . . He was fishing a lot. Trying to find the right sound for his sax section. He never did find it. Probably the guy who came closest was Lennie Niehaus. And the ones he did himself. But at least we got into voicings in the saxes that were different from what other bands were using.

L.A.: You've obviously made sacrifices yourself to stay with music, just as Stan did. So you have something in common with him. Given the choice, he would get experimental, and it seems to me that there's some of that in you too.

HANNA: Sure there is. Anybody who writes music, I'm sure, feels a certain amount of satisfaction from hearing his own work. You get up there in front of a band and rehearse your own music—it never sounds exactly like you expected it to. That's the biggest thrill of all.

15 Jack Elliott

L.A.: *In connection with The New American Orchestra, you said you felt that Stan Kenton's shadow was very much around.*

ELLIOTT: *Well he's there. I mean everybody knows that the Neophonic was in existence.*

L.A.: How well did you know Stan Kenton?

ELLIOTT: I didn't know Stan very well at all. I knew him well enough to shake hands with and say how are you.

L.A.: Where did you meet him?

ELLIOTT: Probably on some show like the Grammys or something like that that I was conducting and he attended.

Jack Elliott in his office, Los Angeles, California. (Photo by the Author.)

I'm not even sure. It could have been a recording studio.

L.A.: Did you ever hear the Neophonic?

ELLIOTT: My former partner, Allyn Ferguson, had written a piece for one of the concerts. So I went to see the concert.

L.A.: What did you think of it?

ELLIOTT: I thought it was terrific. I really don't remember too much about it. I know Johnny Williams wrote a piece for him, I remember Ferg wrote a piece, and after that my memory is totally hazy.

L.A.: There actually were some people who wrote for Stan who also write for you. Bill Russo, Russ Garcia, Dave Grusin, and Dick Grove, to name a few. And Claus Ogerman did an arrangement for Kenton for the Neophonic.

ELLIOTT: That's interesting.

L.A.: So I was wondering just what the connection might be between Stan's Neophonic and your orchestra. Was it just that some of the same composers have written for both?

ELLIOTT: There is no connection.

L.A.: But you're doing the same kind of thing, aren't you? Don't you exist for the purpose of playing new American music?

ELLIOTT: Well we exist for the purpose of really—I guess two or three main reasons. Number one is to commission new music. By composers who are able to write in a certain . . . I guess to sum up what we did was to bridge the gap—there seems to have been a gap that had been created over the years between so-called classical music and American indigenous music, which in essence is really jazz-oriented. The classical is Western European music, and our music is jazz. Which is native to our culture.

L.A.: Well that's just what Kenton wanted to do all his life, wasn't it?

ELLIOTT: I never really was involved in any conversation with Stan or with any—I didn't know what the ethic was, if there was one or—Stan was Stan Kenton. I didn't know Stan Kenton enough to have ever spent any time or to go into it. I know in my own case and in the case of Allyn—we were partners when we formed—when we founded this situation it was a question of really addressing ourselves to what would happen if we got some people to write for the best players around that we could find. Could we continue, could we formalize it, could we keep the orchestra alive, could we have a season. We gave one concert, that was the first

thing, three years ago in April (1979). And we felt we could go forward from there, because we raised enough money to do so.

L.A.: What's the make-up of your orchestra?

ELLIOTT: It's a more or less orthodox symphony-type set-up that gets less orthodox when you examine the nature of the ten woodwinds. There are an awful lot of really jazz-oriented doublers that are in it. Outside of that it has four trumpets, four trombones, four horns, and a tuba. Big string section—24 violins, 10 violas, eight celli, six basses. Two keyboards, four percussion, two guitars, drummers to fit, depending. So there are a lot of similarities, and also a lot of dissimilarities, with Stan's Neophonic. The Orchestra USA with John Lewis and Gunther Schuller was trying to do something similar to what we were doing. There've been attempts, all along the line, to do something like this. And I guess we're just another attempt to do it.

L.A.: You seem to be succeeding, however.

ELLIOTT: Well we're alive. (Laughs.) That's the most important thing. This is the end of the third season and we're still alive and it looks like we'll be able to go forward. I'm hopeful that we will go forward.

L.A.: How many concerts do you give a year?

ELLIOTT: We give four a year.

L.A.: Same as the Neophonic. There's another similarity. You must have it spread out, evidently.

ELLIOTT: It's spread between October and April.

L.A.: One every other month?

ELLIOTT: No, there's nothing really that determines it except—at the beginning it was—we tried to do six one year, we were only able to do five; we tried to do five, we were only able to do four. We did four, and then—we said we were going to do four and did four. This is the first year we didn't have to cancel a concert for lack of funds. It's very difficult to continue to build that audience. It's *very* expensive. And raising funds is probably the single biggest problem, and I'm sure Stan must have run into the same thing.

L.A.: That's why he folded.

ELLIOTT: Ya. I'm sure.

L.A.: He lost forty-five thousand dollars.

ELLIOTT: Well, in those days it was a hell of a lot of money. We lose that almost per *concert.*

L.A.: You're still *losing* money?

ELLIOTT: Oh, my God. These concerts cost in the neighborhood of sixty thousand dollars apiece, when you consider commissions and copying and rehearsals and publicity.

L.A.: And the concert hall.

ELLIOTT: Oh ya.

L.A.: That was a big expense for Stan, the concert hall.

ELLIOTT: The concert hall still remains a big expense. We lose—our average deficit over the three-year period's been about a hundred to a hundred and twenty-five thousand a year, so . . .

L.A.: How do you stay afloat?

ELLIOTT: By constantly being involved in fund-raising. Going out there and trying to raise money.

L.A.: Where do you get your support?

ELLIOTT: Basically it's come from a group of people from the community who are involved, some in the entertainment business, some not. Also a certain amount of corporate support, not very much in the beginning; last year we were able to sell a television show to NBC. Which created enough income for The Foundation (for New American Music) to retire the deficit that we had last year. This year we're negotiating with the Canadian General Life Insurance Company to become a corporate underwriter. And we would then be able to go out and do a series of concerts for them throughout the United States, which would be very very helpful. There will be ten target markets at the beginning, for them, in which The Orchestra would do the first half of the program, and they would be fund-raisers for different organizations. Different performing arts councils and/or organizations, maybe symphony orchestras or ballet companies. That's our biggest problem, getting people to underwrite the cost of these concerts. They're expensive, it's very expensive. It costs about twenty thousand, twenty to twenty-five thousand per evening, exclusive of travel, of course, and hotels and stuff. We have an 84-piece orchestra. They have to take off two or three days to do one concert when we travel. We're talking about studio players who really have to replace that income with something else. That twenty-five thousand is for costs. Nobody's making a thousand dollars an evening or anything like that; those are union costs. The actual concert costs somewhere up to twelve to fifteen thousand dollars. Now you're looking at instrument rentals, and you're looking to the fact that the first violin player and the first trumpet player get time and a half. By the time you're through you've got twenty thousand dollars easily, and that's without any fees or without any—without anything. No dressing at all.

L.A.: Would your orchestra be a forum, let's say, for somebody like Bob Graettinger, if he were still alive?

ELLIOTT: Sure.

L.A.: Let's say some young composer in a clinic someplace reads this and says to himself, "Gee, I wonder if I'd have a chance"—what would he have to do?

ELLIOTT: Pick up the phone, write us a score, send us a tape.

L.A.: And then what do you judge it on? What are the criteria you use?

ELLIOTT: We have a board that consists of people like Henry Mancini and Johnny Williams and Dave Grusin. One of them, let's say Mancini, will call and say "Listen, I heard a guy—he's in town and you ought to listen to him." "Okay." So I'll listen. It's a loose network of people who get here and whose works come here and eventually we make some sort of decision. I guess the buck stops here. But there's no set formula. Hopefully by looking at a score or listening to a tape you can say this one has got the ability to handle a large orchestra. That's one of the biggest criteria—have you written, can you write for a large orchestra. Can you orchestrate it properly, so that it's not a student work. I'm not interested at this point in student works. If we're able to raise enough money, one of the first things we're going to do is have an orchestra that consists of players who are not quite up to the level of the ones that are in our orchestra, who will work in a training situation with our people. And we'll do the same thing with composers. We'll be able to play more stuff as we get the funds for that training orchestra. To bring people up to their ability.

L.A.: So would the composer have to have a group perform his work and send in a tape, or . . .

ELLIOTT: Send in the score.

L.A.: And you can tell by looking?

ELLIOTT: Oh yes.

L.A.: I suppose having your orchestra rehearse it would be prohibitively expensive.

ELLIOTT: Two thousand dollars an hour, union scale.

L.A.: What makes you want to do this kind of thing, personally?

ELLIOTT: It's interesting, number one.

L.A.: But it's financially terribly risky.

ELLIOTT: Well there's no risk in it for me, because I don't make any money doing it. I make my money writing for television or movies. I came out here nineteen years ago—June of '63—to be the chief arranger on the Judy Garland television show. I really came to a point in my life where I said, This is *important*. I just think it's important. There's no other reason to do it.

L.A.: The works that you audition have not been performed elsewhere?

ELLIOTT: Not necessarily; some of them we've played have been performed once or twice elsewhere. But as a rule the thrust is towards newly commissioned works. We commission them, and that's an expensive process. We pay thirty-five hundred dollars for a work, which is certainly not a lot of money, but it is a lot when you consider that it takes another fifteen hundred to copy the work. So there's five thousand dollars right there. Add that to the two-thousand-an-hour rehearsal time and by the time we go with it it's close to ten thousand dollars to play the work. It's very expensive. That's part of the reason that a lot of music doesn't get played. New music.

L.A.: You probably don't have many rehearsals.

ELLIOTT: No. So far we've been averaging three rehearsals for a concert. Well that's—you better have an orchestra as good as this one to be able to do that. You can't do that with the average symphony orchestra. You just can't put it together.

L.A.: Sounds like a Rolls-Royce orchestra.

ELLIOTT: It is Rolls-Royce. The musicians are free-lance players whose jobs really depend on their ability to sight-read very very quickly and play performance level almost instantly. The so-called "red-light players," the studio musicians. For the most part they're very finely tuned, able to shift gears and styles very quickly. That's why they're where they are. There's also great freedom they have in not being stuck playing the literature. If you look at the bios on them you'll find an awful lot of them came out of symphony orchestras, came out of teaching positions. They've done it already. They work here for union scale, on Saturdays and Sundays, giving up time that is very valuable to them. They're there because they want to be. It's done out of love, really. On the other hand, the union rules require that they

get paid. You can't work for nothing, according to the union. They were willing to, but we were not allowed to do it—it might set a precedent in terms of other orchestras. That's a problem that doesn't come up in the universities and schools because you don't have the union situation staring at you. But it does come up in a town like this, where you have a big music industry, and precedent has to be taken into consideration.

L.A.: Are you the only orchestra like this in the country?

ELLIOTT: As far as I know we are. The only one that's organized this way. There are only two places, really, that you could do something like this. One is here, and the other is New York. To have that talent pool of studio players.

L.A.: Don't you think it has something to do with attitude in California being far more receptive to this kind of thing?

ELLIOTT: Well let me put it to you this way. California is probably the easiest place in the country to get something started, and probably also the most difficult to keep it going. Whereas New York might be more difficult to get started, but it would be—there's a larger group with more of a history. Californians tend to burn out quickly. You say, why don't you come to the concert? Oh, we've been there already. You've been there already? It worked once or twice. How do you get them to go again? How do you expand that subscription drive? How do you create a group that starts off with maybe a hundred, hundred and fifty people that are interested, and build on it enough to show two thousand and twenty-five people that are coming constantly, that are subscription ticket buyers.

L.A.: How *do* you do that?

ELLIOTT: By experimenting, really, and by public relations, and by staying alive. It's a real catch-22 situation. The way you build it is by staying alive. And the way you stay alive is by raising money. And the way you raise money is by staying alive.

L.A.: (Laughs.) My gosh.

ELLIOTT: You find a way, in that circle you try to find a little spot, say okay, I'm gonna go here this time, I'll try that, I'll try this. The music is the easiest part of this whole thing.

L.A.: What are your public relations avenues?

ELLIOTT: We've tried radio, television, we've had public relations firms that worked for us. We've tried a little of everything.

L.A.: How do people know that you exist, outside of Los Angeles?

ELLIOTT: Word of mouth. Primarily word of mouth.

L.A.: You're probably well-known in Los Angeles by now.

ELLIOTT: I think in a small circle we are. In musical circles.

L.A.: How can you lend credibility to your organization and really build it?

ELLIOTT: By enlarging support groups. This year you've got three hundred, next year try to make it four or five hundred.

L.A.: Are you really deeply, deeply committed to make this thing work over a long period of time?

ELLIOTT: Well I'm gonna do it until I can't do it. Right now we're at a stage where fund-raising is just the key to the whole thing, the key to keeping it alive, without losing its identity or integrity or the substance of what keeps us together. We're about a hundred thousand dollars in the hole again, which is the figure we have every year—it has been the past three years. That's what we lose. Which, in essence, with inflation and all the rest of it, isn't bad.

L.A.: You lose a hundred thousand dollars . . .

ELLIOTT: Ya, we lose a hundred thousand dollars a year. If we were to continue at the same rate, with inflation we'd be at a hundred and fifty thousand dollars by now. We're not. We're at a hundred. So that's in a way a kind of victory.

L.A.: Are people putting money into you and not expecting ever to see it again?

ELLIOTT: It's a non-profit organization, so it's a tax write-off from the standpoint of their contributions. But why people believe in it is hard to say. I think some of it is personal; some people do believe in the idea or come to recognize it might be of importance.

L.A.: You made a record of your first concert. Will there be more recordings, one a year perhaps?

ELLIOTT: No. We paid for that record ourselves. We thought it important that the first concert be recorded. The record companies are not interested in what we're doing yet. Record companies are interested in hits, and you can't be a hit until you're . . . .

L.A.: What are you going to do about it in the future?

ELLIOTT: Play it by ear and see what happens.

L.A.: Would you want to be nationwide if you could?

ELLIOTT: We could—we will be. I would think the next couple of years we will be. We'll have two programs on National Public Radio's *Jazz Alive* this fall. One is a concert that we did at Royce Hall with Gerry Mulligan, at UCLA. The other was the last concert we did, with Tom Scott and Bill Russo's *Urban Trilogy* and Mancini and Mort Stevens. On 250 stations through NPR.

L.A.: Evidently you feel that this kind of thing fills a need in American culture or you wouldn't be doing it. It's the one thing we don't have.

ELLIOTT: I think it's important to recognize that what we do is of value. I'm talking about the people who write music for a living—in films, in television, in jazz, in records, in so-called popular music, jazz-oriented, whatever you want to call it. It's important that it be given its proper place in American cultural circles, or at least be recognized. If we stop to think about it, American popular music is probably the single most important export we've ever had.

L.A.: What do you suppose American people want of their culture?

ELLIOTT: I don't think they know themselves.

L.A.: Are we still imitating Europe?

ELLIOTT: Absolutely. Every time a major symphony orchestra needs a post filled for a conductor they go to Europe before they look here. The shelves are filled with classical music. Okay, that's fine. But now what the hell's goin' on *here?* What are people doing in this country? And what's going on with contemporary music?

L.A.: How is the kind of thing that you're dealing with, and that Kenton tried to do, ever going to find its proper home? It has such a low threshold of awareness, even—probably not one per cent of the people.

ELLIOTT: I don't think that's important; I think it's important to just go ahead. There's an expression—it's called "Keep on keepin' on." Let somebody else worry about whether it's good or bad, it's gonna survive or can you sell it. Do what you do.

L.A.: There's really no reason to think we can't have more than one kind of American music, is there?

ELLIOTT: Right. I would think so. In essence in this country if it's not classical it's not pure. If it's jazz it's impure. All those things are a luxury we can't afford anymore.

George Roberts, in the Musicians' Union, Los Angeles, California. (Photo by the Author.)

16 George Roberts

We played for the dedication of Stan's memorial, forty trombones and a rhythm section, there on Balboa Beach near the site of the Rendezvous Ballroom. Two thousand people were there. We were playing, the sun was setting . . . it was really neat.

Gazebo and Kenton Memorial, Balboa Beach, California. (Photo by the Author.)

L.A.: Did Stan ever hear your group?

ROBERTS: I wanted very much to have Stan hear them. But I was a little too late. I missed it by a few months.

L.A.: Then you've had the group for . . .

ROBERTS: About two years. I was gonna have him come down and hear us. Just kind of not say anything too much about it; start playing something and have him sit there. He would have gone straight through the ceiling. I really wanted to do that. I'll tell you, it's a hell of a potent sound to hear. They're the greatest.

L.A.: You meet every week?

ROBERTS: Right, from 9 to 1 at Orange Coast College.

L.A.: Where do you concertize?

ROBERTS: We do the Christmas program at Hoag Hospital at Newport Beach—that's a marvelous thing. We do the NAMM Convention—National Association of Music Merchants— every February. We greet the people as they come into the Anaheim Convention Center, in the lobby, like with this big long line of trombones, and we're wailing away and they like that. We play in the lobby of South Coast Plaza. We did that last year, and the people just went ape. And we're going to be doing Concerts By The Sea at Redondo and the Balboa Pavilion.

L.A.: I think Stan would have been thrilled to know this.

ROBERTS: I do too.

L.A.: What do you think he will be remembered for? What do you think was his most important contribution to the American musical scene?

ROBERTS: I think just being the personality that he was. He was the kind of guy that, if you knew him, you would like him. For that kind of a band you damn well better have somebody that was a dynamic guy that people, when they talked to him, would just fall in love with him. He turned a lot of people around to like what he liked. His being the dynamic individual that he was helped a lot of us. With the wrong kind of personality as leader that band wouldn't have been there very long. And he held it together until the day he died.

L.A.: He was the only one in the world that could have held it together.

ROBERTS: I believe that's exactly correct. Really, everybody loved Stan. He had his little differences, personal differences of opinion, but as a man playing with the band you loved the guy. You never had any problems with Stan. When I saw him after he had fallen, it took him a while to get his head together to recognize me—it was very upsetting. Bud Shank and Shelly Manne felt the same thing. He became very personal with all of us. I think we all went off and cried for a second. I'll remember him for his sense of humor, too. I thought I was gonna *die* once. Ahead of time, he told me, "George, you're gonna play 'Stella by Starlight' in Carnegie Hall." I said "You're kidding!" I flipped out of my mind. We get to Carnegie Hall, he introduces it, in this paramount, dramatic fashion. I go *Da-daaa, da-da-da* . . . Then he said something to me—to this day I don't know what it was—and, you know, Carnegie Hall is like . . .

L.A.: Yes.

ROBERTS: And I started laughing.

L.A.: (Laughs.)

ROBERTS: I finally get a chance to play a solo in Carnegie Hall, and I'm standing there, and the people are just sitting there staring at me like "What the hell is he *laughing* at?" Stan's on the floor, screaming. And I'm standing there laughing, and he says, "Go and sit down. Now for our next number . . ." And he went on. I thought "So much for my debut in Carnegie Hall." But that's Stan's humor. That's fun, that's personal. I would dare say everybody in that band sometime or another had some kind of personal thing with Stan, funny or otherwise. Some kind of personal contact with him. Bob Gioga was an important guy on that band. Funny things were always happening. I remember one time we were on a train, I don't know where the hell we were, going somewhere and stopping at all the little cow towns. And these five farmers got on, with their coveralls and boots and caps. Bob and Conte Candoli looked at each other and kinda winked. Bob went up to them and said "Would you boys like to get into a little card game with us?" One of them said "Why, sure would." So they all sit down, they're playing cards. They're playing for like an hour and a half. Gioga is losing something like three, four hundred dollars, Candoli the same thing. And the farmers get up to leave. "Well we'll see you later." "WAIT A MINUTE." These hicks get off the train, Gioga and Candoli are screaming. They'd cleaned 'em out. Funniest thing I ever saw in my life.

L.A.: When did Stan seem most alive to you? Was it when he was fronting the band?

ROBERTS: Oh sure. Sure. That's where he was doing his thing.

L.A.: No matter how tired he was. I'd sure like to know the source of that energy.

ROBERTS: Ah well, so would a lot of people.

L.A.: Do you remember the reaction the first time you played the Innovations?

ROBERTS: I was thrilled to death.

L.A.: I mean the audience reaction. How did they receive that?

ROBERTS: They liked us. Innovations was panned by a lot of critics. But the people who come to see Stan are pretty much gonna like anything he does.

L.A.: Really.

ROBERTS: They knew what Stan was doing.

L.A.: That's an interesting observation. You would think if the critics panned it the people . . .

ROBERTS: Most people who come to see Stan Kenton know before they walk through the door essentially what they're gonna hear. They know they'll have something, sometime through the program, that they'll like. That's why they come. It wouldn't matter if the critics were panning it.

L.A.: When they write all the history books, how do you think they'll rank him?

ROBERTS: I think they'll say that he was one of the great pioneers of American jazz. He made tremendous contributions.

L.A.: Did Stan particularly like your playing? Your tone, or style, or some special quality?

ROBERTS: Stan liked enthusiasm. He liked dedication. He sure had those with me. Soundwise I think I was a different kind of player than what had preceded me on the band.

L.A.: In what sense?

ROBERTS: More a singer.

L.A.: And he liked that?

ROBERTS: I think he did. You know an interesting thing, Stan would go for the dramatic things, where I just wanted to stand up and play the melody of a tune. In the area where the horn belongs. And maybe be very vocal with that horn.

L.A.: What dramatic things?

ROBERTS: He would want me to play up to like a high D. And I'd say "I don't want to play a high D. I want to play a low D." (Laughs.) That's what a bass trombone *is*. I would rather do something unusual where the horn belongs than do this other thing. Like, I'm not *Maynard*.

L.A.: (Laughs.)

116

Kenton Memorial, Balboa Beach, California. Inscription reads:

Dedicated to the memory of Stan Kenton and the members of his original orchestra whose innovative arrangements and unique beat made Balboa and the Rendezvous Ballroom famous and the Summer of 1941 a memorable experience for all of us.

Names on the plaque:

PIANO

STAN KENTON

VOCALIST

KAY GREGORY

SAXAPHONES [sic]

RED DORRIS

BOB GIOGA

BILL LAHEY

JACK ORDEAN

TED ROMERSA

BASS

HOWARD RUMSEY

TRUMPETS

CHICO ALVAREZ

EARL COLLIER

FRANK BLACK [BEACH]

TROMBONES

DICK COLE

HARRY FORBES

GUITAR

AL COSTI

DRUMS

MARVIN GEORGE

(Photo by the Author.)

117

ROBERTS: Going to a high *D*. Why should I play a high D when the guy sitting next to me can play a high D better than I can?

L.A.: I wonder why he wanted you to do that.

ROBERTS: Oh because it was dramatic, I'm sure.

L.A.: It's dramatic to have a high D on a bass trombone?

ROBERTS: Ya. Right. Especially if people are watching you play a high D and your eyes are popping out of your head. That's exciting. (Laughs.) But it's more exciting to me to do something on the horn that's right for it, and make *that* dramatic, than go to extremes.

L.A.: Would you argue with him about it?

ROBERTS: Ya I did.

L.A.: What would happen?

ROBERTS: Well I was thrilled to play anything with the band. You know, like they did with *This Is An Orchestra*? And he had me going down the scale, *Da, da, da, da, dah, dah, dahh!* For years I played a high D, and I said what most people don't know is that it took five people to get the horn dislodged out of my mouth from pressure trying to play the note. (Laughs.) But I wanted to play important things for the horn itself. I wrote an arrangement once. It was the worst thing you ever heard in your life. But Johnny Richards happened to hear us when we rehearsed the thing, and he kind of got the idea of what I was trying to do. And he wrote "Stella by Starlight." Tradition says that a bass trombone's gonna be an elephant, a big dog, an alligator, anything large—except you can turn around and be the greatest vocalist in the world, if you know how to say something nice. I felt the horn as being a very lyric horn. That was the great thing about the Kenton band. It was a place where you could go and maybe sometime in your life establish yourself as an individualist or a stylist. You could have a chance with that band. And that happened specifically for me. I had thoughts about the horn. Thank God I was with Stan.

L.A.: How far back does your love for the trombone go?

ROBERTS: Oh, when I was in school and I first began. I grew up in Des Moines, Iowa. I'd go see every big name band that ever came into town. I'd go up and talk to the players—that was very important to me. Every time I'd hear a band I'd just go out of my mind; I'd see three trombones and think, oh, that's the greatest thing in the world. And Kenton comes in with five! I wanted to be on a big name band. That was my main, really my sole ambition in life.

L.A.: Why did you want to be a trombonist in the first place?

ROBERTS: My mother and father took me to see my brother play in this junior high school band concert. He played saxophone. We went out afterwards and they said, "Would you like to play a musical instrument?" I said "Oh ya. I'd like to play one of those things that goes back and forth like this."

L.A.: (Laughs.)

ROBERTS: They said "That's a trombone." That's where it began. What happened was, I got on Gene Krupa's band, and stayed with him until it broke up in Detroit, in '49 or '50. Gene was a good guy. He was a great band leader. Looked great in front of a band. My first-love trombone player was with Gene. Urbie Green. Marvelous, the most natural trombone player I ever heard in my life. I would love to be able to play just like Urbie, down an octave. That would be one hell of a bass trombone player.

L.A.: And how did you get on Kenton's band?

ROBERTS: I had left Krupa's band and was in Reno playing for about a year. Bart Varsalona had left—I think Johnny Halliburton filled in for a while. Stan said "We should get a new bass trombone player." He talked it over with Bob Fitzpatrick and Milt Bernhart, and they said "How about trying the kid that was with Krupa's band a while back?" Stan called me at the Riverside Hotel where I was playing with Ray Herbeck's band and asked if I'd like to come with the band, and I probably flew right through the phone, like screaming "YES! YES!" I got every Kenton record I had and listened and listened and listened to them. I memorized some of the things—the obvious things, trombone lines. I joined the band at the Oasis Club on Western Boulevard, in Hollywood. That first night we were playing along and doing all right and then Stan said "Let's get out 'September Song,'" which has a very strong bass trombone line where the melody starts. Just as he said that the lights went out. And the whole club was just like a blackout. Stan said "No, we can't play that, we have a new man." I said "Go ahead and play it." And he did, and I played it from memory all the way through, the whole thing, because I'd been listening to that particular thing. When the lights came

back on Stan was looking at me with a big smile on his face, and he motioned for me to come down in front. I kind of reluctantly did so, and he said to the audience, "I would like you to meet our new bass trombone player." He was so aghast that I would walk in the first night and play something from memory. He knew I must want to be with that band awfully bad. It was a knockout; it characterized my relationship with the band for all the years that I was on it.

L.A.: What do you mean by that?

ROBERTS: I loved being with that band. I was very enthusiastic for it. I wanted to do things. Just playing with the band stimulated the hell out of me.

L.A.: This was about the time of the Innovations?

ROBERTS: I did the second Innovations.

L.A.: Oh, it was between the Innovations tours, then, about 1951.

ROBERTS: Yes it was. I think it was right in the middle of that. When I first went on the band Shorty Rogers was there, Chico Alvarez, Buddy Childers, Maynard Ferguson, Shelly Manne, Art Pepper, Bud Shank, Milt Bernhart, Bob Fitzpatrick, Frank Rosolino. It was an unbelievable band. Naturally I was intimidated. I liked that first band better than any band we went through. It was so jolting to me, the players and people . . .

L.A.: Jolting?

ROBERTS: I mean that it was just terribly exciting to me. What a realization—what a marvelous, fantastic bunch of musicians these guys all are. And my God, I'm sitting here on the same stand with them. I never forgot that. I don't think I ever will.

L.A.: How long were you with Stan at that time?

ROBERTS: Two or three years. I left the band about a month before they went to Europe.

L.A.: Then Stan called you back in 1965 to do the Neophonic concerts?

ROBERTS: He called me back to do the second Festival Tour, actually, the one in 1954 (Festival of Modern American Jazz). It's really very funny. He called up and asked if I could come back with the orchestra for about ten weeks. This was when I first came out here (Los Angeles). I said "Well, Stan, you know I'm very busy." Actually I was busy being a box boy in a supermarket, working in a record store, and doing a bunch of stuff like that. (Laughs.) And he thought I

118

meant I was very busy *playing*. He said "If I gave you this much money, would you come back with the orchestra?" I said "Of course." I went out for ten weeks and was able to save some money so I'd have something when I got back here. They were doing the big show, Christy, Charlie Parker, Dizzy Gillespie. After that tour, I came back here, and I've worked here ever since. There's a very interesting story connected with that that illustrates how one thing leads to another. One of the contractors out here at that time was Bobby Helfer, a very powerful man who really controlled the city as far as hiring you for this or that orchestra, motion pictures, tv, film, that kind of thing. I think I was kind of typed as a jazzer, because I'd been with Krupa and Kenton. I'm sitting at home one morning—thank God I stay in practice, that's something I never in my life stopped doing—when the phone rings and it's him. "Mr. Roberts, What Are You Doing Right Now?" I said "I'm having an unemployed cup of coffee."

L.A.: (Laughs.)

ROBERTS: "How Long Would It Take You To Get To Radio Recorders Annex, Mr. Roberts?" I said "Probably about 45 minutes." "Pick Up Your Bass Trombone, Put It In Your Car, Mr. Roberts, And Be Here In 45 Minutes." And he slammed the phone down. So I tore out of there. When I arrived I found they were doing a piece that some of the trombone players had been rehearsing for a couple of months. It was essentially the L. A. Philharmonic. Bob Craft was conducting a piece of Igor Stravinsky's. And *Igor Stravinsky himself* was sitting in the booth observing us.

L.A.: My gosh! Why had he called you?

ROBERTS: A trombone player had walked out on the call. Which is a very big mistake. You don't *do* that in the business. So they asked the trombones who they should get, and the guys said "Why don't you try this new kid that's in town?" He called me, I went down. I walked through the door. I had no time to really think about anything. I went over and sat down with my horn, still kind of like What the hell am I doing here, you know. Bob Craft looked at me and said "You have a solo with the harp at bar so-and-so." The harp was way on the other side of the room, and I said "Oh my God." I thought "I'm gonna bury my head and start counting. I don't care what he's doin', I'm gonna count." So we started playing and a voice interrupted us and it said "He's right. You're

wrong. Play it with him."

L.A.: Meaning *you* were right.

ROBERTS: Yes. We made the record, and that was the end of the day. Now if I'd had time to think any past that, I would have probably been a complete basket case.

L.A.: You mean that was a *recording?*

ROBERTS: That was a recording, ya.

L.A.: *Cold?*

ROBERTS: Cold. And all these other guys had had the part for like a month or however long it was. So as far as Helfer was concerned, all of a sudden now I'm a legitimate trombone player. I'm not just a jazzer. That meant I wasn't restricted to one little box; I could do tv and motion pictures as well. Which is really a very important thing for this business out here. It's a terribly hard business. You've got to try to be as total as you possibly can, cover as much as you can. That way you'll survive.

L.A.: What did you do with Stan's Neophonic Orchestra?

ROBERTS: Dick Nash wrote a piece for tenor trombone and bass trombone that we played. It was quite exciting, a good piece of music. I was also connected with the Junior Neophonic at Cerritos College under Jack Wheaton. We did a color television program for ABC.

L.A.: Boy I wonder if they saved the tape on that one.

ROBERTS: It's probably in a file someplace, I would imagine.

L.A.: How exciting. How did you feel about that kind of music?

ROBERTS: I like any kind of music. I've been through a wild cycle of bands, starting with Ray Robbins, then Gene Krupa, Ray Herbeck, and Stan Kenton. I think the contrasts from one extreme to another in each of those bands helped put me in the commercial business out here. As far as being on Stan's band, I loved every minute of it. Everything that was experimental, I loved. That was great. Where else could I go and make good money, have a lot of fun, and learn to play and do things? And look who I learned to play *with*—all those marvelous players. It was quite a learning process.

L.A.: What did you think of Stan as a band leader?

ROBERTS: I thought he was great. I never had any pressure when I worked with him. Stan was a marvelous guy, a very magnetic person. I saw him at a club once—the people were screaming, "The band's too loud!" He sent the

table a tray of drinks. At intermission he went over and sat with them and talked. Then he came back and played and we couldn't do anything wrong. He just won 'em over.

L.A.: Did you take over into your studio work some of the things you learned with Stan?

ROBERTS: Yes. Nelson Riddle was the first one to pick up on my style, the fact that I wanted to be a melody player. I did a couple of recording dates with him back in the fifties, right after I left Stan's band. Over a period of time he began to write lines and expose the horn line to melody. Nelson's the first one that commercially really started the thing going with bass trombone out here. That was a terribly, terribly important thing to have happen over the years for bass trombone, 'cause there wasn't anything there. Playing a song on bass trombone took it out of the sad, lamentish kind of horn it was up until then, took it out of its box. A number of years went by after that, and Stan called me in to do a record date with him. He came up and this I'll never forget, I loved him for doing it; this is very personal. He put his arm around my shoulder and said "Look what you started." And it was important to me that he said that.

L.A.: What did he mean by that?

ROBERTS: I had started to do that kind of thing with him . . .

L.A.: And now you were doing it in the studios.

ROBERTS: I was doing it in the studios, and it was accepted commercially. The bass trombone had gotten away from roots and fifths and that kind of thing.

L.A.: What are roots and fifths?

ROBERTS: A root is the fundamental bottom note of a band. You'll go *ahh* and everything's built on top of you. You'd play octaves and fifths and stuff—that's kind of what they had thought of the horn.

L.A.: Did Stan start to do that in his band after you'd been with him?

ROBERTS: Yes, I think so. I think other guys wanted to be exposed more that way. Very definitely. They didn't want just to play "Peanut Vendor" and "Intermission Riff." They wanted to stand up and play a tune rather than just be back there in the background someplace.

L.A.: That's where *your* influence on *his* orchestra comes in.

ROBERTS: That's what I hope it would be, yes.

But we have something to give music ourselves.

Allyn Ferguson, in his California home. (Photo by the Author.)

17 Allyn Ferguson

It's no mystery what Stan tried to do. He did the same thing that all composers, all serious artists, have always done. He was trying to extend the form, that's all. He was—he was—the word Innovator is right. Stan was an Innovator.

Unfortunately, we live in a society in which popularity does not equate with excellence. You either learn to deal with it or you in some way destroy yourself. Stan had, I think, a remarkably large audience, for the kind of thing he was doing. Because of his charisma, because of a lot of things that were extramusical. And he was successful—*very* successful, at what he tried to do.

L.A.: How did you first meet him?

FERGUSON: I met him years ago. I met him probably in 1941.

L.A.: Really! All the way back to 1941?

FERGUSON: Oh yeah, absolutely. The old Balboa band, I remember.

L.A.: Did you hear them at Balboa?

FERGUSON: Oh, sure. The band made a big fuss on the West Coast. It was the biggest shock of my life when I heard it for the first time.

L.A.: Why a shock?

FERGUSON: Because it was something I could relate to. He was doing something very, to me, very important. I was only fourteen years old when I first heard that band. It was an emotional *trauma* to hear it. But that's true of every young aspiring artist in this society. You start out with, you know, really wild eyes. If you *don't,* there's no place to go.

L.A.: Oh, elaborate!

FERGUSON: The rhythmic element was different, the real stiff off-the-beat stuff. That was new, but it wasn't the most important thing. What he was doing was really experimenting, that's what was exciting. The band was acting as a unit. There were a bunch of guys together, doing something that they could believe in, and it wasn't what everybody else was doing. It was a West Coast band. I met Stan when the band was in San Jose. I was born there, and I was living up in Northern California in those days. I don't know, I just always knew the band and always knew Stan. At one point, a very good friend of mine, a trombone player, wanted to try out for the band. This must have been 1940, '41. And he asked me to come and play piano for him. Stan loved the way he played but for some reason I don't remember, my friend was never with the band. Stan was impressed with my piano playing. I sat down and we started talking. So that's how he remembered me. Years later I started doing things with him. He wanted to take lessons from me at one time.

L.A.: What did he want you to teach him?

FERGUSON: Film writing, and a lot of things that he felt he lacked.

L.A.: Did he *want* to do film writing?

FERGUSON: Ya. He did a pilot for a couple of series at Warner Brothers. And he didn't have any training for that.

L.A.: He did want to study a few times at certain points in his life, I know.

FERGUSON: Stan never had very much musical education. And he was very much in awe of people who had degrees, for no reason at all. He respected the degree, rather than the person—not always, but the degree meant something to Stan. Those of us who came out of the academic world were not so sure that that was that important. But it did mean a lot to him. So, he always thought of me as something special because I had a Ph.D. from Stanford and I'd studied with Aaron Copland and Nadia Boulanger and all those people. Stan was sort of in awe of not what I could do, particularly, but my background. And so, we were very good friends.

L.A.: Had you written for him prior to the Neophonic?

FERGUSON: Ya, I did charts for him. In the mid-fifties. Ballads and tunes and whatever he wanted. Nothing that he recorded that I can remember.

L.A.: Was this post-Innovations?

FERGUSON: About the same time.

L.A.: Did you write for the Mellophonium Orchestra? That would have been after Innovations. That's a possibility for you, with your classical background.

FERGUSON: Ya, I did some of that. I had a good time. The Neophonic Orchestra of course had French horns in it. And that was fun.

L.A.: How did the Neophonic work come into being?

FERGUSON: Stan knew that for my Chamber Jazz Sextet in the fifties I'd used forms like the *caccia*. When he called me to do the Neophonic thing he said "Will you write something that deals with one of the older forms?" He wanted that specifically. He wanted that fusion. I said, "I've been thinking about doing something with a fugue." And he said "Wonderful!" And so I did, I used a passacaglia and fugue. The passacaglia worked very well. And the fugue, the exposition section is almost strict fugue.

L.A.: How did he feel about your work, once he premiered it? Did he talk to you about it?

FERGUSON: Stan loved it. He recorded only certain works from the concert.

L.A.: That's on the recording, I know.

FERGUSON: I remember he called me, and he said, "Yours is one of the few that I think we should record." The recording was made a year after it premiered. He talked Capitol into doing it.

L.A.: Thank goodness. We have something left of all that.

FERGUSON: Yeah, exactly.

L.A.: There's so much music that's been written that's disappeared. And it's got to be almost as good as what's on records.

FERGUSON: Oh, sure. That's part of the game.

L.A.: Did he quiz you on your "Passacaglia and Fugue"?

FERGUSON: Oh, yeah. He wanted to know all about it. When I said "Well, the exposition in the fugue is an absolutely strict formal exposition" well that didn't mean anything to him. He had never studied fugue-writing. And the passacaglia, he knew what I was talking about when I explained what it was, but he didn't know a passacaglia was a ground bass. None of that was a part of his equipment.

L.A.: What is the passacaglia form, exactly?

FERGUSON: Just a ground bass. It's a bass line, a bass pattern, upon which you build all different kinds of variations. And the pattern, the bass line, just repeats over and over again. The fourth movement of Brahms' Fourth Symphony is a passacaglia, for example. The passacaglia is a very interesting form. It was an obvious thing to do. It came from baroque music, even before, but it's been used by every composer ever since in one way or another.

L.A.: And he was fascinated by all this.

FERGUSON: He would seek people like myself out, that he thought could supply a lot of the technique that he didn't have, a lot of the understanding, the background that he didn't have.

L.A.: From the classical point of view.

FERGUSON: Exactly. That I guess was our attraction for each other. I looked at Stan as a prime mover and he looked at me as a person that probably could help him in areas that he was weak in. 'Cause he was realistic about his education. He always said he was gonna go back to school. Always. He used to threaten to take three years off and go to Stanford, you know. He used to tell me, "Oh, I'm going to Stanford." And he couldn't have taken three years away from that band if his life depended on it. That was his curse. That really is the thing that stopped him from doing anything else. When he wasn't doing it for even six months, he was a banana. I think to the day he died, the biggest heartbreak that he had was the fact that he didn't have any education to speak of. He really wanted that.

L.A.: You mean the whole music school bit? Composition, theory, history of music, and all this kind of thing?

FERGUSON: Sure, everything. Everything.

L.A.: He wanted a comprehensive background in music training.

FERGUSON: Absolutely. He really didn't know much about it. All that Stan knew about writing he had learned the hard way. He had a little bit of training, but pretty much he had learned by doing. He learned to write for his band by writing for his band. And then when other writers would come along, he used to be fascinated, and he'd say, "Why'd you do that?" Or "How come you took the saxophones and did that kind of thing?" And you'd say, you know, and he'd store it away. He was a good learner.

L.A.: Is your Stanford degree in music?

FERGUSON: Um-hm. Composition and theory.

L.A.: What attracted you to jazz?

FERGUSON: I was always interested in jazz. I was brought up with it. My father played with Paul Whiteman. My classical heritage was always a mixture. I studied trumpet with Red Nichols' father when I was four years old.

L.A.: My gosh.

FERGUSON: They were friends of the family. Red Nichols' father was an old,

hard bandmaster out of Ogden, Utah. So I've always had those two elements of music in my background, classical and jazz. As all Americans should! *All* Americans should have that background. They should understand *their* music, they should understand their *roots*, they should understand their musical history.

L.A.: A lot of people think country western is our folk music.

FERGUSON: Well, country western really comes from Scotland and Ireland. It's all British Isles. Of course, it's been adapted and changed and everything, as jazz has, but it's a part of our folk music. I don't put it down. I think it's a very naive music, as is jazz most of the time. But that's what folk music *is*. All shades of it.

L.A.: Jazz was born here, actually, wasn't it?

FERGUSON: It was born here, but it has European harmonic roots. And African rhythmic roots probably. But it is a totally eclectic music. Some of it came from South America, some from Germany. It's all over the place.

L.A.: Stan always used to say that jazz only appealed to a minority audience. Why do you think this is so?

FERGUSON: Because jazz really started out to be utilitarian music. It started out as dance music. Then the musicians that got into jazz started to get serious about the music itself. And, as that happens, the music becomes more codified and it loses touch with its utilitarian purpose. When Stan came along and started changing tempos, for example, how the hell ya gonna dance to that? He lost all the dancers. So did Mozart, when he put a minuet in the third movement of a symphony. It was no longer a minuet. Nobody could dance to that. Bach did the same thing. A gigue in a Bach suite is originally a dance piece.

L.A.: I wonder what Copland would think of your doing music for jazz now.

FERGUSON: I was doing it then—he knew it *then*. I won a scholarship to Tanglewood with a concerto that I had written. It was a crossover piece—it had a lot of jazz rhythms in it. It wasn't harmonically derivative of that idiom. My education was in both idioms. I worked in jazz bands from the time I was 12. I also was a child prodigy on the piano, and I studied composition on the other side, and studied to be a "serious" writer, whatever that meant. The point is that I have always felt, and I still dearly believe, that the first great American composer is going to really understand his *folk* music, as Bartok did, and Stravinsky did. And our folk music is, after all, jazz.

L.A.: A lot of our American composers don't write that way at all.

FERGUSON: That's really where the problem comes. They don't understand *jazz*. They don't understand their own folk music. 'Cause there was a terrible snobbish bifurcation going on, which still exists, between so-called classical and popular, whatever that means— both those terms.

L.A.: Popular is everything else, right? (Laughs.)

FERGUSON: Yeah, I suppose, and classical should refer to a very short specific period in the history of Western music, roughly 1800 to 1840; that's what classical is. The whole thing is insane. Jazz was a poor relative. If you had culture, you didn't pay attention to it; it was dirty. I've thought about it in many ways, and researched it, and I think it has to do with the fact that we're a very young nation and a very insecure one and all of our culture came from Europe. It was transplanted. When I came up I was a serious musician, conductor, composer, in a society in which there is relatively no art. Those of us who are artists living in this society have an enormous problem trying to figure out how to deal with it. There've been great jazz musicians and some great people like Bernstein and Copland and so forth. But they didn't *mix* at all. What *I'm* saying is, that this person's gonna come along who is *both*. He is going to be *steeped* in his *folk* music. Now he's not gonna write *jazz* particularly. But he will have it so imbued within him—and at the same time will have a tremendous background in music and in the music of Western civilization, so that he understands the relationship to his history—that what he writes will come out totally different. It is going to be truly an American music. That will be the first great American composer. We are a young culture. It's maybe fifty years away.

L.A.: Did your thoughts about this lead to your desire to found The Orchestra out here?

FERGUSON: That was a dream I had going way back to 1964. And I used all kinds of forms in my Chamber Jazz Sextet while I was teaching at Stanford in 1956. There was a whole poetry and jazz movement on the West Coast that we started, with Kenneth Patchen, at the old Blackhawk jazz club in San Francisco. Kenneth was one of the great American poets. He's dead now, but he will yet be recognized as one of the great contemporary poets in America. We did an album back then which has recently been reissued. The kids listen to that today and they can't believe we did that in 1957. I mean it's far out by *today's* standards. We did jazz things and jazz-poetry, and it was *all* derivative of other forms of music. I was using forms like *caccia* and—*caccia* is Italian for *chase,* it's an old 13th century form; it's just a canon. An extended canon, one instrument started and the other followed. We did it in an attempt not to *change* jazz but to *expand* it. And to stop calling it "jazz." Which is, you know, really a terrible label. It doesn't mean anything. Everybody means something different when they say "jazz." It's *American music.* The idea that I originally had with The Orchestra was to put together certain instrumentalists who could, given the right kind of compositions or composers, create a new music. Really, a new music. Or a new idiom, if you prefer. The time frame with Stan's Neophonic is interesting, because before Stan did that I talked with Max Herman and the musicians' union, and this was in 1963, I think, or '62, maybe. I did a piece, an album, which has just been reissued. It's a jazz version of Moussorgsky's *Pictures At An Exhibition.*

L.A.: You're kidding!

FERGUSON: No. It's on *Discovery.* It's a very faithful jazz version of the score, all in the same keys and everything. All I did was change it rhythmically a little bit and put some solos in and some improvisation. I'm proud of that. It's one of the best things I've ever done. I wrote it over a period of three years, while I was on the road conducting for Johnny Mathis, and I'd rehearse it with my band whenever I was in town. But I couldn't get a record company interested in it. "Pictures at a *what?"* Nobody could relate to it. Finally the guys in the orchestra said "Let's record it anyway, on our own." So we did. It was a wonderful band. Bud Shank, Paul Horn, who was the Promenader, Bill Perkins, Bill Hood, Jack Nimitz, Johnny Audino, Ollie Mitchell, Stu Williamson, Don Bagley, Johnny Crusano, Frank Capp . . . .

L.A.: There are some good Kenton names in that list.

FERGUSON: It was out about three months, on Fred Astaire's label, *Ava,* and the company went broke. So nobody even heard it until about a year ago.

L.A.: If you were thinking along these lines when Stan called you for the Neophonic, why did you agree to write for him instead of pursuing your own idea?

FERGUSON: I hadn't formed anything at that time. I was thinking about what I wanted to do, but all I wanted to do was write. So when Stan called me I was *delighted.*

L.A.: Did he explain the concept of the Neophonic to you?

FERGUSON: Yeah. As a matter of fact, I recall the conversation. It was a mutual kind of thing, because he knew that's the kind of stuff I was doing and he said "Our ideas are similar."

L.A.: It's a wonder that you weren't even closer to him than you were, because you were two people going parallel toward the same kind of thing.

FERGUSON: You'd be amazed, in the business, people who do the same thing rarely see each other. I almost never see any other writers. I see lots of musicians. I would see Stan a lot. I used to hang out with the band. We were both good friends with Shorty (Rogers) and a lot of people from the band.

L.A.: But Stan knew you were interested in combining classics with jazz.

FERGUSON: Oh yeah. Yeah, we'd had some talks about it. When I wrote the "Passacaglia and Fugue" Stan was very impressed with the fact that I had combined a so-called classical form with a jazz feeling.

L.A.: That's what he loved.

FERGUSON: That's what he loved to think about. Stan couldn't relate to it from the side that I could, because he wouldn't have known a *caccia* if it had hit him in the face. It was all just spontaneous combustion with Stan.

L.A.: (Laughs.)

FERGUSON: It really was. In what I teach, now, I tell my students, this thing is a computer, and it doesn't spit out anything that hasn't been put there some way. Stan had limited input, and a lot of output. He had a lot of energy. Very interesting kinds of energy. He was an incredible human being. A very dramatic person. You remembered everything Stan said. It was his magnetism. Pete (Rugolo) and Stan were ponderous writers. There was nothing delicate

125

about anything that happened in that band. And if it swung lightly it bothered him. It was *huge. ARCHITECTURE.* Pete and Stan were architects. They really built great big things. Stan came up in an age when, if he had been educating himself, he wouldn't have had the band. So he did what he had to do. And he was a wonderful human being.

L.A.: His life really was his music, wasn't it.
FERGUSON: He really didn't have much of a personal life. I used to go over to his house on Alta Drive in Beverly Hills. He had, in the back, a big studio that he had built, I guess in a separate building, right on the back of the lot. And that's where he spent his time. His personal life was a disaster, from start to finish. It's tough to combine the two.

L.A.: Was your orchestra idea similar to Stan's Neophonic?
FERGUSON: Yeah. It's very close. Stan was really dealing with a band. That was the first thing. He was dealing with an expanded instrumental group that he understood. I mean five saxophones and five trombones and so forth.

He could understand that. So he added horns. You know, that was sort of another thing that he could understand.

L.A.: Why didn't he have strings with the Neophonic? Would it have been too expensive?
FERGUSON: It would have been expensive, it is an expensive thing, and secondly I don't think Stan really felt strings. Stan *loved* the *power* of a bunch of horns blowing at him.
L.A.: Although he did have strings in the Innovations orchestras, and everybody loved that.
FERGUSON: Um-hm. Um-hm.
L.A.: The only problem with it being that he lost so much money on it.

FERGUSON: Oh I know. Stan, when Stan believed in something, he did it. And the Neophonic itself lost money. And it was too bad, because it *was* a wonderful idea. The only thing that he really did wrong, he turned people loose. He turned the writers loose a little bit and didn't give them any direction. He didn't point them at all. And some of the guys just couldn't *deal* with that.
L.A.: *Some* of them *loved* it.

FERGUSON: Oh, yeah. It was—it was—
L.A.: From what I've heard. They said "Oh, wow, I can do anything I want."
FERGUSON: Well—ya, but you can't. That's the point. In art, you have to have a parameter. In painting, it's this size canvas, or whatever it is. And Stan didn't set the parameters. That was one of the problems the Neophonic had. But I don't think it had anything to do with the fact that the money was lost, that it was not supported. Those things are not very well supported in this society at all. That had nothing to do with Stan in particular.

L.A.: Stan had as his purposes, as I understand it, the following things: first, to encourage the composition and performance of contemporary music, and to help develop musicians capable of playing it; second, to serve as a clearinghouse for contemporary music, contemporary musicians, and information concerning contemporary music, and to serve in the dissemination of such music to universities, other cities and countries, and third, to sponsor and present

Allyn Ferguson, in his California home. (Photo by the Author.)

the Los Angeles Neophonic Orchestra—which he called "the first permanently established orchestra in the world devoted to contemporary music"—to extend its influence and performance, and to encourage the establishment of similar neophonic orchestras. He wanted to set them up all over. Wouldn't that have been wonderful?

FERGUSON: Absolutely

L.A.: Stan's idea was really international in scope. He even formed what he called the International Academy of Contemporary Music to encompass all this. So this is probably on a broader scale than what you wanted to do. How does it compare with your aims?

FERGUSON: The idea of The Orchestra was to approach a true sort of new musical idiom through an aggregation of players. The idea initially was to put together a very unique combination of instrumentalists who would offer a whole new creative world with which to deal.

L.A.: Because they had the capability of playing anything?

FERGUSON: Exactly. Because they could deal with idioms. Various idioms that most orchestral players today can't deal with.

L.A.: In other words, it's along the lines of what Stan wanted to do, but not exactly the same thing. He wanted to develop musicians capable of playing this new music. That's slightly different from your idea. Rather than help develop them, you were hoping they already had it.

FERGUSON: That's right. My feeling is that the music will come from the players. And Stan more or less thought that the music was gonna come from the writers.

L.A.: He was really more into arrangers and writers.

FERGUSON: Ya, and he was into his band. (Laughs.) And he thought of it in terms of his band expanded. And I don't. I didn't at all. I thought of it in terms of a symphony orchestra, with all that that implies.

L.A.: A symphony orchestra playing indigenous American things combined with classical forms.

FERGUSON: Exactly right. Exactly right. For example, if you take a woodwind section, the same woodwind section that plays Rimsky-Korsakov in let's say a seven-voice chord or passage, if you can imagine those same woodwinds phrasing a thing rhythmically in a way that legitimate players don't do, that's

just a very slight example. When you start to expand the technique of the orchestra you now have some creative ground to deal with that you didn't have before.

L.A.: Yes, I see.

FERGUSON: And that's what my idea was. Trumpet players that can play like Buddy Childers, and at the same time turn around and play a beautiful solo. So now the music that you can bring to this group is an entirely different kind of music. It's *conceived* differently, because you have people who can play in idioms that other symphonic players can't play. And you have opened up the whole creative process. What it is is the ability to walk both sides. If you put together ninety players like that, and you start to think about what this vehicle *is,* you now are *capable* of *writing* for this vehicle in an *entirely different way,* an entirely new way. You can write woodwind passages that don't have rhythmic roots in Europe. They have rhythmic roots *here.* So that through the personnel comes the music, as it's been throughout Western civilization. You could do things you couldn't do with any symphony, anywhere else in the world.

L.A.: Boy that's really—something new. That's strange. You're coming at it from here, let's say from this direction, and Stan was coming at it from here . . .

FERGUSON: Exactly.

L.A.: And you got this close . . .

FERGUSON: That's exactly what happened.

L.A.: . . . and then you split off; he died, and your orchestra thing . . .

FERGUSON: That's exactly what happened. My orchestra—uh—*my* orchestra—doesn't exist anymore. I may yet someday try to do what I'm telling you.

L.A.: You think you'll try to form another orchestra.

FERGUSON: I might. I don't know. The logistics of a ninety-piece orchestra are frightening. Stan's were bad enough at forty, or whatever.

L.A.: Why did you leave your partnership with Jack Elliott?

FERGUSON: I left because it was no longer a musical idea. It became a social idea.

L.A.: In what sense?

FERGUSON: Jack perceived that it was more important to make it a social thing so that it would be supported by a few people in Beverly Hills rather than

an international idea, which is what I had. I think it's an international idea. It's the best idea I ever had. You have to broad-base it. I went to the local union in 1964 and said, "I think there ought to be a Hollywood orchestra that does this kind of thing." Jack and I had a commercial partnership; we shared an office and worked together, doing things like *Charlie's Angels* and *The Rookies* and the Emmys and the Grammys. At a certain point I kept talking about how I wanted to do this and he kept telling me I was crazy. When we first got together there was no thought of doing four concerts a year with foundation support. I don't want a foundation. I think that's totally wrong.

L.A.: How did you want to do it?

FERGUSON: Let's do one concert every once in a while. And let's do it when we can afford it, and let's do it when we've got the music to make it what we say it is.

L.A.: I heard the album of your first concert. I thought it was very good.

FERGUSON: The album was done when we were still together. It's a whole different thing than what's going on now. *That* concert was incredible. There was an electricity at that concert you couldn't believe. Everybody that was there would agree to that. Had we done this as a rehearsal orchestra, just as a musical idea, then I think it would really have lived, I think it would have been a very important thing. We'd have found some good music. It was really basically a problem of different philosophies about what we were doing. We didn't have to pay for rehearsals. That's another enormous argument that we had. When we put The Orchestra together we were entitled to rehearse for nothing.

L.A.: Through the musicians' union's rules?

FERGUSON: Sure. Absolutely. First three rehearsals we had were for nothing. What should have happened, what I wanted to happen with this thing was, the music should come in six months ahead of time. You want to send a score, send me one; okay, we'll look at it, we'll see what its merit is and so forth. And then we will have the time to rehearse it, to work it out, to learn it, to see what it's about; and then we can present it satisfactorily. Jack perceived it as a commercial situation. Now you set up a you-and-me situation, instead of us. I am going to *pay* you for rehearsing in my orchestra. Not: We're gonna build an orchestra together. Follow the difference? And that really I guess is the bottom, basic difference in philosophy as to what the problem was. My feeling about The Orchestra always was: we will get together, the players will all contribute, and so forth and so on. And it will be a learning experience for everybody.

L.A.: So then how did it actually come into being?

FERGUSON: I had done a couple of albums with the Royal Philharmonic Orchestra in England with a friend of mine, in which I experimented, writing an arrangement, for example, of "Here's That Rainy Day" as a symphonic tone poem. I felt that with some things under my arm I could interest somebody in this thing. First I met with some of the main string players in town to see if we couldn't put together a string section like this, in this town, that we could play some of these things with. And they said yes. Then I met with individual players to tell them my idea. We'd sit and talk and have dinner. Bud Shank, Bill Perkins, George Roberts, the brass players, all the way down the line. I got an idea for the instrumentation, how many people I wanted, and so forth. It was a logical outgrowth of what I had been thinking of for a long, long time, since I was at Stanford, which was 1956. So it was roughly twenty years before it came about. At our first three rehearsals we used two of the things from the Royal Philharmonic music and I did a special piece called "Statements for Orchestra," which was just a bunch of sections—bossa nova, pseudo-Dixieland, gospel—different movements that demonstrated what that orchestra could do that other symphony orchestras couldn't do, what it was capable of.

L.A.: I wonder what would have happened if Stan had lived longer and had perhaps got together with you and pursued this idea further.

FERGUSON: The last time I saw him was at Redlands. And we sat and we were drinking coffee, talking about it. He had all these ideas; we gotta do this and we gotta do that. You say, "Oh yeah, we'll do it," and—and you don't. He really was interested in working with anybody who thought kind of the same way he did, and I certainly did, at that time. We always said that we would do something together. We never quite got around to it.

L.A.: The two of you! Oh, how interesting.

FERGUSON: What Stan did was important. Stan made a statement with his life, about jazz or whatever he was doing being more important than most people thought it was. And he was right. I think he had all the right instincts. He was totally a unique person. When Stan took the original, the Balboa band, on the road—now those guys were not extraordinary players, they were all a bunch of guys from Balboa that he got together, and they sat down—well what they did was create an *idea*. Together. And they *performed* the idea *together*. And it became something totally different.

18 Ross Barbour

"You'll never guess who came into the Esquire!" Bob Flanigan said, his eyes as big as saucers.

We knew Stan was in town, we were bitin' our fingernails, we were dyin' that we weren't there. And we said, "Okay, you're gonna tell us Stan Kenton came in to see the Four Freshmen. Ha, ha."

He says, "That's what I . . . Stan is in there!" All gasping and whispery. Well Bob will put you on a little bit, if you let him. So we said, "Sure, sure, sure." And—"No, really!" And then we see that he's—he's—actually, his eyes are goin' around, like the headlights on a train. "Stan—Kenton, quote, 'HE' is here." You know, it's like GOD is in the FRONT ROW.

Ross Barbour and Ken Albers, in Barbour's California home. (Photo by the Author.)

And then we choked, you know, goose pimples, cold sweat. Quaking knees. Sweaty palms . . .

KEN ALBERS: (Laughs.) You wanted to leave town, immediately.

BARBOUR: Oh, ya, out the back door! *Whoo!* We were sittin' in this little place, next door to the Esquire Lounge in Dayton, Ohio. We'd come in through a side door from the lounge right into the place. It was kind of like a White Tower, with a white counter and a hamburger thing behind the short order cook, where they had the fancy "Hey, give me two with their eyes wide open," that kind of thing. Stan was in town, with his Innovations Orchestra. It was a Tuesday night, the kind of night you're not gonna fill the house, especially when people are gonna go see *Stan.* We tried so hard to get off. We're tellin' the boss, "Look. We'll work a Sunday. We'll work *two* Sundays. Let us off so we can go see the Kenton band." "No. We've got people coming in. We've got to keep the doors open." So we went back to the Esquire Lounge and went up on the stage. We didn't even say hi to Stan. He was with George Morte, and Mort Lewis, Frank Pollack, Gene Barry, and Sid Garris, disc jockeys in the town. Gene was a fan of the Freshmen, a fast-talking, rhymer kind of guy: "This is Swing with WING, the Dayton Station, W-I-N-G." And Stan had some players from his band, and fans all around him. We get up there and we're singing like "Poincianna . . ." (*voice trembling*) ". . . Your Branches Speak to Me . . ." Oh, God. Oh, what am I gonna do? Choked. Knees quaking. White knuckles. Playing the wrong chords and everything.

L.A.: Why were you so in awe of him?

BARBOUR: Stan and his band came to town, back when we were all students at Arthur Jordan Conservatory in Indianapolis, in 1947. Of course, we had all been Kenton fans before that, 'cause he was doin' what needed to be *done* in music. The other bands were loafin', just playing the same sounds over and over again. Stan, man, he was out diggin' in, and that's what we were *expecting.* Stan stood out then, like he always did. Well it was something like four dollars a person to get into the concert. Now, in 1947, you'd work all *day* for four dollars, and a college kid might have to work three or *four* days for four dollars. We all wanted to go to the concert, but nobody had any money. Well Ross just happened to have sixteen dollars. And

that's all Ross had. And Ross wasn't really that anxious to split with it to see this *show.* Ross was the one saying "I don't know, it's just a band, we can do without." "But, Ross," and they're shaking him. Well finally the sixteen dollars came loose.

L.A.: (Laughs.)

BARBOUR: And we left the dorm and went to the concert. Well of course it was like Ah-*Spring!* And everything turned new colors. The whole world was this different thing after we realized that this *could happen.* It wasn't some trick. We hadn't just imagined it. It was real. The colors, the excitement that band got, the depth of sound, and the *fierceness,* the *power* they'd generate would just take the paper off the wall. We'd just heard Henry Busse, and Tommy Dorsey'd been in town. And that's nice. And then comes Kenton, and, *wow!* Grabs hold of the curtains and shakes you. And you realize, *ooh,* there *is* something else. It was a different musical dimension. It changed all our lives.

L.A.: Did he play his far-out things that night? In 1947 and '48, that would have been when Pete Rugolo was writing.

BARBOUR: I suppose they did some of that. I remember they did "Eager Beaver." And "St. James Infirmary."

L.A.: Is that when the band was pitching in with . . .

BARBOUR: Yeah. Stan sang "I went down to the St. James Infirmary. I left my ba-bee there . . ." "Whaja leave 'er there for, Stan?"

L.A.: (Laughs.)

BARBOUR: "Laid out on a cold white table. So cold, so white, so bare . . ." "You shoulda covered 'er up, Stan."

L.A.: (Laughs.)

ALBERS: Sounds like Rosolino.

BARBOUR: And Herky Styles was doing a bit with Shelly Manne. He had a drum out front, and he says "All right, Shelly, I'm gonna go (*taps on drum*) 'Rat-tat-a tat tat.' And then I want you to go: 'BOOM BOOM.' Okay? Here I go! 'Rat-tat-a tat! tat.' " And Shelly goes "Boom, boom."

L.A.: (Laughs.)

BARBOUR: And the people fall out! And Herky says, "No, no, no. Look, I want you to go, 'Boom, boom' on the *drum.* Ya *got* it? 'Boom boom' on the *drum,* Shelly." "Oh. Oh, I see." And Herky gets out there, "Rat-tat-a tat! tat!" And Shelly goes "BOOM BOOM! On the drum."

L.A.: (Laughs.)

BARBOUR: Anyhow, before we had

left that night, we were changed. Just changed.

L.A.: How old were you guys at that time? About eighteen? Twenty?

BARBOUR: Eighteen to twenty-one or -two. See, our original group consisted of my brother Don and I, Bob Flanigan, who is our cousin, Hal Kratzsch, and Marvin Pruitt. Marvin sang with us during those early rehearsals. There was a girl, I don't remember her name, who rehearsed with us, until we got a job in Bloomington, and she says "Oh, no, I couldn't go to Bloomington, I would be out to one o'clock in the morning. What would my mother say?" "Ya but why you been rehearsin' all this time?" So we got Marvin. And Marvin kind of choked up in front of an audience. He was a whale of a lot of fun at a party. But you put him in front of an audience and turn a light on him, and he was *deathly afraid.* So when it really came to performing, Marvin didn't want any part of that. And Hal Kratzsch had the car, so he was the leader. (Laughs.)

L.A.: (Laughs.)

BARBOUR: Hal had been in the Navy Air Force in the South Pacific. He'd gotten back and had gone to Indiana University, and then came to Arthur Jordan his *second* year. Marvin had been in the service and came late. My brother came after a couple of years in the service. And I had just gotten out of high school. So—there wasn't any real reason that Don and I would have been in the same freshman class had it not been for the war. And Bob was a little older than Don. And *he* wouldn't have been in my class. And Marvin was older than Bob. And *they* wouldn't have been—*none* of us would have been together. I always said, God is a Freshman. He put it together, and kept it together.

L.A.: I guess *so.*

BARBOUR: And there were so many times that, if it hadn't been for Stan Kenton, it wouldn't have *stayed* together. I don't know, maybe—God *is* Stan Kenton. (Laughs.) He helped us so much, like that. He just used to get involved and make it happen for us. So for us to sing, to Stan Kenton that night, after two and a half years of *idolizing* him, and have him in the audience, actually *listening,* was more than we could *stand.* But we sang our forty-minute show and afterwards got up the courage to come around and shake his hand and thank him for coming. We expected to get up and leave, 'cause we

130

were bad that night, and nobody stays when the group's bad. But Stan had us sit down and he asked if we were recording. At that time we had settled a thing with Woody Herman. Woody was gonna put a band together called "The Band That Plays Music to Dance To," and he wanted a vocal group. He'd heard us at a jam session at the High Note in Chicago, where we'd done background harmony with Mary Ann McCall. During college we had a job where we sang at a nightclub, the Liberal View League Club in Indianapolis. We'd do a song on the show, and then in between the dance sets we'd go sing at the tables, anything they wanted to hear. "Sweet Adeline" or "Nature Boy" or "Dancing in the Dark" or whatever. We knew the song, kind of, and we'd hum along. We were fakers. We were just guys who put it together the way we thought it ought to be—maybe we were right, maybe we were wrong, but we had no lack of guts. So anyway, we were all set to go with Woody. We would go with the band and I would play fifth trumpet—I didn't really know trumpet well enough to play with Woody's band, but I could skate by and I could sing, and Don could play guitar and Bob could play trombone and so forth.

L.A.: So the Freshmen played instruments at this time also?
BARBOUR: Yeah. We had an agent who booked us in the 113 Club in Fort Wayne, Indiana, on September 20th, 1948. That was our first professional job. We went in there and we would sing a song, and then we'd play a song, then sing a song, then play a song. Well there was a pay phone right beside the stage. And the boss is on this pay phone, calling our agent, "GET THESE LOUSY GUYS OUTTA HERE! THEY STINK!!!"

L.A.: My God. That's unbelievable.
BARBOUR: And we're trying to sing and play, you know, and they held us over because the boss's daughter was sweet on the trumpet player. Not that holding us over was such a big deal. It was a six-night week, and they held us over the other five nights, is what it was. But the agent came in, and he says, "Look, I want you guys to learn to play and sing at the same time."
L.A.: Come on. How can you do that?
BARBOUR: That's what we said, "How can you do that? It's a hard thing to sing that style." But he says, "You practice

enough, you'll be able to play and sing at the same time. Play the bass and guitar and drums, let's say, or bass, guitar and piano. Then you can sing with this background. If you do that," he says, "I'll promise you this: I'll have you work in some of the best nightclubs in the Middle West." Well—the best nightclubs in the Middle West in 1948 were toilets. Every one of them. Dingy dives. But—that's where we were—that was our goal. And when Woody Herman offered to take us on the road with his band, that was our promise, that was our fulfillment. And Stan says, "You guys ought not to sing with Woody's band, in my band, or any band. Let's get you a contract on your own."
L.A.: Wow.
BARBOUR: "Oh, Stan, you're kidding, you're kidding." "No. No, you ought to have a contract on your own. You guys have a sound of your own. And I'll do it—I'll call Pete Rugolo. Look, before I leave tonight, I want to give you this number, and that number, and—Morte, write this down: I want Rugolo to meet 'em in New York. He's there with Billy Eckstine." And the plan—in five minutes (snaps fingers)—is set. We are gonna record for Capitol. Stan was a stockholder, he would talk 'em into it. They wouldn't say no to Stan. He'd bulldoze 'em if he had to.
L.A.: Isn't that amazing.

BARBOUR: And—the skies opened up. We called Woody—I never thought we'd call Woody Herman and say, "Sorry, we can't make it." (Laughs.)

L.A.: Weren't you scared, though, I mean . . .
BARBOUR: Oh yeah.
L.A.: . . . not knowing what you were getting into. At least you had the established band behind you with Woody Herman. Not to know what you were getting into, all by yourself, like that, must have been scary.

BARBOUR: No, that wasn't really, we didn't fear that. We knew we could play, and sing, and deliver. We knew we could work, and perform, and entertain people. That had been proved for two years. But—to have—him—saying, "I believe in you. You've got to succeed. You're part of my ego, now." How do you become big enough to do that? You can't let Stan down. So we recorded some test things with Pete Rugolo in New York and later came to California and recorded with Capitol. But Capitol was trying to get rid of their groups.

Bands were dropping them and they were breaking up. Vocal groups were out of style. Stan was out of step again. But he just wouldn't hear no. So they recorded us some things, none of which sounded like us. We had "It's A Blue World" and "Tuxedo Junction" recorded and waiting to be released. And our contract expired and they just let it die. They weren't gonna release "Blue World" and "Tuxedo Junction."

L.A.: To think of being deprived of that. That's all some of us grew up on.
BARBOUR: We bumped into Stan. "Well how the hell are ya!" "Well, Stan, we're all right, but we don't have a recording contract. Capitol let it end." "What!" "Well they didn't sell any of 'em, Stan, you can't blame 'em for that." Right away Stan calls Glenn Wallichs at Capitol. "What the hell are you guys doin' with the Freshmen? Look, they're goin' into Detroit, and they need some dubs of 'Blue World' and 'Tuxedo Junction.' It's the least you can do for 'em, if you're not gonna release 'em. I want those dubs sent to these guys right now, so they can advertise themselves." We got the dubs. Went into Detroit a little early, and Bob Murphy, the deejay from WJBK, had eight or ten copies made and sent them to the college stations and to WXYZ and KMH out in Dearborn. Pretty soon everybody was playing that record. Requests for it started pouring in. It was a hit. Everybody knew it was a hit. Only we weren't signed to Capitol Records.

L.A.: That's a very interesting situation.
BARBOUR: And the line was standing outside the Crest Bowling Lanes, they had a little lounge there, and we were back of the bar, and people were standing in line, trying to get in there because they had heard these records. "It's A Blue World . . ." They didn't know what they were hearin'! They were like us. They figured "Wow. That sound! Where'd that come from?" "Tuxedo Junction" was being played too, so we were a big hit in Detroit. Everybody knew we had a million-seller record goin'! Our career was booming!
L.A.: Except you didn't have a record! (Laughs.)
BARBOUR: No, we didn't even have a record contract! So Capitol sent a territory man, Max Caleson, out to see what was goin' on, out to re-sign the Freshmen. And he tried to get into the nightclub, and he couldn't even get close enough to wave. So he found us the next

131

day at our hotel, and we re-signed with Capitol. And he calls 'em and says, "Look, start making discs." Well they didn't do it then like they do now. In two or three days now they can have a million of them sent to whoever, by air. No, it took six weeks, eight weeks. And after six or eight weeks of playing like a hit and nobody being able to buy it, pretty soon people got interested in something *else*. By the time the records were in the stores, it was too late to sell that much as a single, though later it did well in albums. But—it was an idea that had found its time. Nobody could say no to that sound, right then. That was just what the world needed. And we didn't know what we were doin'!

L.A.: What do you mean, didn't know what you were doing?

BARBOUR: We knew what we loved, but we weren't doing it for *that*. It wasn't meant to be pop, like the Four Aces, or the Mills Brothers.

L.A.: The sound.

BARBOUR: *The* sound.

L.A.: What is *the* sound? How would you describe it to some poor wretch from *Mars,* let's say, who had never heard it?

BARBOUR: Well—most groups at that time had a girl on top with the melody. Or, they had a guy singing the melody in the *middle* of the quartet, like the Mills Brothers, and the rest sang *around* him. We became four guys who sang with the lead on top, which wasn't done, and we sang with so much more of an instrumental phrasing than a vocal one. So many vocalists get the feeling that they are supposed to do nip-ups and be surprising and cute with what they sing. We were trying to sing the genuine work of every chord, every note, every thing we could get out of it. Just like the barbershoppers do, only it wasn't barbershop at *all*. And we were singing *open* voicings. Most groups sang five-part and had the voicing quite close together; the five notes would just play in one hand. But when the Freshmen found this idea of singing with this open *inversion* of chords, so that there was a great, wide *sound,* from four guys, with that blend, then we had heard ourselves sing that *sound,* and we didn't want to sing any other *way* after that.

L.A.: Did you discover this sound before or after Kenton?

BARBOUR: Before. Well, we had heard the Pastels. Of course, everybody had, but most of them didn't know what they were hearing. *We* swallowed it like the bait on a hook. That was what a group was supposed to sound like. But it

was five, you see, and it had a girl on *top*. We were trying to sound like *five voices*. And we were just *four guys*.

L.A.: How do you do that?

BARBOUR: You just spread yourself and leave one of the notes out that your ear accidentally hears when you're singing the other ones right enough.

L.A.: Seriously. (Laughs.)

BARBOUR: And if you're *singing* five notes, then you'll hear five *notes*. But if you're singing the important *four* of those five notes, there is a thing, a *harmonic* sound, that happens in your ear—you *think* you're hearing that fifth note . . .

L.A.: Is that right!

BARBOUR: But it's not even *there*. If

you sing the others *right* enough. And . . .

L.A.: If you have the right intervals between the four . . .

BARBOUR: Ya . . .

L.A.: . . . the fifth one seems to supply it?

BARBOUR: Uh-huh. Yeah! Your ear just will fill that one *in*.

L.A.: (Slyly). Why didn't you just add another guy and save all the trouble?

BARBOUR: Well—the Spartan effect of *getting* that sound—uh—was like performing it with *magic*. Rather than having a guy with a wheelbarrow *haul off* the lion, we made the lion *disappear*. Before the *eyes*. That kind of *magic* is what we were trying for.

L.A.: It *does* sound like more than four.

The Four Freshmen: Ross Barbour, Bob Flanigan, Ken Errair, Don Barbour. 1950s publicity photo. (Collection of the Author.)

BARBOUR: Ya. And there are times—well I know there's one classic chord in "Poincianna" at the end of the bridge, where we sound like *"Oh-oh-oh-oh-ohhh, oh-ohhh, oh-oh-oh-oh-oh-ohhhhhh . . . Poin-ci—"* well, there's a note that appears on *Poin* that's like a fifth above it. *We* didn't sing that note. It just is *there.* Because we sang these so right, you get a harmonic that—I don't know—a physicist could explain it. How one note bangs into the other and causes another vibration.

L.A.: An actual physical sound?

BARBOUR: Uh-huh.

L.A.: Wow.

BARBOUR: You can hear it on the record.

L.A.: How did you arrive at your intervals?

BARBOUR: We did it by ear. We chose those notes by ear, and we chose the notes that sounded best to *us.* Maybe it would be very close. Maybe it would be unison, and suddenly spread. Just 'cause that's what we *liked.* And then back to unison and then half-steps apart to build a chord as it grew. We'd sing "It's A Blue World" and we'd know that's going to start in unison and then *Blue* has got to be *this* way, it's got to be that spread, open sound.

L.A.: What *are* the intervals on *Blue?*

BARBOUR: It's like a D-Major seventh.

L.A.: Did you ever sing a chord larger than an octave?

BARBOUR: Oh, ya! Ya, there are some other chords, like the ending of "This Love of Mine," where the top note is clear up there, and the bass note is down here.

L.A.: Were all of the Freshmen from Indiana?

BARBOUR: Yes. Don and I are from Columbus, and Bob, our cousin, is from Greencastle. We grew up together. Our grandfather was quite a guy—he'd work all day on the farm and then go to the next town to fiddle at a country dance and/or sing harmony or solos all night; a gypsy kind of guy, and the grandchildren were kind of that way too. There are about a hundred of us I guess and most are entertainers of some kind. Bob's younger sister had more talent than any of the rest of us. But we had that dogged devotion to the *sound* that just kept pulling us, and wouldn't let us go.

L.A.: You guys evolved your own style, prior to singing with the Kenton band, and you just happened to be doing the same kind of thing?

BARBOUR: Well, yes. What happened is that we had heard Stan Kenton doing this kind of thing, and we were trying every way we could to do it, with our instruments and our voices.

L.A.: You were trying to imitate him?

BARBOUR: Ya. And we were trying to imitate the Pastels, we were trying to imitate the Kenton sax section, Bob with his trombone sound was trying to be more Kentonish than Kenton, and in the guitar chords, in everything we did, we were trying to be as Kentonish as we could.

L.A.: Now I know why Stan *liked* you. Because that's what *he* does. Stretches the chord.

BARBOUR: He heard the Freshmen trying to sing like the Pastels. And he

Stan Kenton with Willie Maiden in Europe, '70s. (Photo: Courtesy of a Kenton friend.)

Ross Barbour at the record player in his living room. (Photo by the Author.)

liked his Pastels. Somehow it hadn't turned out well and they'd come apart. So Stan didn't have his vocal group when he came to Dayton and heard this bunch of Hoosiers. Who didn't know what they were singin' but they knew they *liked* it. And the *people* knew they liked it. And Stan knew *he* liked it.

L.A.: Was this a case of four individual people getting together who felt the same way about something in life?

BARBOUR: I think a whole lot of it was that way. We loved what we were doing, and we did it from love rather than the way the textbook said groups *do* it now. And it showed. There was an uncomplicated, uncute thing about it. We just sang love songs. With great love. And with jazz feeling. The best things we ever did were the simplest things. We got more involved later on. Some of the things we did we arranged to pieces. And it got so busy it was like *lace.* But it wasn't "Blue World" or "Poincianna."

L.A.: Or "Angel Eyes."

BARBOUR: "Angel Eyes." Songs like that were just so down-center that nobody could ignore 'em, it'd just carry

people with them.

L.A.: Who wrote "Angel Eyes"?

BARBOUR: Matt Dennis and Earl Brent wrote the tune. Pete Rugolo wrote the arrangement with the five trombones.

L.A.: That's a terrific arrangement.

BARBOUR: Oh ya. He sent us those arrangements and—we weren't much as readers. We'd done a lot of faking and memorizing and inventing and making it up as we'd go, and *reading* was just something that other people did. What Pete wrote was four voice parts and five trombone parts, together—nine. Well—he didn't *send* us *their* five. He just sent us our *four.* And you start singing those four notes by themselves, and you think, What kind of a chord is that?

L.A.: Something was missing. (Laughs.)

BARBOUR: Yeah! Terrible! What the—what's he got, man—we were practically in fist fights and smashing a glass against the wall and stamping on it at rehearsals a few times. It was a crisis for us to get that album made. *We* didn't know what the trombones were doing! We're singing these four dumb notes!

"Pete, what have you *done* to us!" Finally when we got the record made, we heard what it sounded like and realized that was just Pete's style.

L.A.: Did the Freshmen do the trombone parts also?

BARBOUR: No, those were done by Milt Bernhart, Frank Rosolino, Harry Betts, Tommy Pederson, and George Roberts. And there was a rhythm section.

L.A.: One of my favorite things you did was Willie Maiden's "Hymn to Her." That was gorgeous.

BARBOUR: That's a whale of an arrangement. But I wish we could have done it over.

L.A.: Why?

BARBOUR: There was a lot of conviction in it. We were trying like crazy. But we didn't get all the good notes that are in there.

L.A.: Did you perform it often?

BARBOUR: No, I don't think so. I think the only time we performed it was that one time, on the *Butler* album. We rehearsed it a lot.

L.A.: How many albums did you do with Stan?

134

BARBOUR: Well, *Butler*, and the *Road Show* albums, and a package with June Christy.

L.A.: And on your own how many?

BARBOUR: We must have about 34 albums. Not counting the groups who *sound* like us.

L.A.: You mean there are people who imitate the Freshmen?

BARBOUR: (Laughs.) Yes. And some you wouldn't *believe*. Come on, I'll play some of these albums for you.

Barbour goes to his living room, and for the next hour plays selections from several diverse groups, all of whom share a remarkable predilection for, and uncanny resemblance to, the style and sound of the Four Freshmen. One is The Vocal Majority, from Dallas, a group made up of "doctors, lawyers, airline pilots and plumbers," Ross explains, who sing "It's A Blue World." Another is The Seventh Sound, a New York group led by Dave Bentley, who sing "Their Hearts Were Full of Spring." A third is The Harlequins, singing "There She Goes, Doesn't Even See Me." Denver Affair sings "Out of Nowhere," "Here's That Rainy Day," and "After You," and dedicates two cuts to the Freshmen, one of which, "Lilacs in the Rain," they've written in the Freshmen style. While the album is playing, Ken Albers says "Who's that, Ross?" and is almost persuaded that it's the Four Freshmen.

Albers, singer, composer and arranger with the Freshmen for 26 years, says he still has his first Kenton album, the original Artistry in Rhythm, on 78's. "Each one is in perfect shape. That album influenced me so much, in my arranging—got me away from the Glenn Miller school of music into a more creative one. Really turned me around. I first met Stan at The Crescendo on Sunset Boulevard one night after our show. He was in the audience. He said his hellos and welcomed me to the group. It was an amazing feeling, meeting him."

At one point, Ross mischievously pops in one of the Freshmen's discs, "I'm Always Chasing Rainbows," and sings along with it. He plays "Julie Is Her Name," and a song written especially for them by Bobby Troup, called "The Four Freshmen," sung and recorded as a return compliment just for them by Julie London at the height of her fame.

Eeriest of all, a group from Japan on an album entitled Time Five sing "Our Love Is Here To Stay." Ross's wife, Sue, comments, "The lead singer kept asking Bob, 'How do you get that much SOUND out of it?'"

L.A.: I never would have believed this if I hadn't heard it!

BARBOUR: Isn't that something?

L.A.: Did Stan continue to come to see the Freshmen perform now and then?

BARBOUR: Yes. He came to Sparks, Nevada, and to the Crest, and to Indian Lake in Ohio, near Akron . . . . Lots of times.

L.A.: One thing one hears quite a bit is how Stan made people play better than they thought they were capable of, that his musicians would want to go out and do everything they had for him.

BARBOUR: The band was his family, his way of measuring his own success. And, right, he raised a lot of these guys, he brought out of 'em more than they ever would have come up with. That was one of the things he took greatest pride in. To see a young kid—bashful, shy—a good player, but—a beginner. And see him spread his wings and fly. And really become a great, great player WHILE he was with Stan's band. He loved to do that.

L.A.: How would he get them to do that? How would he implant the idea that the kid could meet the challenge?

BARBOUR: It was a different thing with each one, and Stan knew how to do it. He would challenge this one guy, and he would cajole the next guy, and he would *trick* the *third* guy.

L.A.: (Laughs.) Trick him how?

BARBOUR: He wouldn't tell him that—well he wouldn't *tell* him that his solo was coming up.

L.A.: Oh, you're kidding!

BARBOUR: He would just say, *"You!"* And the guy'd say "Uh-uh-uh-uh-uh . . . "

L.A.: What, at the *performance?*

BARBOUR: Ya! Stan would do whatever it took to open that kid and make him *bloom*. We were working at Birdland in New York, I guess it was '50. Stan Levey was the drummer. And Stan's a great football player of a guy, great, strong man. Birdland was a basement place at 52nd and Broadway, with a low ceiling, about like a living room. And the band was really juuuuust rippin' people up. There was Levey—*taapatatahh, patatahh, patatahh, patatahh, patatahh!* And—he's got the big end of the stick, and it's a great big thing, and this great big man is goin' *tahhpatatahh, patatahh* and Stan is sayin' "Come on!"

L.A.: (Laughs.)

BARBOUR: "Come *on*! Come on, Stan!" And—*TAHpatatahh, patatahh*—the sweat poppin' out like fountains! I've seen him do this.

L.A.: My gosh.

BARBOUR: And pretty soon, man, the band is swingin'—'cause of *tahpatatahh* man, it's drivin' 'em crazy. (Laughs.) Whenever we played with them, the band would come in behind you, *Paaa!* and you'd just jump right over the footlights at the impact. Stan was a terribly intense guy. Always the first one up. We'd get on the bus and spend all day going somewhere, maybe not even check into a hotel. And Stan'd be out there, getting the band set up. Then you'd do the one-nighter and you'd drive on 'til 3 in the morning, and he'd wake up the sleepers and help 'em get into the hotel and we'd have maybe four hours' sleep and he'd be the one who'd wake 'em up and get 'em on the bus. Or stay up late with some new guy who needed to rehearse or help him get organized. Just—just *intense*. Like a priest to 'em, and like a teacher to 'em. It becomes a society on that bus. It's like an iron lung, somebody said. (Laughs.) And you get your own jokes going. It was like going underground—like being a *mole*. You poke your head up and shout at a thousand people with bright lights in your eyes, then you pop your head down and you're a mole again. For nineteen more hours, then you pop your head up again.

L A.: Would Stan share personal thoughts with you during these long trips?

BARBOUR: I remember one time. We were coming back from a disc jockey show, or something, heading back to the job. I don't even remember who Stan was married to, or connected with. But he had a line like, "I think I fell in love again." Or something like that. And—then that was all there was to that. He didn't go on with it, and I didn't beg him to. You didn't really get inside Stan. He would go into *your* life. Guys would get "Dear John" letters from home, and there they are, trapped on the bus. Whatever personal problems they had, Stan would talk 'em out of it. He'd cheer people up. He was devoted, fatherly, without wavering, without *hesitation*, our friend. Stan would hug ya—didn't matter if you were Roosevelt Grier or if you were a cute little *kid*, Stan would hug ya, and kiss you on the forehead. I imagine Stan has kissed a million foreheads, and hugged a million people. He sure breathed fire into us. Again and again and again. Even before '52, when he went to bat for us with "Blue World," we were working here in Los Angeles—Stan had brought us West—and his manager, Bob Allison, and his publicity agent, Gene Howard, were handling the Freshmen. At no cost. A lot of people will find a group that is going to succeed, or they think they can *make* succeed, and they will take 10 per cent of their success and that's the way the business works. Not with Stan. He didn't ever make a *penny* from us. He loaned us his business manager and his personal manager. And Gene Howard wrote "The Day Isn't Long Enough" for us. Allison took some pictures of us, and they took us under their wing and got us some jobs out here. We were working at Jerry Wald's Studio Club at Sunset and Vine, and we'd go across the street to KNX radio to do Steve Allen's show on intermissions, and when Steve went East to New York to start a career in television, he took us with him. We risked everything to do it; it was the chance of a lifetime. But after a couple of days the musicians' union in New York stopped us, saying we were not "locals." We went to see Stan at the Click Ballroom in Philadelphia and he asked how things were with us and we told him our situation. He was enraged. Next morning he and Steve tried to talk the union into letting us stay, but they wouldn't hear of it. The union guy was surprised even to see Stan there; after all, he wasn't *personally* involved. In fact he was taking great risks. They could have torn up his union card right there. Or sent him a wire forbidding him to make recordings; they've been known to do that. We couldn't win our case, but they did give us a month's salary, so we could get back to L.A. and start all over again. But this was a case, again, of "You must succeed. I've made you part of my ego. We can't let each other fail. We are going to succeed."

L.A.: It's amazing. It's as though he adopted you, almost.

Stan Kenton and his Orchestra, Atlantic City Steel Pier, 1952. Left to right, back row: Kenton, Stan Levey, Conte Candoli, Buddy Childers, George Roberts, Maynard Ferguson, Don Dennis, Sal Salvador, Bob Gioga. Front row (seated), left to right: Ruben McFall, Don Bagley, Dick Meldonian, Bill Holman, Tom Shepard, Frank Rosolino, Bob Burgess, Lee Elliott, Keith Moon, Vinnie Dean. (Photo: Courtesy of Bob Gioga.)

BARBOUR: He had adopted us. We were family.

L.A.: During your association with him, what strikes you as being especially significant about the man?

BARBOUR: I think Stan's the greatest leader of men I ever met. I might say differently if I had met Lincoln or Washington or Roosevelt.

L.A.: You don't mean just bandleader, do you.

BARBOUR: I mean greatest leader of men. Any less of a leader would have been a dismal failure with the complex problems he faced, playing music that was not acceptable—it wasn't—who wants to hear that stuff, that complicated, hard, loud, brassy stuff. Stan kept it goin'. He was a guy would could say it right, and just burn ya up with what he's saying, just set you on fire, *aim* you, *propel* you toward your goal. He led his guys through fire and they'll *still* walk through fire for the name of Stan Kenton. And when you can get that kind of allegiance, you can be a great force for good, or for evil. And he chose to be a great force for music.

Scott Stewart, watching a sectional rehearsal, Madison, Wisconsin. (Photo by the Author.)

19 Scott Stewart

Whitewater, Wisconsin, August 8, 1981. In a dazzling 13-minute display of flash, pizzazz, and full-throttle musicianship, the Madison Scouts Drum Corps take the breath away from a rapt audience with a performance centered on "Malaguena," the Bill Holman-arranged staple of the Stan Kenton repertoire. Rendering it with the kind of fearless horn-work, open emotion and wild excitement that would have brought tears to Stan Kenton's eyes, they drive the 14,000-plus spectators to frenzy, bringing on cheers and standing ovations. Moments later, in the final judging of this much-coveted Midwest Regional competition, the announcer intones, "In second place . . . with a score of 85.75 . . . the Blue Devils!" Screaming peals out from every corner of Warhawk Stadium. If the Devils are second, that means —"In first place . . ." says the barely audible voice ". . . with a score of 86.90 . . . the Madison Scouts!" and the place goes berserk.

L.A.: You've got a *lot* of explaining to do.
STEWART: (Laughs.)

L.A.: Let's start with why you chose "Malaguena" for competition.
STEWART: We played it a few years ago, and we brought it back last year. The reason we picked it was, when you put on "Malaguena," there are very few numbers—I'd still feel this way if we played it for three years and I'd become numb to it, almost, I'd still feel that's one of the most exciting pieces of music ever written.
L.A.: That arrangement or that music?

STEWART: That arrangement. The music itself, Spanish music always holds something, but Stan Kenton's arrangement of it was really just dynamite. Whether you listen to the corps arrangement or his original arrangement, it's just got power, it's got drive, and it's a type of piece of music that—that an educated, musical person can appreciate, but even a person who doesn't understand music but enjoys it would like. It's got everything it takes to be an exciting piece of music.
L.A.: How do you adapt a 19-piece concert arrangement of a work like that—actually it was arranged by Bill Holman for Stan Kenton . . .
STEWART: Um-hm, right.
L.A.: . . . how do you take that and adapt it to your group, which is—how large *is* your group?
STEWART: Brass?
L.A.: No, the whole thing.

STEWART: It's a hundred and twenty-eight. What that breaks down to is 62 brass . . .
L.A.: (Laughs.) I had a vision just now of Stan Kenton listening to 62 brass.
STEWART: He was familiar with drum corps.
L.A.: With your drum corps?

STEWART: Yes. In fact, Stan Kenton did the introduction to one of the earliest drum corps promotional films we made, in 1973.

L.A.: What did he say?
STEWART: He said he felt that drum corps was important in the development of someone as a person, as a musician, because it demanded more intensity and application than did the study of—history, or whatever.
L.A.: More intensity and application. That sounds like Kenton language. He was very much in favor of the concept, then.
STEWART: Um-hm. Right. Anyhow, going on with the breakdown, we march 62 brass, and then 32 percussion, and 32 in the color guard. And the color guard is the visual part, the flags, rifles, whatever props there are to back up the musical part of it. And two drum majors, who are the musical directors and the leaders of the corps while it's on the field performing.
L.A.: How many flags and how many rifles?
STEWART: For us it fluctuates. Sometimes the whole guard is on rifle. Sometimes the whole guard is on flags. Sometimes they're all on different things, so . . .

139

Madison Scouts in performance at DCI North, Ypsilanti, Michigan. (Photos by the Author.)

L.A.: Within the same performance?

STEWART: Right. In our corps they've got to be able to do both. They've also got to be very good at dance and gymnastics. In fact the whole color guard scene has gravitated very much towards theatre and dance, so the guys have got to be very—very much Broadway-oriented, let's say.

L.A.: That rifle sequence last year was unbelievable. They were flashing and whirling and interweaving just *blindingly,* and with such *precision.*

STEWART: That was probably the drum solo. What we had done—we did something that was new. No drum corps

STEWART: Right.

L.A.: You have many kinds of drums and horns.

STEWART: Right. The way it breaks down is, in a horn line we carry what we call soprano horns, which are comparable to trumpets. And then we carry mellophone horns, which are comparable to mellophoniums—which is strange, because Stan Kenton, I think, introduced mellophoniums.

L.A.: Yes! Is it the same kind of instrument?

STEWART: Well, the same—the difference between our horns and a trumpet, say, is that we use only two

is a conical core and the trumpet is cylindrical. In the bore, or inside diameter, the lead pipe, instead of being straight, always expands from the mouthpiece, like a concert baritone or French horn. In a trumpet the lead pipe is the same width all the way down; it's cylindrical. A trumpet and trombone would both be that way. But all bugles are conical. That's what gives a different texture to the sound.

L.A.: In Kenton's band, I know, the mellophones were sort of a bridge between the trumpets and trombones.

STEWART: It's the same with us. Next step we go to is French horns. Beyond

Madison Scouts in a sectional rehearsal. (Photo by the Author.)

had ever done it before. We did it in 1980 and last year. The whole horn line went on flags. And the whole color guard went on rifles. So, in addition to having the color guard good at everything, we had to teach the horn line to be good at doing guard, too.

L.A.: In adapting this 19-piece arrangement, your interpretation probably takes into account all the breakdowns in percussion and horns, right?

valves, instead of three valves. So that puts us in a different key. That also means the arranger has to be very innovative and creative, to make up for his lack of having all three valves. The mellophonium, yes, is very similar to the concert mellophonium, except again, it's in a different key and it's adapted for outside use.

DAVE ELDER: (Scouts staff member.) The real difference between the soprano horn and the trumpet is that the soprano

French horns we go to baritones. And then euphoniums. Then the contrabass. So our whole brass choir is sopranos, mellophones, French horns, baritones, euphoniums, and contrabasses. And then those are split into various parts, too, so we're split generally about fourteen ways.

L.A.: That many sections of sound.

ELDER: What makes it so easy to adapt is the way the choir is split up. In a jazz

141

band you have your saxes, trombones, and trumpets. In drum corps, you've got your sopranos, which are an upper voice, then you've got French horns and mellophones, which would be a saxophone-ranged voice, and then you have baritones, which would be a trombone-ranged voice. Then you have contras for bass instruments, and of course you've got a built-in rhythm section. And the good thing about it is that even though they're all brass instruments, they're not the same. A trumpet and trombone have really the same texture of sound, except that they're in different registers. But each of the bugle sections has its own texture. They're easily distinguishable. You don't get any confusion when parts cross over. That makes it really easy to come in. And it's easier to take a jazz band piece and arrange it for drum corps than it is to take a classical piece, where you have to deal with violins, which play totally out of register for the horns.

L.A.: Are you the one who does that kind of work?
ELDER: I do some of it, but I don't do the field show for it.
L.A.: Who does the adaptation of that 19-piece arrangement?
STEWART: Chris Metzger is our arranger.

L.A.: You're saying it's not as difficult as it would seem.
ELDER: It's not terribly difficult. To get it good and competitive in an arrangement, you have to put a lot of time into it. But it's not an impossible task to make a good adaptation.
STEWART: The biggest switch would be in that mid-voice, where we're switching from a woodwind to a brass, but still, we have our sections that correspond to the sections in the jazz band, so it's . . .
L.A.: It sounds just like it! You know? It sounds like it, only better.
STEWART: Our instrumentation was set up purposely to correspond with the jazz band. See every corps has its own combination of how many horns they use. The way ours is set up, we have an equal number of soprano voices, mid-voices, and baritone-type voices. We're more into the jazz style, the contemporary style. Our instrumentation is set up to accommodate that.
L.A.: You were saying that you had fourteen different shades of sound.
STEWART: That's just in the brass.
L.A.: You have several different kinds of drums.

STEWART: With our percussion we're actually able to do more—far more—than they're usually able to do in a jazz band. We've got a lot more leverage there. Now the reason drum corps percussion is different from anything else, between the snare drums and the quads, which are like tom-toms on a set drum, and the basses, you can imitate a set sound, you know, what you would get out of a set drum.

L.A.: You mean like a soloist with a big band.
STEWART: Trap set, right. But the difference is, when you've got a set drummer playing on those, that's only one guy. Here you've got to have 20 guys doing what a set drummer would do all himself. And the other thing that we add in here that they wouldn't have in a big band is we've also got keyboard.
L.A.: Xylophones.
STEWART: Xylophones, marimbas, vibraphones, concert bells. Those are the four we carry. And we've got a set of timpani, too. Concert timpani that we use. So not only are you having a rhythmic set sound, but on top of that you've got symphonic sounds, with, where you're tuning tunable percussion, we've got a large area that we can work in.
L.A.: And your cymbals.
STEWART: We carry five cymbals.
L.A.: Your six bass drums are pitched differently.

STEWART: That's the other interesting thing with the corps, you take six basses, and you put each one on a different pitch. So you're able to imitate a string bass in a jazz band. You're able to run up and down.
L.A.: In the quads you have four different pitches per set?
STEWART: Right. We have five of those, five guys playing the same part; and ten snares, six bass on different pitches, and four timpani that're all tunable by a foot pedal. Those things can play anything. One guy plays all four, it's like a concert timpanist would play. With those you've got any variety, you can change pitches to anything you want.
L.A.: So you can get a whole bunch more pitches right out of your percussion.
STEWART: Oh ya. Um-hm.
L.A.: I heard them rehearsing. It was like a concert all by itself.
STEWART: Oh ya.
L.A.: I just wonder how all that would

work out with "Malaguena."
STEWART: "Malaguena" was a great one for percussion.
L.A.: Because there's only one drummer in the Stan Kenton Orchestra, would you take the things that he was doing and divide it up among your percussion?

STEWART: To some degree. See we're able to expand on what he was able to do. In Kenton's group, say there was a swing part; the guy that was playing the trap set would probably be playing cymbals with one hand and an off-beat pattern on the snare drum with the other. Well what we would do is that all our snares would be playing on cymbals, so you'd have that same feel there coming through; but then we'd expand, we'd have the bass drums probably covering what was the string bass, so they'd be doing: boom-boom-boom-boom-boom. They'd be backing up the contrabasses out there. Then the timpanis would be written into a melodic passage. Maybe backing up the melody, as would the keyboards. Or— the keyboards may be taking the piano part. Part of the melody, again, may be reinforced by the timpanis, and then the quads—we may have a whole new voice in there that Kenton never had, with our quads playing yet another part. Maybe they're even backing up the saxophone part. Or maybe they're playing a rhythmic thing in there that gives it a little Spanish flavor behind it.

L.A.: That is utterly fabulous. Kenton's music seems in so many ways ideally suited to what you do.
STEWART: Um-hm.
ELDER: Yes.
L.A.: And you personally liked "Malaguena"?

STEWART: Just to get in the way we choose any music is, we'll sit down, as individuals, first of all, and listen to things that we think can sell. Then we sit down as a whole group and say, "Here are my ideas." And you throw 'em on and everybody sits there and goes, "Ya, I think that's got potential; let's put it over here," or else you go, "Euaagh, that'll never work," you know, the crowd won't buy that, or no, this isn't gonna work, and we tear it apart. And "Malaguena," you put that on, everybody just sat there and went: "Phew!"
L.A.: (Laughs.)
STEWART: That's it. I mean I

remember that day we laid it on . . .

L.A.: You mean the Stan Kenton record?

STEWART: Ya, oh ya. Put on his version of it—this was back in '78—and we just all sat there and there was no argument. I mean that very rarely happens. It was just like: "That's it. Let's go on to the next number."

L.A.: It's music with great crowd-appeal.

STEWART: It's got to appeal to the crowd, but it's got to appeal to the judges, too. It's got to be pleasing; at the same time it's got to be creative. And it's got to be something that isn't just a stock number. So you're always looking for things that you can extend your creativity on without losing touch with the person who appreciates music but doesn't necessarily understand it. At least that's our philosophy at Madison.

L.A.: I would think it would relate well to color guard interpretation as well.

STEWART: Right. Our guard interprets music through dance just as they do in a Broadway play. Our coordinator as a visual person has to decide, "This is what this music says," and he's got to do that interpretation with the guard.

L.A.: That must be a lot of fun, figuring out how you're going to do that.

STEWART: Oh, ya. Well all these things are fun. (Laughs.)

ELDER: (Laughs.)

STEWART: I say that facetiously sometimes. The name of the game—the way you win in drum corps now is to be impeccably coordinated. I mean to have it so that all factions, the brass, the percussion, the choreography, the visuals on top of that, everything has to fit. Everything has to make sense, when you sit there and watch it; it's like you were looking at a beautiful painting. And that's what takes time. It's certainly fun, because any time you're being creative it's fun. But it can—it's demanding, because it's got to be done right. Those are what make the corps win and lose. Whoever is the most coordinated should win.

L.A.: Does Stan Kenton's music in a general sense present more challenges or more hard things to work out than let's say the work of another composer that you might want to use?

STEWART: (Pauses.) That was certainly a challenging piece.

ELDER: I wouldn't say it was *more challenging*. Everything is relative.

STEWART: Right.

ELDER: It depends on how you look at it. It's not so much that it was more challenging, it's just that the end product can come out better. Because of the appeal that the music has itself, it lends itself to visual interpretation really easily.

STEWART: It wasn't so much challenging in the sense of intensely articulated passages or technical difficulty. It was challenging in the interpretation of it. It was difficult to pull it off the way he had intended it, to put the right interpretation behind it.

L.A.: You were trying to do that? Play it the way he would have wanted it?

STEWART: Oh, ya. (Laughs.) That's a hot piece.

L.A.: Evidently you both admire Kenton very much yourselves.

ELDER: (Laughs.) Oh, ya.

STEWART: Ya, he's a—

ELDER: Anybody on this corps would, I think. We use him quite a bit.

L.A.: Why?

STEWART: His music is the kind that appeals to a lot of different people. It isn't dry music. It has life to it, it has drive to it.

L.A.: And it has *color*.

STEWART: Oh ya. Um-*hm*. The music that we've used of his has been very, very good for us.

L.A.: How well did you do with "Malaguena" when you first brought it out, in '78?

STEWART: '78 was similar to last year. We were in contention for the number one spot all year. We beat the corps that eventually ended up winning many times throughout the year, same as last year, but we ended up fourth that year in the world championships. There were four of us that were just tight all the way. It was close. I guess my philosophy in the thing is, it's hard to say did you win or lose because when you're competing with other corps that are on an equal level, you can't always win. So long as you stay in that top group, that top four or five, whatever it may be that year, you've got to consider yourself a winner.

L.A.: What other Kenton works have you performed?

STEWART: "MacArthur Park" was like one of our first trademarks. We did it in '75, when we won the championship.

L.A.: Your first world championship

you were playing a Kenton work! *Great.* I think that was arranged for him by Dee Barton.

STEWART: Our soloist in that was Chris Metzger, the guy I mentioned who's now our arranger. He's a really fine player. He did the 1981 arrangement of "Malaguena." We had another version in 1978. Chris is a wonderful arranger, one of the best in the activity. We've done "Granada Smoothie." We did Kenton's "Somewhere" from *West Side Story* for a closer in 1977.

L.A.: What about "Artistry in Rhythm"?

STEWART: That was done by the Anaheim Kingsmen in 1974, when they almost won the world title, and another consistent finalist, the Crossmen, from Philadelphia, are doing it this year for an opener. I can think of at least three corps that have done "Malaga." We've considered doing "Peanut Vendor" and "Chiapas."

L.A.: Do your corps members enjoy playing Kenton? How do they respond to it in relation to other works you perform?

STEWART: Oh, sure, they enjoy it a lot. But generally with all the music we pick we choose things that are entertaining and that our people can really get into playing; they generally enjoy everything they're doing. But Kenton—I guess rather than say they enjoy that more than something else, I'd say that Kenton fits very well into *our* mold, because they *do* enjoy it.

L.A.: I'm sure every drum corps is associated with a certain style and has its own sound. I understand that you are considered more jazz-oriented than most other groups. What would be the Madison sound as such?

STEWART: I would put a bigger umbrella on it than just jazz. It's definitely jazz-oriented, but I would say it's a *contemporary* sound. Also, it's a *powerful* sound. Madison is known for putting out a sound that you not only hear but also you *feel*.

L.A.: Do all drum corps have the same number of personnel?

STEWART: In the top twenty-five, the corps sizes are very similar. Between a hundred and ten and a hundred and twenty-five, twenty-eight is where everybody falls in. Pretty much broken down as ours is, too. About half of the group would be brass, then a quarter color guard and a quarter percussion.

That's pretty standard. Within that, there are variations as to what kind of instrumentations you use and how many of each instrument you use and. . .

L.A.: You can make your own choices on those?

STEWART: Right. Right.

mean that's what he does.

STEWART: It's very similar to what he did, right.

L.A.: What were your other pieces last year?

STEWART: Our opening tune was a chart called "Numero Uno," by Louis

for percussion groups? I guess there's enough color there that you can write specifically for it.

STEWART: Oh yes. Every drum corps features percussion one time in its show, a percussion ensemble presentation.

Madison Scouts in performance at DCI North, Ypsilanti, Michigan. (Photo by the Author.)

L.A.: And do you choose a certain pattern that gives you your particular sound?

STEWART: Right. What we choose is to have our horn line very well balanced. Some of the corps would, say, tend to have a bigger soprano line, and what that would give them is a more upper-end sound. Our whole goal is to have the most balanced sound possible, so that when you hit it, it's like a wall of sound. A fullness.

L.A.: *Wall of sound.* Do you know, that's a Kenton concept.

STEWART: Right. Right. Very much so.

L.A.: From the top to the bottom.

STEWART: Um-hm.

L.A.: You try to do that—I'm sure you came to the idea on your own, but I

Bellson. Then we did "Concierto de Aranjuez," by Rodrigo. When we first put the show together, we had the first tune and then "Malaguena." But we wanted a bridge in there, something that would take us down from the high of the first tune and lead us into "Malaguena," and that was just perfect. Then the drum solo was a number entitled "Downwind," by a percussive group called Gong. And then the closer was the theme from *Ice Castles,* which was a Marvin Hamlisch number.

L.A.: Five pieces altogether.

STEWART: Well, yes, but the drum solo was short, and the "Concierto" was short . . . It was three major numbers.

L.A.: Are they doing that, writing pieces

L.A.: That is fabulous. I guess I thought it was part of something else.

STEWART: That's the object, just have everything so well integrated that the show just flows right along.

L.A.: It did, it felt like one big thing.

STEWART: Yes.

L.A.: And you play the same show all season long, just keep perfecting it?

STEWART: Right. The whole logic of drum corps is to take thirteen minutes and make it as perfect and as well-coordinated as possible. What the average show consists of is six corps going out, putting out, hopefully, six thirteen-minute presentations that are all just really nice little acts.

L.A.: This kind of thing probably couldn't have been possible, say, twenty years ago, could it?

144

STEWART: Oh no no. It could have been played, but it would have been bastardized to the point where it wouldn't have been worth doing. For several reasons. First, the instruments were not good, not comparable to a legitimate instrument, and now they are. Now you've got the tools to do it. And the players—now you have people that are very proficient. College music majors, people who are capable of playing professionally, really fine players. Instructors—you've got very well qualified instructors now. Back in the fifties to a large degree you didn't have any of that. So you could have

L.A.: Did your love of music begin in high school?
STEWART: My interest in music, continued interest in music, was fostered by the corps.
L.A.: Were you a Scout yourself?
STEWART: Yes. Everybody on our staff was. Another thing that's kind of unique about Madison is that we're the only major corps in the country that's got an all-alumni staff. All eighteen guys on the staff were playing members of the corps before they joined.
L.A.: And you've been director for how long?
STEWART: Since 1977.

internationally are all from the United States.
L.A.: This is a relatively new phenomenon, isn't it? I was only conscious of it after seeing one of your competitions on public television a few years ago.
STEWART: Drum Corps as we know it now dates to 1971, and Drum Corps International was formed in 1972.
L.A.: But there've been drum corps around for a long time, haven't there?

STEWART: Yes, it dates back to just after World War I, when the returning

Suncoast Sound, in performance in Port Huron, Michigan. Kenton's famous "wall of sound" lives! (Photo by the Author.)

done a piece, but it certainly would have come off sounding like a high school marching band, rather than the way Kenton had envisioned it.
L.A.: Did you use to listen to his records?
STEWART: Oh ya. I enjoy music very much and I've always enjoyed Kenton's music. I saw him at a concert here, at the technical college, about five years ago.

L.A.: How is the structure of drum corps set up?

STEWART: The main governing body is Drum Corps International, which is made up of the top twenty-five corps, internationally. And the way that's determined is at the International Championship every year. Now the way it sits right now, the best corps

military people starting their American Legion or V.F.W. posts wanted something to keep them busy, so what they did was make little bands, or little drum corps. They were really primitive then; they played on a straight bugle and just snare drums. It was very amateur, very primitive. The biggest problem drum corps has now is that it's advanced to the point where it is definitely an art form.

But so many people haven't seen that advance, and they still think of it in these primitive terms. After a gradual progression in the next few decades, the most dramatic changes have really taken place in the seventies and up to now. That's when it moved from being very amateur to being para-professional, at least. The performances could certainly be qualified as professional-type performances. What's happened over the years is we've got a fewer number of corps, but they're bigger now and much more proficient. One of the reasons for the decline in numbers is just the competitive thing. If your corps isn't going to be competitive at all, it dies out after a while. And the only way to stay competitive is by becoming more and more professional and keeping up with the other corps, and that's just a tough thing to do. It's a real tough thing to keep a corps operating, because the basic laws of society dictate that something like this shouldn't exist. There's just too much effort put in, and there's no monetary return, and most people aren't into that. All our members are under twenty-two. There's only so long without getting paid for it that a guy can continue to sacrifice his whole life to it.

L.A.: Is what makes it international the involvement of Canada, or are other countries involved too?
STEWART: Oh ya. The biggest area of growth right now is probably England, Holland, and Japan. England is at this point really, really developing. I would say they're probably where the American corps were in the sixties. I get correspondence from some foreign person at least every other day, several hundred a year, from people from Japan or England, wanting information. They get the corps publications, the records; they'll invite over two hundred people, say, and watch our videotapes. The more they get into it, the more they like it and the more they improve.

L.A.: Was the formation of Drum Corps International in some way responsible for the advances of the last decade?

STEWART: Yes. From 1971 to 1981, the evolution has been incredible. In 1971 we began to have extensive touring, and it demanded putting in some heavy time to make it good. In 1971 the directors of the top corps at that time met and said, "This is ridiculous. We're putting out superior products right now, yet outside groups are dictating our activity. Let's get together and decide what kind of prize money we get, what rules we're judged under, what kind of situations and touring conditions we have," and so forth, and so they did that. In 1971 the top five corps in the East got together, and then the Midwest and West got together. That was a bold step. They were going against all the veterans' groups that had run everything until that time. I would say 1971 was the year it changed from being a little kid thing to being an art form. Then in 1972, the natural extension of the Eastern and Midwestern unions was the formation of Drum Corps International. That became the governing body that dictated the rules, that set all the tours; and so that was a big change. In 1974 there was a limited tv broadcast out East. Then in '75 there was national coverage of the championship. That was a big step. It opened it up to many people who didn't know what drum corps *was*. They thought—*Wow!* What *is* this? And a whole new market opened up.
L.A.: You mentioned twenty-five corps, but there are more than that, right?

Madison Scouts in a sectional rehearsal. (Photo by the Author.)

Madison Scouts in an outdoor rehearsal. (Photo by the Author.)

STEWART: Yes. In North America there are about 300 drum corps, a hundred in Canada and two hundred in the States. Drum Corps International's schedule is mainly concerned with setting up shows for the top twenty-five corps. They also sponsor the regional competitions, such as the Midwest Regional in Whitewater, Wisconsin; the Northern Regional, in Ypsilanti, Michigan; DCI East in Pennsylvania, and so forth, where any corps can enter, and compete, in the prelims, and the top ones make it to the finals. For the world championships generally about a hundred corps enter, and the finalists are the top twelve. That's Drum Corps International's role. Beyond that, there are regional organizations, such as Drum Corps Midwest, Drum Corps East, and so forth, that are related to the other organization in that the people who run them are involved in both. They set up shows for all the smaller corps within their area, and do the same kind of thing as DCI but on a regional level.

L.A.: How do you account for the fabulous success of the Madison

Scouts? Almost from the beginning, you've been right up there at the top.

STEWART: Madison Scouts have been around since 1938, which makes us one of the oldest corps in the country. And I would say—*my* philosophy, and that of the people before me, has been that longevity and consistency are far more important than being a flash in the pan and fading out after that. In this game, consistency is really an ultimate accomplishment. Madison has always been in the forefront. We want to be good every year, and I guess the ultimate reward is the fact that we just can continue to be good, year after year after year. So that's what *we* shoot for. Out of the top twelve corps in DCI, our budget is tenth. We operate on a budget of two hundred thousand dollars a year, and we compete with corps that spend a million a year. Yet in terms of success we're one of the top three corps. And Madison has always been in the top 20.

L.A.: Usually you're in the top *four*.

STEWART: Out of the last eleven years, ten of the eleven champions have

been from California. We're the eleventh. One advantage we have to keeping on top is that we have a real devotion to it. Here, for example, you've got some classic examples of people who have pretty much disrupted their entire lives, built their entire lives around the activity to make the corps good. You don't find people like that everywhere. And the common tie you find between the guys in the corps and on the staff is that we're all pretty idealistic. I guess we feel that giving up a lot of other things is worth it if we're able to do something we believe in.

L.A.: How much do you have to rehearse to put out such a good program?

STEWART: Well in the winter, we have Sunday rehearsals three times a month. One weekend a month we have a full weekend rehearsal, for all the out-of-town guys. At a camp like this we have guys from Tennessee, Kentucky, Florida, Texas, Massachusetts. It's such an expense, and such a hassle for them to get here, that once they're here, we

147

might as well get a lot done, so we rehearse the hell out of 'em on these weekends. (Laughs.) It's pretty intensive. We start at nine in the morning and work 'til midnight. In addition to that, Dave (Elder) runs a Wednesday night sectional for our local brass people, where they work on individual problems and things like that. And then . . .

L.A.: You mean this is a *whole year* thing?

STEWART: Oh ya. The season ends in August, after the championships. In September, everybody gets to take a break. I don't, I'll keep continuing; the business aspect of it has to go on, and the preparation for what's coming up. In October the staff gets involved again. That's the planning time for setting the final preparation of the program; setting up the schedule for the following year, and how are we gonna attack this whole thing. November, the guys start practicing again. And that continues all the way up until now, which is our final preparation stage before the season, and the season goes June, July and August, and then it just starts over again.

L.A.: Your rehearsals are really fascinating. I was watching a sectional percussion rehearsal earlier today. Was that a corps member acting as a sectional leader? It wasn't an instructor, I don't think. He was so good, getting it down to the finest detail. He said, "Okay, let's get started." They got down to the nitty-gritty and ironed it out. And he was saying "You've got to be precise; if you're too short or too long, you get *mud,* you throw everybody off." And they sat down, and it was the neatest thing, they could have been playing jacks or throwing dice or something. He started slowly, hitting a pattern on his bass drum. Then the number two guy had a pattern, and the number three guy. They gradually worked it out, taking it down to the smallest possible detail.

STEWART: Right, in every section we've got section leaders. When a guy has been here a number of years, and we see the leadership developing in him, we take him aside and say "We want you to take care of this section when we're not around" and so forth. And so that develops him even more.

L.A.: Now that really does contribute to a person's development, 'cause you're making a leader out of him.
STEWART: Oh ya.

L.A.: Is that how you handle this whole thing, just take it down to the smallest detail, every little section, mini-sectionals . . .
STEWART: Right. It starts out in individual practice, at home. A guy has to get to the point where he's good at what he does. Then he comes here, is taught our style, and works within his section. When the individual sections get it together, say the bass drum section, then you throw it in with the whole drum line. *That* takes a long time. Then you've got to put it together with the horns. So *that's* got to work. Then you put it together with the drill outside, so it's just like one. You're just building and building and building.

L.A.: The section leader also said a provocative thing: something like, you have to be in a state of readiness, but you have to be relaxed, too. How in the world do you manage *that,* with all the pressure on you to be perfect?

Madison Scouts in an outdoor rehearsal. (Photo by the Author.)

148

Scott Stewart, posing with the Madison Scouts' truck. (Photo by the Author.)

STEWART: There are different levels of rehearsal. Being ready comes through rehearsal preparation. When you hit the field, you've got to be relaxed; you've got to go out with the thought that, Hey, I know what I'm doing, now it's time to go out and enjoy it and just do my thing. It's the same as with Stan Kenton's group. When those guys went out, they didn't think, I've got a B-flat eighth note to play here. It's got to be almost a normal reaction at that point; the guy feels it. That's the same thing we strive for here. They don't worry about the notes, they just go out and *communicate.*

L.A.: What do you do when you aren't doing this? For a living?
STEWART: I do this all the time. In fact I do live off it. I'm one of the few that does. If you call it living. I've done this now for . . .
L.A.: You make just enough to get by?
STEWART: Ya. In fact since I run the organization, I set my salary, but the way I set it is, what do I need to live—I live on what most people would ask me how do I live. But I live on it, because this is what I want to do.

L.A.: Do you just want to go on being good at it or do you have some kind of big, big dream you're working toward?
STEWART: The dream is just to be able to meet the challenge of keeping this thing going, keeping it perpetuated.
L.A.: Your competition is getting harder all the time.

STEWART: Oh ya. We just keep fighting. You don't win every show. It never gets old. It doesn't get boring. It's just a continuous challenge. I enjoy the activity. I'm an idealist. And because we're dealing with people that are still at a formative age, being seventeen, eighteen, nineteen, twenty, twenty-one, I feel that hopefully we're able to influence them somewhat, to help them out to be a better person, not only as a performer but as a person learning that whatever you want, you've got to work hard at; being able to give them some guidance when maybe they need it—all those type of things. That's important to me. Beyond that, I just enjoy the excitement: being on tour, putting together something where we've got, between the guys in the corps and in our

junior, feeder corps, and the board and all the avenues of support, we're talking 500 people to coordinate. *That's* certainly a challenge. Being able to do that well is certainly something that makes it worthwhile. Then for the last, anywhere from five to ten to fifteen years, our staff, the alumni of the corps, they've been the closest people I've been to, so that keeps me here, wanting to stay with them. This is something that after you've been involved you don't just put it away and say "Okay, that's it." It stays with you. That means so much to me, and we've all worked for the same thing.
L.A.: You have a lot in common with Stan Kenton.
STEWART: In a lot of ways, things that I admire in a person I try to do with myself. I saw Stan as being a very honest person. I think one of the reasons I admire him is, he seemed to be—he definitely cared about other people, and he did things because he thought they were *right,* rather than he thought he could make a buck on it, or this is a fast way to get something by somebody else. He was an idealist for sure.

This music which Americans will create will be a merger of what men are doing in both the contemporary classical field and the modernists in the jazz field.

20 Bud Shank

I would like to perform someday, with an orchestra, a piece of music written for me in which I am able to use my ability as a classical flute player AND as a saxophone player. In one piece of music. And I think it can be done.

L.A.: What would you do, bring them both out on the stage and just switch back and forth?

SHANK: Yeah. It could be done, if I could work with the composer, a composer that knew me.

L.A.: And would you switch from classical to jazz in the same piece?

Bud Shank, in a motel room in Arlington, Virginia, while on concert tour. (Photo by the Author.)

SHANK: Not necessarily. Possibly, I don't know. Where's the dividing line? To a lot of people, as soon as the rhythm section comes in it's jazz. But there's a lot of improvisation that can go along in a piece of music without a rhythm section that can most certainly be considered jazz music, and not *sound* like it. In fact there is a piece of music, a concerto for two flutes, that was written by Martin Kosins for myself and another flute player in Jack Elliott's orchestra, Louise Ditullio. She does what she does, as a classically trained musician, and I do what I do, as an improvising musician; then we switch roles. 'Cause she is very much interested in improvisation. She's not a practicing improviser, but she's interested enough in it that with a little preparation she could do it. That was my idea, incidentally, and I'm the one who got Jack interested in it. As far as I know, Marty has completed the sketches and was waiting for a go-ahead before he finished it, 'cause it's a lot of work and a lot of time, you know.

L.A.: You seem to be in the forefront of this whole idea, in that you're comfortable with jazz, you're comfortable with classical, but you're also comfortable with bringing the two together.

SHANK: Yeh. That's very true, I am.

L.A.: So that it's a very interesting

coincidence, or maybe it's not a co-incidence, that you were with Kenton in what I think are probably the most creative periods of his life. In which he was trying to do this.
SHANK: Yeh. Yeh.
L.A.: He called it jazz. Maybe that's the only way he could define it. But it was not something laid down by a classical composer, where the conductor tells you how to *do* it. The musicians had a certain amount of say about it.

SHANK: Ah. True. That's one of the problems I *still* have, working in an orchestra. I still play a solo *my* way. I just did, on my new album, a couple of things where I phrased them *my* way. And I'm gonna raise a few *eyebrows*. All the tonguing, all the phrasing. It will probably attract some attention. But also there are some people who are gonna say, "Hey. Maybe that's all right too." I hope they do.
L.A.: Don't you think Stan would have approved?
SHANK: Yes. Oh, most certainly. Yes. Yes yes yes yes.
L.A.: He would have wanted you to do this.
SHANK: Yes yes yes yes yes. That's a good point, and it's very true.
L.A.: Have you always had a classical bent or did you pick that up because of your association with Kenton?
SHANK: I think that had a lot to do with it. The Innovations Orchestra was my first experience working with classically trained musicians.
L.A.: That's just when you joined Stan, isn't it, just prior to the forming of the Innovations.

SHANK: That's why I was hired, because I could play flute *and* saxophone. All through 1949 Stan didn't have a band; you remember, he disbanded in 1948. Then when he put together the Innovations Orchestra, he asked the guys to recommend somebody. Someone who did what I did, played sax but also played flute. At the time I had met Buddy Childers, Bob Cooper and Art Pepper in L.A., and we had played together a lot. So they recommended me. Stan came down and heard me play at a theater somewhere in L.A., where I was working a week with an eight- to ten-piece band known illustriously as the Charlie Barnet All-Stars, made up of people who had been with Charlie Barnet. Charlie wasn't there. I was playing all of his solos, which is what I did before when I worked on his band. It

was my job to play his solos when he was off the bandstand, which was most of the time. Stan came down and heard me, but then I still had to audition, because I was being hired to play flute *and* saxophone. I'd only been playing and studying flute for a couple of years and really wasn't that much into it. I knew a couple of weeks in advance about the audition, so I did a lot of hard practicing and got my chops in order. Did the audition, along with a whole lot of other people. And got the job. Not as a soloist. I was the first saxophone player and the flute player with the band. Art Pepper was the soloist. He played second alto. I played first. So Art had all the solo stuff. I enjoyed classical music to *listen* to. All of us, on Stan's band—on Barnet's band, too—we all had Stravinsky and Prokofiev and Ravel on records we carried with us all the time, and after the job we'd listen to those kinds of things, especially from that particular era, 1890 to 1915 or something like that. Up until then I'd never considered being a classical performer, nor did I ever consider working with a symphony orchestra, as a career. What I was doing as a jazz soloist was where I wanted to go. But I was always able to adapt myself very easily to other forms of music.

L.A.: What got you into flute in the first place?
SHANK: It just fascinated me. It was 1946 when I bought my first flute. And the fact that I became interested in the flute when I did showed a little bit of direction toward those kind of things. Back in '46 there was no such thing as a doubling saxophone and flute player, or if there were, there were very few. I practiced it, and all the time I was on Stan's band I improved.

L.A.: That must have been a terribly exciting thing, the forming of the Innovations Orchestra. There was nothing like it in the world.
SHANK: It was a thrill. It was a thrill for everybody. Stan liked the entire spectrum of sound, from the very bottom to the high screaming trumpets, with masses of volume and big sheets of sound. With the Innovations, where he had strings and woodwinds and French horns and a tuba, all of a sudden there were all these new sounds that he hadn't had before, all of a sudden there were more colors added to the spectrum that he could play with, and that his writers could play with.

L.A.: He really was a colorist, wasn't he?
SHANK: Oh yes. Yes. That's what Stan was all about. That's the way he conducted, too. With a paint brush. Like he was painting the *wall.*
L.A.: (Laughs.)

SHANK: He was using an artist's paint-brush when he was laying out these things. Even when other guys wrote the arrangements, that's what he brought out of them, making use of all these colors, and all these things that were available inside the band.
L.A.: Do you recall the first concert?
SHANK: The first—one of the first—one of the things I always remembered about Stan was—we had rehearsed that band from maybe December of '49—and the first concert was—maybe a month it rehearsed. Probably less, I don't know. I was young and excited about it. But it was not a lot of rehearsal, considering what was being done. There was a lot of auditioning going on. Instrumentation was changing. Daily. Especially in the string section. People would come, and people would go. The first concert that *I* remember playing, I think was up in Northern California. I don't exactly remember where. Halfway through the concert, Stan says, "Ladies and gentlemen, I would like you to meet the orchestra." *He introduced everybody by name!*
L.A.: Forty musicians? (Laughs.)
SHANK: One by one. Right through the strings—I didn't even know that he knew *my* name! And he didn't miss one. He didn't miss one.
L.A.: And these were all new people from the last month or so?

SHANK: Yes. (Laughs.) Naturally, some of the older guys were there, but I mean there must have been thirty people there that he had only met within the prior few *days*. And he wasn't on the band bus, either, he didn't meet 'em there, he just—that's the way, that's the kind of person he was. That was one thing that impressed me about the man, just as a man. Musically, it was all new music, it was extremely hard—I was playing a lot of flute, and I wasn't really very good at it, at that time. So I was very much engrossed in what I was doing. I had never played with strings before. And since there were flute parts, that meant you were playing with the string section. A lot, you know, because all of a sudden the strings and wood-winds are one, and the brass section was another and the rhythm section another.

154

That's what writers used, that's the basis of what any composer would do. I had never played with classical musicians before. I did a little bit when I was in college—I played with the college symphony, played clarinet, but that was a different structure, because we were all on equal terms. I was the second chair clarinetist, but I was as damn well good at doing what I was doing as the first violinist was. But in this set of circumstances, the concertmaster was a superb violinist and I was a beginning flute player. So there was a dynamite difference in the thing. There was a lot that I could learn. I had never had to play flute with a violinist, and I got called over in the corner a few times, by the concertmaster. Saying would you phrase this, or would you watch your intonation a little bit.

L.A.: You're kidding.
SHANK: On these kinds of things. Because they're used to playing with—well, he was right. You know. It's all right. I was just learning the instrument. And I learned a lot from him. This didn't happen once; it happened several times over the course of that first three-months tour. There was a lot that I could learn from playing with a person like him. And I did learn. This is totally different from what I was doing and learning as far as the jazz band part was concerned. So that was a thrill. I wasn't the only one; there were a lot of guys having problems like this, 'cause everybody on our side of the band was basically a jazz player. And was learning new things, playing a new kind of music —hard things—but as we got more and more used to the music, then we were able to *appreciate* the music for what it *was*. After playing it every night, three or four weeks of that, then you can really, okay, now I think I know what my part is, I can listen to the *rest* of it. And then you could really enjoy what was being done, even though you might not *agree* with everything musically. Stan lost a tremendous amount of money on those things. But the rest of us all gained. A *whole* lot.
L.A.: Gained in the musical sense?
SHANK: Gained musically. Gained musically. The opportunities—it made us extend ourselves. Into another spectrum of music. It gave me a foundation for a *lot* of things.

L.A.: What was your role as saxophone player in the band? You mentioned that Art Pepper was the soloist. What is the difference in the role, then, between the first alto player and the soloist?
SHANK: Art was soloist and he played second. In Stan's band the solo parts were all in the second alto. That's how his band was set up. I played the top of the saxophone section notes, the lead. I was the leader of the saxophone section, if you wish to put it that way.
L.A.: Of all five? Including the tenors?

SHANK: Ya. Including anything. And also, in the Innovations, when we had the strings and woodwinds, also the woodwind section. I was the first flutist, which meant I was on top. It was my phrasing: I determined where everything was, where everybody breathed, how loud they played or how soft. That was what I was there for. I was not there to be a jazz soloist.
L.A.: Isn't that just as important, or even more so?
SHANK: Yes, of course. That's what *I* said, I was making more money than they were. (Laughs.)
L.A.: Aside from the money. You're the backbone of the orchestra, if you're a lead player, aren't you?
SHANK: Of that section. Yes. Of the saxophones.

L.A.: Well you take the top three lead players, the lead trumpet, the lead sax and the lead trombone, and you're sort of dictating the way the band plays.·
SHANK: We dictate policy.
L.A.: Sure you do. Would Stan entrust that to you?
SHANK: Of course.
L.A.: Or would he have his own ideas?
SHANK: Oh he had some of his own ideas. He most certainly had an idea, that I changed. I was the one that started the saxophone section playing without vibrato.
L.A.: Really!
SHANK: He had had some heavy vibrato players. George Weidler was the one that had been with the band that broke up (in 1948). He had established a sound that was well known with the band, but it was a slurping—
L.A.: (Laughs.)
SHANK: . . . loud, wide, vibrato. And I came in and started playing with no, no inflections like that, and no vibrato, and it shook Stan up. He wasn't ready for that at *all*. And he took me *aside* a few times. He says, "Don't play it like that, play it like this." And I says "Okay," and I went back and did it my *own* way.
L.A.: (Laughs.) I always had heard that he did not like vibrato in his band.

SHANK: After 1950 he *didn't,* but prior to that, listen to all the records that were made from '45, '6, '7, and '8. And you'll find a different thing. It was heavy vibrato, used everywhere. The trombones changed about that time, also, into a no-vibrato thing. The saxophone section solos you'll find on some of those things, all with no vibrato in it, soft and so on, that was all my doing. That was what I was there to do. I was being a soloist in *that* way. I couldn't play that other way if my life depended on it. I would be *fired* first. I would say, "Okay, I'll try, but I don't think I can." And I *can't.* (Laughs.) I couldn't *play* that way.
L.A.: How come?
SHANK: It's not within me. It's not in my principles. I don't like that way.
L.A.: Something about the way you learned your instrument?
SHANK: No. It's just the musical— probably where it came from is that I was heavily influenced by Charlie Parker, and he used very little vibrato.

L.A.: After you left the band Kenton didn't go back to vibrato.
SHANK: No. Stayed that way.
L.A.: Evidently he liked it.
SHANK: Yep.
L.A.: Did Stan like your particular sound, your tone quality?
SHANK: He said I didn't play loud enough. And I says Okay, and then went back and did it my way.
L.A.: You never did play louder?
SHANK: I couldn't.
L.A.: How can you survive on the Kenton band and not play loud? (Laughs.)
SHANK: Well I said this is as loud as I play. It was sufficiently loud. You should see what it's like to sit in the saxophone section, in front of that *brass* section.
L.A.: (Laughs.) Tell me about it.

SHANK: You know. Talk about loud. Sometimes you feel a little *lost*. In *volume*. Because there's no *way* ever, with that instrumentation, with five trumpets and five trombones, that's ten of those, that our five saxophones are gonna come through. Even with one of them we'd never reach the volume of one of the other instruments. So you play your role, in whichever way that may be, depending on which arranger wrote what. And when you're playing the ensemble things, you just let yourself get inside the ensemble and be part of it and let it suffice there.

L.A.: You do have your moments, though. I can't think of anything more dramatic than the entrance of the saxes in "Artistry in Rhythm."

SHANK: Stan did a series of dance arrangements of some songs when I was on the band that featured piano solo and the saxophone section, where the brass played a *minor* role. They were written for recordings, and they were good. Some of 'em we even sang on. He had his own voicings that he used. It was very pretty, simple and basic. He would not require that any of his other writers use that, and none of them did. It was unique to Stan.

L.A.: You were featured as soloist on a number of things that were written for strings and winds. Mainly Rugolo and Kenton things, like "Elegy for Alto," "Monotony," "Salute," "The End of the World," and "Painted Rhythm." That was unusual. Didn't always work, I didn't think, but sometimes it created a different, kind of mysterious, quality.

SHANK: I remember *doing* that album. I'll tell you what, both Stan and Pete liked to take everything as far as it would *go*. That album was made in the middle *fifties,* of music that had been written in the *forties.* They were updating it. Got together a studio orchestra made up of as many ex-Kentonites as they could find, and redid it. A tremendous number of records were being made in Los Angeles in the fifties. All kinds of strange combinations.

L.A.: How did you happen to be on the West Coast just when Stan needed you for the Innovations? What brought you there?

SHANK: I was originally from Ohio, but I had graduated from high school and went to college at the University of North Carolina, where I was with a very very very good band, led by a guy named Johnny Satterfield. This was in 1946. The band was very successful in the South. Got up almost as far as Washington. It was a time when big bands were working quite a bit, right after the war. So the *whole band* quit school together. And the band was gonna be a big suc-

L.A.: The band quit school together? (Laughs.)

SHANK: It was gonna be a *giant success.* It lasted for six weeks.

L.A.: Oh my gosh.

SHANK: And all of a sudden there were no more jobs. And people scattered. Many went back to school. I said the

hell with it and I'm gonna go see if I can make it as a professional musician. I had been to New York to study and I'd read in *Down Beat* that things were happening in Los Angeles. And so I thought, okay. I would like to *see* Los Angeles before I make a decision. I had a chance to get a free ride from the East Coast to California, so I accepted it, got to California, and said, "This is it. As long as I have to serve an apprenticeship," which was obvious, "I would rather be poor in a warm climate than poor in a cold climate!" (Laughs.)

L.A.: What did serving an apprenticeship entail?

SHANK: Parking cars, painting houses, doing anything you could to survive. In becoming a musician in those days, your real apprenticeship was served by getting with a band in college, then getting with a territory band, then as vacancies occurred further up the ladder in better-known bands, creeping up and up until you were with a name band. But I went straight to the source. I went to California. And I had a year—a very questionable year—(laughs)—met a lot of musicians that were in the same position I was in, and we rented an apartment about the size of this *room* we're in right now that the *four* of us lived in.

L.A.: My gosh.

SHANK: It had two single beds and one couch that opened into a double bed. And the only way we made it is we rotated. You rotated from the right-hand side of the double bed . . .

L.A.: (Laughs.)

SHANK: . . . then next week you were on the left, then the following week you were in that single bed, and the next week you were in *this* single bed.

L.A.: (Laughs.)

SHANK: And when we practiced, like it was one guy in the toilet, one guy in the kitchen, one guy in the main room and one guy in the back yard—and *that* rotated! Week by week, you know. After about a year of that, I got the job with Barnet's band, and stayed with him off and on through the end of '47 through '48, doing one-nighters on the road. Then I quit and went back to California to stay. Almost that whole year of '49 I spent doing a lot of jam sessions in clubs around Los Angeles. Free open sessions, where you could play seven days a week, moving from club to club on a circuit. That was a great, great period. It was a great way to play,

and learn, and just enjoy yourself. That's the way you get jobs in the music business, then and now. You have people know you so they can recommend you when there's an opening somewhere. That was when I met Buddy and Shelly and Art and Bob Cooper, playing these sessions. And that's how the association with Stan got started.

L.A.: Do you remember the first time you heard Stan's music?

SHANK: It was when I was in college, right after he went with Capitol. I was spending my time listening to the 52nd Street bebop guys a lot, but I was very favorably impressed with this bunch of people and the record company from the West Coast. I never heard Stan's band live until I worked for it. By that time it had achieved a lot more prominence. Stan's band most certainly was one of the best. Guys my age all had their roots playing with big bands, and when you're doing that you want to go to the top, and that was Stan. So when I got the chance to join him I jumped at it. And I'm glad I *did,* because it turned out to be probably one of the most important associations of my musical career, in what I learned and what I did and the people I met. I was only with him—what, two years, or two and a half years. But I'm still known by people as having been with Stan Kenton. And that's great; even though it was a short period of my life, it was extremely important. I didn't graduate from college, I quit to go on the road as a professional musician, but I've always told people that I got my bachelor's degree from Charlie Barnet and my master's from Stan Kenton.

L.A.: That's neat! When was it you studied with Shorty Rogers?

SHANK: That was in '53 and '54. I left Stan's band at the end of '52 because I got drafted. I'd been 4-F because of a vision problem, and Stan's office had been able to keep me out of the Army. By a strange set of circumstances I reached the draft limit age before I had to serve, and I went back to L.A. Stan wanted me to come back on the band, but by then I was married and I wanted to stay in L.A. I got a job playing tenor sax with a blues and rhythm jitterbug band. It played contests, and it was a roarin' thing. Maynard Ferguson played trumpet with us. That gave me an opportunity to become a soloist again, and brought me out of a shell I had crawled into. Then there was an opening at the Lighthouse in Hermosa Beach, and the same set of guys recommended me.

L.A.: It pays to have a lot of friends. (Laughs.)

SHANK: This was 1954. All this time, all through college and Barnet and the jam sessions and Kenton and several albums I did with the Lighthouse All-Stars and two or three of my own and with Laurindo Almeida, all this time I had never really studied the inner parts of music. And I got to a point where I thought, I have gotten this far, I feel now that I have gone as far as I can go without figuring out what the hell I'm doin'.

L.A.: (Laughs.)

SHANK: So that is why I went to study with Shorty Rogers.

L.A.: You mean you played through two Innovations tours, and you hadn't had any study . . .

SHANK: Not about scores. I had studied my instruments. But as far as being an improvising soloist, I did everything by ear. I did know chord structures, but that wasn't that big a deal. So did a lot of people. I had a lot of catching up to do. My major in college was music, but they taught me a bunch of dumb things that I knew were *wrong*.

L.A.: What did they teach you that was wrong?

SHANK: Like, there's no such thing as parallel fifths.

L.A.: What's a parallel fifth, exactly?

SHANK: Let's say, in cadences at the end of a phrase in traditional music, you want to end in the key of C. An obvious voicing of that C chord would be a C on the bottom and the next note up would be a G, which is a fifth. If you're gonna get there from the dominant, which is G, a G chord, they're saying you cannot write a G and a D, a fifth up there, and go from that fifth to the tonic fifth. Because to their ears it sounds bad. From the G and the D to the C and G, that to their ears is bad. That's called parallel fifths. Now you go to work every night, even with the Johnny Satterfield band, and there's parallel fourths and fifths all over the place! Even Stan Kenton, a typical Stan Kenton voicing would be a G-D to a D-flat-A-flat to a C-G. Parallel fifths all over the place!

L.A.: I just wonder what they would have thought of his *Concerto to End All*

Concertos, with all *those* parallel fifths.

SHANK: Oh yes! As a matter of fact that's full of those kinds of things. Exactly. But about 1954 I realized I could only go so far, with the way music had developed. It was starting to get more sophisticated, more complicated. So I started a program of studying with Shorty. I studied with him for a year or so. And I mean *hard*. Like one or two lessons a week. And some heavy assignments.

L.A.: What would he have you do?

SHANK: We started at the beginning. What is a chord? How is it built? Then the one most important thing I learned from him was a chord sequence known as 2-7-5-7-1. It's used in songs, to modulate from one key center to another. Like, if you're in the key of C, that would be D minor, seventh, G, seventh, C. E. We went through all phases of that, into harmony and into writing, and he had me writing songs. He was a good teacher, very patient. We got along well. It was easy for us to communicate since we knew each other so well. It was a good relationship. And I did learn a lot of things, I learned things from him that I still am applying now.

L.A.: Could any of this have been material that Shorty learned from Kenton? Or that had been used by Kenton?

SHANK: No. But I'm sure he learned things from Stan's band. *Everybody* learned things from Stan. That's one of the great things *about* him. He was a great teacher. Without realizing it. Showing guys how to express themselves.

L.A.: Let's get into that.

SHANK: As far as arrangers are concerned, showing them what works and what doesn't, what will be effective, what will be appealing. Some of Shorty's earlier writing for Stan sounds like the same stuff he wrote for Woody Herman. But that didn't work on Stan's band. When you listen to some of the *later* things that Shorty wrote, they're different. That's when he got into the Afro-Cuban rhythm things, 'cause that really fit with Stan.

L.A.: Yes, Shorty said "He brought out something in me that I had been trying to find," with regard to Kenton.

SHANK: I think *all* of us would say that. There were two fabulous soloists on his band in Art Pepper and Bob Cooper, but still he encouraged me to be

a soloist. Not much of it got on records, but I did play solos on the band. He helped me find myself.

L.A.: You mentioned the Innovations experience as giving you a foundation for a lot of things, and another spectrum of music. I've heard some of your new albums, and they're *fascinating*. One is *Songs of the Seeker,* by Martin Scot Kosins.

SHANK: Surprised you even *found* that, that hasn't had any distribution to speak of. It's a tiny little record company.

L.A.: Yes. *Open Sky Records.* It's beautiful! Then there's one you did with Bill Mays, called *Explorations: 1980.* On one side are original compositions and on the other are works of Debussy, Scriabin, Bach and Ravel.

SHANK: With improvisation.

L.A.: Yes. It's utterly fascinating. I read your program notes, and I thought, What is he going to do with this music. And the changes from classical to jazz, especially in the Bach, are so subtle that I'm almost not aware of them.

SHANK: That's what we were trying to do!

L.A.: It's fabulous. The *jazz* sounds *classical*. Until suddenly it goes back to the real classical—and, hey . . .

SHANK: It took a while, but we're finally getting airplay on the classical stations with that stuff. They rejected it at first. Now there are a couple of things that are getting played a lot. The thing with Marty Kosins has helped—and that's purely classical playing. I just made another album, with Laurindo Almeida, that's pure legit playing.

L.A.: Oh, I like what you did with Bill Mays.

SHANK: I do too. That's combining both of my lives. About six years ago I got really involved in the instrument, doing research, doing *long,* long *long* hours of practice, listening to classical flute players. Galway was an inspiration. I'd never heard an individualist approach in a classical musician before. That's the approach of the *jazz* musician. The first result of all this was that *Explorations* album; it was aimed at that. I commissioned the *Suite for Flute and Piano* and researched the other side, the Bach, Ravel and those things. It's giving me a big inspiration to a whole form of music, which is now opened up to me. At a time when most guys go head for the pasture, I'm on the threshold of a whole new career. And I'm also coming back out as a jazz saxophone player, working with different rhythm groups.

L.A.: As a soloist?

SHANK: As a soloist. And after that time and work spent learning about classical flute, I'm finally learning how to play jazz on the instrument. I'm finally doing some things that make sense to me, as far as jazz is concerned. It's funny. A couple of years ago, in the clubs, I was playing maybe half classical music and half jazz. It got so I was *confusing* people more and more. So the last six months I've taken a different approach, playing all jazz saxophone except for maybe one number a set, on classical flute. Very quickly, and make a production out of it, make it not *too long*—

L.A.: (Laughs.)

SHANK: And—it's working. I'm saving the classical flute playing, which I can do, the real classical stuff, for the *recitals* that I'm doing. You take a regular out-and-out bebop jazz club and if I start doing Debussy or something like that in there, all of a sudden they say "What is that?" (Laughs.) "If he can do that, that means he can't do that other stuff he just *did*."

L.A.: (Laughs.) What if you did it the other way, what if you were playing a recital, and you played jazz?

SHANK: I've tried that. And that upsets the *critics*.

L.A.: Why?

SHANK: I don't *know*. You tell me. I've been trying to figure them out. I'm working on that.

L.A.: They can't put it in a category.

SHANK: No. It doesn't fit in where they think things should be.

L.A.: Well isn't this what Stan Kenton was trying to do.

SHANK: Yes. It's one of the problems that *he* faced. In fact, that's just exactly what we're talking about. Now. Newspapers have a jazz critic, and they have a classical critic. One of them will review it from his approach and the other will review it from *his* approach. They see jazz musicians in there, and they call it a jazz band. Then when it doesn't *swing*, they say it's not *good*. Well it's not *supposed* to swing. Critics have a lot of power. They are telling people, who maybe don't have time to pay more attention to it than to a hobby, let's say, what's good and what's bad. Which of us are acceptable, which are not. That's an unfortunate set of circumstances.

The music that we're involved in is *complex*. It's not the kind of music that can be accepted and understood the first time it's heard.

L.A.: That's true. That's part of the problem too.

SHANK: If it were, then, you know, that's the kind of stuff you hear on AM radio, that has a life span of, what, four weeks? We're dealing in music that has life spans of decades and decades. Sometimes hundreds of years. But the reason it *can* last that long is because it *is* complex.

L.A.: Having been in all three groups, Stan Kenton's Innovations and Neophonic Orchestras, and now the New American Orchestra in Los Angeles, do you see similarities, or distinct differences, or is it all trying to get at the same goal, to take native American music and combine it with classical elements and get a whole new genre? And what should it be called?

SHANK: I don't know. Here we go with labels. I don't know what the hell to call it. I don't even like the term *jazz*. But that's not for me to say or do anything about. As for the goal, yes. Whether the Jack Elliott version will be successful—who knows? With the subsidies that Stan never *did* get, maybe it will be able to hold on long enough to where there *are* some people who will be able to support it. It's on its own, with just contributions from Jack's friends and friends of the orchestra's to support it. Stan never got any kind of subsidy. The Music Center was just opened when Stan's Neophonic thing was there. He got the last of everything. Whatever was left over as far as dates to rehearse and dates to perform. He got *no help* from Dorothy Chandler and her people, because after the first concert, they considered that a threat to the Los Angeles Philharmonic. No help, not in publicity, not in ticket sales, not in anything. All you can do is rent the hall, that's all you get.

L.A.: What about the level of composing in the work that is done for the New American Orchestra?

SHANK: How do you evaluate a piece of music? Even the composers don't know what it's gonna sound like.

L.A.: Allyn Ferguson was saying that the original idea is being gotten away from because of the problems of getting grants and this kind of thing. He feels it's getting away from the musical idea.

SHANK: Yes. I tend to agree with him. And the members of that orchestra are gonna agree. But they also realize what a problem the administration, Jack and his staff, are having financially. So they're willing to go along with playing some things they don't agree with, having some guest stars they don't agree with, just to try to draw an audience. I don't think anybody has gotten into getting, really getting that outside . . .

L.A.: What do you mean, outside? Outside what?

SHANK: Off-the-wall. Avant-garde.

L.A.: Let's talk for a second about Bob Graettinger. Just think back to *City of Glass* for a second. And just think what a mind-blowing thing that was.

SHANK: Of course.

L.A.: And still is. It's not accepted by a lot of people . . .

SHANK: Of course.

L.A.: It was fabulous. If you want to call that off-the-wall . . .

SHANK: The second version of that, that he wrote, was and is a marvelous, fantastic piece of music. I haven't heard that in years. I've got to look that up. Think about what he was writing about. Glass. What is glass? Think of all the things that glass does. Think of what glass sounds like, when it breaks. What it sounds like when you scratch it. He was relating, through his mind, what those things are like. Or looking through it. Think of all the distortions that can happen, looking through glass. Throwing panes this way, that way. Groups of pieces of glass.

L.A.: Do you have anybody writing like that now?

SHANK: (Pauses.) Ahh . . .

L.A.: He's probably as far-out as Stan Kenton ever got.

SHANK: There must be some people *around* doing that, I'm *sure* there are.

L.A.: But not writing for the New American Orchestra.

SHANK: No. No. I think that orchestra, because it is interested in survival, has tried to stay away from writers who would get into extremes like that. *Maybe* that's one of the *problems* with it. Maybe if they *did* have more of that, more people would be . . . I don't know. They're going to have to find that out for themselves. The one thing that is different in 1982 than was the case in 1950 is that, for lack of a better term, and here *I* go, using categories, avant-garde composers are being performed more in the *classical* realm than they were then.

L.A.: That's true.

SHANK: And so a composer such as Bob Graettinger would not, in 1950, have been able to have his works performed by a chamber symphony. In 1982, yes. If he were alive today there are lots of places it could be heard. It *is* interesting, it's a sign of the times. Music like that is being performed by smaller, community orchestras, now. Which it was not in 1950. Graettinger had no choice, really, but to write for a band. If Stan had not *been* there, if there had *been* no such thing as a Stan Kenton band, he would not have been heard.

L.A.: Stan had such a broad career span, really he was involved with music more than fifty years. What do you think was his most important, lasting contribution to twentieth-century music? What would you consider his most outstanding personal characteristic?

SHANK: As far as Stan himself is concerned, in one word, his *strength*. The strength to keep going under adverse circumstances. Vicious attacks in the forties and up through the fifties, from critics and the jazz establishment. Stan hired people for what they were, and brought out the hidden strengths in other musicians, players and composers both. Literally making them extend themselves. Stan had the strength, and guts, to play and perform composers' music that they could not have written for other orchestras, writer after writer after writer. Musicians would come and go, but Stan went on. He had the courage of his convictions, and that led him up to his—whatever the ultimate goal was. We don't know. We don't know that he ever brought it to a conclusion. He might have died too soon. There were probably other things deep down in there that he wanted to do.

L.A.: Just along with what you're saying, he made a statement to a group of jazz educators one time, about the time of his Neophonic Orchestra, something about how he felt that the Neophonic experience, once it had got into the school level, was going to have a far greater impact than . . .

SHANK: Well I already see what you're saying. And one thing you're saying is that the kids coming out of schools now, the past few years, we're just starting to see the results of it.

L.A.: The statement was: "I believe that by having immersed myself in the vitality and enthusiasm of another generation I have created a limitless future for the Neophonic approach to contemporary music—the most exciting thing that's happened to an art form in 20 years." You were part of the Junior Neophonic thing at Cerritos College. You explain to me how those kids could play that Neophonic music! That's weird.

SHANK: It's the quality of musicians that are being turned out in the schools now.

L.A.: But this was 1966!

SHANK: That was the beginning of it, you know. I think that's what Stan meant—college students being able to perform sophisticated, complicated written music, accompanied with improvised music, by the same musician. That's what's different. That's what's happening now. I can wander around in those different fields constantly, easily—and they can do it too. There are a lot of them coming out now that can do it that couldn't before. Whatever those kids become—professional musicians or attorneys or whatever—they have had a Neophonic experience. And they will carry it with them.

Gene Hall, in Stan Kenton Hall, North Texas State University, Denton, Texas. (Photo by the Author.)

21 Gene Hall

Stan would really get wound up and get into things in some of the discussions we had at those Kenton clinics. Sometimes he'd say "Well I always thought—" and somebody else'd say "But what about this—" and he'd say "Oh, ya, but—" and they'd go at it. He had an inquiring mind.

In 1969 a symposium was held at Tanglewood. All the top musicians and music educators in the country were there. People prominent in their field in science and industry were brought in, people like the president of General Motors and others. What they had was a two-week, round-table discussion on music as it applies to our culture. Is it important. All these people were there to participate in this symposium on music and its place in our culture. Stan Kenton was invited.

Well. Why was he invited? Why didn't they invite Woody Herman? Why didn't they invite Les Brown? Or Kay Kyser, or whomever? Why Stan Kenton?

Because he's an intellect. He thinks.

L.A.: I'd give anything to have heard some of those discussions. Is any of that written down anywhere?

HALL: No.

L.A.: What about the clinics, what were those like?

HALL: We used to have a general meeting every day, from one to two, when we'd discuss issues. Rhythmic aspects, melodic aspects, styles, whatever. At least twenty-five of the leading jazz people in the United States would be there, and we'd pick four to be panelists. I'd dream up some question—about the difference between European rhythms and jazz rhythms, let's say—and let all these guys talk about it. The kids would listen and were free to ask questions, and there'd be an interchange of ideas there, about all this. Every day. It was very stimulating, because these twenty-five jazz musicians are creative people in themselves, and they have brains that go like this (*gestures quick snapping motions*). And when they get

started on ideas, you're listening to some really interesting thoughts. Somebody over here says, "Wait a minute, what about so-and-so?" then somebody says, "Yeah, but . . ." and the first thing you know you've got a real issue going there, just from a conversation, with people that are creative and intense about their work.

L.A.: Did your association with Stan start with the clinics?

HALL: Yes. I met Stan in 1959. That's when I went to Michigan State, and that was the first year we had the Stan Kenton Clinics. I was the director of those camps. Ken Morris was really the moving force behind the whole thing. He got Stan to agree to be a part of it, primarily for Stan's name. Stan didn't know what it was and wasn't enthusiastic about it at all. That first year, at Indiana University, he'd be with his band playing a job within a couple of hundred miles, and when it was over he'd drive on in to be at the camp. He'd

come in and he'd be dead on his feet. Then he'd go around and hear these little kids trying to play. He'd been dealing with professional musicians all his life; he didn't really understand what it was all about, for a while. But he stayed with it, and about the second or third year he began to get into it. Later he and Morris had a falling out and he started his own Stan Kenton Clinics. I worked with those for a while. Stan was really, really sold on it; he'd bring his whole band in and keep them there for a week, just playing concerts and being with the kids, so the kids would get an idea what it's like to be professional musicians. Bring in his guys, and pay their salaries, and if there was a deficit in the camp, cover it. I saw him sit down and write out a check for five thousand dollars one afternoon. I said "Stan, you don't have to do this." He says, "Well, I owe it. Music's been good to me. I owe these kids the chance to get into this field if they want to do it. This is something I can do to pay back the fact that I have been successful in this business. If I'd get off my butt and put out another record, I wouldn't have any problems anyway." So he was, in my opinion, a very altruistic man. Young composers, young arrangers, would bring things to him to play. And he'd play them, whether it fitted his style or not, just to give these kids a hearing. He was very honest. One day at the camp he was standing around saying "I wish I had something to do." I said "Why don't you go down and rehearse one of these bands? They'd love it if you'd come, these high school kids, they'd love to have you rehearse their band." So he did, got with a band from Philadelphia that had come in with their leader and their own library. Reached down in the book and said "Let's play this one." Well they'd never played it before, and they couldn't do it. So he came back to the office a little later and was talking about it. I said, "What'd you do?" He said "I didn't know what to do. I didn't know what to tell 'em. If it had been my band, I'd have said, 'You guys play it or I'll get somebody else.' "

L.A.: (Laughs.)

HALL: Now, most of your big-time band leaders won't admit they don't know something. They're very touchy about it. Stan was honest: "I didn't know what to tell 'em. 'Play it or get out.' " A very sincere and honest man.

L.A.: At the time that he was, in effect, paying the bill for some of these things that couldn't make it without him, he had not formed Creative World, had he?
HALL: No. No.

L.A.: So now you're talking about five thousand dollars out of his own pocket.
HALL: Out of his pocket. I suppose. I don't know where else it came from.

L.A.: Isn't that unbelievable.
HALL: I assume that he took it off his income tax that year, certainly. But, even so, that's five thousand bucks.

L.A.: The fact that Stan left his entire music library to North Texas State is a tremendous compliment to you. I'd be interested to know just how your program got started, and how it developed to be probably the finest jazz center in the world. I believe yours was the first accredited jazz program in the country. And since you observed your twenty-fifth anniversary in 1972, this means you got started in 1947, right?

HALL: Yes. We started in 1947, and it's been an uphill struggle all the way. I was

working on my master's degree here in 1942 when school started and three or four boys came in from west Texas who wanted to study arranging. In 1942, the Army was taking the male population very rapidly, and the dean here saw this as a chance to pick up three or four more male students. He knew I'd been writing arrangements for the jazz bands on campus, so he said to me, "Teach 'em arranging." You know, if you don't know any better you think you can do it, so I said, "Sure." When word got out, fifteen people showed up for that class. That impressed the dean, so he put it in the catalog as a regular offering. If you *write* arrangements you have to *hear* them, so every two or three weeks we'd organize a band to play the arrangements we'd written in class. After that year, I went on the road with the band and various things, and by 1947, the arranging class was still going, and a student band, under a student leader, was meeting every day to play the charts. Then the dean moved to Indiana and another dean came in, Walter Hodgson, who thought of that as a peripheral activity that should not be allowed to stand. And he said, "Either we should have this be a part of our regular program or it shouldn't be at all. It's not right to have it hang on like this." He wanted it to be a regular part of the program. Hodgson remembered that I had written arrangements and done things, so he called me up and wanted me to come over here and start this program. At that time I was production director of a 50,000-watt radio station in Fort Worth and had just made arrangements to go to Columbia to work on my PhD. I had a chance of getting with NBC, and I figured I could work there, adjust my classes at Columbia, earn my doctorate and get several years' experience as a producer. But Hodgson said, "Why don't you start the jazz program here and work on your doctorate up there in the summertime?" We finally decided to do it, primarily because by then I had two children, and I didn't want to raise 'em in New York City. So we took this program, and it just seemed to catch on. I wasn't necessarily crusading. It was a job. And to do the job, there're certain things you have to do. A lot of the staff weren't very happy about it.

L.A.: You mentioned that it was an uphill struggle. How did you succeed in spite of the adversities?
HALL: Actually, the kids themselves deserve much of the credit. 'Cause they

stuck it out in spite of roadblocks that were thrown their way by other members of the staff. For instance, in applied music, if you were studying trumpet, the teacher would load you down with material to practice on; then he'd say, "You better drop out of that jazz band. You haven't got time. You've got to work on this." Well the kids would refuse to do it. They'd hang on to it anyway. When we played somewhere, a program at Fort Worth or Dallas or wherever, we paid our own way. I'd say, "I'll meet you there," and we'd all get there on our own and do the thing. I'm *sure* the administration didn't spend more than two hundred dollars for material and supplies during the twelve years I was here.

L.A.: What do you mean, two hundred a year? You don't mean for the entire twelve years that you headed the program?
HALL: Yes.
L.A.: You got a total of two hundred dollars?
HALL: We didn't get *anything*. We had to ask for what we got. The guys furnished their own horns. We used music stands that belonged to the school. We rehearsed in a war assets barracks-type building from Army surplus. Just did it on our own. Wrote our own arrangements. Furnished our own transportation. Did everything ourselves. Just *did* it.
L.A.: The college was not behind you at all?

HALL: No. The last year I was here they gave me a graduate assistant, 'cause I had three bands. A rather pushy fellow, and when I left, he was mad because I didn't give him my job. He was a good composer, but very erratic. And because of the situation here I needed somebody to take over the program who would have the respect of the rest of the staff. I needed a solid educator and a solid musician. Leon (Breeden) seemed to fit the bill, as far as I was concerned. Good musician—a first-rate clarinetist, and he was writing arrangements for the Boston Pops Orchestra. Leon came in, and I went to Michigan. I had told the graduate assistant in the spring that we would not be using him in the fall, and told him to find other support. As far as I was concerned, that ended it. When I left, I made copies of a lot of our arrangements here, to take with me to Michigan State, 'cause I didn't know whether they had anything up there, you see. But all the arrangements were left in the music library. Well apparently this fellow knew where they were and he got 'em all and Leon didn't have anything to work with! He knew the guys and got up a band of his own and all this sort of thing. He undermined the program terribly for Leon, just really gave him a hard time. I didn't know anything about this. If I had I would have done something about it. I was in Michigan and just supposed everything was going along all right. It wasn't 'til later that I found out. Leon fought a lot of battles, just as I did, and deserves tremendous credit for what he did. By *now* it's a common thing for a college to have a jazz program. In those days it was not. For the first twelve years I was very worried that we would get some guys in here that were smokin' pot or something. And that some of them would get caught. And I could just see the headline: "*Jazz Musician—*" you know, whatever. I made an extreme effort to discourage any of those guys from coming in. Word got out that this was not the place to come for the potheads. So that'd mean we got a cleaner type of boy, and we managed to keep things on an even keel around here. But I'm sure that if we'd had one headline like that, the whole thing would have gone down the drain. It was that tenuous as far as administration was concerned. Now Hodgson was behind us. If he hadn't stood behind us we wouldn't have had a program. We'd been in school about six months, the first year, when he called all of the faculty and students together. Made a speech. I was sitting, like this. I didn't know what to expect. But he talked about the new jazz program—its possible worth, not only to the school but to the individuals involved in it, and their place and the place of jazz in our cultural patterns—the whole thing. Just an excellent speech. And he ended by saying, "We're going to have this jazz program here from now on. You may as well make up your mind to it. And quit wearing out my carpet coming to complain about it."

L.A.: What did he mean, complaining about it?

HALL: They would come in and complain that we made a lot of noise, or the students were spending all their time in the jazz program practicing on their horns, or whatever. Anything.

L.A.: The conflict was in the music department itself?

HALL: Yes, the members of the faculty who didn't want a jazz program. One of

them led three expeditions to the president, and was thrown out. Nice fellow, and he didn't object to jazz *itself*. He just didn't think it ought to be in the college program.

L.A.: But the dean stood behind you.

HALL: The dean stood behind us, yes. It finally became established.

L.A.: How did you happen to come to Michigan State?

HALL: Walter Hodgson went to Michigan State to become Dean of Music there, and after a year he wanted me to join him. I didn't much want to leave, but the dean that replaced him had no concept of what a jazz program was. We began to have festivals, where we'd be the host band and bring in high schools, as a recruiting device, really, get 'em all together and see what's happening. The first year with the new dean here, I had twenty-some high school bands coming in. But the auditorium was sewed up for opera rehearsals. Every night for six weeks. Well we needed *one* night for this festival. I went to see the dean, but he didn't have enough authority to do it. So I had to rent the high school auditorium on my own and put on this festival. It just happened that, with the high school bands paying a fee to come in, we came out sixty dollars in the black. And I brought this in, and I said, "What are we supposed to do with this?" "Take it down to the business office." So I did, and I said, "Suppose I'd been sixty dollars in the red?" "Oh. We'd have taken it out of your paycheck."

L.A.: Oh my gosh.

HALL: So you feel that you don't have a lot of support there, you know? So when Hodgson wanted me to come to Michigan State I just said Okay. We'll go to Michigan State. Leon was high school band director in Grand Prairie when I asked him whether he wanted this job and he said yes. I spent half a day telling him why he *should not* take it.

L.A.: (Laughs.)

HALL: (Laughs.) Well, you know, he's a good friend. I didn't want to put him into a bad situation. But Leon is a very careful worker, a perfectionist, he wants things to be right, so he made it work. And I went to Michigan State and started the jazz program there.

L.A.: We have three jazz bands now. Even our marching band seems to have a Stan Kenton sound, a beautiful, wall-

of-brass quality. Are you responsible for starting that, or can it perhaps be traced to the influence you might have had when you were there?

HALL: Well—I don't know about that. (Laughs.) But in 1962 we won the national contest at Notre Dame. We took our band down there and beat everybody. We even beat North Texas.

L.A.: Michigan State beat North Texas?

HALL: Ya.

L.A.: (Laughs.) I don't know why, but there's a certain poetry in that.

HALL: Ya. They had a better band than we did. We just happened to hit the judges just right.

L.A.: Oh, isn't that wonderful. (Laughs.)

HALL: It made me feel good. Leon had won it the year before, playing a concert-type, very polite jazz, with just a beautiful little band. So in 1962, all the bands that came in imitated what he had done the year before. We didn't have a band that was that polished. We couldn't play these polite things. So we just played a sort of a roaring, romping, stomping type of jazz. And the judges, by this time, after two days of hearing all this polite everything, were glad to hear some gutty jazz, so they gave us the award.

L.A.: (Laughs.)

HALL: (Laughs.) There are not a whole lot of schools, not more than fourteen or fifteen in the country, that have a complete degree program in jazz. This was a quirk from the start. That was a bold step in 1947. To offer a whole program in jazz, a degree in jazz. That was really a bold, forward-looking step that Hodgson took.

L.A.: It really impressed me that Kenton thought so highly of your program here that he involved North Texas State with his Neophonic music. How could your students play that music when the professional musicians themselves practically couldn't touch it?

HALL: These guys here play just about as well as the professionals. Now you think—you think I'm kidding.

L.A.: No. I don't.

HALL: As a matter of fact, year before last Leon lost his whole rhythm section in the middle of the semester to Woody Herman. They just all went with the

Herman band. Tony Bennett came by, picked up a band, took them on the road for a couple of weeks. I'm down there in Nacogdoches, in the boondocks. And I got a call from a booker in Dallas, wanting to know if I'd go over and sit in with a band in Shreveport. Everything was happening and they didn't have enough musicians to go around. I said okay and went down there and the band that showed up was the One O'Clock Band from North Texas minus one saxophone player!

L.A.: (Laughs.)

HALL: It was the Jack Benny show. And the guys're playing this music, not missing a *note*. Sitting there with their legs crossed and playing those high F-sharps and little trills and I'm doing my best just to hang *on*. Bandleader said "This is the best band I've ever seen on the road or ever even *come* across." It was the One O'Clock Band. These guys are in and out of those bands all the time. But after six months, if you're a sensitive, creative musician, you get tired of playing those same arrangements, every night, the same way. Well where can they do something more interesting? So they come back to school.

L.A.: And how did they respond to the Neophonic music?

HALL: Well—you see, the Neophonic music is more restrictive of innovation and therefore you've got creative people who are less enthusiastic about that than about something more of their own interest.
L.A.: But the music *itself* was so highly creative.
HALL: Yes. But somebody else created it. See. That's the thing. They were playing somebody else's music.
L.A.: Which do you think is more important, ultimately, or is there room for both?

HALL: There's no way you can get through this life without compromise. You cannot ever play *only* your own things. And you should never have to play always somebody else's things in life. I'm sure it sounds supercilious, but I would hate to be an orchestral clarinet player, let's say, or violinist, who played only what somebody else had written. All my life play somebody else's music. I'd like to play my own, once in a while. I'm sure those people are not unhappy. But think about having to

play what somebody else wrote down, all the time. Ever. That's all. Never get to do a Dixieland job or freewheeling job.

L.A.: Kenton made a quite remarkable statement way back in 1962 when the clinic program was still young in regard to jazz in the universities. This was published in *Down Beat* magazine on September 27, 1962: "Since I became involved in the movement"—I believe he means the clinic movement—"I have come to believe that the future of almost all creative music in the United States"—now that's a big umbrella—"is going to come from the universities. The professional musician today is so bogged down by the demands that are made upon him commercially that he no longer has time to experiment, to work and develop, and music thrives on experimentation—it has to have it." And then in talking about the university orchestras, he says "The music they are composing and arranging in most cases clearly is beyond what is happening in the professional field." In other words, the future is here, where you have the time and the resources and the young, eager minds that aren't going out to make a buck . . .

HALL: I agree. I agree a hundred per cent. Yes.
L.A.: And the other thing he said was "I believe that sooner or later it will be the university orchestras that have the record contracts and will be doing the important recording." Now that is an interesting statement from a professional big band leader.

HALL: Well, I don't know about that last, because the recording business is still managed by people who are out to make a fast buck, and the way to make a fast buck is to give people the things they want. Which is pop—pap. You know.
L.A.: Yes.
HALL: But—the creative aspect, that's true; and I have to give Leon credit for doing the same thing here. Nearly every program he played was all music composed and created by the guys in the band. Nearly all the music they played, giving these guys a chance to experiment and try things. And Stan Kenton did it at a more precarious, professional level, where he had to make bucks to make it pay.
L.A.: Is that why he liked the two of you, and what you were doing here? Because he was just ecstatic about North Texas State and your program.

HALL: Well—you see, I learned to play in a joint. These kids have a chance to learn to play here, in this . . .
L.A.: Beautiful . . .
HALL: This hall . . . with somebody who knows what he's talking about. If you learn the way I did, you learn by experience by getting fired, getting another job, trying again, trying to learn. Learning in a very poor environment. If you come up through the joints, what opportunity do you have? You just learn tunes that the drunks out there want to hear, and play it for 'em. Here you come to a good environment, with good facilities, and a good chance to be with others who know how to play. So when Stan's talking about the future being with the universities, I think there's something to it. It's a valuable opportunity for kids.
L.A.: As far as creativity.

HALL: Creativity, yes. We have two basic kinds of music in our Western culture. One is the European type, wherein the composer decides what is to be. He puts it all down on paper and the conductor tries to "realize" it, tries to bring to life what it is the composer wants. And all the members in the orchestra follow the conductor and try that interpretation of this composer. The other is our *American* style, where the composer is not important at all. We don't use his version. We just want his theme and his chord progression and we'll have our own version. This boy writes an arrangement, I write one, you write one, we all have different versions of how this thing's gonna sound. Or we can play it with a three-piece group, a thirty-piece group, a fifteen-piece group, or a polka band, all different versions of the same tune, which is another creative aspect. American music is creative from the word *go*. How many different versions have you heard of "Stardust"? Endless versions. Which one do you like? Depends on your mood at the time. You don't have the composer telling you what to do. The individual, the *player* decides what to do. Without that creativity the whole thing goes down the tube. Where can you sponsor creativity except in a situation like this? If you're playing in a joint or a club or in a hotel band, you're doing things for the paying public out there, playing "Alley Cat" or whatever it is they want to hear. That's not being creative, though you might innovate some ways of presenting it. But the creative things come with people who don't have pressure from a paying

164

public to do it a certain way. They can sit down here and write something for this band and see what it sounds like.

L.A.: But what happens to them when they go out into the world?

HALL: Hopefully they will learn to direct their ideas according to the situation. I have an arranging class at my school—I teach guitar and arranging at Stephen F. Austin University in Nacogdoches, in east Texas—and out of the twenty students, who are senior music majors, one or two have ideas. You see, when you write an arrangement you have to have an idea of how you want something to be. You may change the harmony; depends on what you want it to be. But these people have for so long been—I guess the word is *taught*—that the way to do it is *this*—do it this way, and, you know, you get your hand slapped if you do it wrong?—that they have had their creativity stifled. They've learned that to make a grade they have to do it a certain way, to please the teacher. Well in these bands you're not graded that way. This is something to try; if you want to try it, try it. If it works, good. If not, take it and try it again. So you see the musical opportunity for somebody in one of these groups, to experiment and try things and become innovative.

L.A.: If you're a student in a lab band here and you want to be an arranger, what do you have to do? You give your chart to the leader?

HALL: Just ask the leader, can you hear this thing. Unless he's got an awfully tight schedule, he'll pass it out and play it, sure. I'm sure that Neil Slater would. Leon would. I would. If you're with Woody Herman or Buddy Rich or someone like that, he might run it through for you one time at a rehearsal, but unless it's in the style that *he* wants, he's not going to put it in his book. He has a public out there that demands certain things, and he has to sell his product.

L.A.: You know you really are in the spirit of Stan Kenton here, aren't you. The one thing all his writers agreed on was that he gave them a crack at writing anything they wanted, and they could *hear* it.

HALL: Sure. With the top musicians playing it.

L.A.: It's almost like a prophecy. It could even be the most important part of the Kenton legacy. It boils down to freedom.

HALL: Ya. Freedom of expression. Now, just as an artist can't just throw paint at the canvas, the musician can't just throw notes around. He's got to understand his craft; he's got to learn what will work and what won't. He doesn't start out and say well I'm gonna do this and away we go. He has to spend a long time learning what has been done, the differences between Stan Kenton's style and Buddy Rich's style and all these styles, and why they're different. And then he begins to understand the man that's behind them who makes the style come out that way. Then he decides, well, my style is going to be *this* way, and he extends his ideas into another area.

L.A.: I heard an exciting thing yesterday, in Bobby Knight's office, a cut from the new lab band album that had a bit of "How High the Moon" right at the beginning, and then the thing went off on its own. I see what you mean, with exposure to that kind of thing, a young composer can pick up on that and from there go off in his own direction.

HALL: That was the tangent he wanted to follow, he wanted to try it and see what it sounded like. In that respect I agree with what Kenton was saying about the cradle of creativity being a place like this. You can experiment, but you also share a cooperative experience and can go a lot faster than finding things out the hard way just on your own.

L.A.: Do you think, in addition to the obvious fact of Mr. Breeden's integrity and dedication to Kenton, all this had something to do with why he left his legacy to North Texas State?

HALL: I assume he left it here because the program is established and it's going to be here, and he had a lot of respect for Leon, knew that Leon was a stable, down-to-earth person who wasn't going to run out and sell arrangements and all that sort of thing.

L.A.: Stan used to talk a great deal about the value of jazz and about how the people who were drawn to it were more creative than usual.

HALL: One aspect of that is in how intricate the music is. The trumpet player plays some sort of little rhythmic melody, the clarinet player joins in with

an antiphonal chord or counter-melody to that, and the trombone player plays a basic part, and it all comes out together. You don't have to have a composer sit down and figure out each note. They agree on a basic chord sequence, and a basic melody, and from there on make music. I think that's tremendous, that you can put three or four or a half dozen fellows together and just off the top of their heads they can play and it sounds good; you like to listen to it. You couldn't do that in any other idiom that I know of. This is the jazz idiom, and that means that players improvise. They listen to one another and pick up ideas and react to each other and it all jells and you've got a thing that holds together because of what each player does. It calls for a great deal of sensitivity and creativity on the part of the people involved.

L.A.: Sounds like a pretty good definition of jazz.

HALL: I suppose if you had a complete definition of jazz it would be a book long before you covered everything. Basically, in music the down beats are 1 and 3. In jazz, the upbeats are important; the emphasis is on the 2 and 4, the weak beats. But the percussion player, or section, plays the *strong* beats while the horns play the *weak* beats, so you've got a *contrasting rhythm* going there. Then if we add another section of horns against the first one, and add a third against the first two, and they're *all* against the *rhythm*, it gets really complex, and we say, *"Man!"*

L.A.: It's exciting.

HALL: Ya. It's a rhythmic projection of melody, really. And then to make it more complex you have counter melodies and harmonies to all of these melodies, and the harmonies themselves create tension. Not usually triads, they're considered too churchy, but four- and five- and six-part harmonies, chords that create tension. Music is tension and release. After so much tension there'll be a partial release. Then more. And this is *harmonic*, on top of the *rhythmic*. We put all that together, and we call it jazz.

L.A.: What got you started in jazz, and why were you able to fight all your battles all through this whole thing?

HALL: It wasn't so much that I wanted to fight. It was a job I had to do, a paycheck next month, stay, do what I had to do . . .

L.A.: You could have picked another field. Why jazz?

HALL: Well—when I got out of high school in 1930, I couldn't get a job. But I did play saxophone. My father was superintendent of a church, and I played it there. Then one night a saxophone player working in a joint about thirty miles from where we lived tried to commit suicide, and they needed a replacement. So I got this job and started playing. Played sheet music off of a wire rack. We had chicken wire in front of the band so we wouldn't get hit by pop bottles.

L.A.: Good grief.

HALL: A big wooden window you could let down and get out if things got too rough.

L.A.: My gosh!

HALL: For umpteen years, because of the depression, there were no jobs. But I could find work playing the horn, so I did. Got into it by doing it, by having to, really.

L.A.: Yes, but obviously there's a development there.

HALL: Oh, sure. If you go into any craft, and stay with it all your life, you're going to develop in it.

L.A.: Then you liked what you were beginning to get out of it, evidently.

HALL: Well when I went to college I thought, I'm going to get out of music. Spent a year and a half majoring in business. We didn't have computers then. You had to add up figures with a pencil and paper. And I added them up as many times as I had to until I had two of them come out the same. Then that was my answer. I decided I didn't want to do that.

L.A.: (Laughs.)

HALL: (Laughs.) I'm sure there are people who are mathematicians, or whatever, who love what they're doing. But it's hard for me to believe that a CPA gets as much fun out of life as a musician.

L.A.: (Laughs.)

HALL: I studied in Spain for six months, picked up quite a bit of Spanish, and thought I'd major in that; that'd be easy. But after a year I thought, What am I going to *do* with it? So I decided to major in English. I didn't have any trouble writing themes. But— what are you going to do with *that*? All this time I was still writing arrangements and playing in bands. I ended up with a double major in education and music. And decided to stay in music.

L.A.: Did Stan talk with you about the appeal of jazz to him?

HALL: If you go into music, if you have aptitude and become skillful enough to produce music yourself, really play it, then you're *hooked*. It's kind of like a drug. You're *into* it. You keep expanding and learning more and challenging yourself further. And this is where *he* was.

L.A.: He used to say, when people sympathized with him because he didn't have a permanent home and was constantly on the road, "I wouldn't trade this. I eat in a different place every day, I sleep in a different place every night."

HALL: Stan was interested in people. You might say he was a humanist. He was also, in my opinion, a very ethical man, musically ethical. I heard somebody ask him once, "How do you get by with playing all that far-out stuff?" His answer was, "I play one for them, and I play one for me." He was an extraordinarily good musician. I think a major contribution he made was that he set the sights high as far as performance levels go. Everybody in his band could play well—and did. You've probably heard that the band sounded different when he was off the stage than when he was on. 'Cause he walks on, the guys in the band know what he expects of them. Stan stands out there with those big arms and he's looking you right in the eye, and he wants you to play. He wouldn't compromise on his musical standards. He had musical integrity.

22 Bobby Knight

I was able to be on a band with Charlie Mariano. And Bob Fitzpatrick. And Kent Larsen. And Sammy Noto. Carson Smith. Bill Trujillo. Jimmy Knepper. Don Sebesky. Jack Nimitz. Bill Perkins. Archie LeCoque. Guys who were stars. They came to him, professional musicians already, with backgrounds of their own. When those guys played it was just—unreal. Jazz history was being made.

Bobby Knight, in his office at North Texas State University, Denton, Texas. (Photo by the Author.)

Charlie Mariano was a *giant* when he was with us. I'd sit there and listen to him, and play. There's nothing *like* that.

L.A.: Stars, you mean, in their improvisation, or in playing the arrangements?

KNIGHT: Both. When they were playing the lead parts, I could hear how they were played. I played under Bob Fitzpatrick and Archie LeCoque and Kent Larsen, and they played different ways, and I *learned* from those guys. I'll tell you, I learned to play my horn on Stan's band.

L.A.: In what sense?

KNIGHT: I wasn't the player when I went on the band that I was when I came off of it. The music was *so* difficult, and when I went on the band, Stan had just had an organization with four trombones and a tuba—played by Jay McAllister—instead of a bass trombone. The *Cuban Fire* album had a tuba on it. And he traveled with a tuba for a while. This was right after that. I was having to play tuba parts. Which I *loved,* because it was the same register. But it was very difficult. So I literally either had to do it or I'd have to leave the band. So that's what I mean, I think I learned to really play my instrument correctly on that band.

L.A.: What were the circumstances of your joining the Kenton band?

KNIGHT: I'd left North Texas, and I went to Michigan State. I was living in East Lansing, on Orchard Street. By you there, right?

L.A.: (Laughs.) I never get over the weird coincidence of that.

KNIGHT: My wife was working for the dean of arts and sciences at Michigan State. Allan Beutler, a baritone player on Stan's band in the early sixties, was there, and was a good friend of mine. We heard Stan's band was going to be playing at the Jackson Jazz Club, which was one of the most formidable jazz clubs in the nation. We spent our whole bankroll of like thirteen dollars driving to Jackson, joining the jazz club, going to the concert, and going to a party somebody was having for the band. It wasn't 'til after I was on Stan's band that I learned Stan's band *never* went to parties. He hated doin' that stuff; he'd always make excuses. But he went to *this* one. I knew a guy on the band, a trumpet player named Frank Huggins, who'd been on Woody's band about eight months before, here in Dallas. I'd

introduced him to a girl from North Texas. At first he didn't remember *me,* though he *did* remember the girl. I told him I wanted to join the band, and he laughed at me. It was a real big thing to be on Stan Kenton's band in 1959. Without knowing how I played or anything, he said **"You kiddin'?** *Everybody* wants to get on this band." Then he said "What do you play?" I said "Bass trombone." He said "Wait a minute. The bass trombone player wants to leave. And Stan's having a tough time trying to find a substitute. Why didn't you tell me?" I was introduced to Bill Smiley, who wanted to move to L.A. and make his mark there, and he said "Let me talk to Stan and we'll see." I went on home and didn't think anything about it. Let's see, that was a Saturday. On Monday morning I got a phone call from Stan Kenton. Just blew my mind! He said "We're in Chicago. Can you be here this weekend?" I said "Yes sir, Mr. Kenton, I sure will." So a friend of mine—guy named Tom Benham, a trumpet player from San Francisco—and I got in the ol' Studebaker Lark and boogied across from Lansing to Chicago. Which is not a small distance, you know.

L.A.: Right, it's about a four-hour drive.

KNIGHT: And I think we'd borrowed twenty dollars from somebody and got there early and killed some time, and then went into the Blue Note, where the band was playing. Stan had to do a television show and the first sets were on, so he asked us to wait. So we sat there all night and listened to the band, which was a *treat.* And Stan came back in the middle of the last set. By that time, things had really gone awry. Several of the band members had gotten bombed. I mean, down the tubes. There was a sub here and there, and I sat in, and a coupla guys were not makin' it, and Stan was a little mad. So afterwards he said, "Bobby, I'm sorry. I just couldn't tell what in the heck was goin' on tonight. Can you come back tomorrow night?" And I didn't have any money! I said, "Stan, I used my credit card to come down here and I've got this friend with me and we had something to eat and now I don't have a dime . . . " He said "Well hell," and he gave me fifty dollars. And in 1959 . . . fifty dollars . . .

L.A.: Was worth about two hundred.

KNIGHT: That's right. He said "Will this help you?" I said "*Yeah.* That'll be

fine." So we stayed over, and I came back the next night and sat in for the first set. And Stan said, "Bobby, I think you'll work out with the band. Can you meet us here two weeks from tonight?" "Sure, Mr. Kenton. Thank you." And so on. And I turned and started to walk off. He says "Just a minute. Don't you want to know what the chair pays?" Well right there I knew that I had lost a lot of money. (Laughs.)

L.A.: (Laughs.)

KNIGHT: I started on the band at a hundred and fifty dollars a week. No rooms, nothing was paid, in those days. That was it. Stan wasn't—I don't know, it's hard to characterize Stan. Stan was a dichotomy. He was *very* generous. And he'd give you anything. Until it came to business. Then it was business. It took me three months to get a five-dollar-a-week raise out of him. Everybody else on the band was making a hundred and seventy-five, and I was making a hundred and fifty, just trying to get along. But—you know, he—Stan was a father figure to most of us. When I came on the band, Stan was, what, 47? That's just about my age right now. Well I think of myself as a virile young *stud,* still like I'm in college.

L.A.: (Laughs)

KNIGHT: And yet, in *those* days, I looked at Stan at 47 as an older guy. I couldn't imagine him being immature at all. He was just super. Really understanding. I was talking to Don Sebesky about two weeks ago. He and I agree, Stan's the best leader that ever was. Stan was a human person. Musically I didn't see eye to eye with Stan on a lot of things. But personally, I loved him. I really did truly love the man. I looked up to him in so many ways. I'm just sorry that I wasn't able to get as close as I'd **have liked to him. I don't think anybody** got really as close as they wanted to. One of the closest guys to him at any time was Bob Fitzpatrick. Fantastic player. He came on and off the band a lot. Bob was on some of those big monster hit bands, and was still on after I left. He was always older than the other guys.

L.A.: I've heard that a lot, about Stan's father image.

KNIGHT: He was the best thing that ever happened to me, in many ways. Other people will say the same thing. They loved him. The greatest leader in the world. But sometimes a pain in the ass. Sometimes you wanted to just stand up and yell at 'im. You know. And vice versa. He had this authoritarian attitude about him. Which was good, because he really—he was a *brilliant* man, *I* think. But—you look at him, and you *expect* him to be *right*. When he was wrong, you just felt like, geez. How can that be? Just like my own dad. My dad I never thought would be wrong about anything in his *life*. 'Til I finally grew up, and realized that he was just a man, too. I think I expected more of Stan than anybody should. Most people did. Not just me. Because he looked, acted—he was bigger than life, to begin with. If you ever met him, he's 6'5, right?

L.A.: Yes.

KNIGHT: Big man. You expected him to be what he was. Well Stan wasn't—Stan was narrow-minded at times. His politics were *horrible. Horrible.* Like just to the right of *Genghis Khan.*

L.A.: (Laughs.)

KNIGHT: We'd be talking, and he'd say "Let's—let's get the band and let's all **join the Air Force!**" *"What?"*

L.A.: (Laughs.)

KNIGHT: (Laughs.) He said "Yeah," he said, "we can do it like Glenn Miller." He said "I can be a colonel or some-thing, and all you guys'd be in it. We'd have bookings and everything."

L.A.: And he was serious.

KNIGHT: *Yes.* "We'd help our country, and—" I said, "But Stan—we're about to go to war." He said "Well hell, let's not fight, let's go *play.*"

L.A.: He did have all those Armed Forces dates in the forties.

KNIGHT: Oh ya. Oh he *loved* the Army. He loved the Air Force. I remember I was on the band the night that Kennedy got elected. In fact I remember it was Schenectady. Stan and I sat down and watched the Kennedy-Nixon debates. And—(laughs)—I never will forget—Stan turned to me and says, "Boy, he sure made a fool of 'im, didn't he?" I said "Yep. Looks like we're gonna have a Catholic President." He says "I mean NIXON made a fool of 'im!" I said, "Stan—you gotta be kidding." He was so one-sided about politics. He couldn't see those things. And he couldn't see, like I told him, the night that Kennedy got elected, he says "Oh, my God, there goes the country." I said "Stan. If you'll stop and look at the history of your band, it's never done any better than

when we've had a Democratic Presi-dent." I think I saw a glimmer of com-prehension. But it was hard for Stan to say some things. Like "Goodbye." That's not putting him down. It was hard for him to say. It was always "Okay, I'll see you." Somebody'd be leaving, he might never see him again. He didn't want to have ties that he was so involved with he couldn't break them easily. You wanted more from him, but he couldn't do it, 'cause it hurt him too much. See Stan didn't like to have anybody leave the band. He didn't like to disclose his feelings too much. Or when it came to saying thank-you's—he taught me something once. He was standing near me when somebody gave me a compliment, something like "You played very well tonight," and I said "Oh no, not really, I didn't do so well." Stan says "A simple 'thank-you' does every-thing you want it to do." And—I watched him after that. For closers, that's all he ever did. He'd say "Thank you." Because—what he said is ab-solutely true.

L.A.: You mentioned not being in agreement with Stan musically at all times. When it came to playing the music, did you have disagreements? I know he didn't always like it when the band was swinging.

KNIGHT: I was on the band one night at the Red Hill Inn, in Pennsauken, New Jersey. And we were playing "Swing House," or some one of Gerry Mulli-gan's things, and just swinging our *ass* off, just having a *ball*—Stan stopped the band—"What the hell's wrong with you guys?"

L.A.: (Laughs.)

KNIGHT: Then the second year I was on the band—we *hated* to play "Peanut Vendor." Stan loved it. Band hated it. You know.

L.A.: Ya they did look kind of bored with it. (Laughs.)

KNIGHT: Tenor trombone players didn't want to learn how to play the lead on it.

L.A.: Why?

KNIGHT: Well they didn't want to *play* it. It was *dumb.* It was *horrid.* You know. So, Stan says "Bobby, you know that?" I said well yeah, he said "Play it for Dick." Dick Hyde. "Well, okay." And Dick's saying "Well I don't quite get that." Stan says "Bobby, I'll tell you what. We're leaving tomorrow—play it until Dick learns it, okay?" I played it

for nine months straight. 'Cause Dick would not learn it. Period. I played bass trombone, and the part went real high. It's not an easy solo for *tenor.* But the point is, it wasn't my place to play it. It was the feature for the tenor trombone player. And they didn't want to play it. So I did. If I missed the high D, the real high note, Stan would go all the way through it and then say to the audience, "We always like to introduce young-sters; it's their chance of a lifetime to really do well. Bobby, will you come back down here?" I'd go back down and he'd make me play it by *myself.* And it was fun. It was shtick. It was show-biz, you know. Stan was good at that. But one thing he wouldn't put up with was players giving him ultimatums. Like "Hey. I don't like so-and-so. Either *he* goes or *I* go." Guess who goes.

L.A.: Did this situation come up?

KNIGHT: It happened to me. I got into a fight with the drummer, Jimmy Campbell, one night. He was an older guy, and I didn't like the way he was playing, and he didn't like the way I was playing. So he tried to get me fired. With Stan you didn't do that. Because if you *do* that, you go to Stan and say that, even if Stan agrees with you, Stan would come closer to firing *you.* He's not gonna allow anyone to *tell* him what he has to do. The best way to operate with him is to say "Stan, what are we gonna do about this?" And let *him* figure it out. One night I saw Billy Root and some of the guys get together and have a kangaroo-court type of thing and they fired the drummer. They told him, "Hey—get lost. Just leave. We want you to split. And don't tell the old man." Well hell, he went to see Stan, and said "These guys don't want me here." Stan fired Billy Root. 'Course, knowing Stan, here was a guy that broke the cardinal rule, and still he gave him eight weeks' notice. (Laughs.)

L.A.: (Laughs.)

KNIGHT: Boy we had some good trumpet players on that band. There was Dalton Smith. And Bill Chase. And Bud Brisbois. They were all on the band about the same time. Sammy Noto. And a guy named Rolf Erickson. He was a fine jazz player. Great trumpet section!

L.A.: Dalton marveled at that high note Bud Brisbois hit on "Lonely Woman" on the *Standards in Silhouette* album.

KNIGHT: That was a *mistake.*

L.A.: It was? Why, had Stan given a cut-off?

KNIGHT: We were playing, and Bud actually went higher than he was supposed to. You ever hear that album? He plays like a triple F-sharp, I don't know what the note is, but he goes (*whistles high*) like that. Everybody started to put their horns down, like Oh Christ, he screwed up. But Stan made a motion and waved us on. And he left it in. It's really a mistake and a goof. But it certainly turned out right. Bud was a phenomenal player. A *phenomenal* player. He could do that all night. And you know he had some very strong . . .

L.A.: He could do *that* kind of high playing?
KNIGHT: *Oh.*
L.A.: Really?
KNIGHT: Ya. After each time at the end of a tune, when he'd play a double C or a triple E or whatever, and just blow the walls down, you couldn't talk to him for like ten, fifteen seconds, because it really did screw him up.
L.A.: Blackout?
KNIGHT: Yeah. I saw him fall down . . .
L.A.: Dalton talked about doing that *routinely. Routinely.*
KNIGHT: Ya. It happened all the time.
L.A.: He said, "You black out, you pass out, you fall over the edge of the stand, then you get up and go back and play."
KNIGHT: With Dalton, Dalton never was sure when he blacked out.
L.A.: (Laughs.)
KNIGHT: You had to tell him, "Hey, Dalton, you're out." "Oh yeah." (Laughs.)
L.A.: (Laughs.) Do you think that was Stan's greatest band, when you were there in '59 through '61?
KNIGHT: No. The best band he *ever* had, in my opinion, was probably in '50, '51, '52. When he recorded the *Prologue* suite—*This Is An Orchestra.*
L.A.: Wasn't that the same personnel that went on the Innovations tours?

KNIGHT: Just about. I separate them. I didn't care for the string thing. I thought those were pretentious. Good music, I guess, but—the band with Lee Konitz and Frank Rosolino and Maynard Ferguson and Conte Candoli and George Roberts. Bob Burgess was playing lead. Those guys. As far as I was concerned, that was the best band he had. When I was on the band, we never had it all together. One of the sections would always be lacking in some respect. Had some good trombone sections, some good sax sections, but never had a good band all at once.

L.A.: I know about 600,000 people who wouldn't agree with that.

KNIGHT: Well, I'm talking about from a musical standpoint, a real solid band, chair by chair by chair. All the way up and down. When I was on the band we had rhythm section problems at times. Either the bass player wasn't quite as strong as he should be, or the drummer. Stan sometimes would hire people that weren't very good players. He hired a trumpet player from Indianapolis one time that literally couldn't play.
L.A.: Then why'd he hire him? (Laughs.)
KNIGHT: I don't know. I've talked to Dalton about that several times, and to other people. Some people think that Stan just had a soft heart. A *real* soft heart.
L.A.: Isn't that interesting.
KNIGHT: And some people think that he didn't know really when a musician was really good.

L.A.: I'd find that hard to believe.

KNIGHT: Well—some people say that the best bands he had were when the guys on the band got other guys on the band, like in 1951 and '52. But it doesn't matter. Stan's strength was being leader of the band. Didn't matter whether he hired 'em or not. I've seen it, though, I saw him hire a bass player, young bass player, that just didn't make it. Had him there for some time. Stan just kept him. Stan stuck with him. Of course we all have our own subjective view, but it's my feeling that there came a point in time, maybe '63, '64, '65, when it became an ex-college band instead of a professional band. After I left, when Dalton was on the band, and Jay Saunders, and Dee Barton, guys like that, it really—really roared. But when you get a *whole band* of youngsters, they play great, but they're not gonna move along like we were able to. What can you learn being on a band where everyone has the same background?

L.A.: But a young band might be more receptive to new ideas.
KNIGHT: See now wait a minute. Like all college bands like this, they're great bands. There's not a better band in the country—I mean that—than this college band right here. It's a *bitch.* Stan's band was never this good, when I was on it. *Never.* Technically, it was never this good.
L.A.: What are we talking about when

we say that it was better?
KNIGHT: We're talking about technically and musically. We're talking about maturity. I mean the musical scene, when Charlie Mariano and those guys played, was incomparable. There's a sterility involved, in youngsters playing, that only with maturity can become something really musical. When there are so *many* people in an organization that're that young, the sterility sort of shows, I think. That's why I was very happy to have been on the band when I was.
L.A.: Let's see, you joined in '59 and were there until '61. Did you return later?

KNIGHT: No. Once I left, that was all. Bud Brisbois and I quit the same night. We were in Denver, and we told Stan, and Stan didn't like that. "Big deal; gonna be a studio musician; where're you gonna be? Why aren't you out here making music with us?" I said "I can't make it on 200 dollars a week, Stan. My wife's pregnant." He didn't like that. He wanted everybody to be a road rat. He told me he was gonna die on that bus. I'm surprised he didn't.
L.A.: He almost did, right?

KNIGHT: Yeah. Several times. (Laughs.) I imagine. The thing of it was, in those days we were on the road for nine, ten, eleven months at a time. One-nighters. It wasn't the way it was the last five or ten years, where he'd be on the road for three months, take a few months off, like that. We followed the band in our car out to Los Angeles in December of 1959 and made our home there. I toured with the band all of 1960 except for the summer. My wife joined me for our last tour of 1960, when she was pregnant, and we traveled with Count Basie, Ann Richards and Joe Williams. In January and February of 1961 I made some recordings with Stan, then in March he went on tour. I guess you could say I was with the band from March of '59 through March of '61. Whereupon a bass trombone player from here, who had taken my place in the North Texas band when I went on Stan's band, took my place on Stan's band.

L.A.: Where were you from originally?
KNIGHT: I was born in Monroe, Louisiana. Where Carl Fontana came from, probably my favorite trombone player of all time. He played on Stan's band at one time, too. I went to high

school in El Dorado, Arkansas, where I continued to get involved in music. When I came to North Texas it was to be a high school band director. But I found out there were other options in life. Graduated from here, got married, and a year and a half later I was on Stan's band.

L.A.: Gene Roland was from North Texas State also, wasn't he?

KNIGHT: Yeah. But now Gene was here before there was a jazz department. Boy, you're talking about a wild man. I could tell you stories about Gene Roland on that bus—oh! See that's why I feel so fortunate having been on the band with all those names, Gene Roland, Johnny Richards, Lennie Niehaus. Great writers. Yet all the money that Johnny and Stan made they just went and blew. Stan could have been wealthy. He consistently surrounded himself with ineptitude. He sometimes was his own worst enemy.

L.A.: In what way?

KNIGHT: One summer we did a pilot for a tv show. A Western. Stan wrote the music. By that time, it was passe. It just didn't work. And I don't know whether Stan was good at it or not, but more important was that he could have done so much . . . .

L.A.: Wait a minute. Stan Kenton, music for a—pilot for a *Western?*

KNIGHT: I believe it was a Western.

L.A.: What did he have in *mind?*

KNIGHT: I'll tell you where we did it. Warner Brothers.

L.A.: How can Stan Kenton music go with a Western?

KNIGHT: It wouldn't have been his band. It would have been just cues, written by Stan Kenton.

L.A.: After you left Stan's band you worked in the studios in L.A.?

KNIGHT: Yes. For eighteen years. Wrote some television scores, like for *Mary Hartman, Mary Hartman, Fernwood Tonight, What's Happening* and *Carter Country.* But I don't miss the studio thing at all, 'cause the pressure, musical pressure, was just enormous.

L.A.: What do you do here at North Texas State?

KNIGHT: I do everything except lead the band. Neil (Slater) does that. Neil took over when Leon (Breeden) left. I produced the last two albums here. Neil and I do the mixing, along with the engineer. I book the band, take care of the travel, and the logistics and the administrative part of the thing, but Neil is the head, and makes all the decisions. It's his program. I'm his assistant. There's so much to the program here; it's really a monumental job. I also have a band on my own. Stan would have broken up to hear this—it's country-western jazz!

L.A.: My gosh. (Laughs.)

KNIGHT: It's good music. We play tunes that are hits on the country-western stations, but we play it our way, and people don't mind.

L.A.: Let's talk about the set-up of the program here.

KNIGHT: There are actually nine bands, plus four rehearsal groups, so there's thirteen groups.

L.A.: It's just staggering to conceive of this. You name them after the clock, right?

Bobby Knight and two students at NTSU—Chris Seiter and Tammy Schultz. (Photo by the Author.)

171

KNIGHT: Right. There's the One O'Clock, Two O'Clock, Three O'Clock, on down. That's what time they rehearse. The four rehearsal bands, or reading bands, meet at 4 o'clock, so the Four O'Clock Band meets at 5 o'clock, along with the Five O'Clock Band. Two bands each meet at 5 o'clock, 6 o'clock, and 7 o'clock, like the Six and Seven O'Clock Bands meet at 6 p.m. and the Eight and Nine O'Clock Bands meet at 7 p.m. And we have two rehearsal halls, so they meet in 5 East, 5 West, 6 East, 6 West, 7 East and 7 West. Same with the reading bands, a band in each hall. But there are so many players that they're divided into two bands each, one that meets on Mondays and Wednesdays and one that meets Tuesdays and Thursdays.

L.A.: You actually have thirteen jazz bands here.

KNIGHT: We actually have thirteen groups, yes.

L.A.: *Cheee.*

KNIGHT: Thirteen 20-piece bands. Not counting ensembles. We have between 1600 and 1700 music majors here in the fall and spring. Of those we have anywhere from 350 to 450 students who have something to do with the jazz department. They're not jazz majors always. We always have around 300 jazz majors, but more students than that get involved in jazz studies. You do have to be a jazz major to be in a lab band. This is the pilot program for the whole nation. Gene Hall started it in 1947. Stan wasn't even aware of it until '59.

L.A.: I don't think *anybody* was.

KNIGHT: No. Not very many people were. When I was a student here I think we worked three outside jobs. This semester they worked sixteen. For a minimum of $1750 bucks a night. Up to $4,000. When I went on the band in March of '59 I kept tellin' Stan about hey, this college band I was in, and he kept saying yeah, sure. 'Cause college bands were a dime a dozen. I kept sayin', "Stan, it's really a good college band!" The lab band came up to New York City in the spring of 1959 to play in the National Stage Band Contest. I'm not sure whether Stan was a judge at that first one or not. We called ours a lab band, they called theirs stage bands; same thing. It was jazz. It was in the Roseland Ballroom. We were back-

stage. I introduced Stan to Gene Hall. And then Stan heard the band and flipped out. First chance he got, later on, he hired Marvin Stamm, who was from NTSU. But that was the first time Stan ever heard the band, and it was the first time he met Gene Hall. I had just left school. All my friends were in New York. That just was hog heaven. That summer of 1959 was the first time I ever met Dalton Smith, at the first jazz clinic at the University of Indiana. People think we're like brothers—well we *are*—but we didn't meet until then. I never will forget that summer. I was just beside myself. I had lunch with Stan, Laurindo Almeida, and Shelly Manne, and just—you know, I was—

L.A.: It's a shame you couldn't have rounded up a few stars.

KNIGHT: Ya. That was in Indianapolis, where the band was playing that night, before we drove over to the clinic. The band didn't play the clinic the first two years. After Stan met Gene Hall, the three of them, Stan, Hall and Ken Morris, got the Kenton Clinics going.

L.A.: Were all three on the ground floor together?

KNIGHT: For the most part. Morris I'm sure was the one who started it, 'cause it meant money. And he made some money out of it.

L.A.: So it was Ken Morris's promotional backing financially?

KNIGHT: I don't know whether he financed it or not. I don't know who financed it. Stan may have been involved with financing. See they had to have three ingredients. They had to have an educator, to round up other educators. And that was Gene Hall, and later Leon Breeden came in. They had to have a name. And that was Stan Kenton. And they had to have a promoter. Somebody at the business end of the thing. That was Ken Morris. Morris was a promoter who booked Stan's band into all those Tom Archer Ballrooms—he had a whole bunch of them in Indiana and Ohio and Michigan and through there.

L.A.: You have the background of having been a professional musician for more than twenty years, and now you're working with young people, observing

their growth. What factors are involved in their development from mere technical proficiency into a more mature musical sensibility? What do they pick up by working with professionals, either through your program here or through a Stan Kenton Clinic experience, that helps in that development?

KNIGHT: It's indefinable. Everybody is looking for that magic thing. That's everybody's dream. What's that magic thing that will make me play like so-and-so? Well that magic thing is generally practice, but nobody wants to hear that. They want to go and get that *spark*. If I could have played like Frank Rosolino, I'd have been beside myself. But he couldn't have told me one thing that I could have gone home and done to be able to do everything he did. So the learning process is very long. What young people could pick up from the clinic experience with Stan and his players, I think, was a kind of emulation. It was an emulatory situation. When you get into a band the next time, you think, well wait a minute, this doesn't sound the way the professional trombone section sounded. So—what do we do to make it change? Or, here's what *they* did. It's not just a matter of watching somebody and learning the specifics. It's the overall professionalism. But if you want to look and see what a tremendous impact Stan had on jazz education, all you have to do is go to any high school or college jazz festival. And look at the bands that are there. Every one of 'em. Every one of 'em is five, five, and five. Which is Stan's size. Some of them even use his set-up, the B-25 set-up.

L.A.: Good grief. What's the B-25 set-up?

KNIGHT: It's what they used to call it with the rhythm section in the middle, piano on the side, and the saxes coming in at an angle on one side and trombones at an angle on the other. Trumpets in the middle, up above the rhythm. Spread out so that the fifth trombone player and the fifth saxophone player were 35 yards apart. Very hard to play like that. It looks great. Looked like it was taking off. Stan was a great one for the dramatics.

Both such factions are moving toward the same goal

and the feeling of admiration and respect between the two expressions

is warm and constant.

Hank Levy, in his office at Towson State University, Towson, Maryland. (Photo by the Author.)

23 Hank Levy

The Kenton band was catching on to this in the fives and sevens and what not. And I thought, well now we can stretch out a little bit. We can't go with just fives and sevens. See we're just—touching the top. They could play seven, very well. So I wrote a chart out and gave it to 'em. And I wrote it in fourteen. And they went crazy again. You know. They see the fourteen, and it drives 'em NUTS.

I said to 'em, now look, the bar is divided into two facets of seven. Now the first seven is divided two-two-three. The second seven is divided two-three-two. Okay. And it's in fourteen. Rather than write it in seven and have to write on top, "This is two-three-two," at the same time I didn't want to put another bar line in, because the phrase ran all the way across two-two-three-two-three-two.

L.A.: Oh I see. All fourteen beats were part of the theme.

LEVY: All of it was one bar. Okay?

L.A.: Um-hm.

LEVY: So you got a feeling of um-dat, um-dat, um-dat, um-dat, um-dah, dah, dah; um-dat, um-dat, um-dah, dah, dah, um-dat, um-dat.

L.A.: What piece was that?

LEVY: I don't remember anymore, because they fell on their fanny, it just didn't go over with them.

L.A.: (Laughs.)

LEVY: I was so disappointed in that. I'd think, "Come on, guys, geez, just do it for me once. And you'll be free. You'll free the shackles, you know? Just fives, sevens or nines are not enough. You can take and extend that." That's why I say it's like you're cutting a piece of pie, and you're just starting at the beginning of this thing, and as you move *outward* it gets more and more wide. You take five,

okay, take five/four time. You *double* that five/four, and you've got ten/eight. When you go in five, in a series of threes and twos, you've only got two and three, or three and two. That's all. When you go into *ten*, you've got *four* different ways. Provided you don't think it in twos. Well you shouldn't. You've got two-two-three-three, you've got two-three-two-three, you've got three-three-two-two, and so forth, you can turn them around any way. Okay. Suppose you go to twenty/sixteen time. The possibilities grow and grow and grow. They become—gigantic. They not only double themselves, they *square* each other. I counted in sevens once. I really went into it and counted out all the possibilities. There were something like 45, in writing a fourteen/four, or fourteen/eight. Suppose you went from fourteen/eight time into twenty-eight/sixteen.

L.A.: (Laughs.) Mind-boggling.

LEVY: Mind-boggling, and the further you go, the wider it gets and the more possibilities there are. And it still narrows down to series of twos and threes! And that's all!

L.A.: So you would take this exotic thing of twenty-eight/sixteen and divide it up . . .

LEVY: Into twos and threes the way I want it.

L.A.: The way you want to, and that would be the thematic material.

LEVY: Um-hm. That would be the root of it, anyway.

L.A.: That's bar one. Bar two . . . does it have to be the same pattern all the time?

LEVY: It wouldn't have to be, but it's a pretty good idea. If it extends out to twenty-eight it's pretty hard to remember what the thing would be.

L.A.: About when did you start to compose in exotic meters like this?

LEVY: I don't know when I first started to experiment. It must have been around '64, '65. I had a kicks band, and I was trying some things at that time.

L.A.: What got into your head? Just look what's become of it.

LEVY: I don't know . . . .

L.A.: (Laughs.)

LEVY: (Laughs.) Not enough has become of it, to tell you the truth.

L.A.: I mean it's really a unique, unique style.

LEVY: It is, and yet it's a very hard thing to sell.

L.A.: Was it any one incident, or some flow of inspiration . . .

LEVY: Nnnnnoo . . . I can remember taking a tune and trying to do it in an odd meter. I even remember what it was. "Speak Low."

L.A.: No kidding!

LEVY: Yeah, and I tried to do it in five,

and I remember writing it out and it looked okay and—and I can remember standing up in front of the band and getting lost. Wasn't able to find one. You know, it just couldn't count to five, it just sounded so *abnormal.* It was terrible.

L.A.: The band couldn't count to five?

LEVY: No. They couldn't do it. And I couldn't either. It just threw me for a loop. At the same time, I had listened to quite a bit of classical music, the Bartok quartets and what not, and saw what they'd do. Then John Richards started to get into these things. They were the biggest influences.

L.A.: *Cuban Fire,* for example?

LEVY: *Cuban Fire,* or the other one is the one I love, it's . . .

L.A.: *Adventures in Time.*

LEVY: *Adventures in Time.* Those influences combined, and I started doin' it. Then another thing—the lead trumpet player that I had here, on my kicks band, was a guy named Glenn Stuart, who was teaching junior high school down at Laurel (Maryland). Glenn used to go on the road in the summertime with one of the semi-name touring bands, and he met Don Ellis, who was playing trumpet on the same band. When Don moved to California Glenn went out there and became lead trumpet player on *Don's* band.

L.A.: Let's talk a little bit about Don Ellis. (Laughs.)

LEVY: Good! Ya, okay.

L.A.: That's a *big name.*

LEVY: Um-hm.

L.A.: I think I first heard the name on one of those albums that you recorded with Kenton, and he talked about how you'd worked with exotic meters with Don Ellis.

LEVY: Um-hm. Oh, Stan was a fan of Don's. Stan used to go see Don's band.

L.A.: Really? I believe he wrote for the Neophonic Orchestra, and made an appearance with it also. And once he led the band when Stan was sick. But he was never actually in the orchestra, was he.

LEVY: No. He never was.

L.A.: Isn't that interesting. And Stan didn't actually buy his charts or anything either, did he.

LEVY: No, he couldn't do that. In the pros, you know . . .

L.A.: Because Don had his own orchestra.

LEVY: That's right.

L.A.: But Stan admired him, as a musician.

LEVY: Very much so. As a matter of fact, Stan thought it was a dynamic kind

of direction to go. I think that's why he got interested in *my* music.

L.A.: He must have been a very interesting character.

LEVY: Oh it's interesting. Don was *beyond* creative. He was *very* experimental. He would try *anything.* He had so many things going at once, he had the adrenaline pumpin' *all* the time.

L.A.: Experimental beyond the time thing, you mean?

LEVY: Don was into time, and I considered that his big thing, but he had eight or ten other things going. Number one, he had a four-valve trumpet. He'd had it made specially for him. With this fourth valve he'd play quarter-tones. And he was *really* into quarter-tones, he had the kind of ear to hear them and use them. The only way for him to get into playing them was on his own solos. If you listen to the early Ellis things you'll hear it. He did it for real.

L.A.: Amazing.

LEVY: He loved it, and everything he had from then on, his fluegelhorns and everything else, could play quarter-tones. He believed in it, very heavily. Then he went in all of a sudden for echoplexes.

L.A.: *What* is an echoplex?

LEVY: It's a piece of machinery that—(laughs)— fits into the mouthpiece of the instrument, an electronic device that runs a tape and will give you a delay. Don could play a line and *record* it, and during his solo he'll play the record back, and play a line *against* that. In other words . . .

L.A.: Coming out of the same *instrument?*

LEVY: Yes, he's playing—he's playing a counterpoint with himself.

L.A.: My God.

LEVY: (Pauses.) Ya.

L.A.: (Laughs.) That is *weird.*

LEVY: Oh ya. Then he used an echoplex which would *repeat* itself, a *reverb* kind of thing, for effects. He used to have all kinds of devices. And he used to *mess* with those things all the *time,* invariably. As a matter of fact he made a mistake on one. He was playing a concert one time. And he pushed the wrong button . . .

L.A.: (Laughs.)

LEVY: . . . And the *weirdest thing* came out. But he *liked* it, so he wrote a *chart* on it. Right? Don was something else again. Had the kind of band that was *wild.* Uninhibited, and a bit crazy. I'm *telling* you, a bit crazy. When he would write, he'd do a chart that would have a head to it, a major theme, and backgrounds, and a finale. But he never knew

what he was gonna do in the middle of those things. He composed his form on the *spot.* His guys never knew where their solos were, they never knew when the backgrounds would occur, and they were *nervous as hell* playing concerts; they never knew what the hell he was gonna come *up* with!

L.A.: Are there recordings of his music?

LEVY: He did maybe fourteen or fifteen albums in his lifetime. Towards the end, around '73, '75 on, he began to mature in his writing and went from wild to more interesting and wrote some really beautiful things. Called me one time and we talked for about three hours and he said, "What do you think about adding strings to the group?" He wrote the music for *The French Connection* — *most* of it was left on the cutting room floor—and for maybe ten or twelve other movies. When I got with Don, I knew damn well if I wanted to stay with that band, I was going to have to lose some of my inhibitions. 'Cause I was an inhibited writer, really, at one time, and Don was the one who helped me over that. He would say, "Gotta stick your neck out, every time you put a note on paper." I joined him in 1965. His first major album was *Live at Monterey,* in 1967. Don really turned that festival on. Got 'em crazy. And one of my tunes was played on that album.

L.A.: What brought you two together?

LEVY: Glenn Stuart called me up one day and said, "You two are experimenting along the same lines. Why don't you send us some charts? We've got a good band out here." And I did. Glenn later on was with Stan; I was instrumental in getting him to play the lead in Stan's band for a while.

L.A.: That's an interesting statement he made, about the two of you experimenting along the same lines. Were you proceeding with the time revolution on your own, then?

LEVY: Don was further ahead, because he had studied this Indian tabla playing. Not only that, he wasn't afraid of it. I was just trying to get my craft together. But I *was* interested in *time* things.

L.A.: Richards had done a lot with time, hadn't he?

LEVY: Yes, but he didn't have time to go far enough. In the same way, **Brubeck was doing some time changes, too, but** *he* **didn't go far enough. Lord knows,** *we* **haven't gone far enough,** *either.* **Because—I can see, just with the little experimenting that we're doing, we're just opening it up a little way.**

When you get inside, there's a whole new *world* out there. In just *that alone. Oh,* it really *is,* and you need some people who can *play* it. When we first started doing it, it was just unreal, because you'd write some charts down, things that you had pretty well up here, and the band falls on its face. And you wonder, is it the charts or is it the concept's fault, or is it the kids' fault, that they can't *play* the thing? You never knew what the real reason was for it. Especially when we were first experimenting with time.

L.A.: When you were first experimenting in Don Ellis's orchestra?

LEVY: With Don's band too, yes, same thing. Hey, he had the same problems out there. He had to teach all of *his* players how to play in these time signatures. And when I first got together with Don, the first things that I sent him out were not odd meters, or exotic meters, whatever you want to call them. When he wrote back he said "Yeah. Let's keep 'em on going, let's keep workin' on 'em. Why don't you try to write some exotic meters?" I called him up and I said "I don't know what the hell you're *talkin'* about."

L.A.: (Laughs.)

LEVY: "What do you mean by exotic meters?" He'd say "Well let's write some things in 5, 7, 9, 11, you know. Thirteen, twelve, whatever." And I said "Gee, that's interesting. Let's try it."

L.A.: Is this always presuming the quarter note is the base, so when you say 5, 7, 9, 11, 13 . . .

LEVY: You can do it in 13/8 if you want to.

L.A.: Does it make a significant difference?

LEVY: The difference is in the way . . .

L.A.: The key thing is the top.

LEVY: It—ya. The difference is in the way you notate it, that's all. But it could come out the same. You could write a thing in 13/8 or 13/4, and it'd be the same—exactly the same thing. The top number, the numerator, can be *anything.*

L.A.: The numerator.

LEVY: The numerator and the denominator. Remember old fractions in the public school system?

L.A.: I've never heard music described in that way before!

LEVY: Well that's the only way I have to describe it.

L.A.: The numerator!

LEVY: The top number can be *anything.*

L.A.: Even *that's* an exciting concept.

LEVY: Yeah, it can be anything you want.

L.A.: 'Cause *I've* never learned music that way.

LEVY: No, well neither did I.

L.A.: I learned "A quarter note gets one beat . . ."

LEVY: (Laughs.)

L.A.: "There are four beats to a measure . . ." (Laughs.)

LEVY: Okay, that's all.

L.A.: The *numerator.* Now that's a space-age concept.

LEVY: (Laughs.) That's elementary school!

L.A.: Well I know, but sometimes you can take an elementary word and give it *glamour* by—doing that.

LEVY: Um-hm. It can be anything, from 2—or 1, even—

L.A.: To 97. (Laughs.)

LEVY: To wherever. I mean it is absolutely—

L.A.: What do you mean, wherever. You don't mean like 5,432.

LEVY: Conceivably. Conceivably, it could. If you could remember the divisions—(laughs)—one bar long, it takes three weeks to play, that's . . .

L.A.: (Laughs.)

LEVY: There are people out there experimenting with no bar lines at all!

L.A.: No bar lines! How can you have rhythm without bar lines?

LEVY: If there are no bar lines there are no primary accents, but you could show accents where you want them placed, which could be anywhere. But it's very very difficult for the player. The other side of that is Stravinsky, who was wedded to the odd meters, but what he would do was rather than write a bar of 7, he would write a bar of 3, another bar of 2, bar of 2; or a bar of 2, bar of 3, bar of 2, to make up the 7.

L.A.: Yes, *The Firebird* is like that.

LEVY: The way I feel about it is, in a jazz value, if you were writing in 7, I think that 7 ought to be *repeated. Because* it's new and fresh and because it's a little bit on the *unusual* side, you better bang that home for a while, in order to get your audience accustomed to it. If you do it long enough, all of a sudden it gets to roll along. Not only that, it helps your musicians to get it, and to play it. So I always believed in that, and I also believe that it is complex to begin with, and to add complexity to it is *wrong.*

L.A.: Using the example of your "Indra," even though the time works out mathematically the same each time, doesn't your syncopation, by coming at different places, make it sound like it's 42 different kinds of time within one piece of music?

LEVY: Well that's part of it. There's a certain influence—if you want it to be Latin, if you want it to be jazz, if you want it to be this and that, you've got to have a certain amount of anticipations into the next thing and a certain amount of syncopations and that kind of thing. But basically, you're talking about separations and subdivisions of the bar. And they're all 2's or 3's. And Don said it very very easily. He said "When you're counting, if you can tap your foot unevenly without it screwing up your equilibrium, you've got it made. If you can tap in 2's and 3's, and just remember where you are, that's all there is to the whole system. And you can play anything there is."

L.A.: But even though you're repeating, say, a measure of 13/4, it sounds different in each measure because you syncopate differently. Is that what I'm hearing?

LEVY: Could be.

L.A.: It sounds *incredibly* complex.

LEVY: And it really isn't, it's really very simple. What I tell my students is, when you begin writing you write difficult and it sounds easy. When you mature, you write easy, and it sounds difficult. Now the reason you want to *do* that is because you get better *performance* when it's easy. And this is really a very easy concept. It can be explained with no strain at all in just a couple of minutes. But getting it done really changes the whole musical habit of the jazz world! Is what it *does.* It scares people—it's *frightening.* And when I got into it I didn't conceive of it that way. But what's *great* about these odd meters is that you can't use the usual licks. We call them licks. The *cliches.* They don't *fit.*

L.A.: What are you referring to?

LEVY: Musical cliches. There are certain jazz motives, thematic material that you can find in most all the tunes you hear. They're accepted as part of a musical habit and they're used, overused, and abused. But they're accepted, because they're an improvised kind of thing that happens in a melodic line. They won't always go the same way, but we've only got twelve notes to work with, so there's got to be some repetition. Well, this kind of repetitive thing doesn't work in a different meter. You've got to coincide with the end of the bar, because you're gonna go into a new chord the next bar. So they don't work anymore. It forces you to create. And that's good. Jazz needs that kind of thing.

L.A.: It really is a revolution, then, isn't it?

LEVY: Yeh.

L.A.: It's breaking up the sound of jazz. You know, you're right. All jazz, even though it's all different, sounds somewhat the same, in that sense. How does the exotic meter concept work out creatively in an improvisation?

LEVY: It might extend that line that you're playing. And that extension, two or three or four notes, even, might be just enough to get you away from this sounding that way. It no longer sounds like that because it's got some extra notes in it, in the middle of it, because you got some more *time* to take up. *Oh, it's mind-boggling,* it's a very, very simple thing—I could spout the whole thing for you in five minutes flat. BUT— it is *deep.* It . . .

L.A.: (Pauses.) It is, isn't it.

LEVY: Yeh.

L.A.: When I listen to your music with an analytical ear, I try to get the handle on it, and I can't. Which is *why* it's *exciting.* I mean it's like finding something *brand-new.* And it *sounds* brand-new *all the time.*

LEVY: That's good. 'Cause that's what it's supposed to do. I make sure—I really take this very very seriously and work on it perhaps harder than I should—make sure that a theme in 5 is not in four plus one. It's not a bar of four with an extra note thrown in. Or a bar of 7 is not a bar of 8 *minus* one note.

L.A.: Gosh! How do you do that?

LEVY: You write it in 7, so that the **thematic material is *really in 7.*** I've been doing this now for fifteen years or better, and the way I am now, I must count *everything.* At one time I could take 4/4 for granted, and I knew where it *was.* Right now, I can get that same kind of thing in 7. If I'm not counting *everything,* 4, 3, 7, 5, whatever it is, I can **get myself *totally lost.*** And—(laughs)— it would be terrifying. Because 7 and 5 now can become as *natural* as 4/4 was at one time.

L.A.: I see what you mean.

LEVY: And I have a feeling with these kids, because they're counting, now, everything, they're better *players* in 4/4 because they're *not* taking it for granted. They're zeroing in and making sure they count it before.

L.A.: I noticed them at your recording session today—listening and counting, and their whole body going with the beat. And that was fabulous to watch. How can you make a 5—7 I can understand a little better, 'cause you talked

about 2 plus 2 plus 3—but how can you keep a 5/4 from becoming 4 plus one? Through thematic material?

LEVY: Well you want your theme to not sound like a 4/4 piece with an extra *beat* in it. It should be a theme in 5 beats to the bar with the primary accent falling on one, and then four more beats and then one again, and four more beats. Now you can do it in 2 and 3. You can do it in 3 and 2. Or you can do it in straight-ahead 5.

L.A.: But the beat should come on the one?

LEVY: The beat will always come on 1, you need the primary accent.

L.A.: What if you syncopate? (Laughs.)

LEVY: Syncopating doesn't hurt it. You still get the primary accent.

L.A.: As in ONE-two-three-four-five, ONE-two-three-four-five.

LEVY: Let me see. "Chiapas" is in 5.

L.A.: I love that wild part that goes da-da-da-da di-da dat-dah.

LEVY: That's in 8. Divided 5 plus 3.

L.A.: Eight? It has a feeling of 5. Though it *does* feel like 5-plus-something.

LEVY: It's 8/4, divided 5 plus 3. ONE-da-da-da-da di-da-da-da ONE-da-da-da-da di-da-da-da MM!-da-da-da-da di-da-da-da It's ONE-two-three-four-five SIX-seven-eight; ONE-two-three-four-five SIX-seven-eight; ONE-two-three-four-five SIX-seven-eight. Just prior to that the trumpets are playing, the background was in five. And when I got to this one spot, it felt like, if I added a couple of extra beats, it would be that much of a kick, so I did a bar of five, and added a three on to it. And it became 8/4 divided 5 and 3. As a matter of fact "Chiapas" was the first thing I ever wrote for Stan.

L.A.: That was the first thing?! Really?

LEVY: Yeah.

L.A.: You had actually been with Stan prior to the time you wrote for him, hadn't you?

LEVY: Yes, for six months in 1953. I was just out of the service and in college and had a little bit of vacation, so I decided to go to California to visit my good friend Ken Hanna. I remember it took me fifteen hours to get there by plane! Single-motor job, made about twelve stops along the way. Ken had always wanted to go to California. Took his wife and two children and left Baltimore when I was in school. I hadn't seen him for a long time, though we corresponded. We were always close.

L.A.: He told me that you used to play Kenton arrangements in his band.

LEVY: Yes, and what a kick it was, getting Kenton *manuscript* charts to work on! Hanna worked for Stan and would bring in these things. I had designs to be a writer. I always wanted to be a writer. I can remember when I was 10 or 11 or 12 years old, I used to—I remember one instance when I wrote a march or something like that. I guess I was—I have no idea how old I was.

L.A.: You wrote a march as a child! (Laughs.) Mozart!

LEVY: Yeah! I can't imagine what the thing would be, because I had no instruction in harmony or theory and didn't know what I was doing. I just knew what the basic concept was, what kind of feeling I wanted and what not, and it was so easy to just go ahead and improvise it.

L.A.: Oh that's exciting. Was that a march in 4/4 time?

LEVY: I imagine so.

L.A.: (Laughs.)

LEVY: At any rate.

L.A.: Gotcha on that one.

LEVY: Yeah. And a lot of the things that Ken was getting ready to send Stan he would bring and we'd play them. I was really scuffling to *play* all these things. I was in high school and I'd just started taking saxophone lessons, and with most of the heavy players drafted into the war I was lucky and got on Ken's band. It got me into big band music, playing in the band and listening to Kenton's records. High school would have been about 1941, '42, '43, somewhere in there.

L.A.: Gosh, that's just when it started.

LEVY: Ya. When he first came in, the *Concerto to End All Concertos* and the theme song always knocked me out. Always. I mean they still do. And "Collaboration." That era was just a complete knockout, the Rugolo-Kenton era. I had all the records. I loved it!

L.A.: It's really strange, Hanna also recruited you into the Navy.

LEVY: Gave me my oath into the service. But he'd said "Don't come. Catch the first bus out of town." He didn't want to see me go in. Well nobody wanted to go in, right at the end of the war. Anyway, Ken and I got to be very close. And I went to see him in California in January of '53, and he said "Let's go down to the Palladium," 'cause the Kenton band was rehearsing there, and I said "Good. I want to take some charts down there and see if Stan'll run one down for me and see what he can do." I was gonna go back home after that; my family were expecting me to go into the business—we had a gourmet

178

store—I was around twenty-two, and hadn't really written anything of great musical caliber yet. Stan was very nice, he gave me some time in front of the band. Naturally I was scared to death. And I talked to Stan, I said "It's no fun to write charts and put them on the shelf. I want to send you some charts; if you run 'em over and don't like 'em, you can ship 'em back to me; if you do like 'em, you can talk to me." And he said, "Well," and he was very kind about it, "you couldn't write for me yet, because you don't know enough about our band. You'd have to be with it for a while to get to know the guys and this kind of thing and write for the band personally. But I see some things. Keep on writing." You know, he was very encouraging. That same day was the day that Bob Gioga gave notice.

L.A.: Isn't that the strangest thing!

LEVY: It sure is, and Stan went to Ken Hanna and said, "I need a baritone player," and Ken turned around and pointed at me and Stan came back and I got the job to go on the road. That fast! Boom! (*Snaps fingers.*) I had *no inkling* about going on that band *at all.* NONE!!

L.A.: Were you a baritone player, or just a saxophone player?

LEVY: I was really a tenor player. But once you play one you can play them all. Now if a guy like Hanna recommends someone, Stan will take that recommendation. He came over and offered me the job right away. And I was new at this kind of stuff, I was really swimming. I said "Stan, if I do take the job with you, which I really want to do, I want you to be happy with what I'm doing. I'd like you to hear me play and *then* give me a judgment." He said, "All right. Sit in with the band." I said "I don't have a horn with me." "You can use Gioga's." So I'm five minutes in the back room with Gioga's horn. Came back onstage. And *scared.* I mean *scared to death.*

L.A.: (Laughs.)

LEVY: First thing I heard right off the bat was a timpani roll, and someone said, "CBS presents, Coast-to-Coast, a Concert in Miniature."

L.A.: Wow.

LEVY: Every Tuesday night they used to give these things, live on the air, and here I am, sitting on the band for the very first time! Stan said, "Come on. Come on, let's go. Not only that, when you're on the band like this and you're writing, you'll get access to the band and you can try your arrangements!" So I called home and said "I'm going with Kenton" and I did.

L.A.: At that time was he using your charts?

LEVY: Well we were using cars at that time instead of buses, so it was hard to write. I submitted a couple of things. One, I think, was accepted. I think that was pretty much tokenism. I think he wanted to encourage me to write. I wasn't really ready to write for the band yet. That goes for not only not knowing the style well enough, but at the same time not having enough of the craft together, myself.

L.A.: So then you left to go back to the family business after six months.

LEVY: Ya. I'd been attending Catholic University in Washington, D.C. when I left, without completing my degree, to go on the road with Stan. But when I got home I decided this was it; I was going to write, and have fun with it. I got a call about 1958 or '59, maybe '60, from Sal Salvador, who had a band up in New York and wanted me to do some writing for him. Sal and I had been pretty close on the road. He had a band that was an unusual kind of thing when it first started. He didn't have any saxes, he used all brass. Had some very heavy people on it and the band was awfully good. In three years I contributed a ton of music for that band. Sal recorded a couple of albums, and I got my first taste of having something of mine on an album in those early years, '60, '61. Meantime I had a kicks band here. We used to get a bunch of musicians around town together and on Sunday morning we'd come in and play some new tunes. We were starting to play some decent things, we were stretching out a little.

L.A.: Were you still in conventional time signatures back then?

LEVY: Yes. I started writing for Don Ellis in 1965.

L.A.: So then, after your association with Ellis and the time revolution, it must have been quite a surprise when Stan encountered this later on, when he took you on as a composer. How did this come about?

LEVY: Stan was the honored guest at the Intercollegiate Jazz Festival in Quinnipiac, Connecticut, in 1969. This was a competition to pick a band to represent the East Coast, one of seven regions, at the National Festival. I had taken our jazz ensemble, from Towson State, and when he heard us, he came down the stairs and said "You should have *won* that!" Funny thing, we lost it that year, but we won it the next three years in a row. But Stan really enjoyed

it, he really liked the music, and that's when he invited me to bring these charts to his band. Said "I'd like to get into that kind of music. I think I'd like to play it."

L.A.: And this is music that you'd composed for the Towson Jazz Ensemble.

LEVY: Yeah. It was probably for Don's band. I used to make a copy for him and keep a copy for us to play. Stan said "You should have won it. You're better than the others." We were in the top three. He kind of thought that because the music was so much more interesting, you know. But the bands were all good there.

L.A.: That's just about the time of the clinics at Redlands, 1969.

LEVY: Yeah. He flew me over there, and I taught one of his clinics. "Chiapas" was first recorded back then, in '69 or '70, with the *Live at Redlands* album.

L.A.: That was the first recording from a Kenton clinic.

LEVY: Yeah.

L.A.: And a few years later, the London album of '72 just took off. That was a sensational album, beautifully recorded and live in presence. In fact it's the first time *I* heard "Chiapas." And I couldn't help but think: This sounds like a whole new phase in Kenton's life. It seemed that there was something absolutely brand-new going on in Kenton's life. And when I think back on it, it can be traced to "Chiapas." "Chiapas" just knocked me cold.

LEVY: *Good.*

L.A.: It was absolutely *sensational.* I thought, *What* is going *on* here? It's as though Stan Kenton is starting all over again. With a whole new thing.

LEVY: I was hoping that's what it would do.

L.A.: And a lot of things are interconnected here. Right about then the *7.5 On the Richter Scale* album came out, and you had a number on that, "Down and Dirty." And the *Chicago* album, with the Blood, Sweat and Tears thing, and Lou Marini, who was with Blood, Sweat and Tears, right? was at one of your Towson clinics.

LEVY: Yeah, he was here at Towson in a clinic with us.

L.A.: And I'm wondering—were you perhaps the single most important thing to happen to Kenton for this last part of his life, with your new revolution in time signatures?

LEVY: Oh, I love to think that, but—I . . . (Laughs.)

179

Stan Kenton posing with billboard promoting his new London album, Memphis, Tennessee, '70s. (Photo: Courtesy of a Kenton friend.)

L.A.: Well that *must* be. Because it was a whole new kind of music all of a sudden.

LEVY: Well—he was always looking for new—you know, he was always looking for something new and fresh. That was his favorite expression. He would never tell his writers what to write. He'd need his ballads and this kind of thing, and everybody can kind of do it. But at the same time we'd ask him, "What are you looking for?" And the answer came back in the form of the words: "New, fresh, and exciting."

L.A.: Exactly. New, fresh, and exciting, and this was the time revolution. Which you really brought on.

LEVY: Geez, I hope so. We had problems. It was difficult to get into. One of the things he feared *most*—after all, he'd been doing 4/4 a lot of years—was my God, if we came *apart,* nobody would ever find their way home. I could sympathize with that. So when I was around, I'd always come out and conduct my own things.

L.A.: During this phase of your relationship with him, were you there pretty much until the end?

LEVY: Yeah.

L.A.: So you would have been witness to his flirtation with the rock spectre.

LEVY: He didn't like it that much.

L.A.: But the album *7.5 On the Richter Scale* is pretty much rock, isn't it?

LEVY: There was a lot of rock music in that. He was trying to say, Okay, we can play this kind of music. He didn't believe in it that much. Maybe he was trying to attract attention to the big band sound, at a time when big bands were hurting.

L.A.: He seems to have been trying to superimpose the Kenton sound on the rock scene.

LEVY: Oh yeah.

L.A.: And it worked.

LEVY: (Laughs.) You always wrote for Stan with his band in mind. Stan has influenced so many people, as far as the writing is concerned and the way of thinking. Stan was awfully good at analyzing charts that were brand-new. As to whether they just sounded good, or whether there was some deep-rooted meaning in them. That's what he was looking for.

L.A.: Really?

LEVY: Oh, he was good at that. He could do it on first listening. When Stan

died, the *Evening Sun* here asked me to do a death write-up. I remembered an incident at a clinic and I called the thing *The Closing Chord.* Each writer would have a day, and we'd have an hour and a half, hour and three-quarters, to submit any of the new charts we'd written, so they would go in the books. We'd have a rehearsal. We'd come up and play the new charts, and the old man would listen to 'em. I remember one session I did one of my tunes. It came off fine; it was all right. I got to the last chord, and I kept it short. And Stan called me over and he said, "Didn't you like that tune?" I said "Sure I like it! Geez, I wouldn't have brought it up if I didn't. Why did you ask that?" He said "Well—that last chord that you played was so damn short it sounded like you were anxious to get it *over* with." I said "What are you talkin' about?" And I said "I have a feeling like you're gonna give me a sermon, now."

L.A.: (Laughs.)

LEVY: And he said, "Well," he says "it just seems to me—that the last chord is a very important thing, in a piece of music. And the last chord, generally

180

speaking, is absolutely very short—or it's super long. And—because of the length of that last chord—it does something for the rest of the chart." It's really true.

L.A.: My goodness.

LEVY: It's really true. And I follow that so much, and I use it—did you notice in any of the music we played today, how long I was holding those last notes? (Laughs.)

L.A.: Yes.

LEVY: The idea that a man would stand up, in concert, and the band would be roarin', high notes and this kind of thing, at the last chord, like this—and they'd be holdin'—and Stan would turn around, take a bow—right? and still hold 'em—and turn back to 'em, and they're still holdin'—they might have to sneak a breath and everything else . . .

L.A.: Or pass out . . .

LEVY: . . . 'cause they're still holdin'—then all of a sudden it's cut off. It's *dynamite!* It was dynamic! That's what I based this whole article on.

L.A.: The last chord. Gee, that is a fascinating thought.

LEVY: Isn't it a fascinating thought? He says "I have that feeling about anybody who plays something and they hold the chord halfway and then cut it off. It's wishy-washy. You might like it, but you don't love it." (Laughs.) "You really ought to do better than that. And when you write, write with depth."

L.A.: Depth as opposed to a lot of flash, did he mean?

LEVY: It can mean sophistication, it can be a sincerity, it can mean that you're putting some things down that you actually mean; that you actually approve of what you've written, and this is *really* the way you feel about the tune, and you're not just—you're not just dredging it out and making it sound good, and chording it right and writing a **nice piece of music—alone. More than that.**

L.A.: Golly, that is interesting.

LEVY: That's one of the main things I felt about Stan, that makes him so unique.

L.A.: He evidently enjoyed talking about his philosophy of music with you.

LEVY: We used to, after everything was over, we'd go to a bar, and sit there and have a couple of drinks, and get real loose. And gab about all kinds of things.

L.A.: What would come out of these sessions like that? Stan's done with the gig, he's relaxed . . . .

LEVY: He could relax with certain people. Sometimes he was on stage because of too many people around, you know? We always had him over to the house for dinner when he was here in Towson. And I'd tell Gloria (Levy's wife), "I don't want any of your friends or any of my friends here, just Stan and some of his immediate family. We'll have a few of 'em over for dinner, and we'll go downstairs and have a couple of drinks and we'll sit around and talk. But **please don't invite the neighbors,"** 'cause right away, it's terrible. He's on stage again. I'd want him to be completely relaxed and just have a night off. So after dinner we're in the basement here. The ceiling was low, and he could just barely make it. And he's lying down on the rug. (Laughs.) Right in front of the fireplace—we had that stereo there. I started playing some Kenton records. '**Cause *he* never got a chance to *hear* his** own records! I'm playing *Adventures in Time* and all. He says "You know, that was pretty Goddamn good music!" I said "You bet your *fanny* it's good **music!" We were playing everybody's favorites. And the old man pulled me** down and says "I'll give you a buck if **you play *Kenton Plays Wagner!*"** (Laughs.)

Hank Levy, in his basement den, Towson, Maryland. (Photo by the Author.)

Hank Levy, conducting one of his jazz bands, Towson State University. (Photo by the Author.)

L.A.: (Laughs.)

LEVY: I said "Would you believe, I've got that record here!" He says "You do!" I said "Yes." We put it on, and he just got such a charge out of that! Meantime I'm playing all these records, and they're *used,* they were scratchy, and Stan says "You mean you play those things for your friends and relatives, scratchy like that?" I said "Stanley, if they were brand-new, you'd accuse me of not playing your music, right?" (Laughs.) Two weeks later, truck pulls up. And I had a copy of every record he ever produced, a clean copy of everything out of Creative World. Ninety-some records. (Laughs.)

L.A.: Gee whiz.

LEVY: Yeah.

L.A.: He's such a generous person. He's bigger than life.

LEVY: There are so many stories. Some that I've had access to, and I don't know how many he never talked about. I don't know how many of them ought to be known. But there are a lot of people that he has helped, *so* much.

L.A.: Practically everybody in music. (Laughs.)

LEVY: Yeah. I mean he's helped them plenty, he's helped them in all kinds of ways. And—that's the way he was.

L.A.: Towson was one of the places that Kenton had a week-long clinic. Were you instrumental in bringing him here because you were teaching here?

LEVY: Stan was looking for a place in the East, and they had about three or four or five spots that wanted it—and I was on the bus at the time, lucky thing, 'cause I went up to him, and I said "Stan, we've got a brand-new building. Absolutely *brand*—it's spanking-new!" It was so new that when we did the clinic, we didn't have a parking lot here. Everybody had to come up from all the way down at the union, up all those stairs! Stan said the first year we were here, "You know there's ten thousand steps in this place, and they're all in front of me!"

L.A.: (Laughs.)

LEVY: "And they're all *up*!" And it really is murder and I hadn't even considered that. The school wasn't even opened yet. We didn't have our first

class in here. One of the first things that we did in here *was* the first Eastern Kenton Clinic. I stuck my neck out so far. We wound up where we used to have anywhere from fourteen to fifteen bands going here, we had 250, 300, 350 students here.

L.A.: Fourteen or fifteen bands at a clinic?

LEVY: Yeah.

L.A.: Wow.

LEVY: Oh—Sacramento. Sacramento was the big one. I remember one time there when we had to move people out of the philosophy building in order to house everybody. We had over 500 **students there, and** *26 bands.* And on Friday, the end of the week, the culmination was that every band played.

L.A.: That's a lot of bands in one day!

LEVY: **And Stan—Stan sat through** (*tapping his desk with finger*), he believed in his heart, the reason they were there was that they wanted him to hear 'em. And he sat through every performance. I remember one started at 2 o'clock in the afternoon and wound up 2 o'clock at night. And he was there—I don't even—I didn't see him go out to

182

the bathroom, fer cryin' out loud. They had an hour off for dinner. He believed he should be there, and by God he was. That's marvelous. That's morality. **That's a real moral kind of thing, and that's the way he was.**

L.A.: How long had you been at Towson?

LEVY: I taught here part-time in '68 and '69. In '70 I came on full.

L.A.: Did Towson's reputation for good **jazz start with you, then, when you came** in with your new music?

LEVY: When I came in I asked for a graded course and for jazz ensemble. We had a little jazz ensemble, everybody did that, but it was voluntary, and there wasn't any program for it. When they put me on full-time, I taught writing. They accepted jazz composition and they accepted improvisation; I taught that, and I had the bands. We have three bands. And now we've got a real degree program. Officially, as of maybe *today.* (Before the interview was over, the official notice did arrive!) That first night of the first Kenton Clinic, for the outdoor concert, there were five, six, seven thousand people sitting on the lawn, cookin'

steaks on their hibachis, drinking wine or a couple of beers. It got to be such a thing that people would call me every spring and want to know the date of the next one. Oh, it was good. It was super. We put a portable stage on the field, set up the lighting, and called in a professional sound system—set it up right there and—*not once* did it threaten rain, it was always absolutely beautiful—it was—it was meant to be.

L.A.: How did you set it up during the week?

LEVY: The kids used to come in on Sunday for registration. They'd get themselves straightened away, get their rooms and all that kind of thing, and then we'd have an outdoor concert, where we would do the first half and Stan would do the second half. That was just for the kids. After they'd had their evening meal we had an open concert outdoors, where everybody came. Then Friday night at the end of the clinic, when the kids had been working with the director all week, they got to play their own fifteen- or twenty-minute programs for everybody.

L.A.: Was there a kind of aura wherever Stan went? Among the students?

LEVY: Not only that. What I loved about him was—I can remember eating lunch. We'd all eat lunch at the same place, and the kids would run up and—I was teaching a course in composition or jazz arranging or something like that; somebody would come, and have a score, and say, "Hey, will this work?" When Stan came in the kids would be around him, talking to him about this and that. And it was just a real close-knit thing.

L.A.: How did he feel about it?

LEVY: He *loved* it! Oh, he loved it. Couldn't keep him off the campus—we **used to try—"Stay home. Go to *sleep.*"**

L.A.: (Laughs.)

LEVY: "For God's sake, stay home." Towards the end, when he was not as well, you know, he was sick and it was an effort for him at times. I used to say, "Everything's running fine. Why don't you stay home and then come in tonight, for rehearsal." No. He'd fight it all the way.

L.A.: He really wanted to be with you.

Hank Levy, conducting one of his jazz bands, Towson State University. (Photo by the Author.)

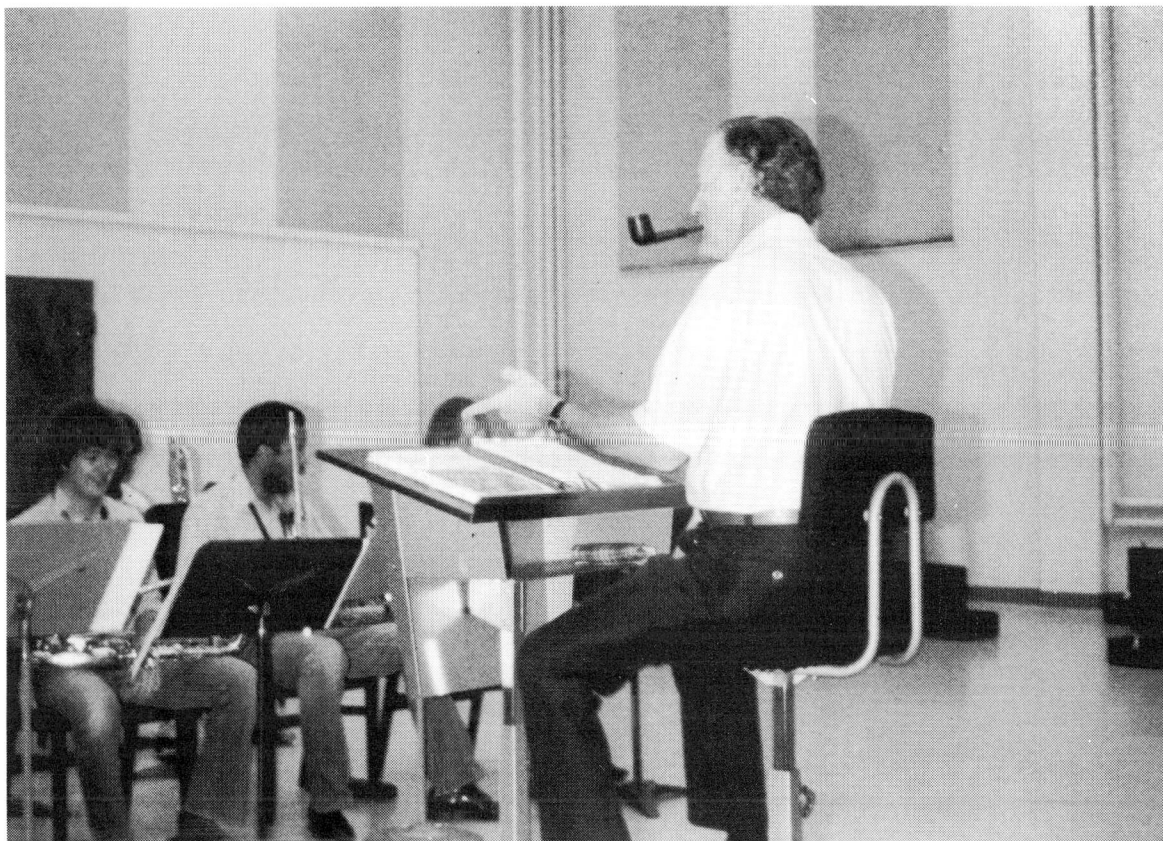

LEVY: Yes he did. And he used to sit around and talk to 'em all—they walk by, "Hi, Stan," you know, these little kids, "Hey Stan!" "Hi! Come on in and let's talk." It was that kind of camaraderie. *Very* nice.

L.A.: Did you have a class for him to teach?

LEVY: He used to teach a special section for the educators. These were teachers from high schools and colleges throughout the area who came in to learn something about jazz, to be a part of the organization, learn what was new on the market, learn new music, and that kind of thing. They had their own band they played on, using the Kenton library.

L.A.: The clinics were really valuable in a lot of ways that one wouldn't think of. There isn't anything that can take their place.

LEVY: Nobody can take *his* place. That kind of feeling for the educators and for the whole music industry is very rare. *Very* rare. We were talking about trying to keep the camp going with the same kind of atmosphere. The major problem is you had to be the type of person who didn't worry about making a buck. If you had somebody who was gonna sponsor this, you're talking about maybe thirty thousand dollars for the week, as a *nut* to crack. Stan used to walk in and say, "Okay, how much do I owe you?" I know he lost money, and a lot of it, and he didn't make a hell of a lot on most of 'em. He certainly could have made more by working his jobs instead. He did it as a moral kind of thing. You can't believe how much money he's endowed various schools with in jazz scholarships.

L.A.: Kenton put his own money into jazz scholarships?

LEVY: I'm sure he did. I know we have two called the Jazz Scholarships of Stan Kenton. And I know we're not the only ones. I learn more and more all the time. He wanted to get to that generation. Rock is a pounding, a constant pounding on your skull, and they pound it into you, saying, "Hey, I'm great," and they're *not*. Jazz takes perception. And that's why jazz and classical music are very very close together. We will always play to limited audiences. And I think it was Bob Curnow who said "Thank goodness."

L.A.: Do you think Kenton had a greatest period?

LEVY: Hmmmm. I liked the mellophones.

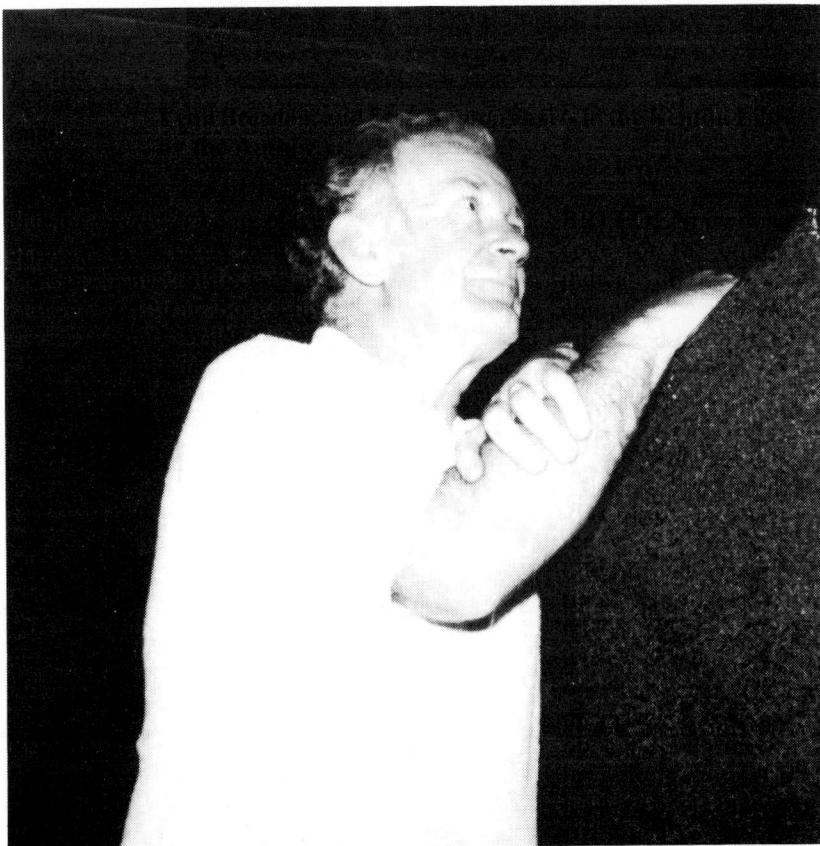

Above: Hank Levy in his recording studio, and, left, listening to a playback. (Photos by the Author.)

184

L.A.: Better than *your* period?

LEVY: Oh. Sure.

L.A.: Because of the ballads?

LEVY: Ya. And the sound of the mellophones. As a matter of fact Curnow and I got on a kick there for a couple of years—he'd played trombone on the Mellophonium band—we'd get together with the old man and try to talk him into adding mellophones to the band again, to the seventies band. And he said "Oh I don't want to get into that now. I don't want to take any more responsibility; it's more people, it costs more money." But that was a damn good band. It was heavy, it was bulky, but I loved that kind of thing. *Adventures in Blues,* that Gene Roland wrote for it and played on it. And *West Side Story.* I mean how heavy can things *get?*

the band one time and they had a hard time with it. But we did it. We used to surprise him when we did our combined concerts. I called it "Tribute." It was a tribute because it sounded like Stan—it was written as John Richards would write it—and yet it was in odd meters.

L.A.: (Laughs.)

LEVY: And Stan said—

L.A.: Only you!

LEVY: Stan said "My God, that's amazing. A lot of people have tried to copy the way John would write."

L.A.: And you got away with it.

LEVY: And you know how far we went with it? We even added mellophones. And we recorded it on one of our albums. It's a dandy piece.

L.A.: Who had the greater influence on whom, you on him or he on you?

say, because you're one of the most creative writers he ever had.

LEVY: (Demurring.) Oh I don't know about that. My things were a little bit off the beaten track. I'm just really that excited that Stan *did* like them and stuck with them, because there were a lot of times the band would be just as happy throwing me out of a second-story *window*

L.A.: (Laughs.) Do you have your own favorite work you've written?

LEVY: I think "Chain Reaction" is one of the best things I've ever done. It's something very special.

L.A.: My favorite composition of yours, among those I've heard, is "Indra." But I can't figure out how to count it.

LEVY: It's in 9. 2-2-3-2. Let's go to the piano. (Plays and counts.) Ba - 2 - baba-

L.A.: That album is not quite Bernstein, it's really Kenton-Bernstein, isn't it?

LEVY: That's true. And that's our boy Johnny Richards again. He wrote *Cuban Fire,* he wrote *West Side Story,* he wrote *Adventures in Time* . . .

L.A.: And he sounds like Stan Kenton. All of you seemed to be able to do that.

LEVY: I wrote a thing once that I was really proud of. It was hard. I took it to

LEVY: Oh, I'm sure, that his influence on me was just . . .

L.A.: Why?

LEVY: Because he was such an encouraging kind of influence. Plus the style of his band was what I liked. I chose that above the Basie, Herman, and the rest of 'em. I liked it as a whole.

L.A.: That's an amazing thing for you to

bababa bababa baa - 2 - baba bababa - (snap snap); ba - 2 - baba-bababa bababa baa - 2 - baba - bababa - eight-nine . . . . You feel it that way?

L.A.: Give me a couple of weeks and maybe I can figure it out. (Laughs.) Let's talk a bit more about how you would work with Stan in presenting new music. Now you said he gave his arrangers just

total free rein to write what they wanted to.

LEVY: Right.

L.A.: But eventually most of you started writing in what was considered the Kenton style.

LEVY: Well we knew that we should. He didn't tell us what to write but he sure wanted to approve of it when we did, and certainly the last word was Stan's word about whether it would be accepted into the band library or not. I always liked him and I always wrote in that particular vein.

L.A.: It's not really a conscious imitation, though, of Kenton. Isn't it more absorbing what you like about him and coming back with it?

LEVY: Oh it certainly is, and, well at the time, now, I had a terrible—I had the job of writing charts and separating the styles between Stan and Don, 'cause I was writing for both of them, at the same time. Just writing something as I felt it, and then having it played back and saying—"Does that belong to Don or Stan?"

L.A.: (Laughs.)

LEVY: (Laughs.) You know. That's right. It's really true. But really I should have one or the other in mind as I write, 'cause they're really very different.

Above, left and preceding page:

Hank Levy in his recording studio. (Photos by the Author.)

L.A.: What would be the dividing line, this is more Don Ellis, or this is more Stan Kenton?

LEVY: Well Stan was an innovator, all right. *Don* was absolutely *berserk.* That's one way of looking at it.

L.A.: Kenton's music to me seems to have a certain form and discipline.

LEVY: Oh, yes.

L.A.: Did you work with him as far as interpretation? Or would he lead the band in your compositions?

LEVY: What would happen is, with all his writers he wouldn't play a piece of music with the band until the *composer* had run it with the band, so he could get all that the composer had in mind, get his idea. And what is strange, and this happens to everyone, later on, after the band played the tune for four or five weeks, little subtle changes would happen, day to day. We call it settling. Something that is different from what was there happens, and everybody says "Yeah, I kind of like it," so they leave it in. They consider it an improvement, certainly.

L.A.: So many composers and arrangers have said that if it hadn't been for Stan Kenton, they wouldn't have become the people they were, that he really championed their cause. Did you admire him for that too?

LEVY: I liked him because when he *heard* something that he *believed* in, he held on like a *bulldog.* He believed in it, and people used to tell him "That isn't for you" or "You would have to invest in it in some way or other; forget it." And that didn't make any difference to him, he *believed* in it, and he went *after* it. That was him, that persevering soul that he was. These odd meters were an absolute *bear* to *impose.* You don't impose them, you just say Okay, here they are, try to accept them and find out what they are. Trouble is, not too many people *knew* what they were, and were thrown so far off balance . . . . We used something that is almost 2,000 years old.

Combining the rhythmic elements of Eastern culture with our jazz of the Western culture. Indian ragas, Greek wedding music, tarantellas, these are all in odd meters, though they're not odd to *them*—they're odd to *us.* We experimented, tried this and tried that—it was very much trial and error. We saw the possibilities and thought, "Let's incorporate it in what we've been doing." Don wrote a thing in thirty-three.

L.A.: He *did?*

LEVY: Yes. There's a thing in thirty-three that he wrote. But he didn't really write it, because it's a Bulgarian folk song that is really in thirty-three.

L.A.: My goodness.

LEVY: He took this thing and he did it in jazz. And there was a kid on Don's band that was a pianist that was dynamite. They corresponded, and Don got him from behind the Iron Curtain. He's Bulgarian—you might have heard of him—his name is Milcho Leviev.

L.A.: I certainly have! I heard him playing with Art Pepper in California.

LEVY: 'Cause he's just an animal. And he sat there and he played not only this thirty-three, but he played jazz on top of it, just as if he's playing the blues! The thing about Don and Stan was, those guys were the messengers. They'd take it out throughout the country, and that's where you became heard, that's where you'd develop a name and reputation.

L.A.: Do you still think about him?

LEVY: I think about him often. Yeah, I really think about him often, it starts cracking me up. I'm just very thankful that we had the ten years together.

L.A.: You mentioned that when he hired you, you were happy that he liked your music, because you wrote like him anyway. What did you mean?

LEVY: I always loved the Kenton sound. So therefore, it became part of my way of thinking, and when I wrote, I wanted to emulate this fellow and to be part of that sound. I wanted to copy it, I wanted to get as close to it as I could get.

L.A.: You sound like him now. You were doing "Over the Rainbow" today.

And *God* that was creepy, because for a minute I thought, now wait a minute—whose orchestra is this anyway? It *sounded* like Stan *Kenton* was there.

LEVY: You want to read my liner notes?

L.A.: Ya.

LEVY: I wrote on there, "I'm sure Stan **would have loved this."**

L.A.: He would have!

LEVY: That, and "I Should Care," and "Time for Love." They're all the Kenton traditional sound. And just because he's not *around* now doesn't mean that we shouldn't take advantage of what he left us. The more people that keep that thing going, the better. I mean, that's personal, that's my way of thinking about it. And his style. I think I will probably write ballads like the Kenton band the rest of my life.

L.A.: Really.

LEVY: Yep.

L.A.: Oh, that's a beautiful tribute to him.

LEVY: It's really the way I feel, I mean, I just feel that strongly about how it's the right way to go. Way underneath, I feel that if I can capture the Kenton ballad, I'm satisfied.

L.A.: I've never understood—Rugolo was another writer that made me feel this way—how you were able to write in such a way as to make a listener feel that *Stan* had written the work. "Chiapas" just sounds like pure Stan Kenton music.

LEVY: It fit in right away, which was marvelous. I couldn't have asked for it better than that. It was odd meter, and the guys took to playing it right away. Except for Willie Maiden. Willie was a character. A great writer. But he didn't believe in odd meters, and he took the part and recopied it and wrote it in 4/4 time, with accents. It was the joke of the band. We were listening to the playbacks at Redlands, and there in the middle of it it's just hard-nosed *five,* and he's sittin' there, conducting it to himself, goin': "ONE-two-three-four, one-TWO-three-four, one-two-THREE-four, one-two-three-FOUR . . . ." (Laughs.)

Leon Breeden, in his den at home, Denton, Texas. (Photo by the Author.)

24 Leon Breeden

"On things like that, there's NO DOUBT about it; those things should be straight eighths. Somebody over here, I hear a little ragtime there. No ragtime. Straight eighths, with accents. 'Cause these things are thrilling when they just come out rolling like that."

The voice is that of Stan Kenton, addressing the 2 O'Clock Lab Band of North Texas State in 1960, then the top band. Kenton has just led them through several opening bars of a student composition.

"When'd you start writing, Bob?" The question is addressed to Bob Pickering, a lab band student and writer of the piece.

"Well, this is my first work. So—it's only been about six months."

"What? It's what! It's your first arrangement?" The band breaks up in laughter. "If you didn't know all the same people I know, I would never believe you. It really is your first arrangement?"

"Yah." (Laughter.)

"Well I'll tell you—everything I tell you guys, you're gonna wind up with egos. You're gonna be unmanageable. But I feel like I should become a used-car peddler, I really do. That's beautiful."

There is a pause, then a voice: "Marv says if you wanna sell cars his dad would..." A big laugh erupts from the band.

"Marv said what?"

Another voice picks it up: "He said if you want to sell cars his dad'll help you out." Everyone laughs.

After a moment's discussion about taking on another work, Stan says, "Let's blow it down once more. Think a little bit more about what I said about the straight eighth notes. Full-value notes."

A student asks, "You mean just play 'em classical style?"

"Well, you're thinking—don't think classical style. It should be eight beats to the bar. It makes for a more thrilling thing in time. It takes away a lot of the guesswork, because time is split evenly. You're splitting the beats in half, you know? For a lot of arrangements, it's true, you want to play them 12/8 time, it gives the thing a triplet feel. But things like this belong in this idiom and they should be played that way. Because if you played this dotted eighth and sixteenth and endeavored to play triplets it would lose its excitement, you know? It's got to be straight eighths, with accents."

Kenton's voice is congenial and explanatory, but underlying the words is a sure sense of authority and he gives them a decided emphatic quality.

"And some of the notes are just throwaway notes but the time is still the same. Okay let's try it once more." He starts snapping his fingers, counting out the first beat—"One-two... Ya, a really delicate beginning. Are you ready? One-two, two-two." The saxes start off smoothly.

Next is a piece in three-quarter time. They discuss tempo. "I'll give you 2 bars in 3," says the student leader, as he begins. After just a few bars Kenton interrupts. "Hold it. Let's take it once much slower." They start again, and the character of the piece changes. Its rhythm is more defined. It has a surer feel to it. It acquires a personality of its own. It comes to life. And it takes off.

L.A.: I think I learned more about Stan Kenton from listening to that tape than I have through all my research. He really had a *remarkable* way with musicians. Treated them with respect, even the students, but still was able to get exactly what he wanted from them.

BREEDEN: Yes. He knew what he wanted.

L.A.: And he emphasized, got so much out of, one little snippet there.

BREEDEN: Attention to detail, yes.

L.A.: Just his style, the way he talked to the musicians, *congenial* . . .

BREEDEN: Oh, always.

L.A.: And yet so *authoritative.* He was *masterful!*

BREEDEN: That's right. He brought it out of the people.

L.A.: That was really exciting, and I thank you for it. Since that was 1960, that was shortly after you met him, then.

BREEDEN: The tape was of a rehearsal Stan had with our top band at Indiana University in 1960. I first really met him at the Notre Dame Jazz Festival earlier that year, though I'd seen Stan from a distance before that, and I'd shaken hands with him. As a young musician, every time Stan got within a hundred, two hundred miles I'd go hear his band. In Fort Worth there was a large ballroom called the Lake Worth Casino, where all the big bands, Tommy Dorsey and Jimmy Dorsey and everybody, would come. When *Stan's* band came, all the *musicians* went to *that* one. All the guys who were in the business felt, "This band is different. It's special."

L.A.: Had you heard his music on records at all?

BREEDEN: I'd never even heard the *name,* I'd *never* heard of him, until—I remember this as if it happened only yesterday. It had to be in the early fifties. At the time I was playing in Houston with the Tony DePardo band from St. Louis. Knowing we were gonna be at the Plantation Club for six weeks, four of us had rented an apartment. We were just working musicians, trying to save money to go back to college, so we'd buy groceries and do our own cooking. We'd been to the store one Saturday afternoon, and we had the radio on as we pulled into the driveway. And we heard "Now from Frank Dailey's Meadowbrook in New Jersey, we bring you the exciting new music of Stan Kenton!" And I'll never forget, there were four of us in the car, two in the back seat and two in the front, and we looked at each other and said "Stan Kenton—who's

that?" Almost like—almost in *unison.* They came on with his theme and the driver started to turn off the motor, and we said "Wait! Wait! Wait!"

L.A.: (Laughs.)

BREEDEN: "Leave it going! Turn it up, turn it up!" And two of us crawled up on the back of the front seat while the fourth guy ran into the house with the groceries so the ice cream wouldn't melt. He turned on the radio, ran back and signalled us, and we all rushed in so we wouldn't miss a single note. And we just sat there like *zombies,* listening.

L.A.: (Laughs.)

BREEDEN: "Eager Beaver" was one of the tunes they were playing. At the end Stan said a few words in that big, powerful voice of his, and when it was over we said, "You know what? Something's gonna come from that. That guy's got the right *answer.*" So you can imagine how what happened at Notre Dame in 1960 affected me. It was incredible.

L.A.: That was soon after you took over the program here, wasn't it?

BREEDEN: I came here in August of '59. Seven months later we went to Notre Dame, and that's when Stan first heard my band. At the time we had a president at NTSU whose favorite word was "No." I had to couch our request for permission to go in terms that he would understand and accept: that it would be good for the teaching tools of these young men, who were going out to be teachers, to know what the other 27 schools represented were doing. He let us go with the stipulation that we pay our own way. So my first big job was to raise money to get us up there. Well, we hit Notre Dame like the Beatles arriving in America. I mean it made papers all over the country. Before we played, I walked through the lobby and I overheard a conversation. Someone said "Who's playing last tonight?" "It's North Texas. Buncha guys probably out in the prairie, down in Texas, I guess." They'd never even *heard* of the school. I knew our band was good, and as I listened to each of the other bands that night I'd think, well we're okay for *that* band. Then we came on. And after our first number, you could feel a buzz in the air. It was just unbelievable. I could sense electricity. And when we finished playing the place literally *exploded.* Three thousand people in the audience. People were standing up in the chairs. They were screaming, they were yelling,

they'd never heard anything like it in their lives. They couldn't believe a college band could play like this. Gene Hall had just gone to Michigan State, and he was in that audience.

L.A.: And Stan Kenton.

BREEDEN: And Stan. When we got through playing, I looked down, and was taking a bow and all that, and out of the semi-darkness, down where the judges were seated, I saw this figure looming toward me . . .

L.A.: (Laughs.)

BREEDEN: . . . with huge strides, and every step he took, he looked a *foot taller* to me. He came up, he did not stop, came right straight up and threw his arms around me, and he had tears flowing from his eyes. And he hugged me real tight, and he said, "My God," he said, "I want to tell you something." He said "Tonight you and your band have renewed my love of music. I was kind of thinking of getting out of the business. I'm *serious* when I tell you, you have put *new life* into me tonight. I see what it's all about. I can't get *over* this! I'm moved clear down to my toes." And he went over and shook hands with all the guys and—from that minute until the day of his death, I felt an affinity for Stan unlike anything I've ever known. And when I was around him with other people, I could sense they felt the same thing I did. He was so special to me—a man of international integrity, who'd played for the Queen of England and all, and yet was just as down-to-earth as he could possibly be, and the great humanity that came out of him and the warmth and all. I just was deeply moved, and while he was telling me, "You've renewed my faith in music," the exact opposite was happening. *He* was renewing *my* faith in music. By just seeing a great man like him *tell* us that. He invited me up to his suite that night, and we talked for about two and a half hours.

L.A.: What did you talk about that first night?

BREEDEN: About music, and about everything. And he turned to me, and I'll never forget it, as long as I live, he said, "Leon—what is your biggest problem? You got that big program down there at North Texas. I don't know how you stand it. With me, if I don't like their playing I just fire 'em. With you, they're students. You've got to *keep* them, don't you?" And I said, "That's right, Stan. We've got to take them where we find them and carry them as far as we can." He said "I don't think I could ever take

Stan Kenton, chatting with North Texas State University band members, April 1965. (Photo courtesy of Leon Breeden.)

Stan Kenton, leading the NTSU band, April 1965. (Photo: Courtesy of Leon Breeden.)

that. My patience is too short." But he said "What do you really need? What's the biggest worry that you've got?" And I was new at North Texas, I'd been there only a few months. I said "Well Stan, I can't get enough music." He reached over and slapped my knee and he said, "That's solved. Now what *else* do you need?" And I had no idea what he was talking about. At that very minute he'd made up his mind to send us his *entire library*. About a year and a half later I was sitting in my office one day when a big Central Van Lines truck pulled up in front of the building. Two men came out with big black carrying cases that said "Stan Kenton Orchestra" on them. And they walked in and knocked on my door. "Mr. Breeden." "Yes?" "We've got something for you, here." And they walked in and sat Stan's whole library down in my office. Prepaid, Stan had paid all the shipping costs, which was a big amount. I carried it all home, the entire library. I put it in a big circle on my living room floor, and I went through part after part. I personally handled, and personally put together, every page. It was about fifty thousand dollars worth of music. I put every copy of "Stompin' at the Savoy" together, every copy of "Peanut Vendor," everything. As I assembled missing parts and studied everything carefully, I had the feeling I was handling something sacred. A trumpet part wasn't labeled "trumpet," it was "Maynard." Conte Candoli's part said "Count." Rosolino's read "Frank." When they were writing, Bill Russo and Bill Holman and all these fellows, they didn't write for first trumpet or first trombone, they wrote for *Maynard* or for the guy they knew was gonna *play* that part.

L.A.: How exciting!

BREEDEN: I went through that, and I carried it to school, five or six things at a time. And we played that entire library. It took us about a year to do it. It was tremendous! As we played each number I heard it for myself and got the reaction of the band, and we'd discuss it. Should this go into the working library, should we use this on the next concert, should we use this for sight-reading with all of our bands. There were guys sending Stan arrangements from all over the country — all over the world, I guess. Sometimes he'd play through 'em one time, and if he didn't like 'em, he'd just put 'em out. They were in loose-leaf folders. Sometimes in the back of a book would be some loose sheets that had got torn off on the road some way,

and the player had just stuck it in the back. So it's a good thing I went through it personally page by page, matching up the manuscript, letter G to letter H or whatever. I handled everything very carefully, one chart at a time. And I started a process of making master copies. I wanted to get copies of the originals before they self-destructed. I kept the masters in one end of the building and the originals in the other, and that worked out well.

L.A.: Your friendship with Stan really blossomed through the years. Many players have told me he could just call you on a moment's notice when he needed a quick replacement on his band, and the guy worked out just great.

BREEDEN: It's true. I would say between 30 and 50 guys from North Texas went on to play with Stan's band. Some may have played just for a short while and then left for other things, but, as I look back now through the years, Stan would call me repeatedly. And I'd recognize that voice. I've got to tell you. The first time he called me, after meeting me at Notre Dame, I had just come in from a hot and heavy rehearsal and I was just beat. And the operator said, "Leon Breeden?" "Yes?" "There's your party; go ahead." "Leon, this is Stan Kenton."

L.A.: (Laughs.)

BREEDEN: My first reaction was to say, "Ya, this is Queen Elizabeth."

L.A.: (Laughs.)

BREEDEN: But something about that voice—

L.A.: (Laughs.) Ya, right.

BREEDEN: . . . had caught me, and I said "I think I recognize your voice." "Ya, it's Stan! Come on!" And "I need a trumpet player. You got somebody?" And I said, "Oh, we got *several*." He said "I'll take *your word* for their musicianship." He said this *many* times. He said, "Leon, you know what I need. If you tell me they can make it, fine. The only thing I'm gonna ask you is, is their wig on straight?" And the first time I didn't know exactly what he meant, I said, "Well, fill me in. Now is their wig on straight . . . " He said "You know. Are they on drugs? Will they embarrass my band? I can't put up with that stuff." Only he used stronger language. I said "I know. We're fighting the same thing here, trying to keep our act clean so one or two guys on their own ego trip don't destroy the whole program." Over the years I recommended so many people to him. And he told me one time, "You never recommended one that did not

come in and, the first time he sat down, just sight-read my book as well as anybody." He was so thankful, so appreciative of it. But in return, Stan did not fail to give us credit at his concerts. And I'll give you an incredible example of what I mean. The most marvelous thing happened to me one time, in England. I was there to conduct an international all-star band, in London and in Paris. I'd gone into the men's room to change for the performance, when someone, noticing my name on the plastic cover of my suit bag, asked if I knew Leon Breeden. I assured him I did; I was he. He rushed out and brought in two companions, and the three of them told me a story about *Stan* that you won't believe. They'd gone to hear Stan at a concert the previous year, and went backstage to talk to him, telling him of their great admiration for him through the years. Suddenly Stan said "Why don't you guys take off, come on, get on the bus with us and make the tour with us?" And they told me, "Can you believe it, we were idiots enough, men with our own businesses and everything, but we got everything set up and we DID. We took off for ten days, got on the bus, went with the band, and had the *time* of our entire *lives*."

L.A.: (Laughs.) And he'd never met them before, right?

BREEDEN: Never met 'em before! That's the kind of man Stan was! At every hotel he worked in some extra rooms for 'em—(laughs). They said "We went with him to many many cities. many concerts, and there was not one concert that he did not introduce the four or five guys in the band that were from North Texas. And he mentioned *you* personally, and how grateful he was that we had this kind of thing going on that would keep this music alive." And— I was just—I almost had *tears* in my eyes. I mean it moved me *so deeply,* and they were so sincere and honest. Stan was over in England, he didn't have to do that. He did it because he sincerely meant it. Now, I ask you, would you not be deeply touched to hear something like that? It just touched me clear to my toes, I couldn't get *over* that. He was a friend to my face, and when he was away. It didn't make any difference *where* he was. He was such a dear human being, and—I don't know, you don't want to hear *that,* I'm just—

L.A.: Yes I do! This is all fascinating. Speaking of your players, you've had some really famous ones come through NTSU.

BREEDEN: Yes. Bud Brisbois was one. He was here with us. He was a soloist with the high school band here in Denton before coming to North Texas. We hung out together. He was just a wonderful, wonderful guy. Phenomenal player. And Dee Barton. Ever heard "Waltz of the Prophets"? That wonderful thing in the whole-tone scale?

L.A.: Oh yes, certainly. I love that.

BREEDEN: Well do you know that *we* recorded it before Stan did?

L.A.: You did?!

BREEDEN: Yes. Unfortunately the master tapes of that album were destroyed in a fire in Dallas. Luckily I still have one copy left. In Europe they're offering up to two hundred dollars for a copy of that album, because it's got Dee as a young kid on it, and Marv Stamm and others. And it's an interesting story how Dee and Stan got together.

L.A.: I'd like to hear that.

BREEDEN: Stan had invited us to come up to Indiana University for a couple of summers, in 1960 and '61. Dee was playing trombone in a little club in Dallas, and didn't want to go. Said "I'm making seventy-five bucks a week. I can't afford to go up there and play with you guys for two weeks for nothin'!" I said "Dee—" and we sat in my old home over here, I had an old two-story house. I said "Dee. I sincerely believe that if you'll meet Stan and get to know him and he can hear your music, it could someday lead to something really great."

L.A.: (Laughs.)

BREEDEN: And he said "I gotta think about it. This club's paying me and I don't have to work too hard and I got long intermissions and everything. It's slow this time of year and I need the money." I said "I believe this could be a good thing for you. All the band members, I'm speaking for all of us, we all want you with us. You're a vital part of our band. We want to take the whole band. You're the *only guy* that said you're not gonna go." "Well—if you put it that way, I guess I can get someone to sub for me for two weeks." He ended up leaving my house that night saying he'd go. He went to Indiana, and met Stan, and it was just click! click! click!, and he joined Stan's band, and Stan did a whole album of *Stan Kenton Presents Dee Barton.* Stan loved the guy, and Dee loved Stan. It ended up being a marvelous thing. And Dee became a vital part of the Kenton organization.

L.A.: What kinds of things would you and Stan talk about?

BREEDEN: He was extremely interested in what I was doing, and I was extremely interested in what he was doing. He was intrigued with academia and would ask me questions about what was happening in school. He really wanted to know how a jazz band could function, surrounded by people who didn't understand it. "Do they give you much trouble? What do you do in faculty meetings? How do they talk about jazz?" I could tell him truthfully that they didn't *talk* about jazz in faculty meetings. They would talk about the symphony concert coming up or whatever would involve the entire faculty. They just weren't involved. I would explain the procedure I went through getting approval for our trips or tours, reporting to the dean, who then went to the academic vice president, who then went to the president of the university if necessary. We went to Mexico on a State Department tour, went to Portugal and the Soviet Union and Germany and Switzerland. Stan had been to

Stan Kenton in conference with Gene Hall (left) and Leon Breeden (right). Probably early '60s. (Photo courtesy of Leon Breeden.)

193

many of the cities where I later took my band and wanted to know how the crowds were reacting, 'cause he was thinking about going back to Germany. I've seen with my own eyes what music can do, and Stan had too, and that's another thing we talked about in our home.

L.A.: They really like Stan Kenton in Europe, don't they. Which is neat, because he was attracted to some of their composers.

BREEDEN: I'll tell you a story that Stan told me himself. One night Stan walked into a club in New York City, where Duke Ellington was playing. Got there a little bit late, and the head waiter, who knew him, seated him at a small table where there was a man sitting with his back to him, watching the performance. Stan noticed after a while that this man would reach around and get a little manuscript pad and he would make a few notes. He'd lay it back down, and listen some more, as Ellington would play certain things, and then he'd reach for the pad and take more notes. Stan could see, when he laid the manuscript down, what he was doing was writing rhythmic patterns. Not melodies, just rhythmic patterns that they were playing. After Ellington finished the set, this man got up and *left*. As he did so, he said hello to Stan— "Oh—I didn't see you there." Something like that. And he walked on out. And the head waiter happened to be walking by, and Stan said to him, "He looked awfully familiar. Who *was* that?" And the waiter said "That was Maurice Ravel."

L.A.: My God!

BREEDEN: Stan said *"Oh my gosh,"* and he tried to find him, but Ravel had already gone out, called a cab or something, and disappeared.

L.A.: That is an *incredible* story.

BREEDEN: And here he'd been sitting, listening to Duke Ellington, and getting ideas, writing down a few little ideas, of his rhythmic patterns. Stan said, "Can you imagine how I felt, knowing I had been sitting there with *Maurice Ravel?* Didn't even know who he was. I knew he looked familiar to me, when he walked by." I've never forgotten that story. To me that's one of the rare stories of all time.

L.A.: It certainly is.

BREEDEN: Because Stan, you know, respected the French writers particularly. He was in our home many times, and we had hours and hours of many, many private talks. He would go

into the kitchen and help Bonna (Breeden's wife) wash the dishes. But if I tried to help him, if I'd say "Get off this bus and let me clean up these beer cans," he'd say "No! You're gonna do my job?" and here he was, with a plastic bag, cleaning up after his band! I'm sure that every single person who knew this man felt as if he belonged to them, as if he was part of them. That was my experience. I was with him many times, and everyone would come up to him like he was their

long lost uncle or brother. Stan, to my dear wife and to me—when I talk of Stan Kenton, I'm talking of my family. I'm talking about my *brother.* I'm talking about someone that was so close, I could pick up the phone and call him anytime, and he never once gave me anything except the deepest warmth. I think Stan understood what we were

going through at North Texas, trying to build our jazz program, because with his own band he had had to struggle, had had to borrow money and fight his way and endure the blasts from the critics. He once told me, "The years I had my finest bands were when they tore me to shreds. But the worse the reviews were, the prouder I was of my band. It didn't help me financially. It made me controversial, when I wasn't *trying* to be controversial. The controversy that sur-

rounded me was because I had firm convictions and I believed, right or wrong, in what I was doing." I said "Stan, you are like a thoroughbred walking down the street with a bunch of little cur dogs barking at your heels. That's the way I see you." "Oh, come on, you don't have to be dramatic, Leon."

L.A.: (Laughs.)

BREEDEN: You know, he was that kind of person. I'm convinced that it drew us close together. I think he really felt an affinity.

L.A.: What were some of the problems you faced here? I think a lot of people assume that, since you have probably the finest jazz program in the *world* here, that it pretty much always was that way.

BREEDEN: I guess for ten or twelve years, I typed every letter personally, 'cause I didn't have anyone I could really trust to do it. I was the only adult in the jazz department here for a number of years. I was teaching all the courses. I was handling all the *auditions* myself, all the trumpets, saxes, trombones, pianos, drummers. My first office was a storage room, where they kept canned goods, and I remember the first day I walked in, there was a lard can with a dead rat in it. I often felt, the day I walked onto the campus of North Texas State, that I had walked into a great, gray area. It wasn't black or white. We were trying to keep jazz alive, keep Gene Hall's program going, in a community of European-trained musicians. That's a little like trying to raise a camel in a hospital. You know, a camel will lift his tail wherever he wants to, and mess things up. But in a hospital you're trying to keep everything pure. In a school of music, that's what you want. You want Mozart played as meticulously and purely as you can. With Stan's band, if it had warts on it and the guys rasped a note, he'd break up laughing about it. I mean, it's just part of the excitement of the music. On days of faculty meetings, I had to make sure I was dressed very neatly, with a tie, and everything had to be right, so when I walked in there, or if I was asked something, I could represent jazz in as high-class a way as any of those other teachers. In other words, they couldn't look at me and say, "Look at that jazzer. He's a fourth-class citizen." Then I'd meet with the guys and I'd try to make sure that my shirt was open and I . . .

L.A.: (Laughs.)

BREEDEN: . . . had on my leather jacket, and I was hangin' out—because *they* would put me down if I walked in there with a *tie* on, see. Just as the faculty would put me down if I walked in there with the motorcycle stuff on. I was very careful. I even kept a detailed record of what I was wearing. I wanted not to wear the same coat in the faculty meetings all the time. I wanted to be sure that I could go in there and look fresh and sharp. I wanted so badly to hang out with the guys, and just be myself.

There's another thing, every rehearsal at North Texas, every single rehearsal, twenty-two years of rehearsals, I never knew who might be sitting behind me—could have been the dean, the president of the university, some of the Board of Regents, the men who had the purse strings. I had my back to the audience, I was watching my band. Couldn't let my hair down and really shout something I felt deep inside. I had to be very cautious and when I corrected something do it in a very judicial, educational, pedagogic way. That's not true of jazz. You know, that's not the best way to get results. I think the guys realized the pressure I was under, in trying my best to put on the best image always. If I'd used the bus terminology we were all used to, it would never have happened. I guarantee it.

L.A.: That's incredible. You're saying you did not have the support of your own administration. And here you have this great international reputation. With all that against you, how in the world did this program grow and prosper?

BREEDEN: I think we grew mainly because of word of mouth. We did not have one penny for advertising. It could not have been for any reason except a beautiful, glowing report in the paper by a reporter who had come to one of our concerts, or a group of musicians who heard us somewhere. Notre Dame was a big thing. And we played for a number of stage band festivals that helped us grow tremendously. We would go and we'd be the guest band, and in our audience would be members of fourteen stage bands, in high schools. I think that enabled us to get our foot in the door and get it started. When I came here in '59, it was not the ideal set-up. There were times in the first few weeks I would have given anything to get out of here. It was absolutely unbelievable. We didn't have a budget. We rehearsed in a choir room, where the reverberation from the horns bounced off a blackboard right behind my head and gave me migraine headaches. We'd have *four* drummers rehearsing in the *same room*. The ingredients for a successful program were not there. Except that that band was something I was proud of.

L.A.: The quality of the program, in other words, was always so good that it kept attracting more people than you could logistically accommodate.

BREEDEN: Always.

L.A.: And you always kept the high level up.

BREEDEN: We had to keep the level

high. These high school kids would hear this excellent band up there and say to themselves "Hey, *I* want to be part of that." That's why we grew. Because we went onstage and we played music at the highest level. That's the only reason.

L.A.: And the naming of the many lab bands after hours on the clock—whose idea was that? Was that Mr. Hall's doing?

BREEDEN: When I came here, we had about two and one-half bands, actually, and Gene had picked the 2 O'Clock Band as his top band. That first year at Notre Dame, we were still using that system, so it was the 2 O'Clock that Stan heard, though it was my top band. It was named that because it met at two o'clock. Gene had a band at one o'clock that was his training band. And there was a 3 O'Clock Band that had to be beefed up a bit with some members out of the One O'Clock. The second year it seemed to just *jump*. Clear out of the sky, I couldn't believe it.

L.A.: Why did you change it around, making the One O'Clock the best band?

BREEDEN: Well I inherited Gene's program of 12 years, and for the first year I did it that way and studied it carefully for that entire year. I was watching, day after day. And here's what was happening. Those young kids were playing at one. And in the middle of the rehearsal, in would walk these heavies. All the 2 O'Clock players — Marv Stamm, and Dee Barton, and all these guys were coming in. And these little kids would start shaking in their boots . . .

L.A.: Oh, I see.

BREEDEN: For several years I insisted on conducting the training band as well as the best band. I wanted to find out where the problems were. Starting in 1961, I changed it around. I said "We're not gonna start the day off with the weakest players. We're gonna start the day off with *One* O'Clock, *The One* sounds better to me than *The Two*."

L.A.: Of course it does.

BREEDEN: So I changed it to One O'Clock, with the idea of starting the day off at the highest possible level as a challenge to all the other bands that came in the afternoon. It worked beautifully.

L.A.: What puzzles me is why all this should have occurred exactly here, in Denton, Texas, out of all possible places in the world. What would have started it off in the first place?

BREEDEN: I think it was a combination of many factors. As far back as

1927, there was a stage show that was going on every Saturday night at a little theater in Denton. The conductor was Floyd Graham. They called him, lovingly, "'Fessor." Their pit orchestra was a group known as the Aces. Gene Hall even played in it. They'd play an overture and some medley from a Broadway show, and then the curtain would open, and they'd have a first-run movie. Then part of the band would get up *on the stage* and set up like a dance band, while down in the pit would be the strings, cello and harp and everything. In those days kids didn't have cars, they all stayed on campus on weekends with nothing to do. So for something like 15 cents they could get this *big orchestra* playing an overture, on stage a band, and comedy acts, jugglers, ventriloquists, singers, trios, and a movie.

L.A.: Is that theater still in existence?

BREEDEN: It's still over there, and they've renovated it. During my first seventeen years, every concert I had at North Texas was in that old theater, on that same stage. "'Fessor" was a wonderful man, though somewhat controversial. I later dedicated one of our albums to him, calling him the "Founder of the Official Dance Band in 1927." Which helped lead to the start of the lab band program because having a dance band on this campus all those years, from '27, helped get people used to the idea of a band playing current charts, Glenn Miller and that sort of thing, and made it a lot easier when the college started experimenting with it. The program started officially in 1947, but the first lab band was actually conducted by Charles Meeks, a graduate student, in 1946. Meantime World War II entered into it. North Texas had a government contract for a V-12 naval officers training program—I guess the "V" stood for "Victory"—and there were GI's all over the place. You could see them on campus, wearing their uniforms. A lot of them ended up marrying students from Texas State College for Women, now Texas Women's University, whose homes were around here. And the musicians among them kind of congregated.

L.A.: Was there a connection between the Aces and North Texas?

BREEDEN: The musicians were all students at North Texas. They called it an official school dance band, but it wasn't a course, they didn't get credit for it. 'Fessor Graham conducted it on his own. They went around and helped raise money to help the war effort in various ways. When 'Fessor's health broke—he had severe diabetes and ended up losing one leg—he had me come in and sub for him with the band. By then it was not the same story; students had cars and would leave on weekends. But we'd play a Wednesday night dance at the Union, and the kids'd get about six dollars for it, and it helped a lot of them stay in school. As for why it happened here, the V-12 and all, it's hard to say; it could be the proximity to Dallas and Fort Worth. We were kind of in the center of things here. You know, I think that name, "stage band," originated here at North Texas because of that Saturday night stage show.

L.A.: I've often wondered about the origin of that term!

BREEDEN: It was innocuous enough that you could call your band that, but still play anything you *wanted* to, at a time when "jazz" was still a dirty word.

L.A.: And now you have well over 400 students in your jazz program, right?

BREEDEN: The one year that I remember the exact number it was 527. Some day I'm going to document all this. I've saved everything; I've got archives on all of it.

L.A.: What I'm wondering is, how do you work in all those students into even thirteen jazz bands, at twenty players per band?

BREEDEN: What we tried to do is give as many a chance to play as possible. Then we'd divide some of the bands—though not the One O'Clock—so that some players came, say, on Mondays and Wednesdays, and the others on Tuesdays and Thursdays. But we encouraged the players to attend rehearsals every day, to observe what the band was playing and to learn from each other. And I'll tell you something interesting. The *Two* O'Clock Band was actually the most difficult band to conduct. These are all the kids who *almost* made the One O'Clock, but didn't quite make it. The Two O'Clock Band several years has been just neck and neck with the One O'Clock. I'd put either one of 'em up against anybody's band. Two O'Clock was a phenomenal band. With the numbers we had, with 135 sax players showing up for auditions, you take the first five out and you still have five more unbelievable players. So those kids were chompin' at the bits, waiting for their chance to get into the One O'Clock. Jim Riggs handled that

band for about nine years, and he built a strong, musical, excellent band. Jim's one of the finest educators and musicians we've ever had at North Texas State. Played lead alto with the One O'Clock Band when we went to Germany in 1970 and just knocked everybody out. We'd have had enough personnel for seventeen bands here, if we'd had the room. I used to kid about that—75 drummers, 105 trumpet players—here in Texas we don't count our players by numbers, we count 'em by *acres*. (Laughs.) And in all our concerts we hardly ever repeated anything; we tried to play different music all the time. Another change I made from Dr. Hall's program was that I made our players audition twice, once in the fall and once in the spring. This encouraged the kids—they knew the door was open. Starting in '60 I gave a fall concert in addition to the spring one. Another thing we did was to sight-read a number on our first album, in '67, our first after I came here—Gene Hall made albums in '57, '58, and '59.

L.A.: Really? Sight-read on an album?

BREEDEN: Yes. We took some chances. Most of the good things we've done here have been because we've been willing to gamble, to stick our necks out. That first album, I just took the bull by the horns, put up the money personally, and without anyone's permission we went to Dallas and just *did* it. Took us a year to pay it off. But we've since sold about four thousand copies of it. I wanted to do an album so we'd have some memory of what the band sounded like, 'cause I knew how good it was. And school was going to let out in a few days, and the players would be gone. We've paid for all our albums ourselves.

L.A.: What were some of the criteria you used to decide on placement?

BREEDEN: There were two. Number one, you had to be a student—couldn't just wander in and say "I want to play in your band." Number two, you had to be able to play your instrument and not hold back the section. And we bent over backwards to be really democratic about it. Sometimes I'd say to our graduate assistants, who were leading the other bands, "*Scare* your band. If they get a little cocky, give 'em a chart, take one of the harder charts in there, and let 'em fall all over themselves. And then say, 'See? You've got some *work* to do, guys. The One O'Clock players can *play* that chart. That's why they're there, and you're here.'" And that worked out well.

L.A.: Sounds like you really challenged 'em.

BREEDEN: I think the *big thing* was motivation. We built a pride up in the guys. I would challenge a player, I'd say "Last year Marv Stamm played in that chair, right there. Now this year *you've* got to carry on that tradition. I want you to play it *better* than he played last year." And yes we challenged the kids. "Rise up! Keep the tradition high. We're not going to this festival or contest to compete against the other people. We're competing against excellence. We're competing against ourselves."

L.A.: In a program of this magnitude, there must have been some special problems unique to you, perhaps that other jazz schools could not dream of.

BREEDEN: As the department grew, one of my biggest sadnesses was that I couldn't know all my kids really well. In the first ten years here I could name every kid in every band. I knew every single one of 'em, first name and last name, and knew and talked to their parents on many occasions. But starting about the eleventh year, it just started growing phenomenally. I could have spent eleven hours a day just in rehearsing. I just couldn't do it. I'd walk into rehearsal with my One O'Clock Band, and there'd be three hundred people in the audience, just wanting to dig the band—kids from the other bands or Ella Fitzgerald's rhythm section or Cannonball Adderley, dropping over from Dallas just to hear them. Rehearsals were more like *concerts* than *rehearsals*. It finally reached a point where we had to close them two days a week, Mondays and Tuesdays, so I could get to know my band, get a better rapport and be more honest with them. But the library was open to all the bands—any leader could come in and check out any music he wanted. And Stan I think was impressed with that, the fact that we were able to take the kids where we found 'em and give them experience. He understood the pressures of a big program like this, and he was quite impressed with it.

L.A.: And there must be some special joys connected with a program like this also.

BREEDEN: My wealth is in the great experiences I've had. I've been able to serve a dual role as an educator and as a professional player. My One O'Clock Band was a family. Those kids were my kids. My wife Bonna and I just love them like they're our own *children*. I can go back to the first band I had when I first came here. Some of those kids write to me as if they're writing to their own father. When your life is touched by somebody you never know what it will lead to. They go off in this direction, you go off in that one, then later in life you come back *together*—it's astounding. I've seen it here, with the young kids. It's been so *great* to see them come out of high school, and the restrictions of home, and all of a sudden feel the freedom they have here. And it's caused some problems, 'cause we've had to kind of—I've—I've often joked with some of my colleagues about going into the One O'Clock rehearsal. I used to eat lunch up here quite a bit until my work got so busy, brought my lunch and just sat here in my office, waiting for long-distance calls and things, and I'd tell 'em, I feel like a—there's a fella named Beatty who used to train lions. World-famous. He would go into the cage, and he carried a—he carried a cane and chair—and a big whip. And I said "I need my chair and my whip, I'm goin' into the One O'Clock Band!" (Laughs.)

L.A.: (Laughs.)

BREEDEN: "I've got to—I've got to train those hungry lions back in shape." And I really felt that way sometimes. I'd walk in there and here they sat, just on the edge of their chairs, like a hungry bunch of *beasts,* you know.

L.A.: (Laughs.)

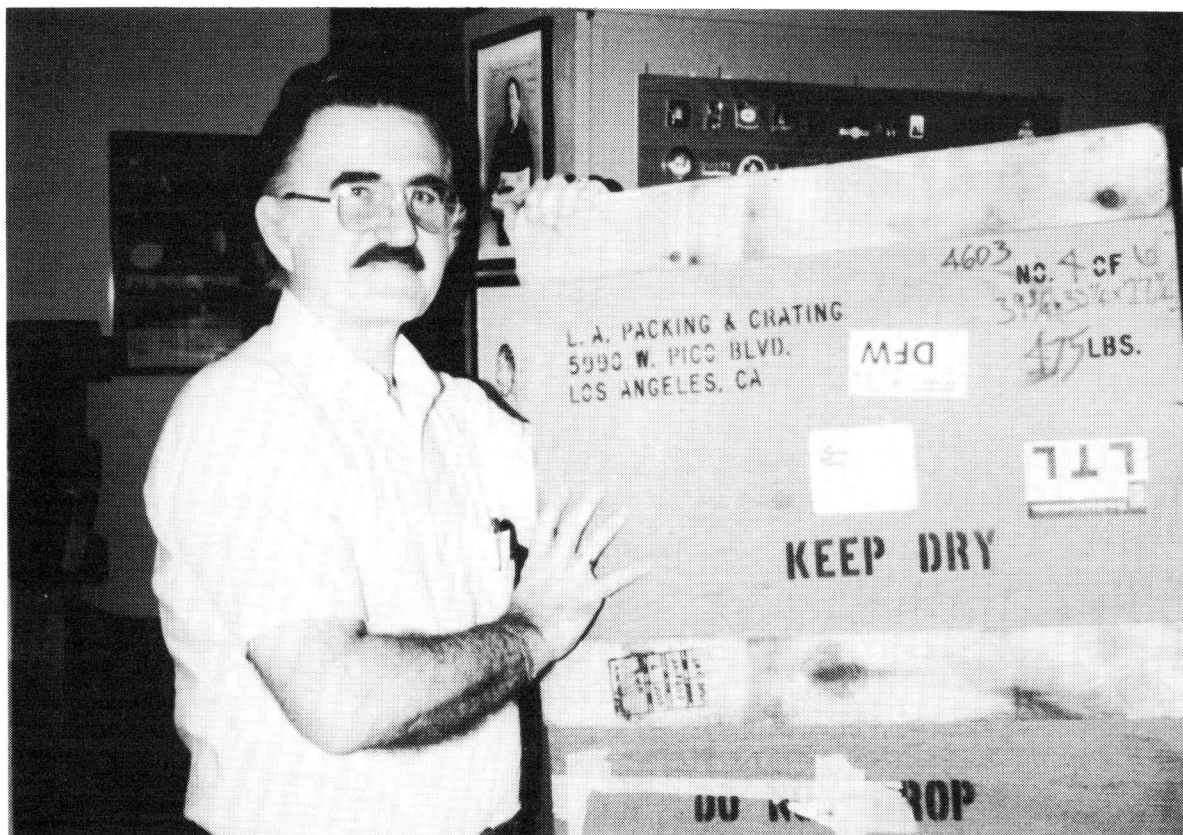

Above photo:

Leon Breeden, posing with crates the Kenton music came in, at North Texas State University. (Photo by the Author.)

Photo on page 194:

Stan Kenton, on his first visit to North Texas State, November 30, 1961. Left is Dave Wheeler, right Leon Breeden, director of the jazz education program at NTSU and conductor of the 1 O'Clock Lab Band. Wheeler had just left NTSU to join the Kenton band. (Photo: Courtesy of Leon Breeden.)

Photo on page 197:

Leon Breeden, with the North Texas library (not the Kenton music – theirs). (Photo by the Author.)

BREEDEN: I felt outnumbered, 20 to 1.
L.A.: (Laughs.) What a picture!

BREEDEN: You know what it's—you know what, in front of the band, and Stan agreed with this, he said "Sometimes it's pretty *lonely* up there, isn't it?" And I said "That's right, Stan. You got that band, you got a big audience out here, waiting for you to be greater than *life.* you know, and maybe the guys are all beat out of their minds, they're so tired from a bus trip or something." He said "How many nights have I had that. When we could hardly put one foot in front of the other, we had to get up there and play those hard charts. I just stood up there and felt sorry for my guys, and for me and for everybody else. And yet we had to make some *history,* so we *did* it."
L.A.: Yes. And now that history lies in your hands. That was a remarkable thing he did, leaving his entire music library to you. Though it's quite obvious *why* he did it.

BREEDEN: I can't think that Stan could have paid us, or education, or jazz studies a greater compliment than that he wanted all of his earthly music to come to us. We've got scores in there, in his own manuscript, that he must have spent hundreds of hours on. When a man is thinking of his will, thinking of leaving this earth, thinking what do I want to do with—and what was Stan's life? His life was music! He *said* so, he said "I wouldn't have lost all my wives and all that if I'd stayed home more. But my music meant too much to me. Given the choice, it'd be my music over my life any day. My music I couldn't *live* without." So—when I found out that he had willed that music to us, I just cried like a baby. I mean it just moved me so deeply. And Audree Coke, who was one of the executors of his will, said "If you knew how many different schools had bugged us to send *them* his music, and he'd never say anything—he just wouldn't comment on it—he already *knew* he was giving it to North Texas. He had already made up his mind, that's where it would go." To me that speaks louder than anything.

L.A.: I'm very curious about what's going to become of this music, and how Stan Kenton is going to shape what happens at North Texas State, now that he's gone.
BREEDEN: I'll give you a copy of the actual minutes at the meeting when the

198

Board of Regents named the rehearsal hall Stan Kenton Hall. Now. Every time a program is scheduled in that hall, it's going to be in *Stan Kenton Hall*. I wanted that Hall to assure, I wanted the *name* of it, to assure young people fifty years from now that they're going to be playing in Stan Kenton Hall. That is *one* way Stan is going to shape it. I wanted to make sure *his* name would be known at this school.

L.A.: Oh, that is beautiful.

BREEDEN: I'll show you the Kenton Library. It's unbelievable. Two thousand, four hundred and forty pounds of music. Says that right on the bill of lading. It came in six big crates. Forty-

he never *once* mentioned that he was leaving his music to us. And though I hesitate to say so, I don't think he would have sent this music to North Texas if he had not believed in me, too. I had assured him that anything he sent I would go through and organize and file properly, and not allow to get diffused and lost and messed up. I assured him his place in education would be known to coming generations. I let him know how much we appreciated his gift in 1962. And he'd say "Aw come on, Leon, that's all I've got. I'd do it again. I wanted to do it for you." But there is no denying that the end result of Stan sending that, which is his *life's work,* to us, is the ultimate compliment of all

destruct from handling, eventually, they won't last forever.

L.A.: What will you do, put them under glass or something?

BREEDEN: Either that or figure out a way to spray them with a plastic covering material that will waterproof them, so fingerprints won't destroy them. With this gift, and the one from '62, we have probably 99% of all Stan's music that was ever written for him. Stan sometimes would just *give away* his music while he was on the road, to some band director or other who would come up to him on the stage and admire an arrangement. But he probably had the masters back in L.A.

Piano and setting, Stan Kenton Hall, North Texas State University. (Photo by the Author.)

some-odd boxes. Inside each box there were stacks of music in envelopes, twenty-five numbers each. I'd estimate there are three to four thousand, five thousand things in there, if you count a score as one entity and the parts as another. At least two or three hundred scores. More than any other school has ever seen. What thrilled me to death, Stan never one time mentioned to me, personally, as many times as we talked,

time. There is nothing a man could *do* that would be more valuable.

L.A.: It would be nice if you could maybe frame some of these scores.

BREEDEN: What we're gonna hope to do is frame those, some way, and have them on a big easel or something, so when a historian or composer wants to study them, he can just flip them and look at them. Otherwise they'll self-

L.A. You have the finest collection of jazz music in the world here.

BREEDEN: Probably so. Here's what we'll do with it. I will personally go through every page here. Some of them are priceless manuscripts that are very old, and they're almost like Egyptian papyrus, they're about to fall apart. *Those* will go into the library behind a

Above: Leon Breeden, in the stage area of Stan Kenton Hall, NTSU.

Below: Stan Kenton Hall, Auditorium, North Texas State University. (Photos by the Author.)

big steel cage into our archives, and will be available—they're kept in tunnels, away from windows, away from light, so they won't turn brown. We may make back-up copies of those. We'll put the *originals* down there for historians, musicologists, arrangers—and they'll have to have some identification, that they're truly involved in research, or they're doing something in relation to some writer. Someday someone may want to do a story on Bill Russo, or Pete Rugolo. They can come in here and see some of the things he wrote back in the forties. Those really valuable things of Stan's will go into the library, under lock and key. But some of the things are *brand-new.* Stan would sometimes play through something—and it might be a great arrangement, but Stan personally didn't *like* it—and he'd say "Pass it in, guys." He'd give it to his librarian and say "Put that back on the shelf." A lot of these things were shelved after *one playing,* they're spankin' brand-new.

L.A. That's a story in itself.

BREEDEN: Those will go into the working library for all of our thirteen bands. I mean it's ridiculous for those things to have been written, brand-new copy-work, and never played by *anybody.*

L.A.: That's the best news I've heard all year.

BREEDEN: So we're gonna put 'em into the working library, so the bands will have a chance to play their music.

L.A.: Fantastic!

BREEDEN: We want to keep—the music is going to be—is going to be both living and respected as archival material. We want Stan to be *alive,* we want the music to be in there *played,* and the kids to get to know his writers and his name. I want to stamp every one of these things, "Stan Kenton Library." Some of them don't even indicate it came from Stan.

L.A.: Fabulous!

BREEDEN: I've recommended to Neil Slater and to the Dean that we keep this library totally separate from the North Texas one—what this is gonna be is the Stan Kenton Music in the North Texas Library. It's going to be housed on different shelving, so that if you want something from Stan's library, you've got to go over to a *different place* to get it. I don't want right next to it a student's arrangement and then Pete Rugolo and then a student arrangement—we're not gonna do that. We're not gonna do that. We're gonna keep it all Stan Kenton. So it'll be living—it'll *all* be living, but you know what I mean. *Active.* It'll be

Leon Breeden, and Stan Kenton charts in the Kenton Library, NTSU. (Photo by the Author.)

actively being played, some of it, as well as actively being *stored* down there, where historians and musicologists can get to it. So I'll have to evaluate every chart. When the music first came, I had a summer band, and I'd take big stacks and we'd just sight-read eight or ten new numbers. And some of them were written for a girl singer or something and were a little *antiquated.* So those will probably just be put in storage. Stan would get a lot of music he didn't even ask for. It would just arrive at his office, and he'd say, "Well, let's *try* it." Some didn't work, and others might be very good. Then there's an envelope that says "Missing Parts." I'm trying to put all that back together, match the part to the score it goes with. Some of those are good charts, and maybe weren't played because they were incomplete.

L.A.: That should be very interesting.

BREEDEN: I will have an instrumental code for the complete listing. It will indicate if it's a score or parts; title; composer or arranger or both, is it in the lab band library or the main library. The lab band library is the working library. Master, do we have a master copy of it. And here's the code for the instrumentation: A 1 means that it's alto, tenor, tenor, bari, bari, ten brass. 1H means this plus 1 horn. A 2 means alto, alto, tenor, tenor, bari. You see? Sometimes he used one alto, sometimes he used two. Sometimes one tenor, and a *bass* sax. This makes a difference to a band director; if it calls for a bass sax and he doesn't have one in his band, he can't play it. A 4 means miscellaneous; there's some flute, oboe, bass clarinet—there's some unbelievable, nice little things there. V means it's a vocal arrangement. S means it's for strings, like the Innovations music.

201

Here, you might enjoy looking at this.

L.A.: "Artistry in Rhythm"? What IS that? It's certainly not the original.

BREEDEN: This is Stan's own manuscript. That's his writing, right there. This is his manuscript. This is his arrangement. It's a different version of his theme. I've never *heard* this version.

L.A.: A different version? When did he write it?

BREEDEN: I have no idea. I wish he'd dated everything, but he didn't. It's fairly new.

L.A.: A newer version of "Artistry in Rhythm." My God. Is your band maybe going to take a crack at it?

BREEDEN: I've got to find out if the parts are over there somewhere. I don't know if it's ever even been copied, see. There's where some of my research has got to be. This may be something never even copied which will later get copied and then played. Stan may never have even heard this. We don't know yet.

L.A.: That's the most exciting thing I've ever *seen!* (Laughs.)

BREEDEN: Isn't that something?

L.A.: You could have that as a graduate project for one of your students!

BREEDEN: Oh ya. We're gonna *involve* the grads in it. It really is amazing. And look at these Graettinger charts. They're *graphs.*

L.A.: Aren't they wonderful. They look so *weird.*

Leon Breeden, posing (triumphantly) with a new version of Kenton's "Artistry in Rhythm," and, below, showing a Bob Graettinger chart, Stan Kenton Archives, NTSU. (Photos by the Author.)

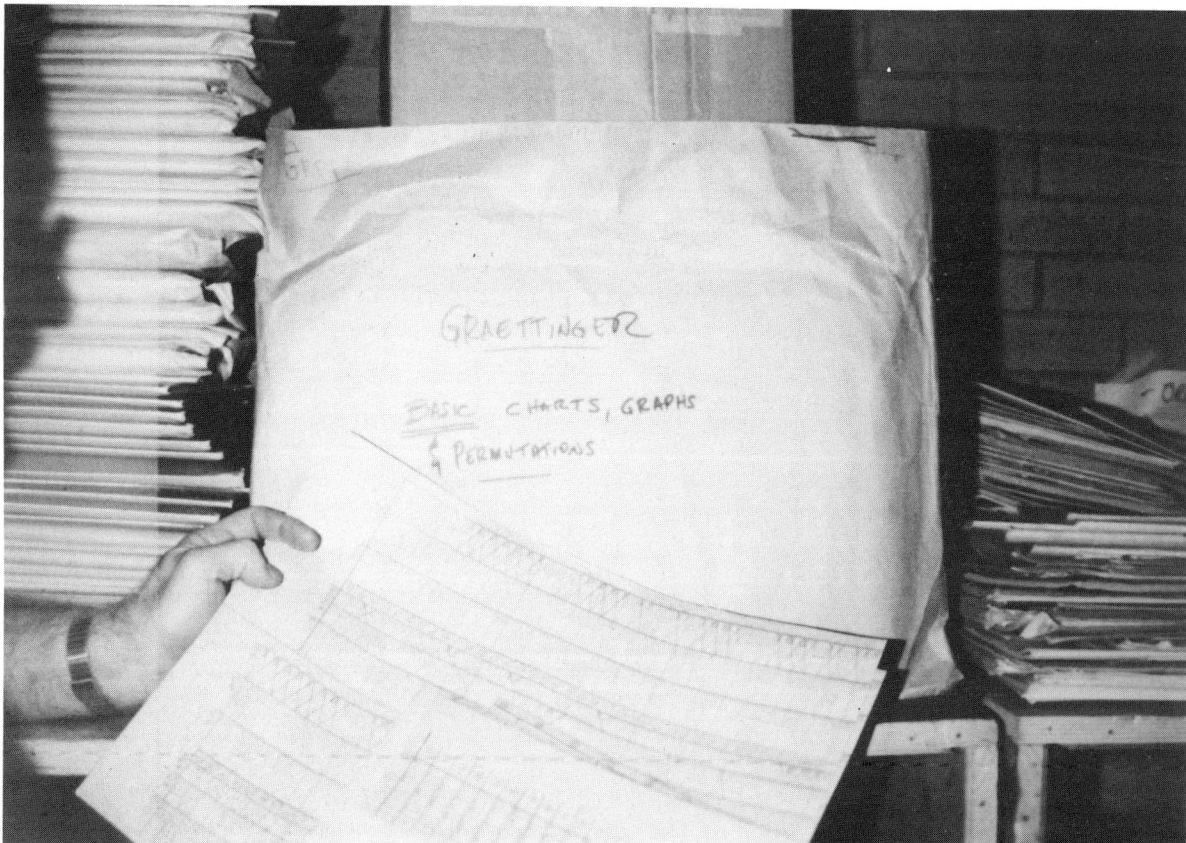

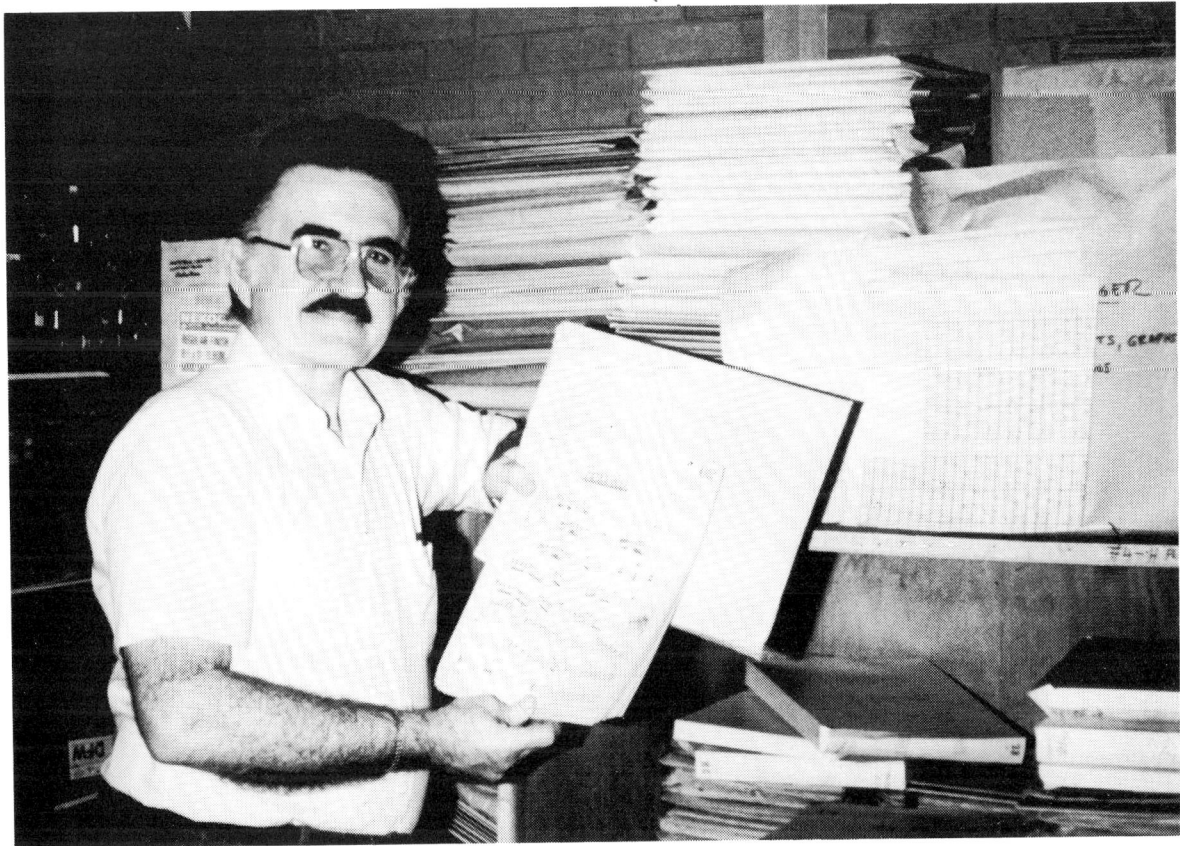

Leon Breeden, holding "Pete's Riff," from the Stan Kenton Library, NTSU. (Photo by the Author.)

BREEDEN: Here's one that says "An Orchestra."

L.A.: That's not the same thing as "This Is An Orchestra," the *Prologue* thing. I don't think I've ever *heard* that.

BREEDEN: Look at this. "Pete's Riff." "Metronome Riff."

L.A.: I haven't heard these either!

BREEDEN: Listen, there are a hundred of 'em in there that you haven't heard. There are at least a hundred and fifty things in here that I've only seen the titles to, and there are about a hundred and fifty that *I've* never heard of. Once it's catalogued, Neil Slater has told me, "We will positively start working them into future concerts." So—that's gonna be great. I would hope in the future that once each year there would be a Salute to Stan Kenton Concert devoted entirely to things out of his library. I would hope so. That's just a dream. I would think it'd be a wonderful thing, myself.

L.A.: That's wonderful. Stan Kenton Concert once a year, played by your lab band.

BREEDEN: I would think it would be marvelous. It could be early in the spring, after the first of the year, before the big spring concert. Or the fall, whenever the best time is. It wouldn't replace any other concerts that are going on. It would be a new addition. We would play different music for each concert. We might do two a year. I mean there's enough music here, you could play—(laughs)—a concert every *week* for the next year. Fifty-two concerts, if you wanted to.

L.A.: In other words, any student who comes here is going to be working with Stan Kenton music. For as long as there is a jazz department here.

BREEDEN: I don't doubt it for a second. It's going to be open to every conductor of every band to play any of the Kenton music . . .

L.A.: Any time he wants to.

BREEDEN: Any of the Kenton music his band feels they can play. Yes, it would be my hope that every student who comes to North Texas will at some time during every year—*every* year—play who knows, ten, twenty, twenty-five, thirty of Stan's things. If only just to *sight-read* it, in a rehearsal. It doesn't mean you have to spend week after week working on it. But they should be *exposed* to this music! We've got some of the greatest music in the *world* here. On these shelves.

L.A.: What about other orchestras in the country? Other high schools and colleges? How would they get access to this, or could they?

BREEDEN: All I can say is this. I'm gonna turn it over. Mr. Slater will have to make that judgment. Some of this involves copyrighted material. Other manuscripts don't even have *titles* on them. We've had inquiries from all over, England, Denmark, Italy—everywhere.

L.A.: You know, learning about all this has made me the happiest person in the whole world. I've been so concerned about where the legacy would go. He just left too much behind for it to die with him.

BREEDEN: That's true.

L.A.: The very fact that you're going to be working with his music . . .

BREEDEN: Is gonna keep it alive.

L.A.: That makes Denton, Texas, the most important little town in the whole world as far as Stan Kenton is concerned now.

BREEDEN: Well—let's put it this way. You spell Denton with a *D* instead of a *K*.

203